Lecture Notes in Economics and Mathematical Systems

Managing Editors: M. Beckmann and H. P. Künzi

164

Ching-Lai Hwang
Abu Syed Md. Masud

In Collaboration with
Sudhakar R. Paidy and Kwangsun Yoon



# Multiple Objective Decision Making – Methods and Applications

A State-of-the-Art Survey



Springer-Verlag
Berlin Heidelberg New York 1979

**Authors**
Ching-Lai Hwang
Dept. of Industrial Engineering
Durland Hall
Kansas State University
Manhattan, KS 66506/USA

Abu Syed Md. Masud
Dept. of Industrial Engineering
and N. M. Solar Energy Institute
New Mexico State University
Box 4230
Las Cruces, NM 88003/USA

**Library of Congress Cataloging in Publication Data**

Hwang, Ching Lai.
Multiple objective decision making, methods and applications.

(Lecture notes in economics and mathematical systems ; 164)
Bibliography: p.
Includes index.
1. Decision-making--Mathematical models.
I. Masud, Abu Syed Md., 1947- joint author.
II. Title. III. Series.
HD3023.H88 658.4'033 79-618

AMS Subject Classifications (1970): 90-02, 90B99, 90C99

ISBN 3-540-09111-4 Springer-Verlag Berlin Heidelberg New York
ISBN 0-387-09111-4 Springer-Verlag New York Heidelberg Berlin



Printing and binding: Beltz Offsetdruck, Hemsbach/Bergstr.
2142/3140-543210

## Acknowledgment

We would like to thank all the researchers in this field. The scope of this survey cannot be done without many fine researchers carrying out and publishing their research. Many have supplied us their reprints, preprints, technical reports and computer codes; in this respect we wish to thank professors J. P. Dauer (Nebraska), J. P. Ignizio (Penn State), S. M. Lee (Nebraska), D. E. Monarchi (Colorado), R. E. Steuer (Kentucky), H. Wallenius (Helsinki School of Economics), P. L. Yu (Kansas), M. Zeleny (Columbia), and S. Zionts (SUNY - Buffalo). Professor Reza S. Lashkari (Windsor, Canada) read most of the second draft of this monograph and gave us many suggestions. The first draft was used in the first author's Spring 1978 class of "Advanced Topics in Operations Research". The two collaborators, S. R. Paidy and K. Yoon, were among others in the class, T. L. Applegate, M. M. Babiker, D. M. Chow, H. Gianto, W. Kuo, H. B. Lee, K. S. Raju, J. M. Tiao, R. G. Wagner and W. K. Wei, who tested many methods and reviewed various fields of applications. Marie Davis and Cheryl Lynn Hoseney typed most of the manuscript, and Jean Burnham assisted in editing.

This study was started when the first author (Hwang) was a guest professor at the Technical University of Denmark (Danmarks Teknisk Højskole) during the academic year 1974-75. The visit was arranged by Professors Anders Björkman and Mogens Bundgaard-Nielsen; the housing at Nyhavn 18 in Copenhagen for foreign scholars and scientists was provided by Danmarks Nationalbank.

This study was partly supported by the Office of Naval Research, Contract No. N00014-76-C-0842.

C. L. Hwang
Kansas State University
Manhattan, Kansas
Fall 1978

A. S. M. Masud
New Mexico State University
Las Cruces, New Mexico
Fall 1978

## ABSTRACT

Literature on Multiple Objective Decision Making (MODM) methods and their applications have been reviewed and classified systematically.

This survey provides readers with a capsule look into the existing methods, their characteristics, and applicability to analysis of MODM problems.

The basic MODM concepts are defined and a standard notation is introduced in Part II to facilitate the review.

A system of classifying about two dozen major MODM methods is presented. Most of these methods have been proposed by various researchers in the last few years, but here for the first time they are presented together. The basic concept, the computational procedures, and the characteristics of each of these methods are presented concisely in Part III. The computational procedure of each method is illustrated by solving a simple numerical example.

Part IV of the survey deals with the actual or proposed applications of these MODM methods. The literature has been classified into 12 major topics based on the area of applications. Summary of each reference on applications is given.

An updated bibliographical listing of 24 books, monographs or conference proceedings, and 424 papers, reports or theses is presented.

TABLE OF CONTENTS

## LIST OF FIGURES

## LIST OF TABLES

## I. INTRODUCTION

Decision making is the process of selecting a possible course of action from all the available alternatives. In almost all such problems the multiplicity of criteria for judging the alternatives is pervasive. That is, for many such problems, the decision maker (DM) wants to attain more than one objective or goal in selecting the course of action while satisfying the constraints dictated by environment, processes, and resources. Another characteristic of these problems is that the objectives are apparently non-commensurable. Mathematically, these problems can be represented as:

$$\left.\begin{array}{l} \text{Max } [f_1(\underline{x}), f_2(\underline{x}), \ldots, f_k(\underline{x})] \\ \text{subject to: } g_i(\underline{x}) \leq 0, \qquad i = 1, \ldots, m \end{array}\right\} \qquad (1.1)$$

where $\underline{x}$ is an n dimensional decision variable vector. The problem consists of n decision variables, m constraints and k objectives. Any or all of the functions may be nonlinear. In literature this problem is often referred to as a vector maximum problem (VMP).

Traditionally there are two approaches for solving the VMP. One of them is to optimize one of the objectives while appending the other objectives to a constraint set so that the optimal solution would satisfy these objectives at least up to a predetermined level. The problem is given as:

$$\left.\begin{array}{l} \text{Max } f_i(\underline{x}) \\ \text{subject to: } g_j(\underline{x}) \leq 0, \quad j = 1, \ldots, m \\ \qquad\qquad f_\ell(\underline{x}) \geq a_\ell, \ \ell = 1, \ldots, k, \text{ and } \ell \neq i \end{array}\right\} \qquad (1.2)$$

where $a_\ell$ is any acceptable predetermined level for objective $\ell$. The other approach is to optimize a super-objective function created by multiplying each objective function with a suitable weight and then by adding them together. This approach leads to the solution of the following problem:

$$\left.\begin{aligned} &\text{Max} \sum_{i=1}^{k} w_i f_i(\underline{x}) \\ &\text{subject to:} \quad g_i(\underline{x}) \leq 0, \; i = 1, \ldots, m \end{aligned}\right\} \qquad (1.3)$$

The weights are usually normalized so that $\sum_{i=1}^{k} w_i = 1$.

Both of the above approaches are ad hoc at best. Often they lead to a solution which may not be the best or most satisfactory. Because of the incommensurability and the conflicting nature of the multiple criteria, the problem becomes complex and it becomes difficult to choose the acceptable levels, $a_\ell$'s, in (1.2) that will result in a nonempty constraint set in the first attempt for the solution. In the first approach, the implied value trade-off between $f_\ell$ and $f_i$ is as follows:

$$\text{Value Trade-off} = \begin{cases} 0 \, , & f_\ell \geq a_\ell \\ \infty \, , & f_\ell < a_\ell \end{cases}$$

This may not be the actual value structure of the DM and this value structure is sensitive to the level of $a_\ell$. For the second approach, the major problem is in determining the proper weight, $w_i$. The $w_i$'s are sensitive to the level of the particular objective as well as the levels of all other objectives.

Multiple objective decision making (MODM) methods are the result of the desire to eliminate the above difficulties as well as to treat the objectives independently. Most of the progress in this area has taken place within the last decade even though one of the earliest considerations of multiple objectives can be found in 1951 by Kuhn-Tucker [200]. The rapid progress in such a short time necessitates a thorough review of the existing literature and a systematic classification of methods for the guidance of future users. Such is the purpose of this paper. In addition to reviewing the methods, we will also review the actual or proposed applications of these methods and discuss the basic concepts and terminology. The result will provide researchers with a capsule look into the existing methods, their characteristics, and applicability to different problems.

Multiple objective (or criteria) decision making problems have been presented in books and monographs. Table 1.1 shows the classification. Earlier research monographs have been written by Ijiri in 1965 [BM-10] and Johnsen in 1968 [BM-11], and they have been followed by those of Zeleny [BM-22], Wilhelm [BM-21], Wallenius [BM-19], and Haimes, Hall, and Freedman [BM-8] in recent years (1974-76). Text books have been written by Lee [BM-13], Easton [BM-3], Ignizio [BM-9], and Keeney and Raiffa [BM-12] during 1972-76. Several symposium proceedings and collected papers presenting recent progress (1973-77) in theory, methods, and applications have been edited by Cochrane and Zeleny [BM-2], Leitmann and Marzollo [BM-15], Wendt and Vlek [BM-20], Thiriez and Zionts [BM-18], Zeleny [BM-23], Leitmann [BM-14], Starr and Zeleny [BM-17], and Bell, Keeney, and Raiffa [BM-1a]. Books and monographs indirectly related to multiple criteria decision making are also listed in Table 1.1.

Of course this is not the first attempt at surveying this area of research. Table 1.2 presents the classification of the previous surveys. Some of the earlier attempts have been carried out by Johnsen in 1968 [BM-11], and Roy in 1971 [280]. Starr and Zeleny in 1977 [317] present a good review of the methods and outlook of this research topic. Some of the previous reviews are limited in their scope or area covered; e.g. Fishburn in 1974 [113] reviewed the literature on lexicographic orders, utilities and decision rules, and Cohon and Marks in 1975 [68] considered the literature on multiple objective decision making applied to water resources management problems. Literature on multiple attribute decision making, which is excluded in the present review, has been reviewed extensively by MacCrimmon in 1968 [227] and in 1973 [229], Green

Table 1.1

Classification of books, monographs and conference proceedings

| Class | References |
|---|---|
| A. Directly related to the topic | |
| Books | BM-3, BM-9, BM-12, BM-13 |
| Monographs | BM-8, BM-10, BM-11, BM-16a, BM-19 BM-21, BM-22 |
| Edited Conference Proceedings | BM-1a, BM-2, BM-14, BM-15, BM-17 BM-18, BM-20, BM-23, BM-24 |
| B. Indirectly related to the topic | BM-1, BM-4, BM-5, BM-6, BM-7, BM-16 |

Table 1.2

Classification of references related to literature survey

| Class | References |
| --- | --- |
| Survey of Literature on Multiple Objective | BM-8, BM-11, 37, 54, 68, 180, 206, 280, 317. |
| Survey of Literature on Multiple Attribute | BM-7, BM-12, 227, 229 |
| Survey of Literature on Multiattribute Utility Theory | 103, 111, 113, 162, 361 |
| Survey of Literature on Applications | |
| Water Resources Management | 68, 225 |
| Business Management | 251 |
| Compiled Bibliographical Lists | BM-12, BM-19, 103, 376, 381 |

and Wind in 1973 [BM-7], and Keeney and Raiffa in 1976 [BM-12]. Some of the literature reviews concerned with multiple attribute decision making have been carried out in the field of multi-attribute utility theory; eg. by Huber in 1974 [162], Winterfeldt and Fisher in 1975 [361], Farquhar in 1977 [103] (see Table 1.2). Compiled lists of bibliography on multiple criterion decision making have been presented by Zeleny in 1973 [376] and in 1975 [381], Wallenius in 1975 [BM-19], Keeney and Raiffa in 1976 [BM-12], and Farquhar in 1977 [103].

The methods for various Multiple Criteria Decision Making (MCDM) problems are widely diverse. However, even with the diversity, all the methods which are concerned here share the following common characteristics: (1) a set of criteria of judgment; (2) a set of decision variables; and (3) a process of comparing the alternatives. The problems of MCDM can be broadly classified into two categories: (1) Multiple Attribute Decision Making (MADM), and (2) Multiple Objective Decision Making (MODM).

The distinguishing features of the MADM are that there are usually a limited (and countably small) number of predetermined alternatives. The alternatives have associated with them a level of the achievement of the attributes (which may not necessarily be quantifiable) based on which the final decision is to be made. The final selection of the alternative is made with the help of inter- and intra-attribute comparisons. The comparisons may involve explicit or implicit trade-off.

Multiple objective decision making, on the other hand, is not associated with the problem where the alternatives are predetermined. The thrust of these models is to design the 'best' alternative by considering the various interactions within the design constraints which best satisfy the DM by way of attaining some acceptable levels of a set of some quantifiable objectives. The common characteristics of MODM methods are that they possess: (1) a set of quantifiable objectives; (2) a set of well defined constraints, (3) a process of obtaining some trade-off information, implicit or explicit, between the stated quantifiable objectives and also between stated or unstated nonquantifiable objectives. Thus MODM is associated with design problems (in contrast to selection problems for the MADM).

Scope of This Study: In most previous surveys of multiple criteria decision making, the major emphasis has been on multiple attribute methods. However, in this paper we shall focus our attention on the multiple objective methods. Table 1.2 lists some of the extensive reviews on the MADM.

In the process of decision making, some preference information articulation from the DM may be required. If so then the type of information and when it is given plays a key role in the actual decision methods. We classify methods for MODM based upon these considerations. A taxonomy of the MODM is shown in Fig. 1.1. The classification has been made in three steps: Step I: the stage at which the preference information is needed; Step II: the type of information needed; Step III: the major methods in any branch formed from Steps I and II. Also indicated in Step III are all other methods which resemble these major methods. Finally in Table 1.3, all references are classified according to the methods in Step III.

As shown in Figure 1.1, there are four possible stages at which the information is needed from the DM (Step I). They are: (1) no articulation

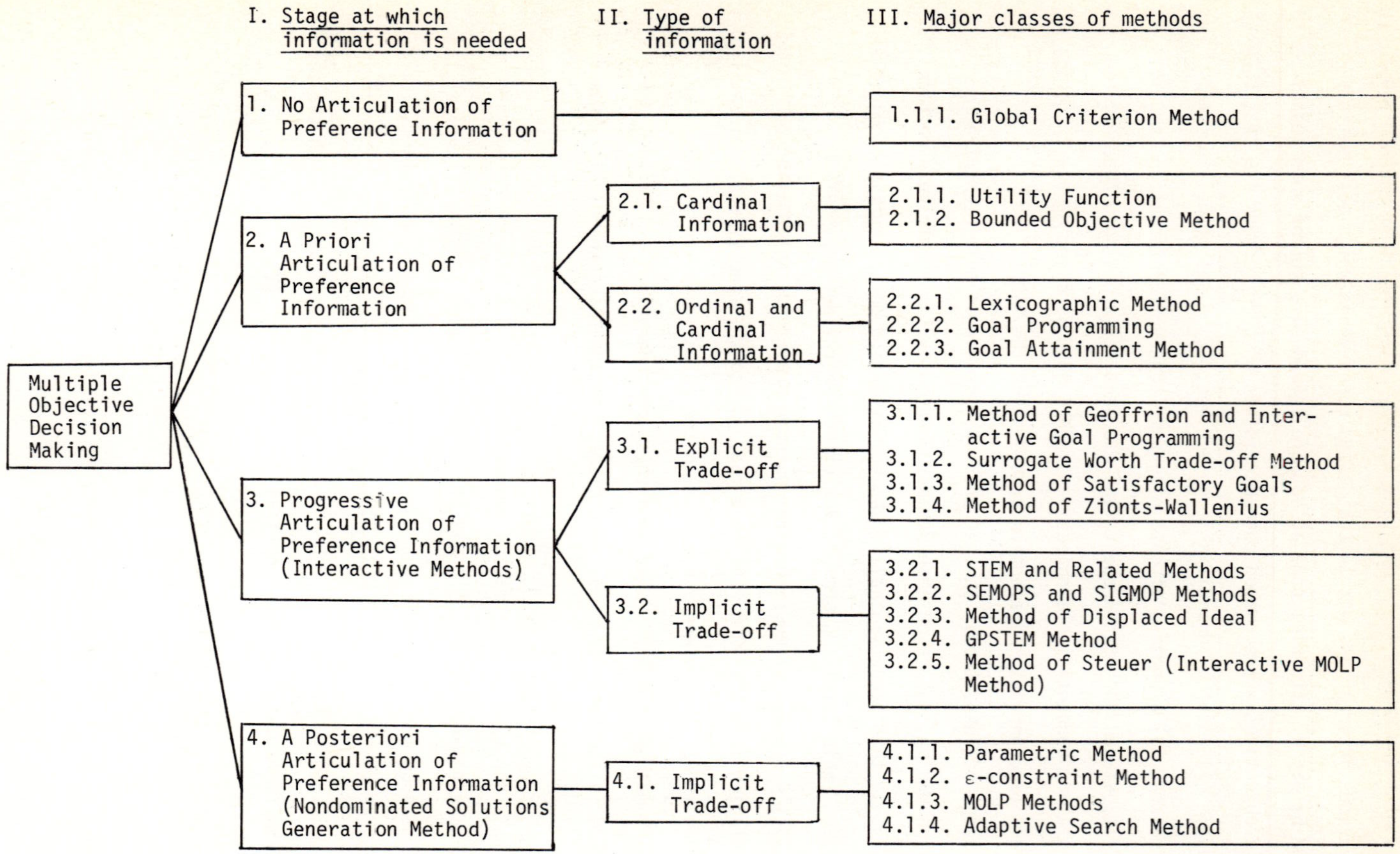


Fig. 1.1 A taxonomy of methods for multiple objective decision making.

Table 1.3 Classification of references on multiple objective decision methods.

| Class | References |
|---|---|
| 1. Methods for no articulation of Preference Information Given: | |
| 1.1 Global Criterion Method | 37, 206, 289-292 |
| 1.2 Others | 278 |
| 2. Methods for 'A Priori' Articulation of Preference Information Given: | |
| 2.1.1 Utility Function Method | BM-12, 42a, 86, 103, 113, 122, 162, 187, 224, 279, 287-288 |
| 2.1.2 Bounded Objective Method | |
| 2.1.3 Others | 10, 39, 141-142, 262, 314, 353 |
| 2.2.1 Lexicographic Method | BM-12, 64, 113, 239, 304, 353 |
| 2.2.2 Goal Programming | |
| Linear Goal Programming | BM-9, BM-10, BM-13, 8, 49, 53-59, 71, 78, 78a, 134, 137, 146, 149-150, 154, 163, 173, 190-191, 212-218, 252, 257, 269, 271, 294, 300, 310, 327a, 332, 347, 352, 356, 363-364 |
| Linear Integer Goal Programming | BM-9, 219 |
| Nonlinear Goal Programming | BM-9, 8, 49, 56, 146, 165-168, 201, 275 |
| Nonlinear Integer Goal Programming | 211a |
| 2.2.3 Goal Attainment Method | BM-8, 125 |
| 2.2.4 Others | 193 |
| 3. Methods for Progressive Articulation of Preference Information Given (Interactive Methods): | |
| 3.1.1 Method of Geoffrion and Interactive Goal Programming | BM-19, 1, 89-92, 105, 130-131, 255a, 348-350, 353a |

Table 1.3 (continued)

| | | |
|---|---|---|
| 3.1.2 | Surrogate Worth Trade-off Method | BM-8, 140, 143 |
| 3.1.3 | Method of Satisfactory Goals | 19a |
| 3.1.4 | Method of Zionts-Wallenius | BM-19, 254, 349, 351, 385-386 |
| 3.1.5 | Others | 43-44, 115a |
| 3.2.1 | STEM and Related Methods | BM-19, 1, 17-19, 86a, 349-350 |
| 3.2.2 | SEMOPS and SIGMOP Methods | 247-249 |
| 3.2.3 | Method of the Displaced Ideal | BM-22, 378-380 |
| 3.2.4 | GPSTEM Method | 109 |
| 3.2.5 | Method of Steuer (Interactive MOLP Method) | 323-324 |
| 3.2.6 | Others | 5, 16, 87, 156, 179, 270, 281-282, 338, 344, 377 |
| 4. | Methods for 'A Posteriori' Articulation of Preference Information Given (Nondominated Solutions Generation Methods): | |
| 4.1.1 | Parametric Method | BM-22, 9, 70, 126-128, 265, 277, 305, 345, 374 |
| 4.1.2 | $\varepsilon$ - Constraint Method | BM-8, 66-67, 141-142 |
| 4.1.3 | MOLP Methods | BM-22, 20, 95, 99-100, 122a-122c, 170-171, 198-199, 209-211, 261-262, 320-322, 327, 369, 372-373, 383 |
| 4.1.4 | Adaptive Search Method | 15, 69, 241 |
| 4.1.5 | Others | 36, 46, 61, 98, 120, 172, 221-222, 259, 266, 276, 306, 319, 343, 354a, 366, 371, 384 |
| 5. | Miscellaneous Methods | 34, 84a, 134a, 148, 176, 240, 278, 326, 331, 357a |

of preference information is needed from the DM, (2) "a priori" articulation of preference information from the DM, (3) "progressive" articulation of preference information from the DM, and (4) "a posteriori" articulation of preference information from the DM.

Before going into the actual review, some key concepts and notations will be defined in Part II so that we can explain the literature with a unified notation of the most used terms. This will facilitate later discussion. In Part III, the literature dealing with the techniques of multiple objective decision making will be reviewed and classified. In part IV, the literature dealing with the actual or proposed applications will be reviewed.

Although we have tried to give a reasonably complete survey, those papers not included were either inadvertently overlooked or considered not to bear directly on the topics in this survey. We apologize to both the readers and the researchers if we have omitted any relevant papers.

## II. BASIC CONCEPTS AND TERMINOLOGY

The four words most used in multiple criteria decision making literature are: attributes, objectives, goals and criteria. There are no universal definitions of these terms as stated by Keeney and Raiffa [BM-12]. Some authors make distinctions in their usage while many use them interchangeably. We shall make some distinctions among these words in terms of their usage. They are defined as follows:

Definition 1: Attributes

Attributes are the characteristics, qualities or performance parameters of alterantives.

Multiple attribute decision parоblems involve the selection of the "best" alternative from a pool of preselected alternatives described in terms of their attributes. As an example, consider the problem facing a city commission where the issue is to select the direction of future expansion of the city. Due to the geography of the area, the planners have determined that the city can only grow in one of three directions - east, south-east and west. Here the decision makers are presented with three alternatives and they must choose the one they think best for the city. The alternatives will be compared based on the attributes settled on by the commission. The attributes may be cost of service expansion, effect on downtonw vitality, possibility of flooding, preservation of balance in city neighborhoods, proximity to existing recreational facilities, etc.

Definition 2: Objectives

Objectives are the directions "to do better" as perceived by the decision maker.

Thus objectives are reflections of the desires of the decision maker (DM) and they indicate the direction in which the DM wants the organization to work. MODM problems, as a result, involve the design of alternatives which optimize or "best satisfy" the objectives of the DM. Consider the problem of making development plans for the government of a developing country. The objectives of the government in devising the acceptable plan would be: to maximize the national welfare; to minimize dependence on foreign aid; to minimize unemployment rate, etc.

Definition 3: Goals

Goals are things desired by the decision maker expressed in terms of a specific state in space and time.

Thus, while objectives give the desired direction, goals give a desired (or target) level to achieve. However, in the literature this distinction gets blurred and these two words are used interchangeably. We will also use them interchangeably.

Definition 4: Criteria

Criteria are standards of judgement or rules to test acceptability.

This is the dictionary definition of the term. However, as used in the MCDM literature, it indicates attributes and/or objectives. In this sense, an MCDM problem includes either multiple attributes, or multiple objectives or both. This is used to indicate the general class of problems with which we are concerned here.

The notations that will be used throughout this review are defined next. This will save us from confusion and provide a notational uniformity.

The multiple objective decision problem will be defined mathematically as follows:

Problem 1:

$$\text{Max } [f_1(\underline{x}), f_2(\underline{x}), \ldots, f_k(\underline{x})]$$

subject to $g_j(\underline{x}) \leq 0, \; j = 1, \ldots, m$

or in a vector notation,

$$\text{Max } \underline{f}(\underline{x})$$

subject to $\underline{g}(\underline{x}) \leq \underline{0}$

where $\underline{x}$ is an n-dimensional vector. The problem indicates that there are k number of objectives which are to be maximized, m number of constraints, and n number of decision variables. Any or all of the functions $f_i(\underline{x})$ and $g_j(\underline{x})$ can be nonlinear. As already mentioned, this problem is also referred to as a Vector Maximum Problem (VMP).

The symbol $\leq$ will be defined as follows for use in vectors:

Definition 5: Two vectors which are $\underline{x} \leq \underline{y}$

For any two vectors $\underline{x}$ and $\underline{y}$, $\underline{x} \leq \underline{y}$ iff $x_i \leq y_i$ for all i for which the two vectors are defined. Similarly $\underline{y} \geq \underline{x}$ iff $y_i \geq x_i$ for all i.

For the VMP the constraints $\underline{g}(\underline{x}) \leq \underline{0}$ define a feasible set X where X is defined as follows:

Definition 6: A Feasible Set X

The feasible set X is the set of decision variables $\underline{x}$ which satisfy the constraint set $\underline{g}(\underline{x}) \leq \underline{0}$, i.e., $X = \{\underline{x} | \underline{g}(x) \leq \underline{0}\}$.

With each point in X there is an associated $\underline{f}(\underline{x})$ vector. So, it is possible to map X into a set S in the objective function space. S can be formally defined as follows:

Definition 7: A Set of Functional Values S

S is a set of functional values $\underline{f}(\underline{x})$ for each vector $\underline{x}$ in X, i.e., $S = \{\underline{f}(\underline{x}) | \underline{x} \in X\}$.

As a result, a VMP can be represented in any of the following three equivalent notations:

(a) Max $\underline{f}(\underline{x})$

subject to $\underline{g}(x) \leq \underline{0}$

(b) Max $\underline{f}(\underline{x})$

subject to $\underline{x} \in X$

(c) Max $\underline{f}(\underline{x})$

subject to $\underline{f}(\underline{x}) \in S$

We shall now introduce the idea of optimal solution, nondominated solution and preferred solution in the context of a VMP. A clear notion of these concepts is crucial to the understanding of the solution methodologies for multiple criteria decision problems. We will clarify these concepts with the help of numerical examples 1 and 2.

Example 1:

$$\begin{aligned} &\text{Max} \quad f_1 = x_1 + x_2 \\ &\text{Max} \quad f_2 = x_2 - x_1 \\ &\text{subject to} \quad x_1 \leq 3 \\ &\qquad x_2 \leq 3 \\ &\qquad x_1, x_2 \geq 0 \end{aligned}$$

Example 2:

$$\begin{aligned} &\text{Max} \quad f_1 = x_2 \\ &\text{Max} \quad f_2 = x_2 - x_1 \\ &\text{subject to} \quad x_1 \leq 3 \\ &\qquad x_2 \leq 3 \\ &\qquad x_1, x_2 \geq 0 \end{aligned}$$

Figure 2.1 shows the decision variable space representation of both examples. Figure 2.2 shows the objective function space representation of Example 1; let us call this $S_1$. Figure 2.3 shows the objective function space representation of Example 2; let us call it $S_2$. Of course, this kind of figure can be drawn only with such simple examples.

Definition 8: An Optimal Solution

An optimal solution to a VMP is one which results in the maximum value of each of the objective functions simultaneously. That is, $\underline{x}^*$ is an optimal solution to the VMP iff $\underline{x}^* \varepsilon X$ and $\underline{f}(\underline{x}^*) \geq \underline{f}(\underline{x})$ for all $\underline{x} \varepsilon X$.

Since it is the nature of MODM problems to have conflicting objectives, usually there is no optimal solution to a VMP. Looking at our examples we notice that Example 2 has an optimal solution. This optimal solution is located at $(x_1,x_2) = (0,3)$ where $(f_1,f_2) = (3,3)$; this is shown by point B in Fig. 2-3. For Example 1, there is no optimal solution. The maximum value of $f_1 = 6$ which occurs at $(x_1,x_2) = (3,3)$; the maximum value of $f_2 = 3$ which occurs at $(x_1,x_2) = (0,3)$. Point F in Fig. 2.2 gives $f_1 = 6$ and $f_2 = 3$, however, the point is outside the feasible region $S_1$. It may be noted that the optimal solution is also known as the superior solution or the maximum solution.

In the absence of an optimal solution of a VMP, the idea of a preferred solution has been introduced. However, before defining a preferred solution, a nondominated solution is introduced in the context of a VMP.

Definition 9: A Nondominated Solution

A nondominated solution is one in which no one objective function can be improved without a simultaneous detriment to at least one of the other objectives of the VMP. That is, $\underline{x}^*$ is a nondominated solution to the VMP

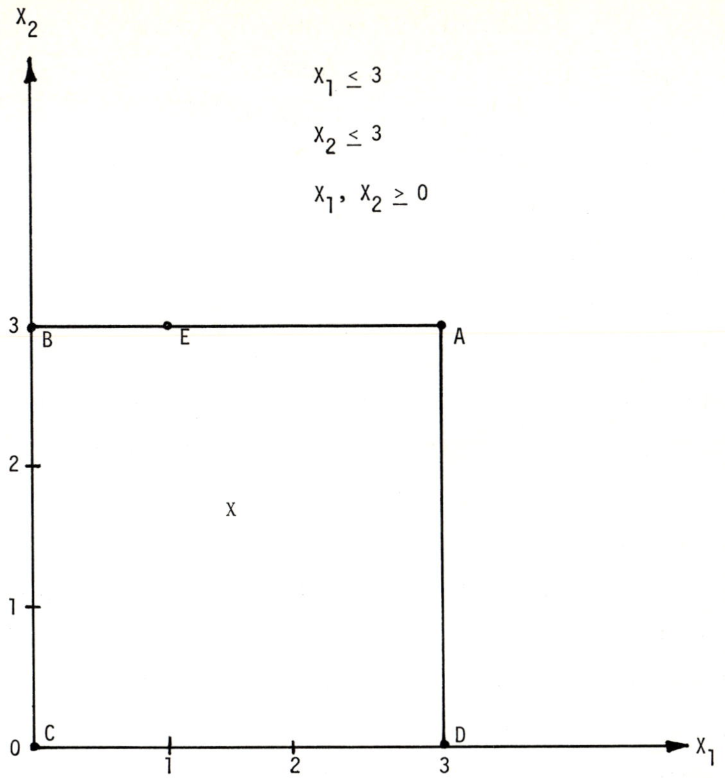


Fig. 2.1 Decision variable space representation of the feasible area of Examples 1 and 2.

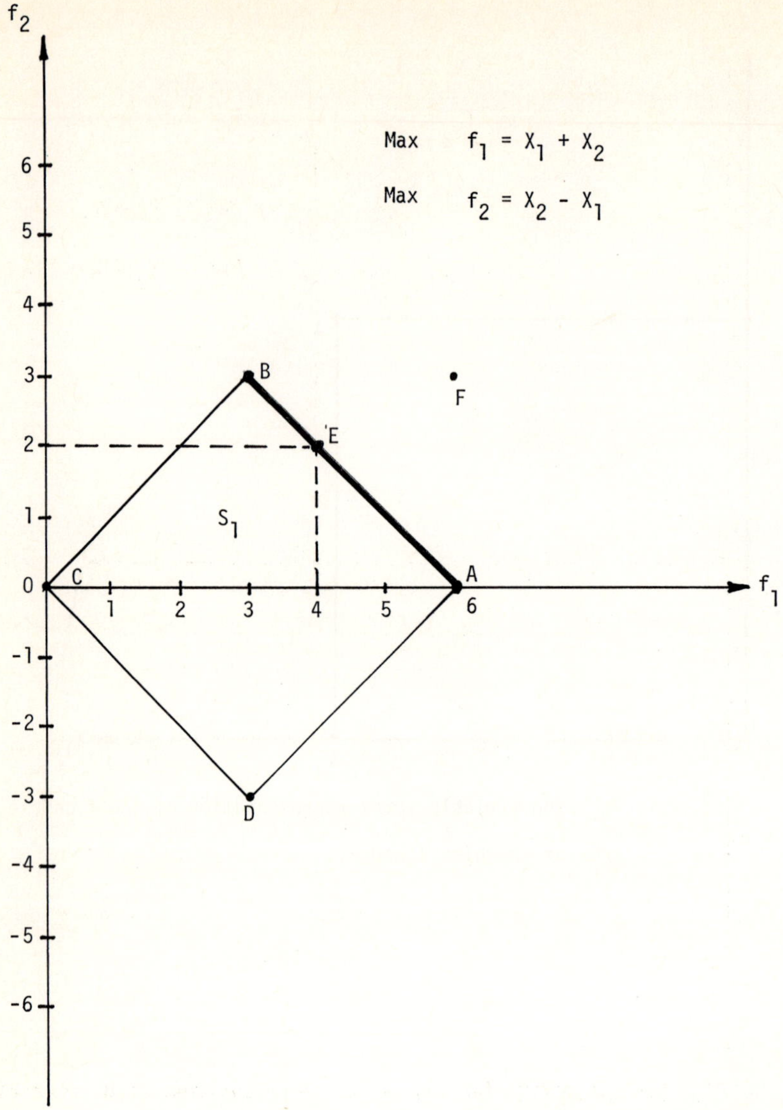


Fig. 2.2 Objective function space representation of the feasible area of Example 1.

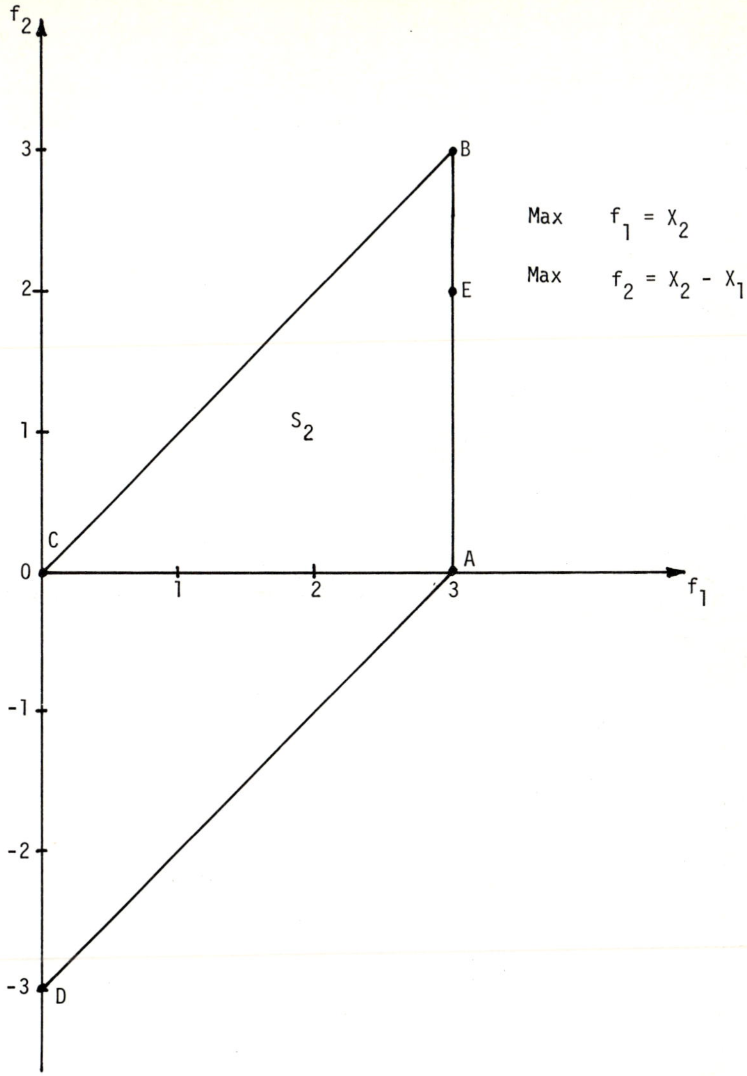


Fig. 2.3 Objective function space representation of the feasible area of Example 2.

iff there does not exist any $\underline{x} \in X$ such that $f_i(\underline{x}^*) \leq f_i(\underline{x})$ for all i and $f_j(\underline{x}^*) < f_j(\underline{x})$ for at least one j.

The nondominated solution is also known as Pareto-optimal solution, noninferior solution, or efficient solution. For Example 1, all solutions for $x_2 = 3$ and $0 \leq x_1 \leq 3$ are nondominated. In Fig. 2.2, these nondominated solutions are represented by the straight line BA. It is obvious that all the nondominated solutions must lie on the boundary BA of $S_1$ because any point interior to $S_1$ is dominated by at least one point on the boundary BA. This is a very important characteristic of the set of nondominated solutions of a VMP. Reid and Citron [276] give a rigorous proof for this.

For most of the VMPs, the number of solutions in the set of nondominated solutions is quite large. So, the decision maker must make a final selection of the most satisfactory solution by using some other criteria. This final solution thus chosen is known as the preferred solution. It is defined as follows:

Definition 10: A Preferred Solution

A preferred solution is a nondominated solution which is chosen by the DM, through some additional criteria, as the final decision. As such, it lies in the region of acceptance of all the criteria values for the problem. A preferred solution is also known as the best solution.

Definition 11: A Satisficing Solution

A satisficing solution of Simon [307a] extended to a VMP is a reduced subset of the feasible set, which exceeds all of the aspiration levels (goals) of each objective. Satisficing solutions need not be nondominated. This solution is credited for its simplicity which matches the behavior processes of the DM whose knowledge and ability are limited.

## III. METHODS FOR MULTIPLE OBJECTIVE DECISION MAKING

### 1. Methods for No Articulation of Preference Information Given

This means that methods following this approach do not need any interobjective or other subjective preference information from the DM once the problem constraints and objectives have been defined. Thus this approach requires that the DM be able to accept the solution obtained from the method. The advantage of this route is that in the process of obtaining the solution the DM will not be disturbed by the analyst, which is preferable from the point-of-view of the DM. But a major disadvantage then is the necessity for the analyst to make many assumptions about the DM's preference. This is difficult to do with even the best and most knowledgeable analyst.

#### 1.1.1. THE METHOD OF GLOBAL CRITERION

The major method of this category is the method of global criterion. An optimal vector is a vector that minimizes some global criterion; for example, the sum of the squares of the relative deviation of the criteria (objective functions) from the feasible ideal points.

The solutions of the following k problems:

$$\begin{cases} \max f_j(\underline{x}) \\ \text{s.t. } g_i(\underline{x}) \leq 0, \; i = 1, 2, \ldots, m \end{cases} \tag{3.1}$$

$$j = 1, 2, \ldots, k.$$

are defined as the ideal solutions, $f_j(\underline{x}^*)$, $j = 1, 2, \ldots, k$. Then the method of global criterion for the vector maximum problem (VMP) of (1.1) solves the problem given by (3.2):

$$\min \sum_{i=1}^{k} \left(\frac{f_i(\underline{x}^*) - f_i(\underline{x})}{f_i(\underline{x}^*)}\right)^p \tag{3.2}$$

$$\text{s.t. } g_i(\underline{x}) \leq 0, \quad i = 1, 2, \ldots, m$$

Boychuk and Ovchinnikov [37] have suggested $p = 1$, and Salukvadze [289-292] has suggested $p = 2$ for the global criterion. These are only two of the many possible expressions that can be used in the context of (3.2). The 'best' solution chosen for the VMP will differ greatly according to the criteria chosen. These criteria locate points which are geometrically different from one another. The problem with this approach is to determine which p would result in a solution that is the most satisfactory solution to the DM. It is also possible that whatever p is chosen, (3.2) might give a solution which has a particular objective value, $f_i(\underline{x})$, that is totally unacceptable to the DM.

Case 1. $p = 1$; $\underline{f}(\underline{x})$ and $\underline{g}(\underline{x})$ are linear functions

When all the objectives, $f_i(\underline{x})$, $i = 1, 2, \ldots, k$, and all the constraint functions, $g_i(\underline{x})$, $i = 1, \ldots, m$, are linear functions, and $p = 1$, then (3.2) becomes a linear programming problem. The simplex method for L.P. can solve the problem.

Case 2. $p = 2$; $\underline{f}(\underline{x})$ and $\underline{g}(\underline{x})$ are linear functions

When both $\underline{f}(\underline{x})$ amd $\underline{g}(\underline{x})$ are linear functions and $p = 2$, (3.2) becomes a convex programming problem; more precisely, a quadratic programming problem.

As is well known, in a convex programming problem, a local minimum is absolute (or global). The convex programming problem can be solved by using any method of finding a local extreme, including the gradient method, quadratic programming, or nonlinear programming methods.

Case 3. $\underline{f}(\underline{x})$ and $\underline{g}(\underline{x})$ are nonlinear functions

If any one or all of the objectives, $f_i(\underline{x})$, i = 1, 2, ...,k, and the constraints, $g_i(\underline{x})$, i = 1, 2, ..., m, are nonlinear functions, (3.2) is a nonlinear programming problem (for both p = 1 or p = 2). A variety of nonlinear programming methods (e.g. the sequential unconstrained minimization technique (SUMT) [165a], or the generalized reduced gradient method (GRG) [1a,165b] can be used for solving the problem. A new approach which is called iterative nonlinear goal programming is an effective method for solving this problem (see Sec. 2.2.2.b).

NUMERICAL EXAMPLE (Production scheduling of the Hardee toy company)

The Hardee toy company makes two kinds of toy dolls. Doll A is a high quality toy and Doll B is of lower quality. The respective profits are \$0.40 and \$0.30 per doll. Each Doll A requires twice as much time as a Doll B, and if all dolls were of type B, the company could make 500 per day. The supply of material is sufficient for only 400 dolls per day (both A and B combined). The problem assumes that all the dolls for type A and type B the factory can make could be sold, and that the best customer of the company wishes to have as many as possible of type A doll. The manager realizes that two objectives: (1) the maximization of profit, and (2) the maximum production of Doll A, should be considered in scheduling the production.

This VMP can be formulated as follows:

$$\max f_1(\underline{x}) = 0.4x_1 + 0.3x_2$$

$$\max f_2(\underline{x}) = x_1$$

subject to

$$g_1(\underline{x}) = x_1 + x_2 \leq 400$$

$$g_2(\underline{x}) = 2x_1 + x_2 \leq 500$$

$$x_1, x_2 \geq 0$$

where $x_1$ and $x_2$ are the number of Doll A and that of Doll B produced respectively.

The method of global criterion follows three steps: Step 1. Obtain the ideal solution; Step 2. Construct a pay-off table; Step 3. Obtain the preferred solution.

<u>Step 1. Obtain the ideal solutions</u>

1) $$\max f_1(\underline{x}) = 0.4x_1 + 0.3x_2$$

$$\text{s.t. } g_1(\underline{x}) = x_1 + x_2 \leq 400$$

$$g_2(\underline{x}) = 2x_1 + x_2 \leq 500$$

$$x_1, x_2 \geq 0$$

This is a linear programming problem. The solution is:

$$x_1 = 100, \qquad x_2 = 300$$

$$f_1(\underline{x}^*) = 130$$

Point B is the ideal solution for $f_1(\underline{x})$ (see Figs. 3.1 and 3.2).

2) $$\max \; f_2(\underline{x}) = x_1$$

$$\text{s.t.} \quad g_1(\underline{x}) = x_1 + x_2 \leq 400$$

$$g_2(\underline{x}) = 2x_1 + x_2 \leq 500$$

$$x_1, x_2 \geq 0$$

This is again a linear programming problem. The solution is:

$$x_1 = 250, \qquad x_2 = 0$$

$$f_2(\underline{x}^*) = 250$$

The ideal solution for $f_2(\underline{x})$ is point C in Figs. 3.1 and 3.2.

Step 2. Construct a pay-off table

The results of Step 1 are summarized in the following pay-off table.

| | $f_1$ | $f_2$ | $x_1$ | $x_2$ |
|---|---|---|---|---|
| $f_1$ | 130 | 100 | 100 | 300 |
| $f_2$ | 100 | 250 | 250 | 0 |

Note that in this pay-off table, row 1 gives the solution vector $\underline{x}^* = (100, 300)$ which maximizes the objective $f_1(\underline{x}^*) = 130$; $f_2\,(100, 300) = 100$ is the value taken on by the objective $f_2$ when $f_1$ reaches its maximum. Similarly, row 2 gives the solution vector $\underline{x}^* = (250, 0)$ which maximizes $f_2\,(\underline{x}^*) = 250$; $f_1\,(250, 0) = 100$ is the

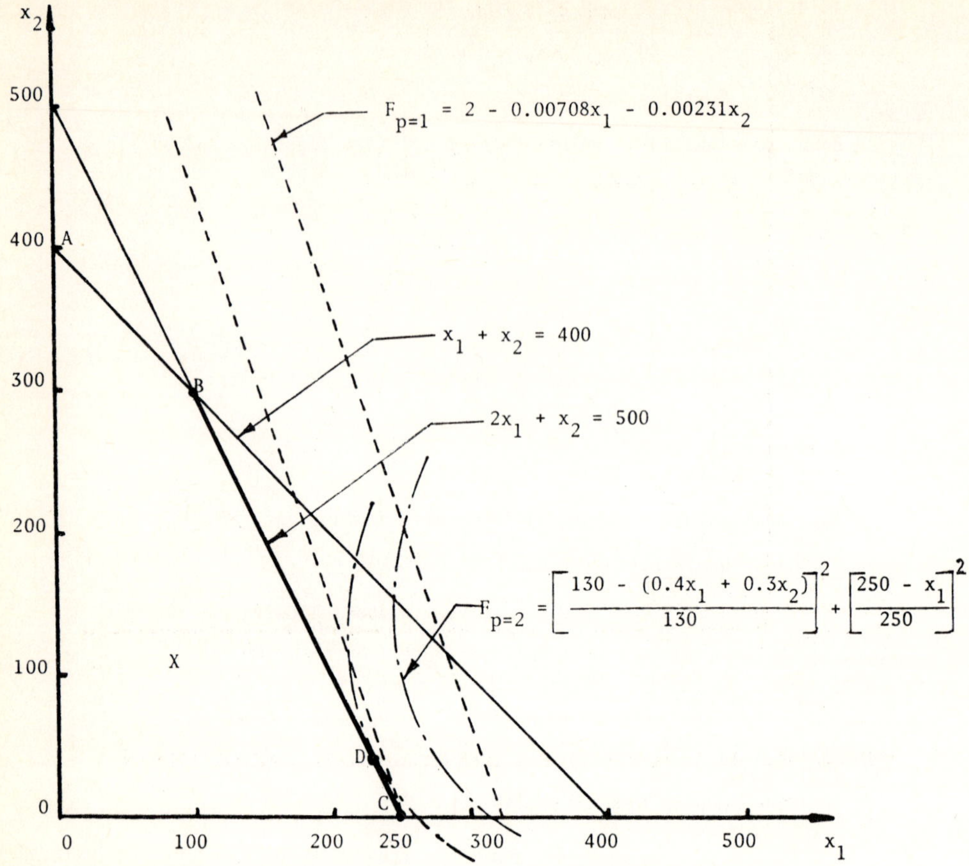


Fig. 3.1 Illustration of the method of global criterion for two variables with p=1 and p=2 in the decision variable space for the numerical example.

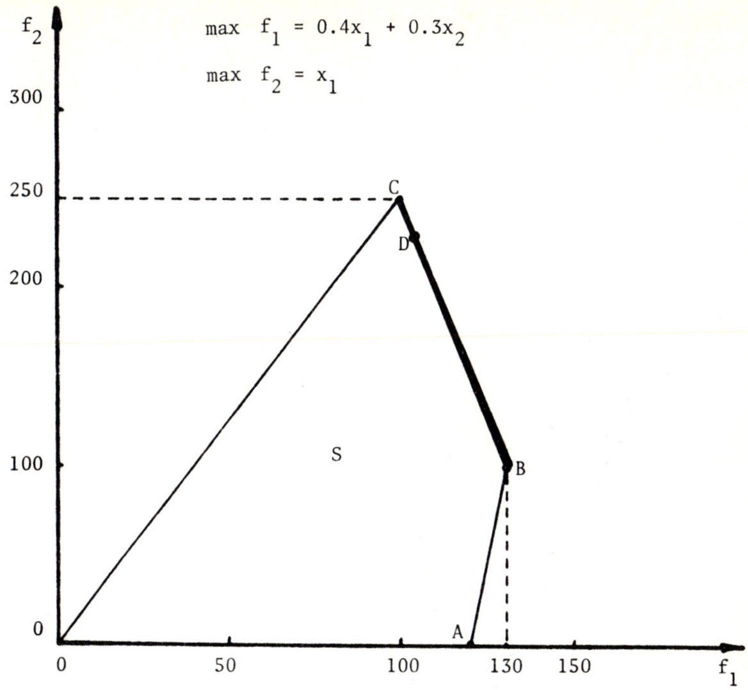


Fig. 3.2 Objective function space representation of feasible area of the numerical example.

value taken on by $f_1$ when $f_2$ reaches its maximum.

Step 3. Obtain the preferred solution

A preferred solution is a non-dominated solution which is a point on the segment of straight line BC. (In Figs. 3.1 and 3.2 all points on the segment of straight line BC are non-dominated solutions).

Case 1. p = 1

The preferred solution for p = 1 in (3.2) is to find $\underline{x} = (x_1, x_2)$ so as to

$$\min F_{p=1} = \frac{130 - (0.4x_1 + 0.3x_2)}{130} + \frac{250 - x_1}{250}$$

$$= 2 - 0.00708x_1 - 0.00231x_2$$

$$\text{s.t.} \quad g_1(\underline{x}) = x_1 + x_2 \leq 400$$

$$g_2(\underline{x}) = 2x_1 + x_2 \leq 500$$

$$x_1, \; x_2 \geq 0$$

This is a linear programming problem. The solution is given by

$$x_1 = 250, \qquad x_2 = 0$$

$$f_1 = 100, \qquad f_2 = 250$$

which is point C in Figs. 3.1 and 3.2.

Case 2. p = 2

The preferred solution for p = 2 in (3.2) is to find $\underline{x}$ so as to

$$\min F_{p=2} = \left(\frac{130 - (0.4x_1 + 0.3x_2)}{130}\right)^2 + \left(\frac{250 - x_1}{250}\right)^2$$

$$\text{s.t.} \quad g_1(\underline{x}) = x_1 + x_2 \leq 400$$

$$g_2(\underline{x}) = 2x_1 + x_2 \leq 500$$

$$x_1, \; x_2 \geq 0$$

This is a nonlinear programming problem. The sequential unconstrained minimization technique (SUMT) [165a] is used for solving the problem. The solution is

$$x_1 = 230.7, \qquad x_2 = 38.6$$

$$f_1 = 103.9, \qquad f_2 = 230.7$$

which is point D in Figs. 3.1 and 3.2.

As shown in Fig. 3.1, for p = 1, the function to be minimized $F_{p=1}$, is a linear function; therefore the preferred solution is determined by the slope of line BC and that of $F_{p=1}$. Since the slope of $F_{p=1}$ is less than that of line BC (the line representing the non-dominated solutions), point C is the preferred solution. For p = 2, the function to be minimized, $F_{p=2}$, is a nonlinear (quadratic) function, and the minimum point for $F_{p=2}$ is point D in Fig. 3.1, which is the point where the $F_{p=2}$ curve touches the segment of line BC.

The DM's preferred solution for this example should be one of the non-dominated solutions (represented by points on the segment of straight line between B and C in Figs. 3.1 and 3.2). The solutions for $F_{p=1}$, point C, and for $F_{p=2}$, point D, derived by this method may not satisfy the DM at all.

2. Methods for A Priori Articulation of Preference Information Given

'A Priori' means the preference information is given to the analyst (who is responsible for solution of the VMP) before he/she actually solves the problem. The DM provides the information during or after the actual mathematical formulation of the problem. The information may be either: (1) cardinal information, or (2) mixed (ordinal and cardinal) information. In the case of cardinal information, the DM must give some judgement about specific objective preference levels or specific trade-offs. But if the information is mixed, the DM must rank the objectives in the order of their importance.

2.1. Methods for Cardinal Information Given

The two major methods under this category are: (1) utility function methods, and (2) bounded objective methods.

2.1.1. UTILITY FUNCTION METHODS

In all of the utility function methods the VMP is converted to (3.3):

$$\left.\begin{array}{ll} \max & U(f_1, f_2, \ldots, f_k) = U(\underline{f}) \\ \text{s.t.} & g_j(\underline{x}) \leq 0, \quad j = 1,2, \ldots, m \end{array}\right\} \qquad (3.3)$$

where $U(\underline{f})$ is the utility function of the multiple objectives. Thus the methods require that $U(\underline{f})$ be known prior to solving the VMP. The rationale for using $U(\underline{f})$ is that from a realistic point-of-view the DM must have some utility associated with the objectives. This approach is similar to that of using utility functions in consumer theory in economics. The utility function would take into consideration the DM's preferences. However, the determination of $U(\underline{f})$ for even a simple problem is difficult. For a complex problem with multiple objectives the process of determining $U(\underline{f})$ is very difficult. The literature on utility function methods and on problems of determining $U(\underline{f})$ is discussed and reviewed in Farquhar [103], Fishburn [113], Huber [162], Keeney [187], Keeney and Raiffa [BM-12], and Winterfeldt and Fischer [361].

The major advantage of utility function methods is that if $U(\underline{f})$ has been correctly assessed and used, it will ensure the most satisfactory solution to the DM. The solution will be a point at which the nondominated set of solutions and the indifference curves of the DM are tangent to each other. (The indifference curves can be considered as contours of equal utility). Thus, the solution will have the highest utility for the DM, and it will also be nondominated. The major difficulty with the methods is that the DM is required to articulate preference judgement in an information vacuum. Moreover, like the single objective utility functions, the multiobjective utility functions suffer from their intransitivity in terms of time and state.

The utility function $U(\underline{f})$ can be of many forms. The common form assumes that the DM's utility function is additively separable with respect to the objectives [113]. The assumptions behind the additive utility function method are: (i) if $\underline{f}^1 = (f_1^1, f_2^1, \ldots, f_k^1)$ and $\underline{f}^2 = (f_1^2, f_2^2, \ldots, f_k^2)$ are two vectors of $\underline{f}$, then $\underline{f}^1$ is preferable to $\underline{f}^2$ if $U(\underline{f}^1) > U(\underline{f}^2)$, and (ii) $U(\underline{f}) = U_1(f_1) + U_2(f_2) + \ldots + U_k(f_k)$ where $U_i$'s are utility functions for each $f_i$, $i = 1,2, \ldots,k$. For this additive utility function method, the VMP is given by (3.4):

$$\left.\begin{aligned} &\max \quad U = \sum_{i=1}^{k} U_i(f_i) \\ &\text{s.t.} \quad g_i(\underline{x}) \leq 0, \qquad i = 1,2, \ldots, m \end{aligned}\right\} \tag{3.4}$$

A special form of (3.4), which has been widely used in MODM problems, is to use the weights $w_i$ to indicate the importance of each objective. The problem then is given by

$$\left.\begin{aligned} &\max \quad \sum_{i=1}^{k} \cdot w_i \ f_i(\underline{x}) \\ &\text{s.t.} \quad g_i(\underline{x}) \leq 0, \qquad i = 1,2, \ldots, m \end{aligned}\right\} \qquad (3.5)$$

It has been shown [232] that the line passing through the point of tangency of indifference curve and nondominated solution set is a source of the optimal values for weight $w_i$'s; i.e., the slope of the tangent is proportional to the ratio of the optimal values of the $w_i$'s. Thus if the optimal $w_i$'s can be determined, (3.5) will ensure the most satisfactory solution. However, in practice the $w_i$'s often are the DM's subjective estimate of the importance of different objectives, and not necessarily the optimal values.

The advantage of using (3.4) or (3.5) is the simplicity. It is easier to assess k unidimensional $U_i$'s than to assess $U(\underline{f})$ directly; similarly, it is easier to get $w_i$'s from the DM, who may believe these values are correctly known before the actual solution. The disadvantages of this approach are: (1) there are very few cases where utility functions are really additively separable; (2) the $w_i$'s depend upon both the achievement level of $f_i(\underline{x})$ itself, and the relative achievement of $f_i(\underline{x})$ compared to the achievement levels of the other objective functions.

Some other forms of $U(\underline{f})$ may be used; for example, $U(\underline{f}) = \prod_{i=1}^{k} U_i(f_i)$. However, all other forms do not alleviate the basic weakness of utility function methods - the difficulty in assessment and intransivity of utility functions.

<u>NUMERICAL EXAMPLE</u> (Production scheduling of the Hardee toy company)

<u>Example 1 (Weighting Method)</u>

We again consider production scheduling of the Hardee toy company presented in Sec. 1.1.1. The VMP problem is:

$$\begin{aligned} \max \quad & f_1(\underline{x}) = 0.4x_1 + 0.3x_2 \\ \max \quad & f_2(\underline{x}) = x_1 \\ \text{s.t.} \quad & g_1(\underline{x}) = x_1 + x_2 \leq 400 \\ & g_2(\underline{x}) = 2x_1 + x_2 \leq 500 \\ & x_1, x_2 \geq 0 \end{aligned}$$

Let $\underline{x} \in X$ represent the constraints set.

Assume that the DM gives the weights, $\underline{w} = (w_1, w_2) = (0.6, 0.4)$, to indicate the importance of each objective. Then the problem in the form of (3.5) is:

$$\max_{\underline{x} \in X} \quad 0.6f_1(\underline{x}) + 0.4f_2(\underline{x})$$

or

$$\max_{\underline{x} \in X} \quad 0.64x_1 + 0.18x_2$$

The solution of this problem is:

$\underline{x} = (250, 0)$, $f = (100, 250)$.

This solution is the same as the ideal solution of $f_2(\underline{x})$ which solves (see Sec. 1.1.1):

$$\max_{\underline{x} \in X} \quad f_2(\underline{x}) = x_1$$

That is, the solutions for weights $\underline{w} = (0.6, 0.4)$ and $\underline{w} = (0, 1.0)$ are the same; therefore, the weights do not reflect the relative importance of each objective in the proportional sense. One way to eliminate the difficulty of estimating the weights of objectives is to use the parametric method (see Sec. 4.1.1) for generating a nondominated solution set by varying $\underline{w}$. From this set the DM then selects the preferred solution. The nondominated solution set obtained by the parametric method is presented in Table 3.1. All the solutions are on the line segment of BC in Fig. 3.3.

Tabel 3.1 The nondominated solutions set of Example 1.

| $w_1$ | $w_2$ | $-w_1/w_2$ | $x_1$ | $x_2$ | $f_1$ | $f_2$ | Location* of $\underline{f}$ |
|---|---|---|---|---|---|---|---|
| 0. | 1.0 | 0. | 250. | 0 | 100. | 250 | C |
| 0.2 | 0.8 | -0.25 | 250. | 0 | 100. | 250 | C |
| 0.4 | 0.6 | -0.67 | 250. | 0 | 100. | 250 | C |
| 0.6 | 0.4 | -1.5 | 250. | 0 | 100. | 250 | C |
| 0.8 | 0.2 | -4. | 250. | 0 | 100. | 250 | C |
| 0.833 | 0.167 | -5.** | - | - | - | - | Segment BC |
| 1.0 | 0. | ∞ | 100. | 300. | 130. | 100 | B |

* Locations in Fig. 3.3

** It is equal to the slope of BC in Fig. 3.3, hence the solutions set has infinite points.

$$\max \quad f_1 = 0.4x_1 + 0.3x_2$$

$$\max \quad f_2 = x_1$$

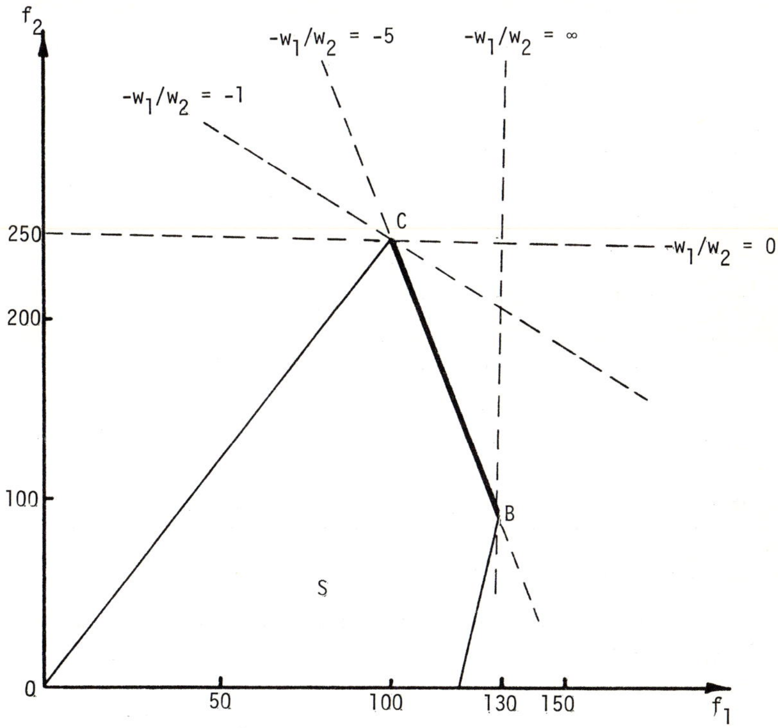


Fig. 3.3 The nondominated solution set of Example 1.

The additively separable utility function of (3.5) is the simplest form among the utility functions. However, as Example 1 shows, the solutions do not necessarily reflect the DM's subjective estimation of the relative importance of each objective.

The next example will illustrate the assessment of the manager's utility function for the Hardee toy company.

Example 2 (Assessing the utility function)

The manager's objectives are (1) to maximize the profit, and (2) to improve the relationship with the best customer by producing as many of Doll A as possible. Then the manager's overall preference can be represented by the two attributes (objectives): "profit Y" and "number of Doll A produced Z". The multiattribute (multiobjective) utility function $U(y,z)$ is introduced to quantify the manager's preference.

Prior to assessing the manager's preference, note that Y cannot exceed \$130 and that Z cannot exceed 250 dolls; these values are obtained by optimizing $\max_{\underline{x} \varepsilon X} Y = \max_{\underline{x} \varepsilon X} f_1(\underline{x})$ and $\max_{\underline{x} \varepsilon X} Z = \max_{\underline{x} \varepsilon X} f_2(\underline{x})$. Thus the consequence space is limited by $\{(y, z) \mid 0 \leq y \leq 130, \; 0 \leq z \leq 250\}$.

It is necessary to check whether Y is utility independent of Z. Given $U(y,z)$, we shall say Y is utility independent of Z if the DM's preference over any lotteries on Y for a fixed $z_o$ in Z are the same regardless of the amount of $z_o$. Thus if Z is the same for all possible consequences, the DM's relative preferences for lotteries involving these consequences depend only on Y. To simplify the process, it is assumed that Y is utility independent of Z; for example, manager's lottery $[(130, 0) : (0, 0)] \sim (55, 0)$ is also the same as $[(130, 100) : (0, 100)] \sim (55, 100)$. The notation [P : Q] means a lottery yielding either P or Q with equal probability. And also assumed is that Z is utility independent of Y. Thus the attributes (objectives) are mutually utility independent; and Keeney's theorem [183] is applicable. If Y and Z are mutually independent, then

$$U(y,z) = U(y,z_o) + U(y_o,z) + kU(y,z_o)\ U(y_o,z)$$

where k is a constant evaluated empirically by

$$k = \frac{U(y_1,z_1) - U(y_1,z_o) - U(y_o,z_1)}{U(y_1,z_o)\ U(y_o,z_1)}$$

where all subscripts indicate a specific value for y and z.

Next we assess a conditional utility function for (y, 0). It is certain that the DM's preference is monotonically increasing in Y. Previously the lottery [(130, 0) : (0, 0)] is shown to be indifferent to (55, 0). In addition [(55, 0) : (0, 0)] is indifferent to (25, 0), and [(130, 0) : (55, 0)] to (90, 0). Thus it seems that the conditional utility function for (y, 0), which will be denoted by $U_1(y, 0)$, is risk averse (i.e., $U_1(\cdot)$ is concave).

We may arbitrarily set the origin and unit of measure of $U_1(y, 0)$ by

$$U_1(0, 0) = 0 \quad \text{and} \quad U_1(130, 0) = 1 \tag{3.5a}$$

For simplicity, we use a utility function of the form $a(1 - e^{-by})$ to fit the data as plotted in Fig. 3.4a. The utility of specific values is calculated as:

$$U_1(55, 0) = 1/2\ U_1(130, 0) + 1/2\ U_1(0, 0) = 0.5$$

$$U_1(25, 0) = 1/2\ U_1(55, 0) + 1/2\ U_1(0, 0) = 0.25$$

$$U_1(90, 0) = 1/2\ U_1(130, 0) + 1/2\ U_1(55, 0) = 0.75$$

By fitting curves, the resulting utility function is

$$U_1(y, 0) = 2.1545\ (1 - e^{-0.0048y}) \tag{3.5b}$$

The utility function is monotonically increasing and risk averse.

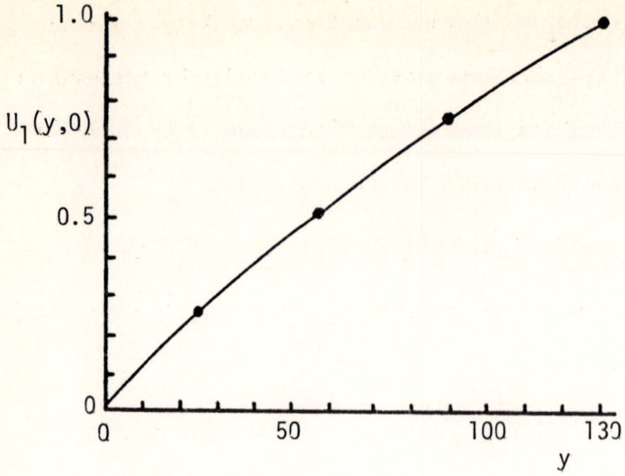


Fig. 3.4a Conditional utility function for profit.

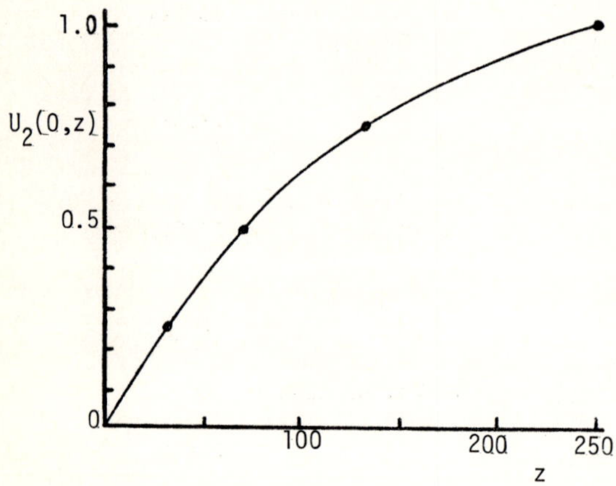


Fig. 3.4b Conditional utility function for Doll A production.

Similarly, in assessing $U_2(0, z)$ the conditional utility function for Z, [(0, 250) : (0, 0)] is given indifferent to (0, 75) by the manager; [(0, 75) : (0, 0)] indifferent to (0, 35); and [(0, 250) : (0, 75)] indifferent to (0, 135). Thus by scaling

$$U_2(0, 0) = 0 \quad \text{and} \quad U_2(0, 250) = 1 \tag{3.5c}$$

the data can be plotted as indicated in Fig. 3.4b. Again by fitting curves, this utility function becomes

$$U_2(0, z) = 1.1982\ (1 - e^{-0.0072z}) \tag{3.5d}$$

The next step of the assessment involves the consistent scaling of $U_1(y, 0)$ and $U_2(0, z)$. It is determined that (100, 0) is indifferent to (0, 250). Now, it is possible to scale the utility function for (y, z), which will be denoted by U(y, z). First, set

$$U(0, 0) = 0 \tag{3.5e}$$

and

$$U(130, 250) = 1 \tag{3.5f}$$

and define $a_1$ and $a_2$ by

$$U(130, 0) = a_1 \tag{3.5g}$$

and

$$U(0, 250) = a_2 \tag{3.5h}$$

From eqs. (3.5a), (3.5e), and (3.5g), it follows that

$$U(y, 0) = a_1\ U_1\ (y, 0) \tag{3.5i}$$

Likewise, from eqs. (3.5c), (3.5e), and (3.5h), we have

$$U(0, z) = a_2\ U_2\ (0, z) \tag{3.5j}$$

Also, since U(100, 0) = U(0, 250)

or by substituting from eqs. (3.5c), (3.5i), and (3.5j), we have

$$a_1\, U_1(100, 0) = a_2\, U_2(0, 250) = a_2 * 1 = a_2 \qquad (3.5k)$$

Using eq. (3.5b), $U_1(100, 0) = 2.1545\,(1 - e^{-0.0048*100}) = 0.8213$,

which can be substituted into eq. (3.5k), we obtain

$$a_2 = 0.8213 a_1 \qquad (3.5\ell)$$

Because of mutual utility independence between Y and Z,

$$U(y, z) = U(y, 0) + U(0, z)$$

$$+ \left\{\frac{U(130, 250) - U(130, 0) - U(0, 250)}{U(130, 0)\, U(0, 250)}\right\} * U(y, 0)\, U(0, z)$$

$$= a_1\, U_1(y, 0) + a_2\, U_2(0, z)$$

$$+ \left(\frac{1 - a_1 - a_2}{a_1 a_2}\right) a_1\, U_1(y, 0)\, a_2\, U_2(0, z)$$

$$= 2.1545 a_1\, (1 - e^{-0.0048y}) + 1.1982\, a_2 (1 - e^{-0.0072z})$$

$$+ 2.1545 * 1.1982\, (1 - a_1 - a_2)(1 - e^{-0.0048y})(1 - e^{-0.0072z}) \qquad (3.5m)$$

The only parameter needed in eq. (3.5m) to completely specify U(y, z) is $a_1$. To calculate $a_1$, it is found that the DM is indifferent between [(130, 250) : (0, 0)] and (80, 150). Then using eqs. (3.5e) and (3.5f), we have

$$U(80, 150) = 1/2\, U(130, 250) + 1/2\, U(0, 0) = 0.5 \qquad (3.5n)$$

Equ. (3.5m) now can be evaluated at (80, 150) and equal to 0.5 to yield

$$a_1 = -0.1257 \qquad (3.5o)$$

We obtain the desired utility function by substututing eq.(3.5o) into eqs. (3.5ℓ) and (3.5m).

$$U(y, z) = -0.2708(1 - e^{-0.0048y}) - 0.1237(1 - e^{-0.0072z})$$

$$+ 3.1725 (1 - e^{-0.0048y})(1 - e^{-0.0072z}) \qquad (3.5p)$$

The obtained utility function (3.5p) is assumed to be satisfactory for the necessary consistency.

We know the following relationship between the attributes and their associated decision variables.

$$y = f_1(\underline{x}) = 0.4\, x_1 + 0.3\, x_2$$

$$z = f_2(\underline{x}) = x_1$$

By substituting these relationships into eq. (3.5p), we obtain

$$U(f_1, f_2) = -0.2708\ [1 - e^{-0.0048(0.4x_1 + 0.3x_2)}]$$

$$-0.1237\ [1 - e^{-0.0072x_1}]$$

$$+3.1725\ [1 - e^{-0.0048(0.4x_1 + 0.3x_2)}][1 - e^{-0.0072x_1}] \qquad (3.5q)$$

After assessing the utility function, the VMP problem is converted to (3.3) format:

$$\max\ U(f_1, f_2)$$

$$\text{s.t. } x_1 + x_2 \leq 400$$

$$2x_1 + x_2 \leq 500$$

$$x_1, x_2 \geq 0$$

This is a nonlinear programming problem, since $U(f_1, f_2)$ given by (3.5q) is a nonlinear function. The sequential unconstrained minimization technique (SUMT) [165a] was used to solve the problem. The solution is:

$$U(f_1, f_2) = 0.8004$$

$$\underline{x} = (223, 53)$$

$$\underline{f} = (105, 223)$$

Note that the solution is one of the nondominated solutions on the line segment of BC in Fig. 3.3.

2.1.2. BOUNDED OBJECTIVE METHODS

These methods require that the DM give at least the minimum acceptable level of achievement for each objective function. The VMP then is converted to (3.6):

$$\left.\begin{aligned} &\max \ f_r(\underline{x}) \\ &\text{s.t. } g_i(\underline{x}) \leq 0, \quad i = 1,2, \ldots, m \\ &\qquad f_j(\underline{x}) \geq L_j, \quad j = 1,2, \ldots, k; \ j \neq r \end{aligned}\right\} \tag{3.6}$$

Another variation is that the DM specifies both the minimum level $L_j$, and the maximum acceptable achievement level $H_j$ if so desired. Thus the problem becomes (3.7):

$$\left.\begin{aligned} &\max \ f_r(\underline{x}) \\ &\text{s.t. } g_i(\underline{x}) \leq 0, \quad i = 1,2, \ldots, m \\ &\qquad f_j(\underline{x}) \geq L_j, \quad j = 1,2, \ldots, k; \ j \neq r \\ &\qquad f_j(\underline{x}) \leq H_j, \quad j = 1,2, \ldots, k; \ j \neq r \end{aligned}\right\} \tag{3.7}$$

The main difficulty with these methods is to find $L_j$ (and $H_j$) values from the DM prior to any preliminary solution. Since the DM has to give these values in an information void, they may result in turning (3.6) or (3.7) into problems with inconsistent constraints. Even if the DM is well informed and the problems are not turned into inconsistent ones, the solution of (3.6) or (3.7) may not necessarily provide the satisfactory solution for the DM. Another question in this approach is which objective should be used for $f_r(\underline{x})$.

Because of the above difficulties these methods are now rarely used alone; rather they are used in conjunction with other solution methods. This is why there is no mention of any literature under this category in Table 1.3.

NUMERICAL EXAMPLE

Examples of how bounded objective methods are incorporated in other solution methods are: as a part of the surrogate worth trade-off method (see Sec. 3.1.2, Example 2, Step 2); as a part of the method of satisfactory goals (see Sec. 3.1.3, Numerical Example, Step 2).

## 2.2 Methods for Mixed Ordinal and Cardinal Information Given

The most important information needed for lexicographic method, goal programming, and goal attainment method is the ordinal inter-objective preference information, although some of these methods also require some cardinal information.

### 2.2.1 LEXICOGRAPHIC METHOD

This method requires that the objectives be ranked in order of importance by the DM. The preferred solution obtained by this method is one which maximizes the objectives starting with the most important and proceeding according to the order of importance of the objectives. (See Table 1.3 for references).

Let the subscripts of the objectives indicate not only the components of the objective vector, $\underline{f}(\underline{x})$, but also the priorities of the objectives, i.e., $f_1(\underline{x})$ is the first component of $\underline{f}(\underline{x})$ and the most important objective, $f_2(\underline{x})$ is the second component and the second most important objective, and so on. Then the first problem to be solved is:

$$\left.\begin{array}{lll} \max & f_1(\underline{x}) & \\ \text{s.t.} & g_j(\underline{x}) \leq 0, & j = 1, 2, \ldots, m \end{array}\right\} \qquad (3.8)$$

Let $f_1^*$ be the solution to (3.8). If (3.8) gives a unique $\underline{x}$ for $f_1^*$, the solution is considered as the preferred solution to the entire problem. Otherwise, the second problem is to be solved, i.e.,

$$\left.\begin{array}{lll} \max & f_2(\underline{x}) & \\ \text{s.t.} & g_j(\underline{x}) \leq 0 & j = 1, 2, \ldots, M \\ & f_1(\underline{x}) = f_1^* & \end{array}\right\} \qquad (3.9)$$

Let $f_2^*$ be the solution to (3.9). If (3.9) gives a unique $\underline{x}$ for $f_j^*$, the solution is the preferred solution to the entire problem. Otherwise the procedure is repeated until all k objectives have been considered. In general, the ith problem is:

$$\left.\begin{array}{lll} \max & f_i(\underline{x}) & \\ \text{s.t.} & g_j(\underline{x}) \leq 0, & j = 1, 2, \ldots, m \\ & f_\ell(\underline{x}) = f_\ell^*, & \ell = 1, 2, \ldots, i-1 \end{array}\right\} \qquad (3.10)$$

Since the procedure is terminated when a unique solution is obtained at the ith problem, the solution will be the preferred solution to the entire problem; the objectives ranked less important than $f_i(\underline{x})$ are ignored by this method. The rationale for this method is that individuals tend to make decisions in this manner.

Let us consider an example with two objectives and one decision variable as illustrated in Fig. 3.5. All possible solutions for the first problem which maximize $f_1(x)$ are in the region of $x_b \leq x \leq x_c$. $f_2(x)$ is maximized at $x = x_c$ in this region. Therefore, $x_c$ is the preferred decision.

If the priorities of $f_1(x)$ and $f_2(x)$ are changed in this example (Fig. 3.5), $x_e$ becomes the preferred decision instead of $x_c$. All decisions in the region $x_c \leq x \leq x_e$ are non-dominated. Note that the solution is very sensitive to the ranking of the objectives given by the DM; the analyst should exercise caution in applying this method when two objectives are of nearly equal importance.

A variation of the method proposed by Waltz [353] may reduce the sensitivity. After the first objective is maximized, the second objective is maximized subject to keeping the first objective within a certian percentage of its optimum. The third objective is then maximized keeping the first two within a certain percentage of the optimum values found in the previous step. The ith problem then is:

$$\left.\begin{array}{lll} \max & f_i(\underline{x}) & \\ \text{s.t.} & g_j(\underline{x}) \leq 0, & j = 1, 2, \ldots, m \\ & f_\ell(\underline{x}) = f_\ell^* - \delta_\ell\ , & \ell = 1, 2, \ldots, i-1 \end{array}\right\} \qquad (3.11)$$

where $\delta_\ell$'s are tolerances determined by the DM.

With this modification, the feasible region for the second problem in the example (Fig. 3.5) expands to $x_a \leq x \leq x_d$; $x_d$ yields the maximum value of $f_2(x)$ in this region and becomes the preferred decision. Therefore, the sensitivity of the ranking to the solution is reduced.

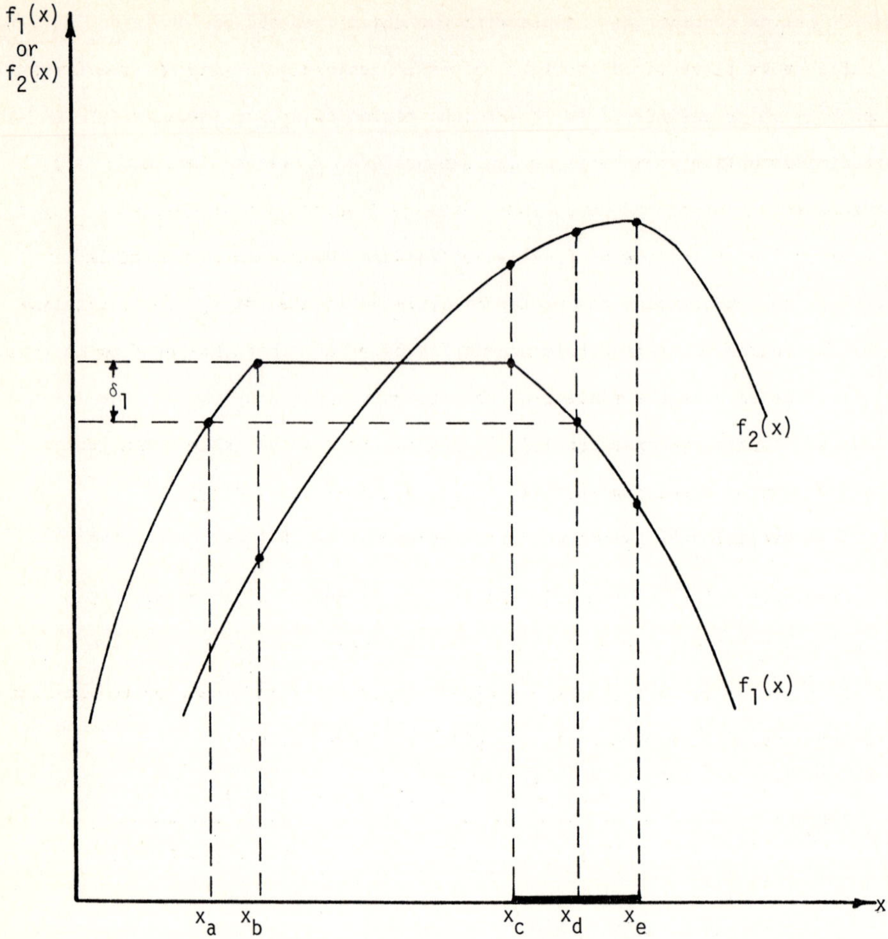


Fig. 3.5 Lexicographic method for a problem with two objectives and one decision variable.

NUMERICAL EXAMPLE (Optimal scheduled maintenance policy)

For every piece of military or commercial equipment, there exist critical components whose failure could result in the shutdown of the equipment, hazardous conditions for individuals using the equipment, or failure of the tactical functions of the equipment. As a consequence, it is desirable to use multiple criteria in determining the replacement age of such critical items.

The problem is to determine the preventive replacement age for a critical item of a complex system (e.g. an aircraft) based on the following four criteria:

(1) minimize the replacement cost per unit time, $C(t_p)$

(2) maximize the mission reliability of the complex system, $R(t_p,H)$

(3) maximize the availability of the critical item, $A(t_p)$

(4) minimize the expected mission failure cost, $E_{t_p}$

When the failure of the critical item is distributed according to the Weibull distribution, the replacement cost per unit of time, $C(t_p)$, the mission reliability, $R(t_p,H)$, the availability, $A(t_p)$, and the expected mission disaster cost, $E_{t_p}$, are respectively given by [167a, 353b]:

$$C(t_p) = \frac{C_1 \exp(-\frac{1}{A} t_p^B) + C_2 [1 - \exp(-\frac{1}{A} t_p^B)]}{\int_0^{t_p} \exp(-\frac{1}{A} t_p^B) dt_p + t_1 \exp(-\frac{1}{A} t_p^B) + t_2 [1-\exp(1 - \frac{1}{A} t_p^B)]}$$

$$R(t_p,H) = \frac{\exp [-\frac{1}{A} (t_p + H)^B]}{\exp(-\frac{1}{A} t_p^B)}$$

$$A(t_p) = \frac{\int_0^{t_p} \exp(-\frac{1}{A} t_p^B) dt_p}{\int_0^{t_p} \exp(-\frac{1}{A} t_p^B) dt_p + t_1 \exp(-\frac{1}{A} t_p^B) + t_2 [1 - \exp(-\frac{1}{A} t_p^B)]}$$

$$E_{t_p} = C_3 F(t_p,H) = C_3 \left\{ 1 - \frac{\exp [-\frac{1}{A} (t_p + H)^B]}{\exp(-\frac{1}{A} t_p^B)} \right\}$$

An aircraft engine is found to have failure characteristics which are closely represented by a Weibull distribution with two parameters: $A = 2.6954 \times 10^9$, $B = 3.0$. It is also reasonable to assume the following numerical values:

$C_1$ = \$25,000 = the cost of a preventive replacement

$C_2$ = \$37,500 = the cost of a failure replacement

$C_3$ = \$2,500,000 = the cost of a mission failure

$t_1$ = 8 hrs = the mean replacement time for the preventive replacement

$t_2$ = 16 hrs = the mean replacement time for the failure replacement

H = 16 hrs = the mission length

$F(0,H) = 1 - R(0,H)$ = the probability of mission failure of newly replaced critical item.

With these numerical values, the replacement cost per unit of time, $C(t_p)$, the mission reliability, $R(t_p,H)$, the availability, $A(t_p)$, and the expected mission cost, $E_{t_p}$, are shown in Fig. 3.6.

Optimal policy by the basic algorithm

Assume the DM ranks the importance of four criteria as: (1) mission reliability, (2) expected cost of inflight failure cost, (3) replacement cost per unit of time, (4) the availability of the equipment. Then the first problem to be solved is (instead of $\max_{t_p} R(t_p,H)$) as follows:

$$\left.\begin{array}{ll} \text{Find} & t_p \\ \text{s.t.} & R(t_p,H) \geq R(t_p,H)_{min} \\ & t_p \geq 0 \end{array}\right\} \qquad (3.12)$$

where $R(t_p,H)_{min} = 0.985$.

The solution is $t_p \leq 913$ hrs (see Fig. 3.6). Since this is not a unique solution, the second problem to be solved is (instead of $\min_{t_p} C_3F(t_p,H)$) as follows:

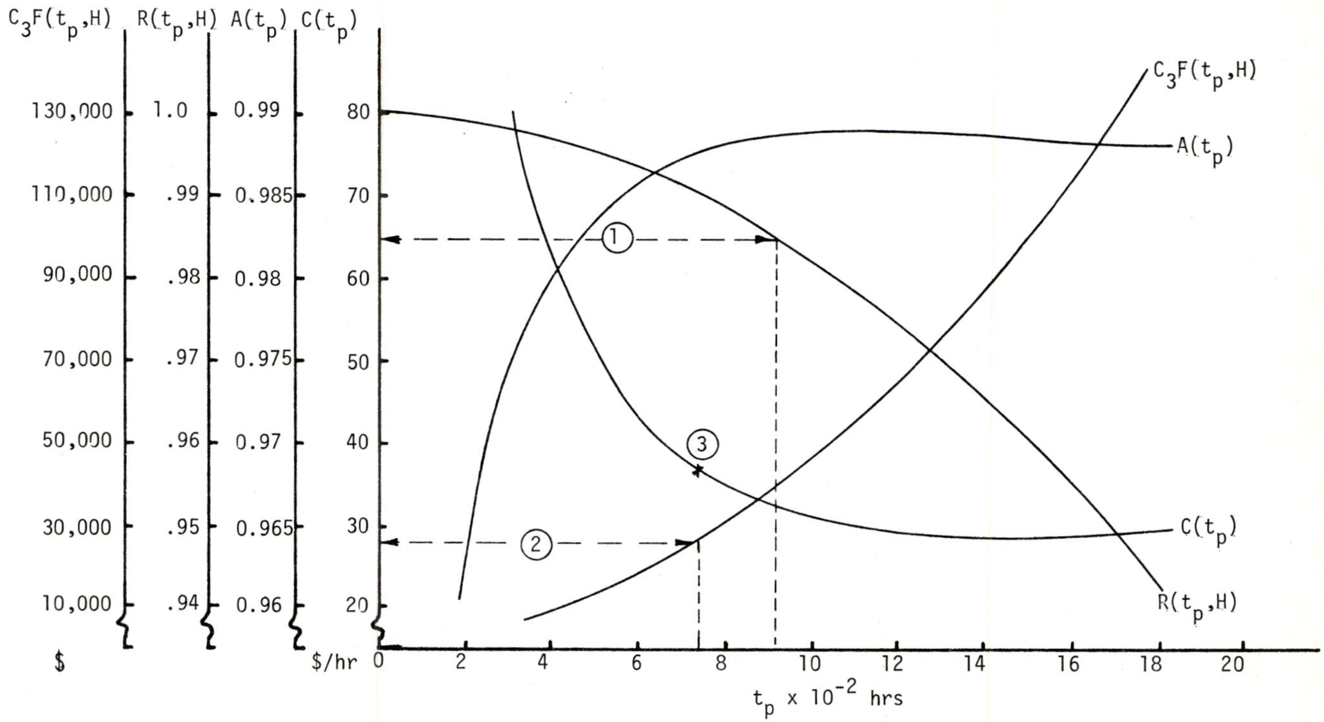


Fig. 3.6 Finding replacement age by lexicographic method

$$\left.\begin{array}{ll} \text{Find} & t_p \\ \text{s.t.} & C_3F(t_p,H) \leq C_3F(0,H) + C_1 \\ & R(t_p,H) \geq 0.985 \\ & t_p \geq 0 \end{array}\right\} \quad (3.13)$$

The solution to (3.13) is $t_p \leq 743$ (see Fig. 3.6). Since this is still not a unique solution, the third problem to be solved is:

$$\left.\begin{array}{ll} \min\limits_{\{t_p\}} & C(t_p) \\ \text{s.t.} & R(t_p,H) \geq 0.985 \\ & C_3F(t_p,H) \leq C_3F(0,H) + C_1 \\ & t_p \geq 0 \end{array}\right\} \quad (3.14)$$

The solution to (3.14) is $t_p$ = 743 hrs. Since this is a unique solution the procedure is terminated. The $t_p$ = 743 hrs is the preferred solution to the entire problem. The less important criterion, availability of the equipment, is ignored by this method. The optimal replacement age of this specific example obtained by the lexicographic method is illustrated in Fig. 3.6. Since there are four criteria in the problem, the DM may rank their importance in 4! = 24 different ways. The results for these 24 different ways of rankings are shown in Table 3.1a. Results in Table 3.1a indicate that for this specific numerical example, the preferred solution is dominated by the first priority or the first and second priorities. It is noted that the preferred solution will be different if the priorities of the four criteria are changed. Since the solution is very sensitive to the ranking of the objectives given by the DM, the analyst should exercise caution in applying this method when some objectives are of nearly equal importance.

Table 3.1a The results of different rankings of criterion importance by lexicographic method

| Priority 1 | Priority 2 | Priority 3 | Priority 4 | $t_p^*$(hr) |
|---|---|---|---|---|
| $C(t_p)$ | | Those criteria in this area will not affect the solution | | 1455 |
| $A(t_p)$ | | | | 1129 |
| $R(t_p,H)$ | $A(t_p)$ | | | 913 |
| $R(t_p,H)$ | $C(t_p)$ | | | 913 |
| $R(t_p,H)$ | $C_3\ F(t_p,H)$ | | | 743 |
| $C_3F(t_p,H)$ | | | | 743 |

Optimal policy by Waltz's lexicographic method

A variation of the method proposed by Waltz [353] may reduce the sensitivity of the DM's priority of criteria. After the first objective is maximized, the second objective is maximized subject to keeping the first objective within a certain percentage of its optimum. The third objective is then maximized keeping the first two within a certain percentage of the optimum values found in the previous step, and so on.

Now, if the DM decides that the importance of four criteria are ranked as (1) the replacement cost per unit of time, (2) the availability of the equipment, (3) the mission reliability, and (4) the expected inflight failure cost, then the first solution to be solved is:

$$\left.\begin{aligned} &\min_{\{t_p\}} && C(t_p) \\ &\text{s.t.} && t_p \geq 0 \end{aligned}\right\} \tag{3.15}$$

The solution is $t_p^* = 1455$ hrs, and $C(t_p) = 28.92$ \$/hr (see Fig. 3.7). However, the DM decides the replacement cost per unit time, $C(t_p)$, is satisfactory when it is less than 30.5 \$/hr. Then the second problem to be solved is:

$$\left.\begin{aligned} &\max_{\{t_p\}} && A(t_p) \\ &\text{s.t.} && C(t_p) \leq 30.5 \\ & && t_p \geq 0 \end{aligned}\right\} \tag{3.16}$$

The solution to (3.16) is $t_p^* = 1129$ hrs. and $A(t_p^*) = 0.9888$ (see Fig. 3.7). The DM thinks that it is acceptable when the availability of the item is higher than 0.9875. Then the third problem to be solved is:

$$\left.\begin{aligned} &\max_{\{t_p\}} && R(t_p,H) \\ &\text{s.t.} && C(t_p) \leq 30.5 \\ & && A(t_p) \geq 0.9875 \\ & && t_p \geq 0 \end{aligned}\right\} \tag{3.17}$$

The solution to (3.17) is $t_p^* = 1057$ hrs, $R(t_p^*,H) = 0.98$ (see Fig. 3.7). At this point, the DM finds that the value of mission reliability can not be relaxed. So a unique solution is obtained and the procedure is terminated. The preferred solution is:

$$t_p^* = 1057 \text{ hrs} \qquad \begin{aligned} C(t_p) &= 30.5 \text{ \$/hr} \\ A(t_p) &= 0.98877 \\ R(t_p,H) &= 0.98 \\ C_3F(t_p,H) &= \$50000 \end{aligned}$$

It is noted that the sensitivity of the priority ranking to the solution is reduced. The optimal replacement age of this specific example obtained by Waltz's lexicographic method is illustrated in Fig. 3.7.

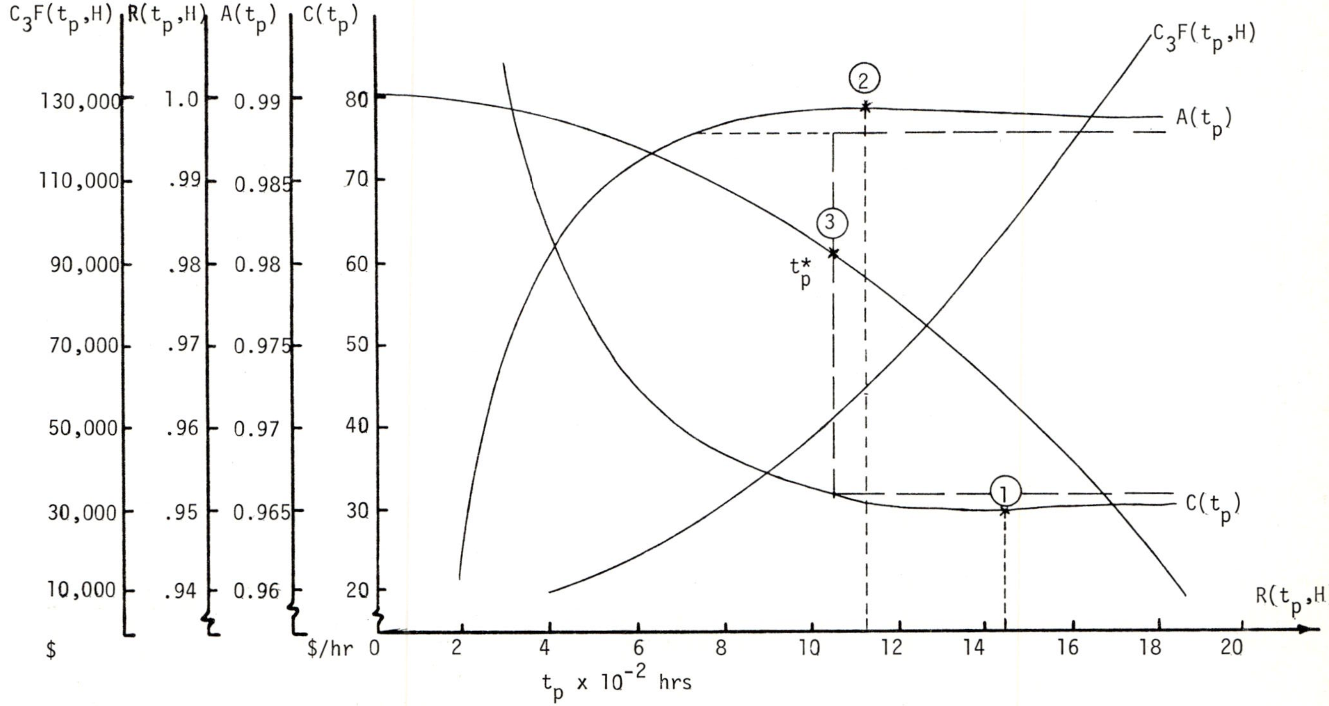


Fig. 3.7 Finding replacement age by Waltz's lexicographic method

2.2.2 GOAL PROGRAMMING

The goal programming was originally proposed by Charnes and Cooper [50] for a linear model. It has been further developed by Ijiri [BM-10] , Lee [BM-13] , and Ignizio [BM-9] , among others. (See [54] for Charnes' and Cooper's review of this method). The method requires the DM to set goals for each objective that he/she wishes to attain. A preferred solution is then defined as the one which minimizes the deviations from the set goals. Thus a simple GP formulation of the VMP is given by (3.18):

$$\left.\begin{array}{ll} \min & \left[ \sum_{j=1}^{k} (d_j^- + d_j^+)^p \right]^{\frac{1}{p}}, \qquad p \geq 1 \\ \text{s.t.} & g_i(\underline{x}) \leq 0, \qquad i = 1, 2, \ldots, m \\ & f_j(\underline{x}) + d_j^- - d_j^+ = b_j, \qquad j = 1, 2, \ldots, k \\ & d_j^-, d_j^+ \geq 0, \qquad \forall_j \\ & d_j^- \cdot d_j^+ = 0 \qquad \forall_j \end{array}\right\} \tag{3.18}$$

where $b_j$, $j = 1, 2, \ldots, k$ are the goals set by the DM for the objectives, $d_j^-$ and $d_j^+$ are respectively the under-achievement and over-achievement of the jth goal. The value of p is based upon the utility function $U(\underline{f})$ of the DM.

The most common form of GP formulation requires that the DM, in addition to setting the goals for the objectives, also be able to give an ordinal ranking of the objectives. The GP formulation of the VMP for such a case is:

$$\left.\begin{array}{ll} \min & [P_1 h_1(\underline{d}^-, \underline{d}^+), P_2 h_2(\underline{d}^-, \underline{d}^+), \ldots, P_\ell h_\ell(\underline{d}^-, \underline{d}^+)] \\ \text{s.t.} & g_j(\underline{x}) \leq 0, \; j = 1, 2, \ldots, m \\ & f_i(\underline{x}) + d_i^- - d_i^+ = b_i, \qquad i = 1, 2, \ldots, k \\ & d_i^-, d_i^+ \geq 0 \qquad \forall_i \\ & d_i^- \cdot d_i^+ = 0 \qquad \forall_i \end{array}\right\} \tag{3.19}$$

where $h_i(\underline{d}^-, \underline{d}^+)$, $i = 1, 2, \ldots, \ell$, are linear functions of the deviational variables and are called achievement functions. The $P_i$'s are preemptive weights; that is, $P_i >>> P_{i+1}$. This implies that no number W, however large, can make $W*P_{j+1} > P_j$.

The solution algorithm for (3.19) is that $h_1(\underline{d}^-, \underline{d}^+)$ is minimized first; let min $h_1 = h_1^*$. Next $h_2(\underline{d}^-, \underline{d}^+)$ is minimized, but in no circumstances can $h_1$ be greater than $h_1^*$. Thus a lower ranking achievement function cannot be satisfied to the detriment of a higher ranking achievement function. This process continues until $h_\ell(\underline{d}^-, \underline{d}^+)$ is minimized. Some special computer codings for linear models are available; for example, in Ignizio [BM-9] . It is basically a modified simplex algorithm for linear programming problems. However, for a moderate size problem the modified simplex algorithm approach is time consuming, and it needs a large capacity computer. The same problem can be solved iteratively by the basic simplex algorithm [see Dauer and Krueger, 78; 364] .

If any of $f_i(\underline{x})$ and $g_i(\underline{x})$ functions in (3.19) are nonlinear, (3.19) becomes a nonlinear goal programming problem. Any single objective nonlinear optimization technique can be used iteratively to solve the problem [165-167, BM-9] . Using the method of linear approximation of nonlinear functions, as presented by Griffith and Steward [138a] , then the nonlinear GP problem can be solved by linear GP [BM-9] . Linear integer goal programming [BM-9] and nonlinear integer goal programming [211a] are also considered.

Note that GP method is quite similar to lexicographic method; the difference is that GP requires goals for the objectives be set by the DM and achievement functions to be minimized in the order they are formed.

Advantages of GP in (3.19) are that the DM does not need to give the numerical weights for the objectives; he/she needs to give only an ordinal ranking of them. However, this implies a value trade-off assumption: that in minimizing $h_{i+1}(\underline{d}^-, \underline{d}^+)$, the value preference for $h_i$ over $h_{i+1}$ is zero if $h_i \leq h_i^*$ and infinity if $h_i > h_i^*$, where $h_i^*$ is the minimum value obtained for $h_i$ when (i-1) previous achievement functions have already been minimized. This value trade-off assumption is a very strong one and is very sensitive to the goal vector set for the objectives and ordinal ranking given by the DM.

GP method has been widely used in many MODM problems (see Table 1.3 for the references).

2.2.2a LINEAR GOAL PROGRAMMING

The general linear goal program model (LGP) takes on the following form:

Find $\underline{x} = (x_1, x_2, \ldots, x_n)$ so as to minimize

$$\underline{a} = \{h_1(\underline{d}^-, \underline{d}^+), h_2(\underline{d}^-, \underline{d}^+), \ldots, h_\ell(\underline{d}^-, \underline{d}^+)\}$$

such that

$$\sum_{j=1}^{n} c_{ij}x_j + d_i^- - d_i^+ = b_i \qquad i = 1, \ldots, m$$

$$\underline{x}, \underline{d}^-, \underline{d}^+ \geq 0, \qquad d_i^- \cdot d_i^+ = 0 \quad \forall_i$$

Graphical Analysis

The technique for solving LGP problems may be easily understood if we first consider a simple graphical approach. Although graphical analysis is only appropriate for a problem having no more than 3 decision variables, it does serve to aid in the understanding of the basic concept and method to be used in large problems.

NUMERICAL EXAMPLE (Production scheduling of the Hardee toy company)

Example 1

The Hardee Toy Company makes two kinds of toy dolls. Doll A is a high quality toy and Doll B is of lower quality. The respective profits are \$0.40 and \$0.30 per doll. Each doll of type A requires twice as much time as a doll of type B, and if all dolls were of type B, the company could make 500 per day. The supply of material is sufficient for only 400 dolls per day (both A and B combined). Assuming that all the dolls for type A and type B the factory can make could be sold, how should the manager schedule production to achieve the most profit?

This problem is a typical linear programming problem which is formulated as below:

$$\max \quad f_1 = 0.4x_1 + 0.3x_2$$

subject to

$$x_1 + x_2 \leq 400$$

$$2x_1 + x_2 \leq 500$$

$$x_1, x_2 \geq 0$$

where $x_1$ and $x_2$ are the numbers produced of Doll A and Doll B respectively. The optimum solution is,

$$x_1^* = 100 \qquad x_2^* = 300$$

$$f_1^* = \$130$$

This profit maximization problem can be formulated as a goal programming problem.

$$\min \quad \underline{a} = \{(d_1^+ + d_2^+),\ (d_3^-)\}$$

such that

$$G_1: \quad x_1 + x_2 + d_1^- - d_1^+ = 400$$

$$G_2: \quad 2x_1 + x_2 + d_2^- - d_2^+ = 500$$

$$G_3: \quad 0.4x_1 + 0.3x_2 + d_3^- - d_3^+ = 240$$

$$\underline{x}, \underline{d}^-, \underline{d}^+ \geq 0$$

The achievement function consists of two priorities. The first priority is given to the minimization of $(d_1^+ + d_2^+)$ because $G_1$ and $G_2$ are absolute objectives (i.e., they come from physical constraints). The second priority factor is assigned to the minimization of $d_3^-$; that is, to minimize the under-attainment of some arbitrarily chosen target value, say \$240. This value is set arbitrarily, knowing that we will never be able to achieve a higher profit (\$0.4 x 400 = \$160 < \$240 and \$0.3 x 400 = \$120 < \$240).

In order to solve this goal programming by the graphical method, all the objective functions must be plotted on graph as shown in Figure 3.8. No feasible region is found to satisfy all three goals; i.e., $G_3$ is completely conflicting with $G_1$ and $G_2$. By introducing priority levels in goal programming this difficulty could be handled. The solution space satisfying the objective set of priority level 1 ($P_1$) is indicated by the corss-hatched area (I) of Figure 3.8. Here both $d_1^+$ and $d_2^+$ are set to zero. Next we attempt to satisfy priority level 2($P_2$) without degrading the solution of $P_1$. In this situation $d_3^-$ can be minimized until $d_3^- = 110$. If $d_3^-$ becomes smaller than this, it degrades $P_1$. Consequently the final solution is point A shown in Figure 3.9 and is,

$$x_1^* = 100 \qquad x_2^* = 300$$

$$\underline{a}^* = \{0, 110\}$$

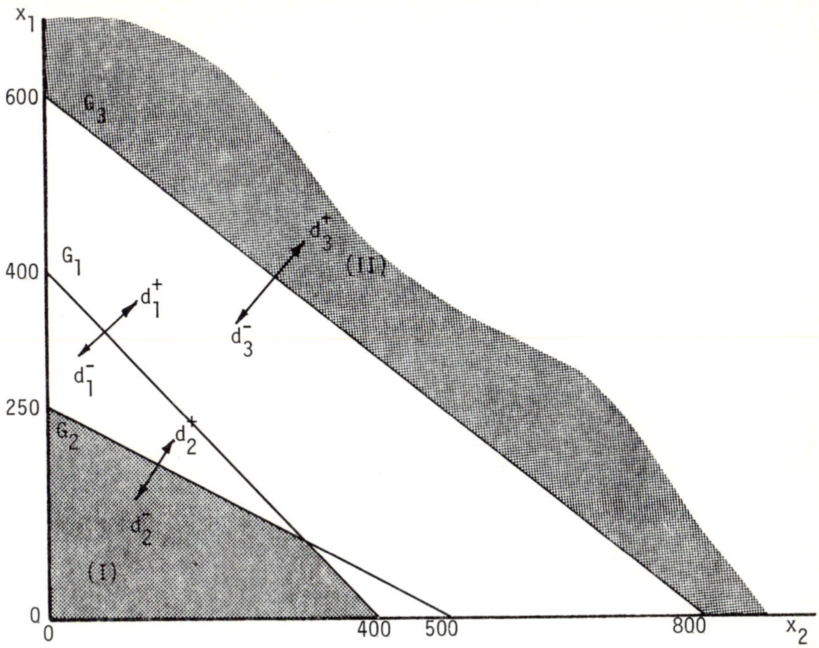


Figure 3.8 No feasible region for satisfying three goals.

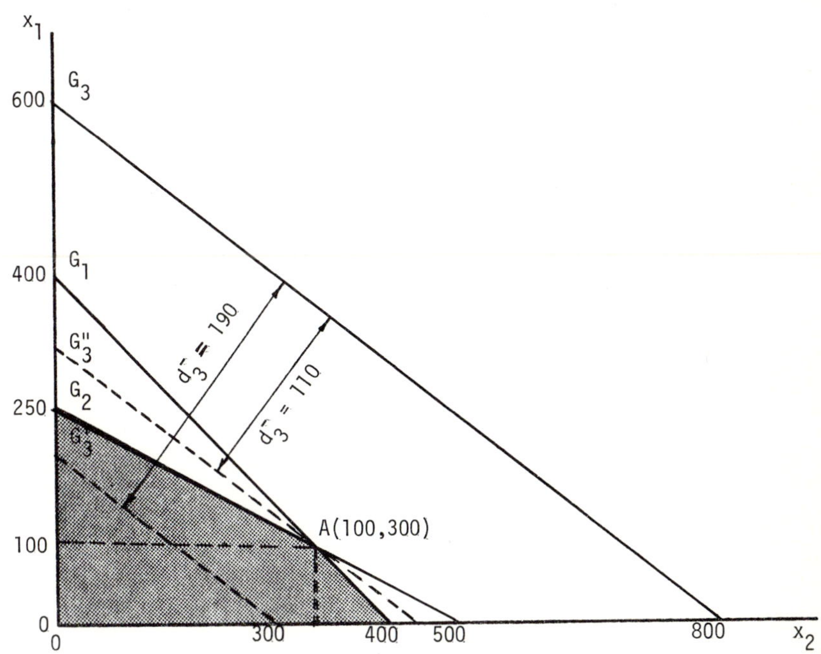


Figure 3.9 Final solution for Example 1

Example 2

Suppose the best customer of the toy company ordered 300 dolls of type A. For various reasons the manager could not decline this order. How should the manager switch the production schedule to meet the sudden demand? Assume that the other conditions are the same as Example 1.

If we attempt to utilize linear programming to maximize profit, the problem is formulated as below:

$$\max \quad f_1(\underline{x}) = 0.4x_1 + 0.3x_2$$

subject to

$$x_1 + x_2 \leq 400$$

$$2x_1 + x_2 \leq 500$$

$$x_1 \geq 300$$

$$x_1, x_2 \geq 0$$

The graphical presentation of the model is shown in Fig. 3.10. Obviously, there is no area of feasible solution and consequently the above problem is unsolvable by linear programming. In simple words, the company does not have enough capacity to satisfy the customer's demand.

This difficulty can be handled - if the manager wishes to satisfy his desires as closely as possible rather than absolutely satisfy all goals. Let's assume that his priorities are:

$P_1$: Avoid the overtime operation of the plant (500 dolls/day)

$P_2$: Meet the best customer's order as closely as possible (i.e. produce at least 300 dolls of type A)

$P_3$: Satisfy, as much as possible, the \$240 profit.

Now the linear goal programming model becomes:

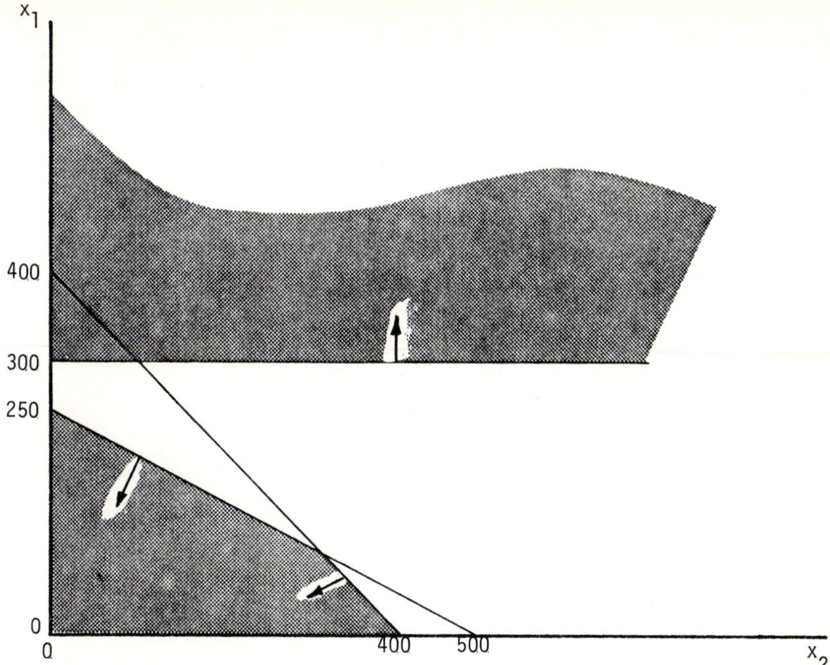


Figure 3.10 Infeasible solution for linear programming model

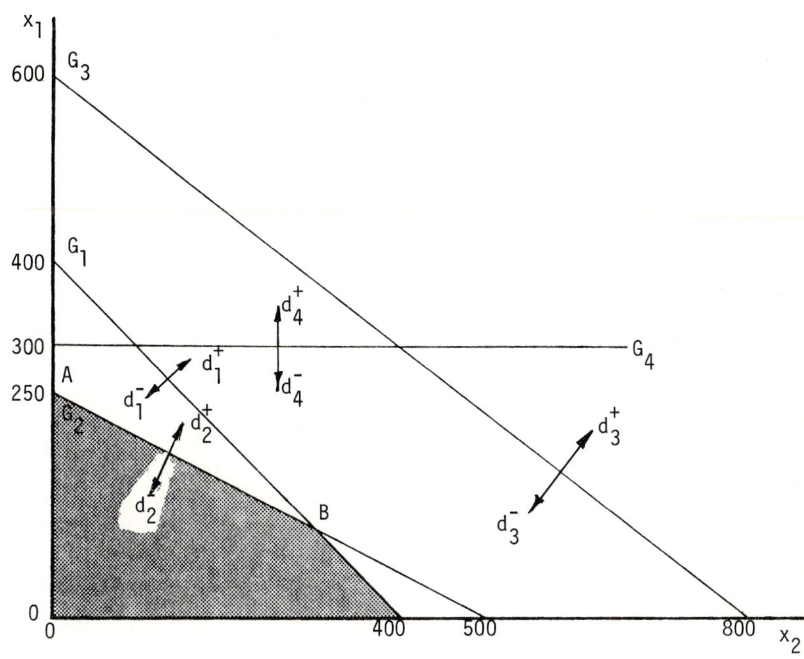


Figure 3.11 Final solution for Example 2

Find $\underline{x} = (x_1, x_2)$ so as to

min $\quad \underline{a} = \{(d_1^+ + d_2^+), (d_4^-), (d_3^-)\}$

such that

$$G_1: \quad x_1 + x_2 + d_1^- - d_1^+ = 400$$

$$G_2: \quad 2x_1 + x_2 + d_2^- - d_2^+ = 500$$

$$G_3: \quad 0.4x_1 + 0.3x_2 + d_3^- - d_3^+ = 240$$

$$G_4: \quad x_1 + d_4^- - d_4^+ = 300$$

$$\underline{x}, \underline{d}^-, \underline{d}^+ \geq 0$$

The above model is shown in Figure 3.11. Now our first goal is to avoid the overtime operation and the over use of material by minimizing $(d_1^+ + d_2^+)$. That is $d_1^+ = d_2^+ = 0$. Hence the feasible solution must be in the cross-hatched area. Our second goal calls for production of 300 type A dolls by minimizing $d_4^-$. We can proceed until we reach point A (that is $d_4^- = 50$) without degrading the solution to priority level 1. Finally, to achieve the profit maximization goal of priority level 3, we must minimize $d_3^-$. We can proceed from point A to point B, but this movement is against priority level 2. Hence point A has to be the final solution. That is,

$$x_1^* = 250, \qquad x_2^* = 0$$

$$\underline{a}^* = (0, 50, 140)$$

Linear goal programming by iterative approach

The mathematical formulation of a Multiple Objective Linear Programming (MOLP) problem, in general, is:

$$\max \quad [f_1(\underline{x}),\ f_2(\underline{x}),\ \ldots,\ f_k(\underline{x})]$$

$$\text{s.t.} \quad g_j(\underline{x}) \leq c_j, \qquad j = 1, 2, \ldots, m$$

$$x_i \geq 0, \qquad i = 1, 2, \ldots, n$$

where

$$f_t(\underline{x}) = \sum_{i=1}^{n} c_{ti}x_i, \qquad t = 1, 2, \ldots, k$$

$$g_j(\underline{x}) = \sum_{i=1}^{n} a_{ji}x_i, \qquad j = 1, 2, \ldots, m$$

The LGP formulation of the above problem is:

$$\left.\begin{array}{lll} \min & [P_1a_1(\underline{d}^-, \underline{d}^+),\ P_2a_2(\underline{d}^-, \underline{d}^+),\ \ldots,\ P_\ell a_\ell(\underline{d}^-, \underline{d}^+)] & \\ \text{s.t.} & g_j(\underline{x}) + d_j^- - d_j^+ = c_j, & j = 1, 2, \ldots, m \\ & f_t(\underline{x}) + d_t^- - d_t^+ = b_t, & t = 1, 2, \ldots, k \\ & d_i^-,\ d_i^+ \geq 0, & d_i^- \cdot d_i^+ = 0 \quad \forall_i \end{array}\right\} \qquad (3.20)$$

where $g_j(\underline{x}) + d_j^- - d_j^+ = c_j$ are the absolute constraints, and $f_t(\underline{x}) + d_t^- - d_t^+ = b_t$ are goal constraints.

The basic solution algorithm for (3.20) is that $a_1(\underline{d}^-, \underline{d}^+)$ is minimized first, let min $a_1 = a_1^*$. Next $a_2(\underline{d}^-, \underline{d}^+)$ is minimized but in no circumstances can $a_1$ be greater than $a_1^*$. Thus, a lower ranking achievement function cannot be satisfied to the detriment of a higher ranking achievement function. This process continues until $a_\ell(\underline{d}^-, \underline{d}^+)$ is minimized. The problem can be solved iteratively [see Dauer and Krueger, 78] by the basic simplex algorithm for which many efficient computer codes are available.

By an iterative approach, the GP model can be decomposed into $\ell$ number of single objective problems as follows:

Problem 1: To find $\underline{x} = (x_1, x_2, \ldots, x_n)$ so as to

$$\min \quad a_1(\underline{d}^-, \underline{d}^+)$$

$$\text{s.t.} \quad g_i(\underline{x}) + d_i^- - d_i^+ = c_i \qquad i = 1, 2, \ldots, m$$

$$\underline{d}^-, \underline{d}^+ \geq 0$$

Notice that the first priority level (Problem 1) is associated with the achievement of the absolute constraints.

Let $a_1^*$ be the optimal solution for Problem 1, i.e., $a_1^* = \min a_1(\underline{d}^-, \underline{d}^+)$. Usually $a_1^*$ is zero, since the absolute constraints must be satisfied, and if so, a solution for the GP problem does exist. If $a_1^* \neq 0$, then the GP problem has no solution; i.e., the feasible region formed by the absolute objectives (constraints) is empty.

If $a_1^* = 0$, then the attainment problem for goal 1 is equivalent to problem 2.

Problem 2. To find $\underline{x}$ so as to

$$\min \quad a_2(\underline{d}^-, \underline{d}^+)$$

$$\text{s.t.} \quad g_i(\underline{x}) + d_i^- - d_i^+ = c_i, \qquad i = 1, 2, \ldots, m \tag{3.21}$$

$$a_1(\underline{d}^-, \underline{d}^+) \leq a_1^* \tag{3.22}$$

$$f_1(\underline{x}) + d_{m+1}^- - d_{m+1}^+ = b_1$$

$$\underline{d}^-, \underline{d}^+ \geq 0$$

Notice that constraints (3.21) and (3.22) imply that in trying to achieve goal 1 we will not sacrifice the previously determined attainment of Problem 1.

Let $a_2^*$ be the solution of this problem. We can then proceed to goal 2.

Problem 3: To find $\underline{x}$ so as to

$$
\begin{aligned}
\min \quad & a_3(\underline{d}^-, \underline{d}^+) \\
\text{s.t.} \quad & g_i(\underline{x}) + d_i^- - d_i^+ = c_i, \qquad i = 1, 2, \ldots, m \\
& a_1(\underline{d}^-, \underline{d}^+) \leq a_1^* \\
& f_1(\underline{x}) + d_{m+1}^- - d_{m+1}^+ = b_1 \\
& a_2(\underline{d}^-, \underline{d}^+) \leq a_2^* \\
& f_2(\underline{x}) + d_{m+2}^- - d_{m+2}^+ = b_2 \\
& \underline{d}^-, \underline{d}^+ \geq 0
\end{aligned}
$$

Let $a_3^*$ be the solution for problem 3.

We can now write a general goal attainment problem (j+1) for attaining goal j, $0 \leq j \leq \ell-1$ as follows:

Problem (j+1): To find $\underline{x}$ so as to

$$
\begin{aligned}
\min \quad & a_{j+1}(\underline{d}^-, \underline{d}^+) \\
\text{s.t.} \quad & g_i(\underline{x}) + d_i^- - d_i^+ = c_i, \qquad i = 1, 2, \ldots, m \\
& a_i(\underline{d}^-, \underline{d}^+) \leq a_i^*, \qquad i = 1, 2, \ldots, j \\
& f_i(\underline{x}) + d_{m+1}^- - d_{m+1}^+ = b_i, i = 1, 2, \ldots, j \\
& \underline{d}^-, \underline{d}^+ \geq 0
\end{aligned}
$$

NUMERICAL EXAMPLE (Production scheduling of the Hardee Toy Company)

Example 2 is used again for the illustration of the iterative linear goal programming approach. This problem is composed of three priority levels; hence it can be decomposed into three single objective problems.

Problem 1 (for the absolute constraints)

$$\min \quad a_1 = d_1^+ + d_2^+$$

$$\text{s.t.} \quad x_1 + x_2 + d_1^- - d_1^+ = 400$$

$$2x_1 + x_2 + d_2^- - d_2^+ = 500$$

$$\underline{x}, \underline{d}^-, \underline{d}^+ \geq 0$$

The ordinary simplex procedure gives multiple solutions for decision variables ($\underline{x}$) and $d_1^+ = d_2^+ = 0$ for deviational variables. Hence it is certain that the absolute constraints form a nonempty set. Now we can proceed to the 2nd priority level.

Problem 2 (for the 2nd priority level)

$$\min \quad a_2 = d_4^-$$

$$\text{s.t.} \quad x_1 + x_2 + d_1^- = 400$$

$$2x_1 + x_2 + d_2^- = 500$$

$$x_1 + d_4^- - d_4^+ = 300$$

$$\underline{x}, \underline{d}^-, \underline{d}^+ \geq 0$$

or simply,

$$\min \quad a_2 = d_4^-$$

$$\text{s.t.} \quad x_1 + x_2 \leq 400$$

$$2x_1 + x_2 \leq 500$$

$$x_1 + d_4^- - d_4^+ = 300$$

$$\underline{x}, \underline{d}^-, \underline{d}^+ \geq 0$$

Its solution gives $x_1 = 250$, $x_2 = 0$, and $d_4^- = 50$. With this result we can go to the 3rd priority level.

Problem 3 (for the 3rd priority level)

$$\min \quad a_3 = d_3^-$$

$$\text{s.t.} \quad x_1 + x_2 \le 400$$

$$2x_1 + x_2 \le 500$$

$$x_1 + d_4^- - d_4^+ = 300$$

$$d_4^- \le 50$$

$$0.4x_1 + 0.3x_2 + d_3^- - d_3^+ = 240$$

$$\underline{x}, \underline{d}^-, \underline{d}^+, \ge 0$$

or simply

$$\min \quad a_3 = d_3^-$$

$$\text{s.t.} \quad x_1 + x_2 \le 400$$

$$2x_1 + x_2 \le 500$$

$$x_1 \ge 250$$

$$0.4x_1 + 0.3x_2 + d_3^- - d_3^+ = 240$$

$$\underline{x}, \underline{d}^-, \underline{d}^+ \ge 0$$

The solution is $x_1 = 250$, $x_2 = 0$, and $d_3^- = 140$.

The results of the above three sub-problems are a solution of linear goal programming, and are:

$$x_1^* = 250, \qquad x_2^* = 0$$

$$\underline{a}^* = (0, 50, 140)$$

2.2.2 b NONLINEAR GOAL PROGRAMMING

Although the real world is nonlinear, it can often be approximated by a linear model. The solution methods for nonlinear models are not as simple as the simplex method for the linear model. There are two algorithms for solving Nonlinear Goal Programming (NLGP) problems. They are an Iterative Nonlinear Goal Programming (INGP) and the Griffith - Stewart linear approximation approach to NLGP problems.

In the INGP approach, the NLGP problem is decomposed into a set of single objective nonlinear optimization problems and solved iteratively. An effective computational procedure is presented which integrates the iterative approach and a modified Hooke and Jeeves pattern search into an efficient solution procedure for the NLGP [166] . One interesting feature of this iterative procedure for solving NLGP problems is that the problem is solved by a traditional nonlinear search technique that is originally intended for solving the so called "unconstrained" problems.

If all the nonlinear functions of the constraints and the objectives in an NLGP problem are differentiable, then these functions can be approximated by linear functions using the Griffith and Stewart approach [138a] . The NLGP problem is approximated and solved by the linear goal programming approach. The Girffith - Stewart linear approximation approach is presented by Ignizio [BM-9] .

In this section, the INGP approach is presented.

Formulation of an iterative nonlinear goal programming problem

The complete GP model formulation is given below: To find $\underline{x} = (x_1, x_2, \ldots, x_n)$ so as to

$$\left.\begin{array}{ll} \min & \underline{a} = \{a_1(\underline{d}^-, \underline{d}^+), a_2(\underline{d}^-, \underline{d}^+), \ldots, a_\ell(\underline{d}^-, \underline{d}^+)\} \\ \text{subject to} & g_i(\underline{x}) + d_i^- - d_i^+ = c_i, \quad i = 1, \ldots, m \\ & f_i(\underline{x}) + d_{m+i}^- - d_{m+i}^+ = b_i, \; i = 1, \ldots, k \\ & \underline{d}^-, \underline{d}^+ \geq 0, \; d_i^- \cdot d_i^+ = 0 \quad \forall_i \end{array}\right\} \quad (3.23)$$

Each achievement function, $a_j(\underline{d}^-, \underline{d}^+)$, is a linear function of the appropriate deviational variables. Each deviational variable is determined "independently" from the corresponding constraint equation as follows:

$$d_i^- = \begin{cases} d_i^- & \text{if } d_i^- \geq 0 \\ 0 & \text{if } d_i^- < 0 \end{cases}$$

$$\left.\begin{array}{ll} \text{where} & d_i^- = c_i - g_i(\underline{x}) \\ \text{or} & d_i^- = b_i - f_i(\underline{x}) \end{array}\right\} \qquad (3.24)$$

similarly

$$d_i^+ = \begin{cases} d_i^+ & \text{if } d_i^+ \geq 0 \\ 0 & \text{if } d_i^+ < 0 \end{cases}$$

$$\left.\begin{array}{ll} \text{where} & d_i^+ = g_i(\underline{x}) - c_i \\ \text{or} & d_i^+ = f_i(\underline{x}) - b_i \end{array}\right\} \qquad (3.25)$$

Notice that in the process of determining "each" deviational variable, the corresponding absolute or goal constraint, which is a function of the decision variables, $\underline{x} = (x_1, x_2, \ldots, x_n)$, is utilized, so that the constraints in (3.23) are no longer the constraints to the minimization problem in the sense of constraints in single objective nonlinear programming problems.

By an iterative approach, the GP model can be decomposed into $\ell$ number of single objective problems ($\ell \leq k + 1$) as follows:

Problem 1: To find $\underline{x} = (x_1, x_2, \ldots, x_n)$ so as to

$$\min\ a_1(\underline{d}^-, \underline{d}^+)$$

$$\text{s.t.} \quad g_i(\underline{x}) + d_i^- - d_i^+ = c_i, \qquad i = 1, 2, \ldots, m$$

$$\underline{d}^-, \underline{d}^+ \geq \underline{0} \text{ and } d_i^- \cdot d_i^+ = 0 \quad \forall_i$$

Notice that the first priority level (Problem 1) is associated with the achievement of the absolute constraints. The last constraint, $d_i^- \cdot d_i^+ = 0$, implies that only one deviational variable, either positive or negative, exists in the solution.

Let $a_1^*$ be the optimal solution for problem 1, i.e., $a_1^* = \min a_1(\underline{d}^-, \underline{d}^+)$. $a_1^*$ is usually zero, since the absolute constraints must be satisfied. If so, there exists a solution for the GP problem. If $a_1^* \neq 0$, then the GP problem has no solution, i.e., the feasible region formed by the absolute objectives (constraints) is empty.

if $a_1^* = 0$, then the attainment problem for goal 1 is equivalent to problem 2.

Problem 2. To find $\underline{x}$ so as to

$$\min \ a_2(\underline{d}^-, \underline{d}^+)$$

$$\text{s.t. } g_i(\underline{x}) + d_i^- - d_i^+ = c_i, \qquad i = 1, 2, \ldots, m \tag{3.26}$$

$$a_1(\underline{d}^-, \underline{d}^+) \leq a_1^* \tag{3.27}$$ [+]

$$f_1(\underline{x}) + d_{m+1}^- - d_{m+1}^+ = b_1$$

$$\underline{d}^-, \underline{d}^+ \geq \underline{0} \text{ and } d_i^+ \cdot d_i^- = 0 \quad \forall_i$$

Notice that constraints (3.26) and (3.27) imply that in trying to achieve goal 1 we will not sacrifice our previously determined attainment of Problem 1.

Let $a_2^*$ be the solution to this problem. We can then proceed to goal 2.

---

[+]The value of $a_1$ is always greater or equal to zero (why?).

In the above problem, only one objective $f_1(\underline{x})$ is being considered at priority level 2. However, any number of "commensurable" objectives with the same rank may be grouped into one priority level, and the corresponding deviational variables can be added to the achievement function of the same level. The order of priority level and the goal number may not necessarily be in the same order. However, in the following problems, for simplicity, the order of priority level and the goal number is the same order, and only one objective is considered in each priority.

Problem 3: To find $\underline{x}$ so as to

$$\min \; a_3(\underline{d}^-, \underline{d}^+)$$

$$\begin{aligned}
\text{s.t. } & g_i(\underline{x}) + d_i^- - d_i^+ = c_i, \qquad i = 1, 2, \ldots, m \\
& a_1(\underline{d}^-, \underline{d}^+) \leq a_1^* \\
& f_1(\underline{x}) + d_{m+1}^- - d_{m+1}^+ = b_1 \\
& a_2(\underline{d}^-, \underline{d}^+) \leq a_2^* \\
& f_2(\underline{x}) + d_{m+2}^- - d_{m+2}^+ = b_2 \\
& \underline{d}^-, \underline{d}^+ \geq \underline{0} \text{ and } d_i^+ \cdot d_i^- = 0 \quad \forall_i
\end{aligned}$$

Let $a_3^*$ be the solution for Problem 3.

We can now write a general goal attainment problem (j+1) for attaining goal j, $0 \leq j \leq \ell-1$ as follows:

Problem (j+1): To find $\underline{x}$ so as to

$$\min \; a_{j+1}(\underline{d}^-, \underline{d}^+)$$

$$\begin{aligned}
\text{s.t. } & g_i(\underline{x}) + d_i^- - d_i^+ = c_i, \qquad i = 1, 2, \ldots, m \\
& a_i(\underline{d}^-, \underline{d}^+) \leq a_i^*, \qquad i = 1, 2, \ldots, j \\
& f_i(\underline{x}) + d_{m+i}^- - d_{m+i}^+ = b_i, \qquad i = 1, 2, \ldots, j \\
& \underline{d}^-, \underline{d}^+ \geq \underline{0} \text{ and } d_i^+ \cdot d_i^- = 0 \quad \forall_i
\end{aligned} \tag{3.28}$$

Computational procedure of the iterative nonlinear goal programming

The preceeding "$\ell$" single objective decision making problems can be solved by any proper nonlinear programming method. The iterative approach to the nonlinear goal programming problem presented here follows closely that of Dauer and Drueger [78] . A computational procedure using Hooke and Jeeves pattern search for NLGP is presented by Ignizio [BM-9] . We will present a new computational procedure which integrates the iterative approach and our modified Hooke and Jeeves pattern search into an effective solution procedure for NLGP.

One interesting feature of this procedure for solving the iterative nonlinear goal programming problem is that the problem is solved by traditional nonlinear search techniques that are originally intended for solving the so called "unconstrained" problem.

The original direct search method of Hoode and Jeeves is a sequential search routine for minimizing an "unconstrained" function $h(\underline{x})$ of more than one variable $\underline{x} = (x_1, x_2, \ldots, x_n)$. The argument $\underline{x}$ is varied until the minimum of $h(\underline{x})$ is obtained. The search routine determines the sequence of values for $\underline{x}$. The successive values of $\underline{x}$ can be interpreted as points in a nondimensional space. The procedure consists of two types of moves: Exploratory and Pattern.

A move is defined as the procedure of going from a given point to the following point. A move is a success if the value of $h(\underline{x})$ decreases (for minimization); otherwise, it is a failure. The first type of move is an exploratory move designed to explore the local behavior of the objective function $h(\underline{x})$. The success or failure of the exploratory move is utilized by combining it into a pattern move which indicates a probable direction for a successful move.

Since the NLGP problem is associated with constraints and deviational variables, the original Hooke and Jeeves pattern search method cannot be applied directly for solving the problem. The method is modified. In the modified Hooke and Jeeves pattern search for NLGP, the procedure is to minimize an achievement function vector, $\underline{a} = (a_1, a_2, \ldots, a_\ell)$. In the iterative approach of the NLGP, the solution to Problem (j+1) is to find $\underline{x} = (x_1, x_2, \ldots, x_n)$ so as to minimize the achievement function, $a_{j+1}(\underline{d}^-, \underline{d}^+)$, such that the jth goal, $f_j(\underline{x}) + d^-_{m+j} - d^-_{m+j} = b_j$, is satisfied and the previously attained achievement functions are not violated; that is, $a_t(\underline{d}^-, \underline{d}^+) \leq a_t^*$, $t = 1, 2, \ldots, j$. Therefore, the problem is a constrained problem. However, checking the constraints, $a_t(\underline{d}^-, \underline{d}^+) \leq a_t^*$, $t = 1, 2, \ldots, j$, can be integrated into a move of the modified Hooke and Jeeves pattern search.

A move is a success for the modified Hooke and Jeeves pattern search if the value of $a_{j+1}(\underline{d}^-, \underline{d}^+)$ decreases and $a_t(\underline{d}^-, \underline{d}^+) \leq a_t^*$, $t = 1, 2, \ldots, j$ are satisfied; otherwise, it is a failure. This modification is incorporated into the exploratory move and pattern move. The exploratory move is performed as follows:

1) Introduce a starting point $\underline{x}$ with a prescribed step length $\delta_i$ in each of the independent variables $x_i$, $i = 1, 2, \ldots, n$.

2) Compute the achievement function, $a_{j+1}(\underline{d}^-, \underline{d}^+)$, where $\underline{d}^-$ and $\underline{d}^+$ are functions of the decision variables, $\underline{x} = (x_1, x_2, \ldots, x_n)$. Let $a_{j+1}(\underline{d}^-, \underline{d}^+) \equiv a_{j+1}[\underline{x}]$. Set $i = 1$.

3. Compute $a^i_{t+1}$ [$\underline{x}$] , $t = 1, 2, \ldots, j$, at the trial point $\underline{x} = (x_1, x_2, \ldots, x_i + \delta_i, \ldots, x_n)$. The superscript i on the achievement function, $a_{t+1}$, corresponds to the variable, $x_i$, being perturbed.

4. Compare $a^i_{j+1}$ [$\underline{x}$] with $a_{j+1}$ [$\underline{x}$] :

(i) If $a^i_{j+1}$ [$\underline{x}$] $<$ $a_{j+1}$ [$\underline{x}$] , and $a^i_t$ [$\underline{x}$] $\leq a^*_t$ for $t = 1, 2, \ldots, j$, set $a_{j+1}$ [$\underline{x}$] $= a^i_{j+1}$ [$\underline{x}$] $= (x_1, x_2, \ldots, x_i, \ldots, x_n) = (x_1, x_2, \ldots, x_i + \delta_i, \ldots, x_n)$,

and $i = i+1$. Consider this trial point as a starting point, and repeat from step 3.

(ii) If $a^i_{j+1}$ [$\underline{x}$] $\geq a_{j+1}$ [$\underline{x}$] and/or $a^i_t$ [$\underline{x}$] $> a^*_t$ for any $t = 1, 2, \ldots, j$, set $\underline{x} = (x_1, x_2, \ldots, x_i - 2\delta_i, \ldots, x_n)$. Compute $a^i_{t+1}$ [$\underline{x}$] , $t = 1, 2, \ldots, j$, and see if $a^i_{j+1}$ [$\underline{x}$] $< a_{j+1}$ [$\underline{x}$] and $a^i_t$ [$\underline{x}$] $\leq a^*_t$ for all $t = 1, 2, \ldots, j$. If this move is a success the new trial point is retained. Set $a_{j+1}$ [$\underline{x}$] $= a^i_{j+1}$ [$\underline{x}$] , $\underline{x} = (x_1, x_2, \ldots, x_i, \ldots, x_n) = (x_1, x_2, \ldots, x_i - 2\delta_i, \ldots, x_n)$, and $i = i+1$, and repeat from step 3. If again $a^i_{j+1}$ [$\underline{x}$] $\geq a_{j+1}$ [$\underline{x}$] and/or $a^i_t$ [$\underline{x}$] $> a^*_t$ for any $t = 1, 2, \ldots, j$, then the move is a failure; $x_i$ remains unchanged, that is, $\underline{x} = (x_1, x_2, \ldots, x_i, \ldots, x_n) = (x_1, x_2, \ldots, x_i + \delta_i, \ldots, x_n)$. Set $i = i+1$ and repeat from step 3.

The point $\underline{x}_B$ obtained at the end of the exploratory moves, which is reached by repeating step 3 until i=n, is defined as a base point. The starting point introduced in step 1 of the exploratory move is a starting base point or point obtained by the pattern move.

The pattern move is designed to utilize the information aquired in the exploratory move, and executes the actual minimization of the function by moving in the direction of the established pattern. The pattern move is a simple step from the current base to the point

$$\underline{x} = \underline{x}_B + (\underline{x}_B - \underline{x}_B^*) \qquad (3.29)$$

$\underline{x}_B^*$ is either the starting base point or the preceding base point. Following the pattern move a series of exploratory moves is conducted to further improve the pattern. If the pattern move followed by the exploratory moves brings no improvement, the pattern move is a failure. Then we return to the last base which becomes a starting base and the process is repeated.

If the exploratory moves from any starting base do not yield a point which is better than this base, the lengths of all the steps are reduced and the moves are repeated. Convergence is assumed when the step lengths, $\delta_i$, have been reduced below predetermined limits.

A descriptive flow diagram for the iterative NLGP algorithm with the modified Hooke and Jeeves pattern search is given in Fig. 3.12.

After initializing a base point, the achievement functions $a_j\ [\underline{x}]$ , $j = 1, 2, \ldots, KP$ are evaluated. In the process of evaluation, we start with $j = 1$ and check $a_1 = 0$. If so, $a_2$ is calculated and checked if $a_2 = 0$. This process will proceed until $j = KP$ when $a_{KP} \neq 0$. If KP is greater than the total number of the priorities, NPRIOR, then we get a solution. If KP is not greater than NPRIOR, then the modified Hooke and Jeeves pattern search is used for searching the solution for the single objective decision problem, Problem KP, which is Problem (j+1) defined in (3.28). The procedures will be applied until KP = NPRIOR.

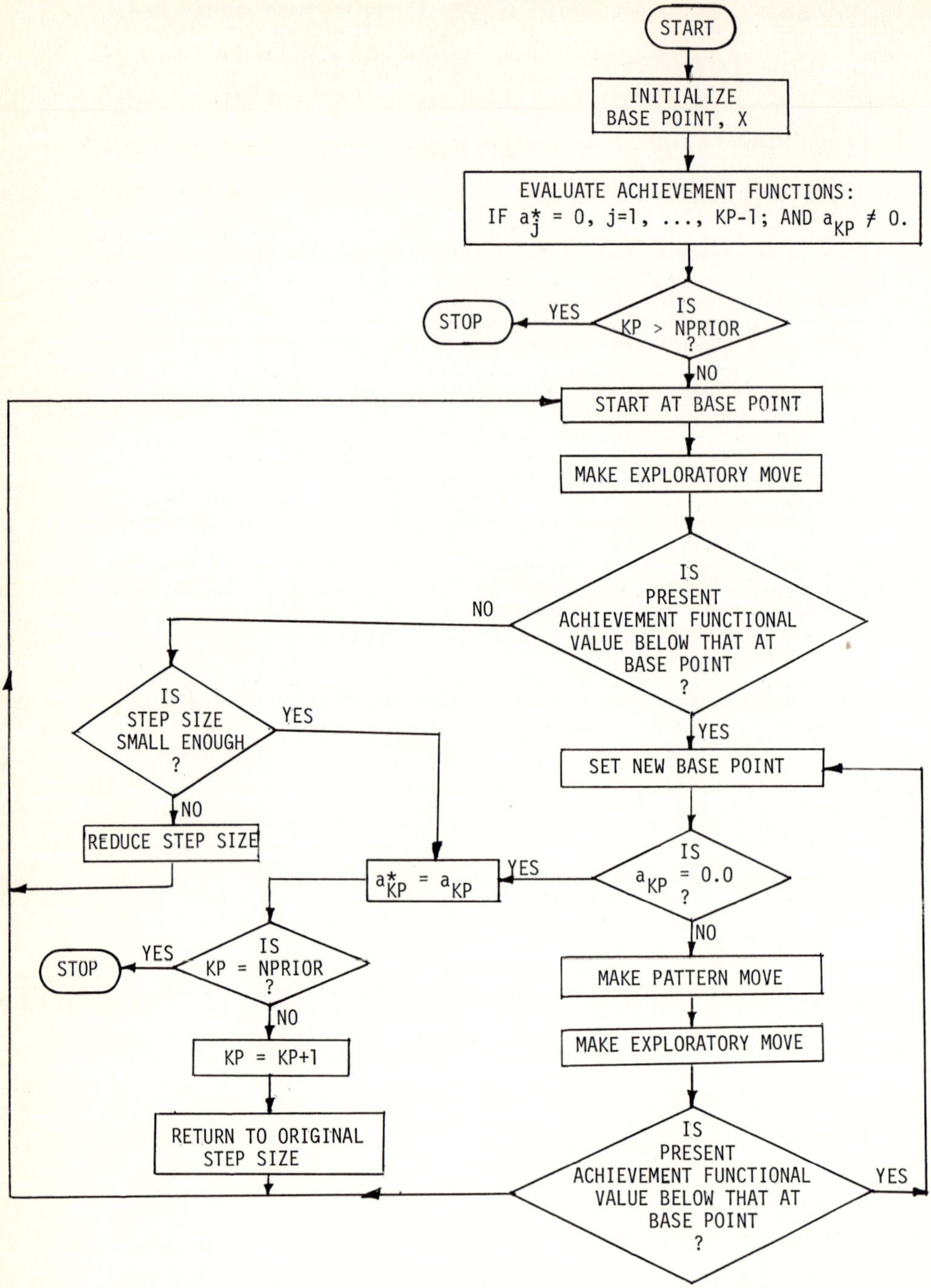


Fig. 3.12 Flow diagram for the iterative NLGP algorithm with a modified Hooke and Jeeves pattern search.

NUMERICAL EXAMPLE

The ABC Company produces two similar products A and B. Both products are equally important. The total profit, in hundreds of dollars, can be approximated by the mathematical product of the two products in tons $(x_1x_2)$, where $x_1$ and $x_2$ are daily productions of A and B in tons, respectively. The inprocess inventory costs of each product, in hundreds of dollars per ton, are $(x_1 - 4)^2$ and $(x_2)^2$ for products A and B, respectively. The labor cost of production is \$500/ton and \$400/ton for products A and B, respectively.

The president of the company has set the following goals in the order of their importance to the company.

(1) Limit the total cost of inprocess inventory to \$1025/day.

(2) Achieve the profit of at least \$300 per day, and limit the total labor cost to \$2,000 per day.

(3) Production of product B to be twice that of product A, and combined production should be more than 8 tons per day.

The problem may be formulated mathematically as follows:

Priority 1: The absolute objectives (constraints) are:

$$g_1(\underline{x}) = x_1 \geq 0$$

$$g_2(\underline{x}) = x_2 \geq 0$$

Priority 2: The first goal is to limit the inprocess inventory cost.

$$f_1(\underline{x}) = (x_1 - 4)^2 + x_2^2 \leq 10.25$$

Priority 3: Achieving the profit and limiting the total labor cost are in the same priority level.

$$f_2(\underline{x}) = x_1x_2 \geq 3$$

$$f_3(\underline{x}) = 5x_1 + 4x_2 \leq 20$$

Priority 4: The last priority is to achieve the daily production goal.

$$f_4(\underline{x}) = x_1 + 2x_2 \geq 8.$$

The NLGP problem in format of (3.23) will be: To find $x_1$ and $x_2$ so as to

$$\min \quad \bar{a} = [a_1, a_2, a_3, a_4] = [(d_1^- + d_2^-), (d_3^+), (d_4^- + d_5^+), (d_6^-)]$$

$$\text{s.t.} \quad x_1 + d_1^- - d_1^+ = 0$$

$$x_2 + d_2^- - d_2^+ = 0$$

$$(x_1-4)^2 + x_2^2 + d_3^- - d_3^+ = 10.25$$

$$x_1x_2 + d_4^- - d_4^+ = 3$$

$$5x_1 + 4x_2 + d_5^- - d_5^+ = 20$$

$$x_1 + 2x_2 + d_6^- - d_6^+ = 8$$

$$\underline{d}^-, \underline{d}^+ \geq \underline{0}, \quad d_i^- \cdot d_i^+ = 0 \quad \forall_i$$

By the iterative NLGP approach, the problem is decomposed into the following 4 single objective problems.

Problem 1. To find $x_1$ and $x_2$ so as to

$$\min \quad a_1 = d_1^- + d_2^-$$

$$\text{s.t.} \quad x_1 + d_1^- - d_1^+ = 0$$

$$x_2 + d_2^- - d_2^+ = 0$$

$$\underline{d}^-, \underline{d}^+ \geq \underline{0}, \quad d_i^- \cdot d_i^+ = 0 \quad \forall_i$$

Problem 2. To find $x_1$ and $x_2$ so as to

$$\min \quad a_2 = d_3^+$$

$$\text{s.t.} \quad x_1 + d_1^- - d_1^+ = 0$$

$$x_2 + d_2^- - d_2^+ = 0$$

$$a_1 \leq a_1^*$$

$$(x_1-4)^2 + x_2^2 + d_3^- - d_3^+ = 10.25$$

$$\underline{d}^-, \underline{d}^+ \geq \underline{0}, \quad d_i^- \cdot d_i^+ = 0 \quad \forall_i$$

<u>Problem 3.</u> To find $x_1$ and $x_2$ so as to

min $\quad a_3 = d_4^- + d_5^+$

s.t. $\quad x_1 + d_1^- - d_1^+ = 0$

$x_2 + d_2^- - d_2^+ = 0$

$(x_1-4)^2 + x_2^2 + d_3^- - d_3^+ = 10.25$

$a_i \leq a_i^*, \qquad i = 1, 2$

$x_1x_2 + d_4^- - d_4^+ = 3$

$5x_1 + 4x_2 + d_5^- - d_5^+ = 20$

$\underline{d}^-, \underline{d}^+ \geq \underline{0}, \quad d_i^- \cdot d_i^+ = 0 \quad \forall_i$

<u>Problem 4.</u> To find $x_1$ and $x_2$ so as to

min $\quad a_4 = d_6^-$

s.t. $\quad x_1 + d_1^- - d_1^+ = 0$

$x_2 + d_2^- - d_2^+ = 0$

$(x_1-4)^2 + x_2^2 + d_3^- - d_3^+ = 10.25$

$x_1x_2 + d_4^- - d_4^+ = 3$

$5x_1 + 4x_2 + d_5^- - d_5^+ = 20$

$a_i \leq a_i^*, \qquad i = 1, 2, 3$

$x_1 + 2x_2 + d_6^- - d_6^+ = 8$

$\underline{d}^-, \underline{d}^+ \geq \underline{0}, \quad d_i^- \cdot d_i^+ = 0 \quad \forall_i$

The NLGP problem is solved by the algorithm, presented in Fig. 3.12, which integrates the iterative approach and the modified Hooke and Jeeves pattern search.

Let a starting base point be $(x_1, x_2) = (8,6)$.
Then the achievement function of Problem 1, $a_1(\underline{d}^-, \underline{d}^+) = d_1^- + d_2^-$, is evaluated as follows (see (3.24) and (3.25)):

Since $d_1^- = c_1 - g_1(\underline{x}) = 0 - x_1 = -8 < 0$

set $d_1^- = 0$.

Similarly

$$d_2^- = c_2 - g_2(\underline{x}) = 0 - x_2 = -6 < 0$$

set $d_2^- = 0$.

Therefore, $a_1(d_1^-, d_2^-) = d_1^- + d_2^- = 0$, which satisfies the absolute constraints.
Let $a_1^* = \min a_1 = 0$. As shown in Fig. 3.13a, any point in the first quadrant (the shaded area) will satisfy the absolute constraints and gives $a_1 = 0$.

The value of the achievement function of Problem 2 at the base point, $a_2 = d_3^+$, is: $d_3^+ = f_1(\underline{x}) - b_1 = (x_1 - 4)^2 + x_2^2 - 10.25 = 41.75 \neq 0$
Therefore, KP = 2, and the modified Hooke and Jeeves pattern search is applied to find $\underline{x}$ so as to minimize $a_2 = d_3^+ = (x_1 - 4)^2 + x_2^2 - 10.25$.

To illustrate the modified procedure, the cost curve, $(x_1 - 4)^2 + x_2^2 = 10.25$, is drawn in Fig. 3.13b. The numbers on the points indicate the sequence in which they are selected. The number on each point also corresponds to the number of functional values searched from the beginning of Problem 2 up to and including that point. Table 3.2b presents the step by step results of applying the modified Hooke and Jeeves procedure for NLGP to Problem 2.

The point $\underline{x}^1 = (8,6)$, is the starting base $(B_{20})$ which is also the last base point of Problem 1. The step length is $\delta = (\delta_1, \delta_2) = (0.5, 0.5)$. At

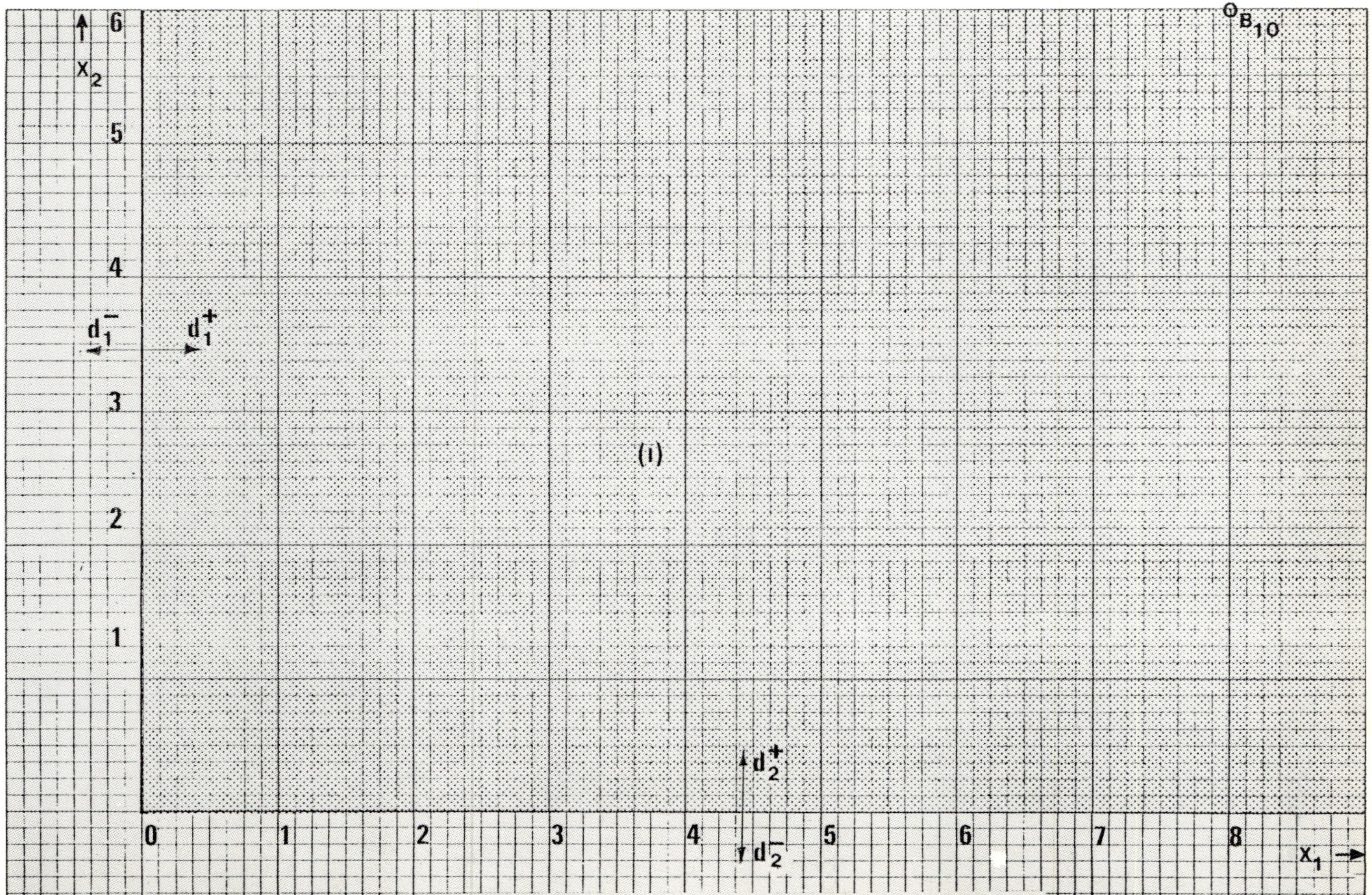


Fig. 3.13a Solution to Problem 1 of the NLGP problem.

Table 3.2a Step by step results of Problem 1 of the iterative NLGP problem.

| n | Base point $X_B$ | Step size | Better point $X$ | $a_1$ | Trial point $X^n$ | $a_1$ | Comments |
|---|---|---|---|---|---|---|---|
| 1 | $B_{10}$ | (.5,.5) | (8.0, 6.0) | 0.0 | | | Priority 1 satisfied. |

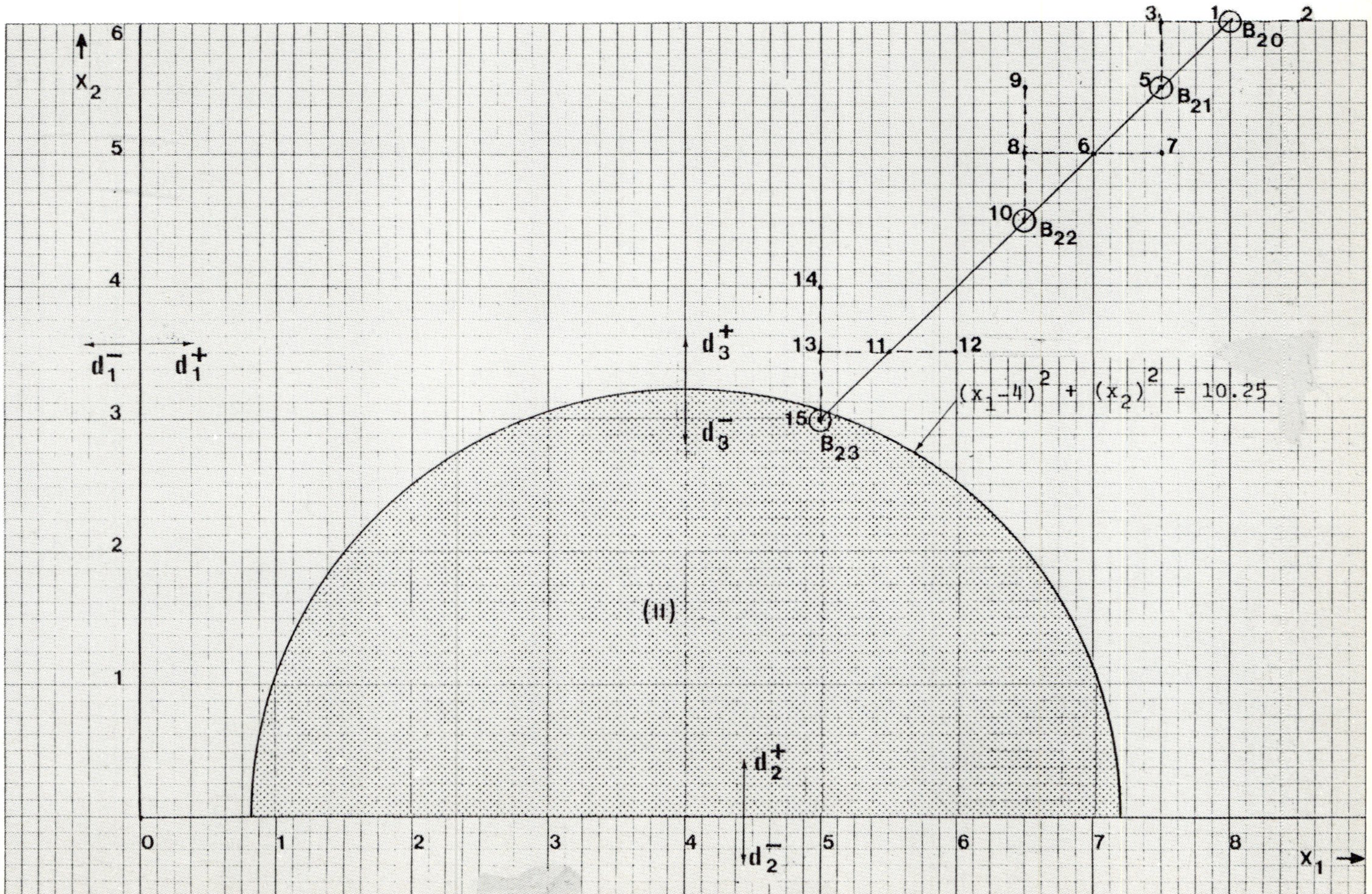


Fig. 3.13b  Solution to Problem 2 of the NLGP problem.

Table 3.2b Step by step results of Problem 2 of the iterative NLGP problem.

| n | Base point $x_B$ | Step size | Better point $x$ | $a_j^*$: $a_1^*$ | $a_j^*$: $a_2$ | Trial point $x^n$ | $a_j$: $a_1$ | $a_j$: $a_2$ | Comments |
|---|---|---|---|---|---|---|---|---|---|
| 1 | $B_{20}=B_{10}$ | (.5,.5) | (8.0, 6.0) | 0.0 | 41.75 | | | | Starting Base Pt. |
| 2 | | | (8.0, 6.0) | 0.0 | 41.75 | (8.5, 6.0) | 0.0 | 46.0 | Exp. Failure |
| 3 | | | (8.0, 6.0) | 0.0 | 41.75 | (7.5, 6.0) | 0.0 | 38.0 | Exp. Success |
| 4 | | | (7.5, 6.0) | 0.0 | 38.0 | (7.5, 6.5) | 0.0 | 44.25 | Exp. Failure |
| 5 | | | (7.5, 6.0) | 0.0 | 38.0 | (7.5, 5.5) | 0.0 | 32.25 | Exp. Success |
| 5 | $B_{21}$ | | (7.5, 5.5) | 0.0 | 32.25 | | | | |
| 6 | | | (7.5, 5.5) | 0.0 | 32.25 | (7.0, 5.0) | 0.0 | 23.75 | Pattern Move Success |
| 7 | | | (7.0, 5.0) | 0.0 | 23.75 | (7.5, 5.0) | 0.0 | 27.0 | Exp. Failure |
| 8 | | | (7.0, 5.0) | 0.0 | 23.75 | (6.5, 5.0) | 0.0 | 21.0 | Exp. Success |
| 9 | | | (6.5, 5.0) | 0.0 | 21.0 | (6.5, 5.5) | 0.0 | 26.25 | Exp. Failure |
| 10 | | | (6.5, 5.0) | 0.0 | 21.0 | (6.5, 4.5) | 0.0 | 16.25 | Exp. Success |
| 10 | $B_{22}$ | (.5,.5) | (6.5, 4.5) | 0.0 | 16.25 | | | | |
| 11 | | | (6.5, 4.5) | 0.0 | 16.25 | (5.5, 3.5) | 0.0 | 4.25 | Pattern (Success) |
| 12 | | | (5.5, 3.5) | 0.0 | 4.25 | (6.0, 3.5) | 0.0 | 6.0 | Exp. Failure |
| 13 | | | (5.5, 3.5) | 0.0 | 4.25 | (5.0, 3.5) | 0.0 | 3.0 | Exp. Success |
| 14 | | | (5.0, 3.5) | 0.0 | 3.0 | (5.0, 4.0) | 0.0 | 6.75 | Exp. Failure |
| 15 | | | (5.0, 3.5) | 0.0 | 3.0 | (5.0, 3.0) | 0.0 | 0.0 | Exp. Success |
| 15 | $B_{23}$ | (.5,.5) | (5.0, 3.0) | 0.0 | 0.0 | | | | Priorities 1 & 2 satisfied. |

the starting base point, $\underline{x}^1$, exploratory moves are conducted first in $x_1$ direction. At the point $\underline{x}^2 = (8.5, 6.0)$, the values of achievement functions $a_2^1[\underline{x}^2]$ and $a_1^1[\underline{x}^2]$ are compared with $a_2[\underline{x}^1] = 41.75$ and $a_1^* = 0$; $a_2^1[\underline{x}^2] = 46 > a_2[\underline{x}^1] = 41.75$ and $a_1^1[\underline{x}^2] = 0 = a_1^*$. So the point $\underline{x}^2$ is a failure. At $\underline{x}^3 = (7.5, 6.0)$, $a_2^1[\underline{x}^3] = 38 < a_2[\underline{x}^1] = 41.75$ and $a_1^1[\underline{x}^3] = 0 = a_1^*$. So the point $\underline{x}^3$ is a success, because both conditions are satisfied. Let $a_2[\underline{x}] = a_2[\underline{x}^3] = 38.0$. Again exploratory moves are conducted in $x_2$ direction at the point $\underline{x}^3$. The point $\underline{x}^4 = (7.5, 6.5)$ is a failure because $a_2^2[\underline{x}^4] = 44.25 > a_2[\underline{x}^3] = 38$ although $a_1^2[\underline{x}^4] = 0 = a_1^*$. The point $\underline{x}^5 = (7.5, 5.5)$ is a success because $a_2^2[\underline{x}^5] = 32.25 < a_2[\underline{x}^3] = 38$ and $a_1^2[\underline{x}^5] = 0 = a_1^*$. $\underline{x}^5 = (7.5, 5.5)$ is the end of the exploratory moves and since $\underline{x}^5$ is better point than $\underline{x}^1$, $\underline{x}^5$ is set as a new base point ($B_{21}$). Point $\underline{x}^6 = (7, 5)$ is obtained by the pattern move based on (3.29).

From $\underline{x}^6 = (7, 5)$ exploratory moves are performed again; $\underline{x}^{10} = (6.5, 4.5)$ becomes the new base point because $a_2^2[\underline{x}^{10}] = 16.25 < a_2[\underline{x}^5] = 32.25$ and $a_1^2[\underline{x}^{10}] = 0 = a_1^*$.

Point $\underline{x}^{11} = (5.5, 3.5)$ is reached by the pattern move according to equation (3.29) where the last base point $\underline{x}_B$ is $\underline{x}^5$ and the new base point is $\underline{x}^{10}$.

Point $\underline{x}^{15} = (5.0, 3.0)$ is the result of the exploratory moves starting from point $\underline{x}^{11}$, where moves to $\underline{x}^{13}$ and to $\underline{x}^{15}$ are successes because $a_2^1[\underline{x}^{13}] < a_2[\underline{x}^{11}]$ and $a_1^1[\underline{x}^{13}] = a_1^*$ and becuase $a_2^2[\underline{x}^{15}] < a_2^1[\underline{x}^{13}]$ and a $a_1^2[\underline{x}^{15}] = a_1^*$. Since $a_2^2[\underline{x}^{15}] < a_2^2[\underline{x}^{10}]$ and $a_1^2[\underline{x}^{15}] = a_1^*$, $\underline{x}^{15}$ becomes a new base point.

Because $a_2[\underline{x}^{15}] = 0$ and $a_1[\underline{x}^{15}] = 0$, $\underline{x}^{15} = (5, 3)$ is a solution to Problem 2.

Let $a_2^* = a_2[\underline{x}^{15}] = 0$ (minimum of $a_2$). As shown in Fig. 3.13b, any point in the shaded area (II) will satisfy priority levels 1 and 2 completely. Now we will set KP = 2 + 1 = 3, and Problem 3, min $a_3 = d_4^- + d_5^+$, is solved by starting at the last base point obtained in Problem 2; i.e. letting starting base point ($B_{30}$), $\underline{x}^1 = (5, 3)$.

The step by step results of Problem 3 are presented in Table 3.2c and Fig. 3.13c. After a series of pattern and exploratory moves, point $\underline{x}^{13} = (3.0, 1.0)$ is obtained where priorities 1, 2, and 3 are completely satisfied because at this point, $a_1 = 0$, $a_2 = 0$ and $a_3 = 0$. Let $a_3^* = \min a_3 = 0$. As shown in Fig. 3.13c any point in the shaded area (III) satisfies the priority levels 1, 2, and 3.

The search procedure is again continued for solving Problem 4, min $a_4 = d_6^-$, after setting KP = 3 + 1 = 4 and starting base point $B_{40}$ as the last base point obtained in Problem 3; i.e., $B_{40} = (3.0, 1.0)$.

The step by step results of Problem 4 are presented in Table 3.2d and in Fig. 3.13d. Minimum value for $a_4$ is obtained at the point $\underline{x}^{27} = (2.0, 2.5)$ where $a_1 = 0$, $a_2 = 0$, $a_3 = 0$ and $a_4 = 1.0$. All attempts to reduce the value of $a_4$ from 1.0 have failed because $a_1^*$, $a_2^*$, and $a_3^*$ are increasing at any other point where $a_4$ is less than 1.0, which is highly undesirable. The shaded area III in Fig. 3.13d represents the feasible region for priorities 1, 2, and 3; shaded area (IV) represents the feasible region for priority level 4. It is evident that we cannot attain priority level 4 (goal 3) completely because there is no common region formed by the feasible regions (III) and (IV). So the optimal solution for the GP problem is $x_1 = 2$, and $x_2 = 2.5$. All absolute constraints are satisfied and goals 1 and 2 are completely achieved, but goal 3 is not achieved fully.

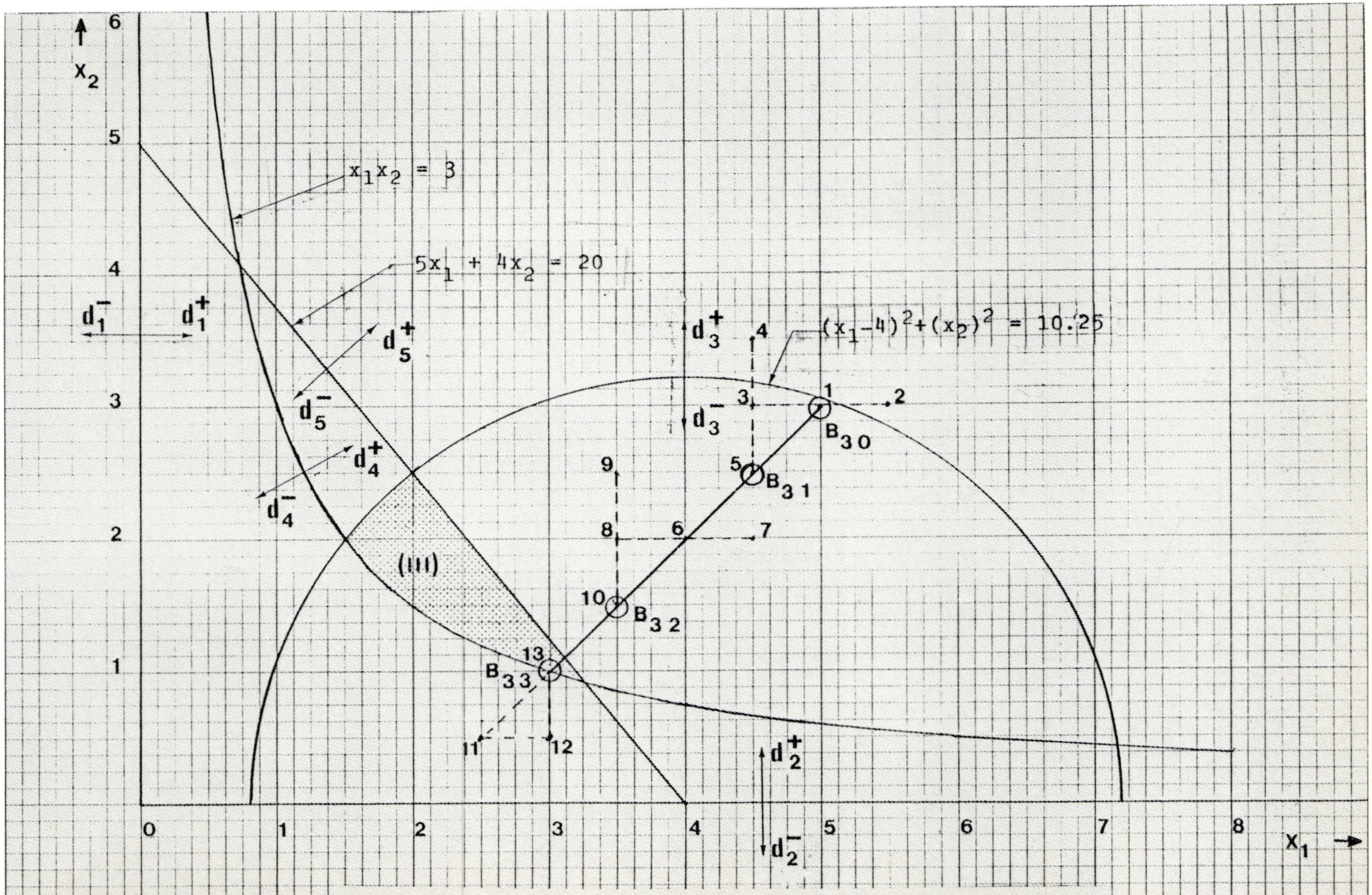


Fig. 3.13c Solution to Problem 3 of the NLGP problem.

Table 3.2c Step by step results of Problem 3 of the iterative NLGP problem.

| n | Base point $x^n$ | Step size | Better point x | $a_j^*$: $a_1^*$ | $a_2^*$ | $a_3$ | Trial point $x^n$ | $a_j$: $a_1$ | $a_2$ | $a_3$ | Comments |
|---|---|---|---|---|---|---|---|---|---|---|---|
| 1 | $B_{30} = B_{23}$ | (.5,.5) | (5.0, 3.0) | 0.0 | 0.0 | 17.0 | | | | | Starting Base Pt. |
| 2 | | | (5.0, 3.0) | 0.0 | 0.0 | 17.0 | (5.5, 3.0) | 0.0 | 1.0 | 19.5 | Failure |
| 3 | | | (5.0, 3.0) | 0.0 | 0.0 | 17.0 | (4.5, 3.0) | 0.0 | 0.0 | 14.5 | Success |
| 4 | | | (4.5, 3.0) | 0.0 | 0.0 | 14.5 | (4.5, 3.5) | 0.0 | 2.25 | 16.5 | Failure |
| 5 | | | (4.5, 3.0) | 0.0 | 0.0 | 14.5 | (4.5, 2.5) | 0.0 | 0.0 | 12.5 | Success |
| 5 | $B_{31}$ | | (4.5, 2.5) | 0.0 | 0.0 | 12.5 | | | | | |
| 6 | | | (4.5, 2.5) | 0.0 | 0.0 | 12.5 | (4.5, 2.0) | 0.0 | 0.0 | 8.0 | Pattern Success |
| 7 | | | (4.0, 2.0) | 0.0 | 0.0 | 8.0 | (4.5, 2.0) | 0.0 | 0.0 | 10.5 | Failure |
| 8 | | | (4.0, 2.0) | 0.0 | 0.0 | 8.0 | (3.5, 2.0) | 0.0 | 0.0 | 5.5 | Success |
| 9 | | | (3.5, 2.0) | 0.0 | 0.0 | 5.5 | (3.5, 2.5) | 0.0 | 0.0 | 7.5 | Failure |
| 10 | | | (3.5, 2.0) | 0.0 | 0.0 | 5.5 | (3.5, 1.5) | 0.0 | 0.0 | 3.5 | Success |
| 10 | $B_{32}$ | | (3.5, 1.5) | 0.0 | 0.0 | 3.5 | | | | | |
| 11 | | | (3.5, 1.5) | 0.0 | 0.0 | 3.5 | (2.5, 0.5) | 0.0 | 0.0 | 1.75 | Pattern Success |
| 12 | | | (2.5, 0.5) | 0.0 | 0.0 | 1.75 | (3.0, 0.5) | 0.0 | 0.0 | 1.5 | Success |
| 13 | | | (3.0, 0.5) | 0.0 | 0.0 | 1.5 | (3.0, 1.0) | 0.0 | 0.0 | 0.0 | Success |
| 13 | $B_{33}$ | | (3.0, 1.0) | 0.0 | 0.0 | 0.0 | | | | | |
| | | | | | | | | | | | Priorities 1,2&3 satisfied. |

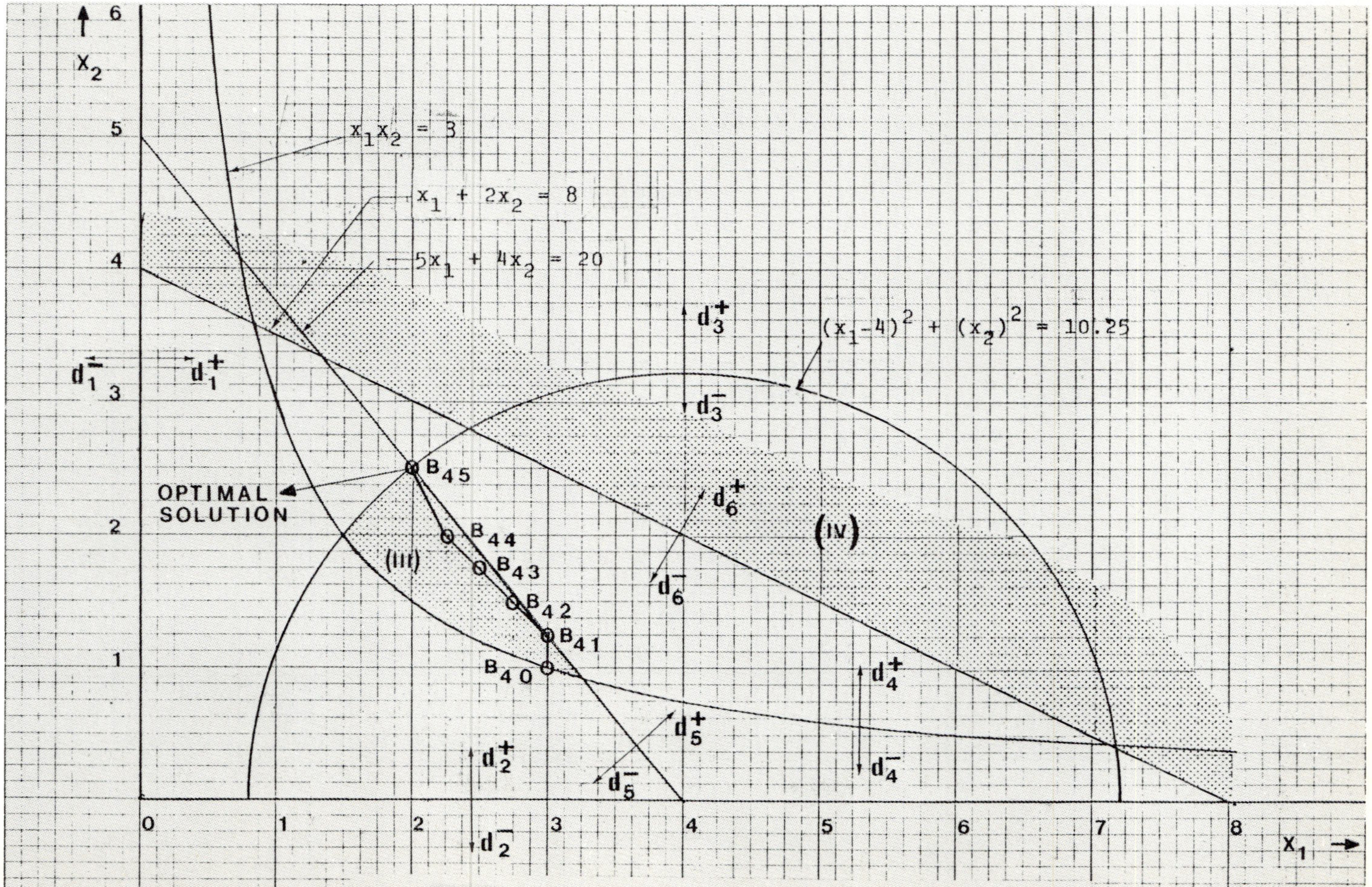


Fig. 3.13d Solution to Problem 4 of the NLGP problem.

Table 3.2d Step by step results of Problem 4 of the iterative NLGP problem.

| n | Base point $x_B$ | Step size | Better point x | $a_j^*$: $a_1^*$ | $a_2^*$ | $a_3^*$ | $a_4$ | Trial point $x^n$ | $a_j$: $a_1$ | $a_2$ | $a_3$ | $a_4$ | Comments |
|---|---|---|---|---|---|---|---|---|---|---|---|---|---|
| 1 | $B_{40} = B_{33}$ | (.5,.5) | (3.0, 1.0) | 0.0 | 0.0 | 0.0 | 3.0 | | | | | | Starting Base Pt. |
| 2 | | | (3.0, 1.0) | 0.0 | 0.0 | 0.0 | 3.0 | (3.5, 1.0) | 0.0 | 0.0 | 1.5 | 2.5 | Failure |
| 3 | | | (3.0, 1.0) | 0.0 | 0.0 | 0.0 | 3.0 | (2.5, 1.0) | 0.0 | 0.0 | 0.5 | 3.5 | Failure |
| 4 | | | (3.0, 1.0) | 0.0 | 0.0 | 0.0 | 3.0 | (3.0, 1.5) | 0.0 | 0.0 | 1.0 | 2.0 | Failure |
| 5 | | | (3.0, 1.0) | 0.0 | 0.0 | 0.0 | 3.0 | (3.0, 0.5) | 0.0 | 0.0 | 1.5 | 4.0 | Failure |
| 1 | $B_{40}$ | (.25,.25) | (3.0, 1.0) | 0.0 | 0.0 | 0.0 | 3.0 | | | | | | Starting Base |
| 6 | | | (3.0, 1.0) | 0.0 | 0.0 | 0.0 | 3.0 | (3.25,1.0) | 0.0 | 0.0 | 0.25 | 2.75 | Failure |
| 7 | | | (3.0, 1.0) | 0.0 | 0.0 | 0.0 | 3.0 | (2.75,1.0) | 0.0 | 0.0 | 0.25 | 3.25 | Failure |
| 8 | | | (3.0, 1.0) | 0.0 | 0.0 | 0.0 | 3.0 | (3.0,1.25) | 0.0 | 0.0 | 0.0 | 2.5 | Success |
| 8 | $B_{41}$ | (.25,.25) | (3.0,1.25) | 0.0 | 0.0 | 0.0 | 2.5 | | | | | | |
| 9 | | | (3.0,1.25) | 0.0 | 0.0 | 0.0 | 2.5 | (3.0, 1.5) | 0.0 | 0.0 | 1.0 | 2.0 | Pattern Move Failure |
| 10 | | | (3.0,1.25) | 0.0 | 0.0 | 0.0 | 2.5 | (3.25,1.5) | 0.0 | 0.0 | 2.25 | 1.75 | Failure |
| 11 | | | (3.0,1.25) | 0.0 | 0.0 | 0.0 | 2.5 | (2.75,1.5) | 0.0 | 0.0 | 0.0 | 2.25 | Success |
| 12 | | | (2.75,1.5) | 0.0 | 0.0 | 0.0 | 2.25 | (2.75,1.75) | 0.0 | 0.0 | 0.75 | 1.75 | Failure |
| 13 | | | (2.75,1.5) | 0.0 | 0.0 | 0.0 | 2.25 | (2.75,1.25) | 0.0 | 0.0 | 0.0 | 2.75 | Failure |

Table 3.2d (cont'd).

| n | Base point $x_B$ | Step size | Better point $x$ | $a_j^*$ | | | | Trial point $x^n$ | $a_j$ | | | | Comments |
|---|---|---|---|---|---|---|---|---|---|---|---|---|---|
| | | | | $a_1^*$ | $a_2^*$ | $a_3^*$ | $a_4$ | | $a_1$ | $a_2$ | $a_3$ | $a_4$ | |
| 11 | $B_{42}$ | | (2.75, 1.5) | 0.0 | 0.0 | 0.0 | 2.25 | | | | | | |
| 14 | | | (2.75, 1.5) | 0.0 | 0.0 | 0.0 | 2.25 | (2.5, 1.75) | 0.0 | 0.0 | 0.0 | 2.0 | Pattern (Success) |
| 15 | | | (2.5, 1.75) | 0.0 | 0.0 | 0.0 | 2.0 | (2.75,1.75) | 0.0 | 0.0 | 0.75 | 1.75 | Failure |
| 16 | | | (2.5, 1.75) | 0.0 | 0.0 | 0.0 | 2.0 | (2.75,1.75) | 0.0 | 0.0 | 0.0 | 2.25 | Failure |
| 17 | | | (2.5, 1.75) | 0.0 | 0.0 | 0.0 | 2.0 | (2.5, 2.0) | 0.0 | 0.0 | 0.0 | 2.0 | Failure |
| 18 | | | (2.5, 1.75) | 0.0 | 0.0 | 0.0 | 2.0 | (2.5, 1.5) | 0.0 | 0.0 | 0.0 | 2.5 | Failure |
| 14 | $B_{43}$ | (.25,.25) | (2.5, 1.75) | 0.0 | 0.0 | 0.0 | 2.0 | | | | | | |
| 19 | | | (2.5, 1.75) | 0.0 | 0.0 | 0.0 | 2.0 | (2.25, 2.0) | 0.0 | 0.0 | 0.0 | 1.75 | Pattern (Success) |
| 20 | | | (2.25, 2.0) | 0.0 | 0.0 | 0.0 | 1.75 | (2.5, 2.0) | 0.0 | 0.0 | 0.5 | 1.5 | Failure |
| 21 | | | (2.25, 2.0) | 0.0 | 0.0 | 0.0 | 1.75 | (2.0, 2.0) | 0.0 | 0.0 | 0.0 | 2.0 | Failure |
| 22 | | | (2.25, 2.0) | 0.0 | 0.0 | 0.0 | 1.75 | (2.25,2.25) | 0.0 | 0.0 | 0.25 | 1.25 | Failure |
| 23 | | | (2.25, 2.0) | 0.0 | 0.0 | 0.0 | 1.75 | (2.25,1.75) | 0.0 | 0.0 | 0.0 | 2.25 | Failure |
| 19 | $B_{44}$ | | (2.25, 2.0) | 0.0 | 0.0 | 0.0 | 1.75 | | | | | | |
| 24 | | | (2.25, 2.0) | 0.0 | 0.0 | 0.0 | 1.75 | (2.0, 2.25) | 0.0 | 0.0 | 0.0 | 1.5 | Pattern (Success) |
| 25 | | | (2.0, 2.25) | 0.0 | 0.0 | 0.0 | 1.5 | (2.25,2.25) | 0.0 | 0.0 | 0.25 | 1.25 | Failure |

Table 3.2d (cont'd).

| n | Base point $x_B$ | Step size | Better point x | $a_1^*$ | $a_2^*$ | $a_3^*$ | $a_4$ | Trial point $x^n$ | $a_1$ | $a_2$ | $a_3$ | $a_4$ | Comments |
|---|---|---|---|---|---|---|---|---|---|---|---|---|---|
| | | | | $a_j^*$ | | | | | $a_j$ | | | | |
| 26 | | | (2.0, 2.25) | 0.0 | 0.0 | 0.0 | 1.5 | (1.75,2.25) | 0.0 | 0.0 | 0.0 | 1.75 | Failure |
| 27 | | | (2.0, 2.25) | 0.0 | 0.0 | 0.0 | 1.5 | (2.0,2.5) | 0.0 | 0.0 | 0.0 | 1.0 | Success |
| 27 | $B_{45}$ | | (2.0, 2.50) | 0.0 | 0.0 | 0.0 | 1.0 | | | | | | |
| 28 | | | (2.0, 2.5) | 0.0 | 0.0 | 0.0 | 1.0 | (1.75,3.0) | 0.0 | 3.81 | 0.75 | 0.25 | Pattern Failure |
| 29 | | | (2.0, 2.5) | 0.0 | 0.0 | 0.0 | 1.0 | (2.0, 3.0) | 0.0 | 2.75 | 2.0 | 0.0 | Failure |
| 30 | | | (2.0, 2.5) | 0.0 | 0.0 | 0.0 | 1.0 | (1.5, 3.0) | 0.0 | 5.0 | 0.0 | 0.5 | Failure |
| 31 | | | (2.0, 2.5) | 0.0 | 0.0 | 0.0 | 1.0 | (1.75,3.25) | 0.0 | 5.38 | 1.75 | 0.0 | Failure |
| 32 | | | (2.0, 2.5) | 0.0 | 0.0 | 0.0 | 1.0 | (1.75,2.75) | 0.0 | 2.38 | 0.0 | 0.75 | Failure |
| 27 | $B_{45}$ | (.125, .125) | (2.0, 2.5) | 0.0 | 0.0 | 0.0 | 1.0 | | | | | | Starting Base |
| 33 | | | (2.0, 2.5) | 0.0 | 0.0 | 0.0 | 1.0 | (2.125, 2.5) | 0.0 | 0.0 | 0.63 | 0.88 | Failure |
| 34 | | | (2.0, 2.5) | 0.0 | 0.0 | 0.0 | 1.0 | (1.875, 2.5) | 0.0 | 0.52 | 0.0 | 1.13 | Failure |
| 35 | | | (2.0, 2.5) | 0.0 | 0.0 | 0.0 | 1.0 | (2.0, 2.625) | 0.0 | 0.64 | 0.5 | 0.75 | Failure |
| 36 | | | (2.0, 2.5) | 0.0 | 0.0 | 0.0 | 1.0 | (2.0, 2.375) | 0.0 | 0.0 | 0.0 | 1.25 | Failure |

Table 3.2d (cont'd).

| n | Base point $x_B$ | Step size | Better point x | $a_j^*$ | | | | Trial point $x^n$ | $a_j$ | | | | Comments |
|---|---|---|---|---|---|---|---|---|---|---|---|---|---|
| | | | | $a_1^*$ | $a_2^*$ | $a_3^*$ | $a_4$ | | $a_1$ | $a_2$ | $a_3$ | $a_4$ | |
| 27 | $B_{45}$ | (.0625, .0625) | (2.0, 2.5) | 0.0 | 0.0 | 0.0 | 1.0 | | | | | | Starting base |
| 37 | | | (2.0, 2.5) | 0.0 | 0.0 | 0.0 | 1.0 | (2.0625, 2.5) | 0.0 | 0.0 | 0.31 | 0.94 | Fail |
| 38 | | | (2.0, 2.5) | 0.0 | 0.0 | 0.0 | 1.0 | (1.9375, 2.5) | 0.0 | 0.25 | 0.0 | 1.06 | Fail |
| . | | | . | . | . | . | . | . | . | . | . | . | |
| . | | | . | . | . | . | . | . | . | . | . | . | |
| . | | | . | . | . | . | . | . | . | . | . | . | |
| | $B_{45}$ | | (2.0, 2.5) | 0.0 | 0.0 | 0.0 | 1.0 | | | | | | Optimal solution |

Note

The algorithm for Iterative Nonlinear Goal Programming (INGP) is an effective procedure for solving a set of constrained minimization problems sequentially in one attempt. The effectiveness of INGP is based on the Goal Programming characteristic that there exist many solutions which satisfy the constraints at each priority level, and that solutions become fewer and fewer as the number of priority levels of the achievement functions being minimized increases. The INGP does not require the derivatives of objectives or constraints. Another interesting feature of this algorithm is that it combines the iterative procedure for solving NLGP problems by traditional nonlinear search technique that is originally intended for solving the so called "unconstrained" problems.

The INGP can also be used to solve the classical (single objective constrained) nonlinear programming problem effectively by reformulating the problem into a nonlinear goal programming problem which has the absolute constraints in the first priority level and the single objective to be optimized in the second priority level (see Sec. 3.2.2 Example).

A listing of the FORTRAN program of the algorithm is available. We have solved several single and multiple objective problems with the proposed algorithm. Some of the recent applications include production scheduling, reliability problems, and water resources management. The algorithm has been found to be effective for small to moderate size (say up to 25 variables and 50 constraints/objectives) nonlinear problems.

### 2.2.3 GOAL ATTAINMENT METHOD

This is a variation of the GP method proposed by Gembicki [125, also see BM-8]. The method requires that the DM gives a goal vector, $\underline{b}$, and a vector of weight $\underline{w}$ relating the relative under- or overattainment of the desired goals. The mathematical formulation of the problem is:

$$\left.\begin{array}{lll} \min & z & \\ \text{s.t.} & g_j(\underline{x}) \leq 0, & j = 1, 2, \ldots, m \\ & f_i(\underline{x}) - w_i z \geq b_i, & i = 1, 2, \ldots, k \\ & \underline{w} > 0 & \end{array}\right\} \quad (3.30)$$

where z is a scalar variable unrestricted in sign, and $\underline{w}$ is generally normalized so that $\sum_{i=1}^{k} |w_i| = 1$. In the case of underattainment of the desired goals, the smaller weighting coefficient is associated with the more important objectives. For overattainment of the desired goals, the smaller weighting coefficient is associated with the less important objectives.

The goal attainment method for two objectives is illustrated in Fig. 3.14. The direction of the preferred solution vector, $\underline{b} + \underline{w}z$, is fixed by the goal vector $\underline{b}$ and the weight vector $\underline{w}$. The minimum value of z occurs where $\underline{b} + \underline{w}z$ vector intersects the upper bound of S (for maximizing $\underline{f}(\underline{x})$).

This method has the same disadvantages as those of GP; namely, the preferred solution is sensitive to the goal vector and the weighting vector given by the DM. When some of the desired goals are under- and some overattained, this method has difficulty in determining the proper weighting coefficient $w_i$. However, (3.30) has fewer variables to work with, so it will be computationally faster.

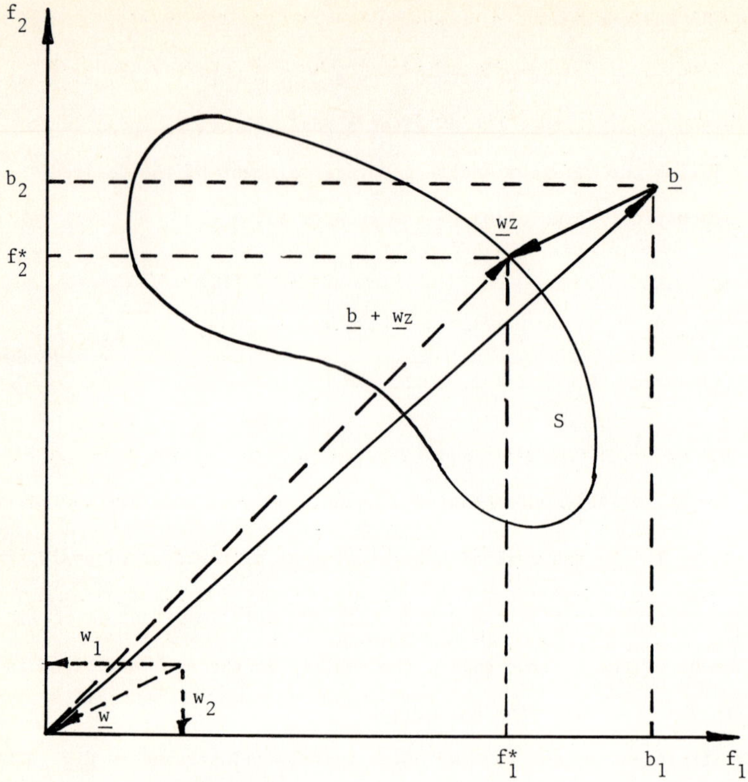


Fig. 3.14 Goal attainment method for two objectives.

<u>NUMERICAL EXAMPLE</u> (Production scheduling of the Hardee Toy Company)

To illustrate the use of this method, consider again the management of the Hardee Toy Company. The VMP problem is given by:

$$\max \quad f_1(\underline{x}) = 0.4x_1 + 0.3x_2$$

$$\max \quad f_2(\underline{x}) = x_1$$

$$\left.\begin{aligned} \text{s.t.} \quad g_1(\underline{x}) &= x_1 + x_2 \leq 400 \\ g_2(\underline{x}) &= 2x_1 + x_2 \leq 500 \\ x_1, x_2 &\geq 0 \end{aligned}\right\} \quad \text{Let these constraints be denoted by } \underline{x} \in X.$$

The method requires that the DM gives a goal vector $\underline{b}$ and a vector of weight $\underline{w}$ relating the relative under- or overattainment of the desired goals. Let $\underline{b} = (b_1, b_2) = (180, 200)$, and the relative underattainment of $f_2$ should be one-half the underattainment of $f_1$. Then $\underline{w} = (w_1, w_2) = (-0.67, -0.33)$. The mathematical formulation of the problem is:

$$\min \quad z$$

$$\begin{aligned} \text{s.t.} \quad g_1(\underline{x}) &= x_1 + x_2 \leq 400 \\ g_2(\underline{x}) &= 2x_1 + x_2 < 500 \\ & 0.4x_1 + 0.3x_2 + 0.67z \geq 180 \\ & x_1 + 0.33z \geq 200 \\ & x_1, x_2, z \geq 0 \end{aligned}$$

The solution to this LP problem is:

$$z = 95.4, \ (x_1, x_2) = (168.2, 163.6)$$

$$(f_1, f_2) = (116.4, 168.2)$$

This solution is depicted as point D in Fig. 3.15.

<u>Note</u>

In the example, if the DM gives the goal vector, $\underline{b}^1 = (180, 100)$, $\underline{b}^2 = (180, 50)$, or $\underline{b}^3 = (150, 0)$, with a weight vector $\underline{w} = (-0.67, -0.33)$, the solution to the LP problem of (3.30) is always point B; that is

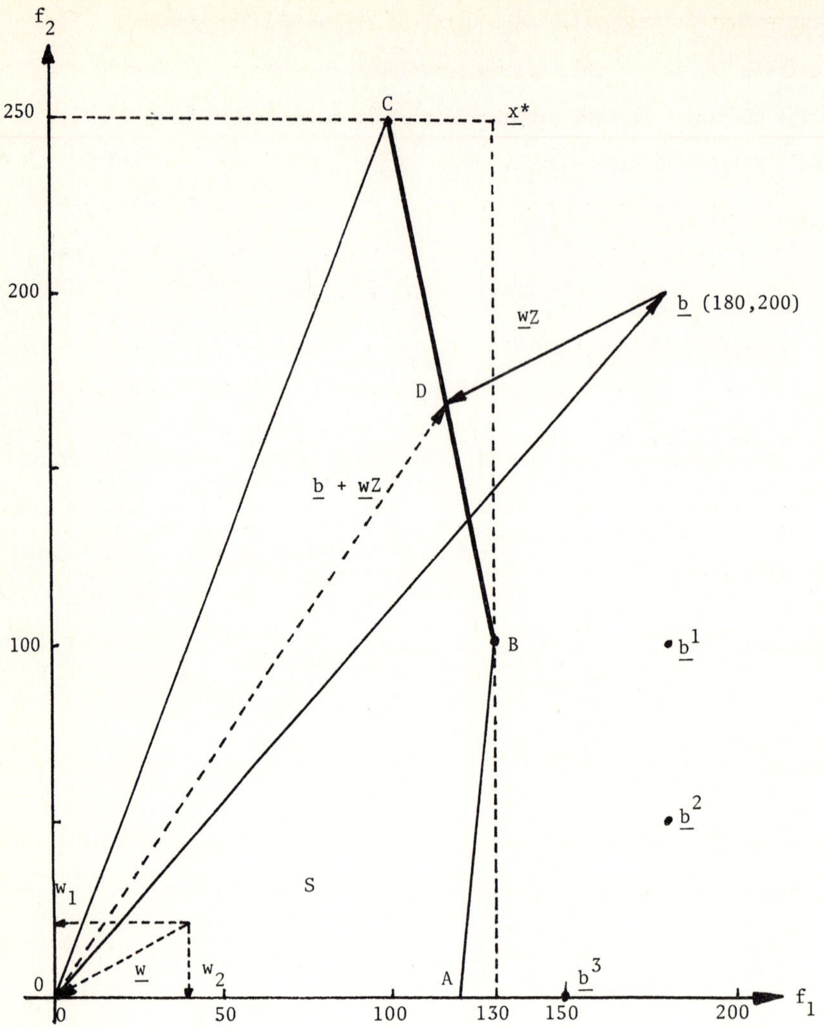


Fig. 3.15 Illustration of goal attainment method applied to the example.

$(x_1, x_2) = (100, 300)$, $(f_1, f_2) = (130, 100)$. In this case, the weight vector $\underline{w}$ does not dictate the solution, but the nearest nondominated point (Point B) from these goals ($\underline{b}^1$, $\underline{b}^2$, or $\underline{b}^3$) determines the solution (see Fig. 3.15).

The basic goal attainment method may be modified. A payoff table (see Section 1.1.1 Steps 1 and 2) may be constructed and the information is given to the DM before he/she decides the goal vector.

As the payoff table is shown to the DM, who will realize that the nondominated solutions for this problem will be: $f_1$ takes the values between 100 to 130, and $f_2$ takes 100 to 250. Then the DM may give a reasonable goal vector of $\underline{b}$ (e.g. $\underline{b} = (120, 200)$) and a weight vector $\underline{w}$. The basic goal attainment method can be applied to obtain the solution to the problem.

3. Methods for Progressive Articulation of Preference Information Given (Interactive Methods)

This class of methods, generally referred to as "Interactive Methods", relies on the progressive definition of the DM's preferences along with the exploration of the criterion space. Much work has been done recently on this class of methods (see Table 1.3 for references.) The progressive definition takes place through a DM-Analyst or DM-Machine dialogue at each iteration. At each such dialogue, the DM is asked about some trade-off or preference information based upon the current solution (or the set of current solutions) in order to determine a new solution. Some methods require explicit information regarding the trade-off between the attainment levels of objectives at each stage; others require the implicit trade-off information in the form allowing the DM to indicate acceptability of the current achievement level.

These methods assume that the DM is unable to indicate 'a priori' preference information due to the complexity of the problems, but that he/she is able to give preference information on a local level to a particular solution. As the solution process progresses, the DM not only indicates his/her preferences, but also learns about the problem. Some methods allow the DM to reverse the order of his/her preferences; a few methods guarantee a preferred solution after a limited number of interactions.

The advantages of the methods are: (1) there is no need for 'a priori' preference information; (2) it is a learning process for the DM to understand the behavior of the system; (3) only local preference information is needed; (4) since the DM is part of the solution process, the solution obtained has a better prospect of being implemented; and (5) there are less restrictive assumptions as compared to methods described previously. The disadvantages are: (1) solutions depend upon the accuracy of the local preference the DM can indicate; (2) for many methods there is no guarantee that the preferred solution can be obtained within a finite number of interactive cycles; and (3) much more effort is required of the DM than is so with methods presented previously.

### 3.1. Methods for Explicit Trade-Off Information Given

The methods require that the DM be able to indicate his/her preferable trade-offs on a specific achievement level of the objectives. Some methods provide a set of feasible trade-offs from which the DM can choose.

### 3.1.1 METHOD OF GEOFFRION AND INTERACTIVE GOAL PROGRAMMING

#### 3.1.1.a METHOD OF GEOFFRION

The trade-off ratios are difficult to obtain when there are more than two objectives, but the DM can rather easily assess the trade-off between two objectives on a specific achievement level of the objectives. Hence the improvement of an overall utility function through successive trade-offs can be made by using an efficient interactive optimization technique.

The method proposed by Geoffrion, Dyer and Feinberg [105, 130] demonstrates that a large-step gradient algorithm can be used for solving the VMP if the DM is able to specify an overall utility function defined on the values of the objectives. However, the method never actually requires this function to be identified explicitly. Instead, it asks only for such local information as is needed to perform the computations. The procedure is described in the context of the Frank-Wolfe algorithm [117a] which is a specific nonlinear programming method.

The problem is formulated as follows:

$$\left.\begin{array}{l} \max\ U(f_1(\underline{x}),\ f_2(\underline{x}),\ \ldots,\ f_k(\underline{x})) \\ \text{s.t.}\quad \underline{x} \in X \end{array}\right\} \qquad (3.31)$$

The objective functions $f_i(\underline{x})$ and the feasible set X, $X = (\underline{x}|\underline{g}(x) \leq \underline{0})$, are assumed to be explicitly known, but the utility function $U(\underline{f})$ is assumed to be only implicitly known. (If U were explicitly known, the problem would be an ordinary nonlinear optimization problem, see Sec. 2.1.1.). To be able to solve (3.31) using the Frank-Wolfe method, the following convexity and differentiability assumptions have been postulated: (1) the constraint set is convex and compact; (2) $U(\underline{f})$ is differentiable and concave on $\underline{x}$; (3) each $f_i$ is concave; (4) $\partial U/\partial f_1 > 0$, (i.e., positive marginal utility) in the neighborhood of $\underline{x}^i$ ($\underline{x}$ at the ith iteration) where $f_1(\underline{x})$ is the reference objective.

The algorithm

Among the gradient methods, Geoffrion et al. [130] selected the well-known Frank-Wolfe algorithm for its simplicity, and its robust convergence properties. The Frank-Wolfe approach for the solution of problem (3.31) is by linear approximations. Given a feasible point $\underline{x}^i$, let $\underline{y}^i$ be the solution to the problem that uses the same constraints as problem (3.31) but whose objective function is a linear approximation of $U(\underline{f})$ at $\underline{x}^i$. Then the direction of improvement of the solution, $\underline{z}^i = \underline{y}^i - \underline{x}^i$, is a direction to seek an increased value of $U(\underline{f})$.

The basic Frank-Wolfe algorithm as applied to (3.31) is (ignoring for the moment the fact that $U(\underline{f})$ is not explicitly known):

Step 0. Choose an initial point $\underline{x}^i \in X$. Set $i = 1$.

Step 1. Determine an optimal solution $\underline{y}^i$ of the direction-finding problem:

$$\left.\begin{aligned} &\max \; \nabla_{\underline{x}} U(f_1(\underline{x}^i), f_2(\underline{x}^i), \ldots, f_k(\underline{x}^i)) \cdot \underline{y}^i \\ &\underline{y} \in X \end{aligned}\right\} \qquad (3.32)$$

Set $\underline{z}^i = \underline{y}^i - \underline{x}^i$

Step 2. Determine an optimal $t^i$ of the step-size problem:

$$\left.\begin{aligned} &\max \; U(f_1(\underline{x}^i + t^i z^i), \ldots, f_k(\underline{x}^i + t^i z^i)) \\ &0 \le t^i \le 1 \end{aligned}\right\} \qquad (3.33)$$

Set $\underline{x}^{i+1} = \underline{x}^i + t^i \underline{z}^i$, $i = i+1$, and return to Step 1.

The theoretical termination criterion is satisfied if the solutions $\underline{x}^i$ and $\underline{x}^{i+1}$ are equal.

The interpretation of the algorithm in the spirit of the steepest ascent algorithm is that it determines the best direction of movement from the current point $\underline{x}^i$ (Step 1), and the DM is asked to determine how far to move in this direction (Step 2). A sequence of improving feasible solutions $\underline{x}^i$ to (3.31) is obtained which converges to an optimal solution.

Method for determining the direction of improvement: Since $U(\underline{f})$ is not known explicitly, carrying out Steps 1 and 2 requires the DM's assistance. The acquisition of information necessary to complete these steps forms the interactive portion of this method. Although $U(\underline{f})$ is not known explicitly, it is assumed that the DM can estimate the trade-off between any two objectives among all objectives at a particular solution point. The trade-off can be used to estimate the direction of the gradient of $U(\underline{f})$ at that solution point.

In Step 1, the objective function can be expressed by the chain rule which yields:

$$\nabla_{\underline{x}} U[f_1(\underline{x}^i), \ldots, f_k(\underline{x}^i)] \cdot \underline{y}^i$$

$$= \left.\frac{\partial U}{\partial(f_1, \ldots, f_k)}\right|_{\underline{f}^i} \cdot \left.\frac{\partial(f_1, \ldots, f_k)}{\partial(x_1, \ldots, x_n)}\right|_{\underline{x}^i} \cdot \underline{y}^i$$

$$= \left(\frac{\partial U}{\partial f_1}, \ldots, \frac{\partial U}{\partial f_k}\right)_{\underline{f}^i} \cdot \begin{pmatrix} \frac{\partial f_1}{\partial x_1} & \cdots & \frac{\partial f_1}{\partial x_n} \\ \vdots & & \vdots \\ \frac{\partial f_k}{\partial x_1} & \cdots & \frac{\partial f_k}{\partial x_n} \end{pmatrix}_{\underline{x}^i} \cdot \underline{y}^i$$

$$= \left[ \sum_{j=1}^{k} \left(\frac{\partial U}{\partial f_j^i}\right) \nabla_{\underline{x}} f_j(\underline{x}^i) \right] \cdot \underline{y}^i$$

where $\frac{\partial U}{\partial f_j^i}$ is the partial derivative of U with respect to objective j which is evaluated at the point $[f_1(\underline{x}^i), \ldots, f_k(\underline{x}^i)]$, and $\nabla_{\underline{x}} f_j(\underline{x}^i)$ is the gradient of $f_j$ evaluated at $\underline{x}^i$. The solution of problem (3.32) will not be affected by multiplying the objective function by a scalar. Hence we divide the objective function by $\left(\frac{\partial U}{\partial f_j^i}\right)$. Then, the direction – finding problem (3.32) is equivalent to:

$$\left.\begin{aligned} &\max \sum_{j=1}^{k} w_j^i \; \nabla_{\underline{x}} f_j(\underline{x}^i) \cdot \underline{y}^i \\ &\underline{y} \in X \end{aligned}\right\} \tag{3.34}$$

where $w_j^i$ is defined as

$$w_j^i = (\partial U/\partial f_j^i) \,/\, (\partial U/\partial f_1^i), \qquad j = 1,2, \ldots, k \tag{3.35}$$

The weights $w_j^i$ reflect the DM's trade-off between $f_1$ (arbitrarily chosen as the reference criterion) and $f_j$ at the current point $\underline{x}^i$, and must be elicited before the problem can be solved. One way to obtain $w_j^i$ is to determine an infinitesimal change $\Delta f_1$ in the first objective which exactly compensates for a change $\Delta f_j$ in the jth objective, while all other objectives remain constant. Then (3.35) is approximated by

$$w_j^i = -\frac{\Delta f_1}{\Delta f_j}$$

This is the DM's indifference trade-off or marginal rate of substitution between objectives.

<u>Methods for step size selection</u>: Since U is not explicitly available, Step 2 must be done by the DM. This is not as difficult as it sounds because there is only one variable, t, and plots can be made of the values of all k objectives $\underline{f}\,(\underline{x}^i + t\underline{z}^i)$ as a function of t between 0 and 1.

There are two ways of displaying the values of $\underline{f}(\underline{x}^i + t\underline{z}^i)$ for various values of t, $0 \leq t \leq 1$. The computer can tabulate the values of the objectives at selected intervals of t, and present the table (e.g. Table 3.3) to the DM. Another way is the graphical method. The values of $\underline{f}(\underline{x}^i + t\underline{z}^i)$ are calculated and plotted over a grid of points for $0 \leq t \leq 1$. Although each objective can have a different scale, all objectives can be superimposed on a single graph with the scale of each marked separately as shown in Fig. 3.16. Given the tabular or graphical display, the DM must determine a value of t for which the objectives are most preferred. For example, the dotted vertical line in Fig. 3.16 indicates the selection of $t^i$ and the most preferred values of objectives.

Termination criterion: As mentioned, the theoretical termination criterion is satisfied if the solutions $\underline{x}^i$ and $\underline{x}^{i+1}$ are equal. But as this rarely happens, a practical criterion is presented here.

From the concavity of U, it is known that $U(\underline{f})$ nowhere exceeds it tangent hyperplane at any point $\underline{f}^i$; i.e.,

$$U(\underline{f}) \leq U(\underline{f}^i) + \Delta_{\underline{f}} U(\underline{f}^i) \cdot (\underline{f} - \underline{f}^i), \forall f_i, f_i \in S$$

or

$$U(\underline{f}) - U(\underline{f}^i) \leq \Delta_{\underline{f}} U(\underline{f}^i) \cdot (\underline{f} - \underline{f}^i). \quad \forall f_i, f_i \in S$$

Hence the amount of improvement made from $\underline{f}^i$ to $\underline{f}^{i+1}$, i.e., $U(\underline{f}^{i+1}) - U(\underline{f}^i)$

Table 3.3 Tabular presentation of multi-objective results for step-size selection

| t | 0 | 0.1 | 0.2 | ..... | 0.9 | 1 |
|---|---|---|---|---|---|---|
| $f_1$ | | | | | | |
| $f_2$ | | | | | | |
| ⋮ | | | | | | |
| $f_k$ | | | | | | |

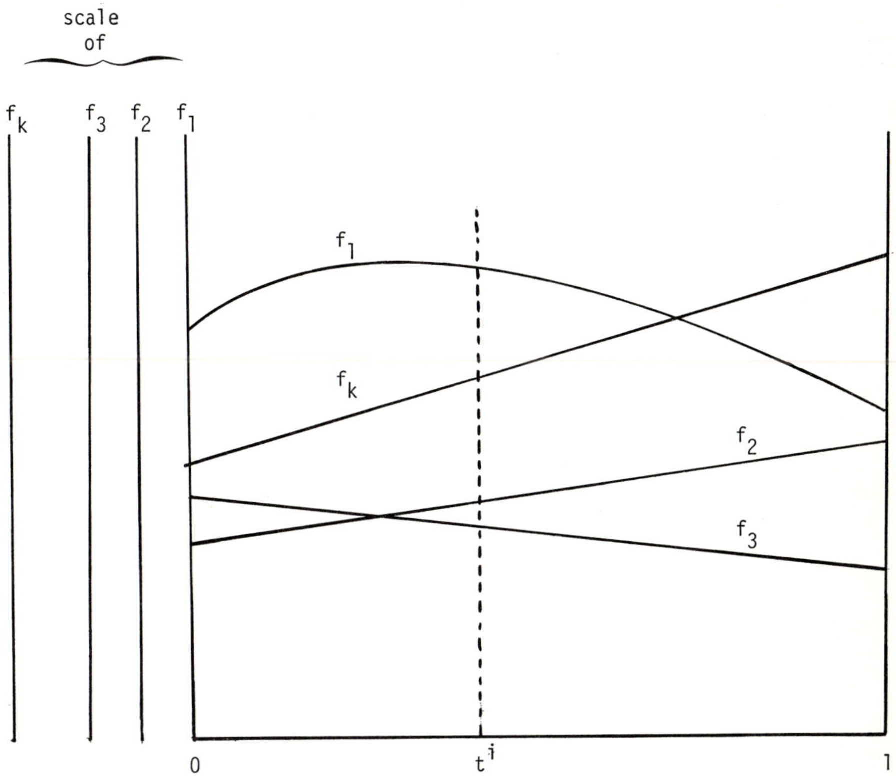


Fig. 3.16 Graphical representation of multi-objective relults for step-size selection

is bound by $\nabla_{\underline{f}} U(\underline{f}^i) \cdot (\underline{f}^{i+1} - \underline{f}^i)$. Although the gradient of U is not known, we can make meaningful comparisons of the relative magnitudes of the factors $\underline{w}^i = (1, w_2^i, \ldots, w_k^i)$ at different points. Since $\frac{\partial U}{\partial f_1} = c > 0$ at all feasible points, the gradient at each point $\underline{f}^i \in S$ is

$$\nabla_{\underline{f}} U(\underline{f}^i) = c \cdot (1, w_2^i, \ldots, w_k^i)\Big|_{\underline{f}^i}$$

Then we have

$$\nabla_{\underline{f}} U(\underline{f}^i) \cdot (\underline{f}^{i+1} - \underline{f}^i) = c(1, w_2^i, \ldots, w_k^i) \cdot (\underline{f}^i - \underline{f}^{i-1}).$$

The ratio of improvement in the ith iteration to that in the first iteration is

$$\frac{\Delta^i}{\Delta^1} = \frac{c \cdot (1, w_2^i, \ldots, w_k^i) \cdot (\underline{f}^i - \underline{f}^{i-1})}{c \cdot (1, w_2^1, \ldots, w_k^1) \cdot (\underline{f}^1 - \underline{f}^0)} \qquad (3.37)$$

Since the unknown c is canceled out in (3.37) the value of $\Delta^i/\Delta^1$ can be calculated. We may preset the termination criterion as:

$$\text{terminate if } \frac{\Delta^i}{\Delta^1} \leq \alpha, \text{ for } i > 1.$$

NUMERICAL EXAMPLE (A Nutrition Problem)

The nutrition problem is to find the quantities of certain foods that should be eaten to meet certain nutritional requirements at a minimum cost. Information on six foods is given in Table 3.4.

The problem is to find the quantities of these foods that satisfy: (*i*) the minimum daily requirement of vitamin A and iron; and the balanced daily requirement of food energy and protein; (*ii*) at a minimum cholesterol daily intake; (*iii*) at a minimum carbohydrate daily intake; and (*iv*) at a minimum cost.

The maximum daily intakes of the foods are: 6 pints of milk, 1 pound of beef, 1/4 dozen eggs, 10 ounces of bread, 10 ounces of lettuce and salad, and 4 pints of orange juice.

Let the daily diet requirements of milk (in pints), beef (in pounds), eggs (in dozens), bread (in ounces), lettuce and salad (in ounces), and orange juice (in pints) be $x_1$, $x_2$, $x_3$, $x_4$, $x_5$, and $x_6$, respectively. Then, the MODM problem is to find $\underline{x} = (x_1, x_2, \ldots, x_6)$ so as to:

$$\max \quad f_1(\underline{x}) = -0.225\, x_1 - 2.2\, x_2 - 0.8\, x_3 - 0.1\, x_4 - 0.05\, x_5 - 0.26\, x_6$$

$$\max \quad f_2(\underline{x}) = -10\, x_1 - 20\, x_2 - 120\, x_3$$

$$\max \quad f_3(\underline{x}) = -24\, x_1 - 27\, x_2 - 15\, x_4 - 1.1\, x_5 - 52\, x_6$$

$$\text{s.t.} \quad g_1(\underline{x}) = 720\, x_1 + 107\, x_2 + 7080\, x_3 + 134\, x_5 + 1000\, x_6 \geq 5000$$

$$g_2(\underline{x}) = 0.2x_1 + 10.1x_2 + 13.2x_3 + 0.75x_4 + 0.15x_5 + 1.2x_6 \geq 12.5$$

$$g_3(\underline{x}) = 344x_1 + 460x_2 + 1040x_3 + 75x_4 + 17.4x_5 + 240x_6 = 2500$$

$$g_4(\underline{x}) = 18x_1 + 151x_2 + 78x_3 + 2.5x_4 + 0.2x_5 + 4x_6 = 63$$

$$g_5(\underline{x}) = x_1 \leq 6.0$$

$$g_6(\underline{x}) = x_2 \leq 1.0$$

Table 3.4 Nutrition and cost information of six foods

| | Milk (pint) | Beef (pound) | Eggs (dozen) | Bread (ounce) | Lettuce salad (ounce) | Orange juice (pint) | Recommended Daily Allowance for Adults |
|---|---|---|---|---|---|---|---|
| Vitamin A (I.U.) | 720 | 107 | 7080 | 0 | 134 | 1000 | 5000 |
| Food energy (calories) | 344 | 460 | 1040 | 75 | 17.4 | 240 | 2500 |
| Cholesterol (unit) | 10 | 20 | 120 | 0 | 0 | 0 | |
| Protein (g) | 18 | 151 | 78 | 2.5 | 0.2 | 4 | 63 |
| Carbohydrate (g) | 24 | 27 | 0 | 15 | 1.1 | 52 | |
| Iron (mg) | 0.2 | 10.1 | 13.2 | 0.75 | 0.15 | 1.2 | 12.5 |
| Cost ($) | 0.225 | 2.2 | 0.8 | 0.1 | 0.05 | 0.26 | |

$g_7(\underline{x}) = x_3 \leq 0.25$

$g_8(\underline{x}) = x_4 \leq 10.0$

$g_9(\underline{x}) = x_5 \leq 10.0$

$g_{10}(\underline{x}) = x_6 \leq 4.0$

$x_i \geq 0, \; i=1, 2, \ldots, 6$

Let this constraint set be denoted by $\underline{x} \in X$.

Iteration No. 1:

Step 0 Choose an initial point $\underline{x}^1$

Let an initial point $\underline{x}^1 \in X$ be

$$\underline{x}^1 = (3.0, 0.5, 0.15, 5.0, 5.0, 3.0)$$

Set i = 1.

Step 1 Determine the direction of improvement

a) Calculate the weights.

With the initial point, we have

$$\underline{f}^0 = (f_1(\underline{x}^1), f_2(\underline{x}^1), f_3(\underline{x}^1)) = (-3.43, -58., -322.).$$

To determine weights, $w_i^1$, i = 2, 3, the DM indicates the following trade-off to be equivalent.

For $f_1$ and $f_2$:

$$(-3.43, \; -58., \; -322.) \sim (-3.43 + 0.5, \; -58.-20, \; -322.)$$

For $f_1$ and $f_3$:

$$(-3.43, \; -58. \; -322.) \sim (-3.43 + 0.5, \; -58., \; -322.-30.)$$

That is,

$$w_2^1 = -\frac{\Delta f_1}{\Delta f_2} = -\frac{0.5}{-20.} = 0.025$$

$$w_3^1 = -\frac{\Delta f_1}{\Delta f_3} = -\frac{0.5}{-30.} = 0.017$$

b) Compute an optimal solution $\underline{y}^1$ and $\underline{z}^1$.

Then the objective function of (3.34) becomes,

$$\sum_{j=1}^{3} w_j^1 \nabla_{\underline{x}} f_j(\underline{x}^1) \cdot \underline{y}^1$$

$$= 1 \cdot (-0.225, \quad -2.2, \quad -0.8, \quad -0.1, \quad -0.05, \quad -0.26) \cdot \underline{y}^1$$

$$+ 0.025 \, (-10, \quad -20, \quad -120) \cdot \underline{y}^1$$

$$+ 0.017 \, (-24, \quad -27, \quad 0., \quad -15., -1.1, -52.) \cdot \underline{y}^1$$

$$= f_1(\underline{y}^1) + 0.025 \, f_2(\underline{y}^1) + 0.017 \, f_3(\underline{y}^1)$$

where

$$\underline{y}^1 = (y_1^1, y_2^1, y_3^1, y_4^1, y_5^1, y_6^1)^T.$$

The value of $\underline{y}^1$ can be obtained by solving the following LP problem.

$$\max \quad f_1(\underline{y}^1) + 0.025 \, f_2(\underline{y}^1) + 0.017 \, f_3(\underline{y}^1)$$

$$\text{s.t.} \quad \underline{y}^1 \in X$$

The solution is:

$$\underline{y}^1 = (5.12, \quad 0.66, \quad 0.25, \quad 0., \quad 10., \quad 0.)$$

The direction of improvement, $\underline{z}^1$, is:

$$\underline{z}^1 = \underline{y}^1 - \underline{x}^1 = (2.12, \quad 0.16, \quad 0.1, \quad -5., \quad 5., \quad -3.)$$

Step 2. Determine the step-size, $t^1$

To determine an optimal $t^1$, we calculate $f_j(\underline{x}^1 + t \, \underline{z}^1)$ values for the 0.2 interval of t:

| t | 0 | 0.2 | 0.4 | 0.6 | 0.8 | 1.0 |
|---|---|---|---|---|---|---|
| $f_1$ | -3.43 | -3.40 | -3.34 | -3.35 | -3.33 | -3.31 |
| $f_2$ | -58. | -65.3 | -72.6 | -79.8 | -87.1 | -94.4 |
| $f_3$ | -322. | -287.9 | -253.9 | -219.8 | -185.8 | -151.8 |

The above results are presented to the DM; he/she chooses $\underline{f}^1 = (-3.35, -79.8, -219.8)$ as the best solution for the first iteration, then $t^1 = 0.6$. Set

$$\underline{x}^2 = \underline{x}^1 + t^1\underline{z}^1 = (4.27,\ \ 0.60,\ \ 0.21,\ \ 2.,\ \ 8.,\ \ 1.2)$$

$$i = i + 1 = 2$$

Go to the next iteration.

Iteration No. 2:

Step 1 Determine the direction of improvement

a) Calculate the weights.

At the achieved level of $\underline{f}^1 = (-3.35, -79.8, -219.8)$, the analyst notices that both $f_1$ and $f_3$ values increase as $t^1$ increases (see the table in Step 2 in Iteration No. 1); i.e., no trade-offs can be estimated. The analyst advises the DM to change the reference objective from $f_1$ to $f_2$ because $f_2$ conflicts with both $f_1$ and $f_3$ at the neighborhood of $\underline{f}^1$. Then the DM gives the following trade-offs at the level of $\underline{f}^1$. For $f_2$ and $f_1$:

$$(-3.35, -79.8, -219.8) \sim (-3.35 + 0.5, -79.8 - 15, -219.8)$$

For $f_2$ and $f_3$:

$$(-3.35, -79.8, -219.8) \sim (-3.35, -79.8-15, -219.8 + 20)$$

That is,

$$w_1^2 = -\frac{\Delta f_2}{\Delta f_1} = -\frac{-15}{0.5} = 30$$

$$w_2^2 = 1$$

$$w_3^2 = -\frac{\Delta f_2}{\Delta f_3} = -\frac{-15}{20} = 0.75$$

Hence the weight vector is,

$$\underline{w}^1 = (30,\ 1,\ 0.75)$$

which is also equivalent to

$$\underline{w}^1 = (\ 30/30,\ 1/30,\ 0.75/30)$$
$$= (\ 1,\ 0.033,\ 0.025)$$

b) Calculate $\underline{y}^2$ and $\underline{z}^2$.

The value of $\underline{y}^2$ is obtained by solving the following LP problem.

$$\max\ f_1(\underline{y}^2) + 0.033\ f_2(\underline{y}^2) + 0.025\ f_3(\underline{y}^2)$$
$$\text{s.t.}\quad \underline{y}^2 \in X$$

The solution is:

$$\underline{y}^2 = (5.12,\ 0.66,\ 0.25,\ 0.,\ 10.,\ 0.)$$

which is equal to $\underline{y}^1$. Set

$$\underline{z}^2 = \underline{y}^2 - \underline{x}^2 = (0.85,\ 0.06,\ 0.04,\ -20.,\ 2.,\ -1.2)$$

<u>Step 2 Determine $t^2$</u>

The value of $\underline{f}(\underline{x}^2 + t\ \underline{z}^2)$ is given below for 0.2 interval of t.

| t | 0 | 0.2 | 0.4 | 0.6 | 0.8 | 1.0 |
|---|---|---|---|---|---|---|
| $f_1$ | -3.35 | -3.34 | -3.33 | -3.32 | -3.31 | -3.31 |
| $f_2$ | -79.8 | -82.8 | -85.1 | -88.6 | -91.5 | -94.4 |
| $f_3$ | -219.8 | -206.2 | -192.6 | -178.9 | -165.3 | -151.8 |

The DM chooses $t^2$ = 0.2, and $\underline{f}^2$ = (-3.34, -82.8, -206.2).

The ratio of improvement on the 2nd iteration to that on the first iteration is:

$$\frac{\Delta^2}{\Delta^1} = \frac{(1,\ w_2^2,\ w_3^2)\ (\underline{f}^2 - \underline{f}^1)}{(1,\ w_2^1,\ w_3^1)\ (\underline{f}^1 - \underline{f}^0)}$$

$$= \frac{(1,\ 0.033,\ 0.025)\ (-3.34 + 3.35,\ \ -82.8 + 79.8,\ \ -206.2 + 219.8)^T}{(1,\ 0.025,\ 0.017)\ (-3.35 + 3.34,\ \ -79.8 + 58.,\ \ 219.8 + 322.)^T}$$

$$= \frac{0.25}{1.27} = 0.20$$

If we set $\alpha = 0.15$ the termination criterion is not satisfied. Set

$$\underline{x}^3 = \underline{x}^2 + t^2\ \underline{z}^2 = (4.44,\ 0.61,\ 0.22,\ 1.6,\ 8.4,\ 0.96)$$

and $i = i + 1 = 3$. Go to the next iteration.

Iteration No. 3:

Step 1 Determine the direction of improvement

a) Calculate the weights.

The DM makes the following trade-offs with $f_2$ as the reference objective:

For $f_2$ and $f_1$:

$$(-3.34,\ \ -82.8,\ \ -206.2) \sim (-3.34-0.025,\ -82.5+5.,\ -206.2)$$

For $f_2$ and $f_3$:

$$(-3.34,\ -82.8,\ \ -206.2) \sim (-3.34,\ \ -82.8 + 5,\ \ -206.2 - 10)$$

That is,

$$w_1^3 = -\frac{5}{-0.025} = 200$$

$$w_2^3 = 1$$

$$w_3^3 = -\frac{5}{-10} = 0.5$$

The weight vector is equivalent to

$$\underline{w}^3 = (200/200,\ \ 1/200,\ \ 0.5/200)$$
$$= (1,\ 0.005,\ 0.0025)$$

b) Calculate $\underline{y}^3$ and $\underline{z}^3$.

$\underline{y}^3$ is obtained by solving the following LP problem.

$$\max \quad f_1(\underline{y}^3) + 0.005\ f_2(\underline{y}^3) + 0.0025 f_3(\underline{y}^3)$$

$$\text{s.t.} \quad \underline{y}^3 \in X$$

The solution is:

$$\underline{y}^3 = (3.78,\ \ 0.,\ \ 0.25,\ \ 10.,\ \ 0.,\ \ 0.79)$$

and

$$\underline{z}^3 = (-0.63,\ -0.61,\ 0.03,\ 8.4,\ -8.4,\ -0.17)$$

<u>Step 2 Determine $t^3$</u>

The value of $\underline{f}\ (\underline{x}^3 + t\underline{z}^3)$ is given below for 0.2 interval of t.

| t | 0 | 0.2 | 0.4 | 0.6 | 0.8 | 1.0 |
|---|---|---|---|---|---|---|
| $f_1$ | -3.34 | -3.12 | -2.91 | -2.67 | -2.47 | -2.26 |
| $f_2$ | -82.8 | -79.7 | -76.7 | -73.8 | -70.8 | -67.8 |
| $f_3$ | -206.2 | -220.7 | -236.0 | -251.3 | -266.5 | -281.7 |

The DM chooses $\underline{f}^3 = (-2.91, -76.7, -236.0)$, then $t^3 = 0.4$.

The ratio of improvement on the 3rd iteration is,

$$\frac{\Delta^3}{\Delta^1} = \frac{(1,\ w_2^3,\ w_3^3)\ (\underline{f}^3-\underline{f}^2)}{(1,\ w_2^1,\ w_3^1)\ (\underline{f}^1-\underline{f}^0)}$$

$$= 0.303$$

which is larger than $\alpha = 0.15$. Hence set

$$\underline{x}^4 = \underline{x}^3 + t^3\underline{z}^3 = (4.16,\ 0.37,\ 0.23,\ 4.96,\ 5.04,\ 0.89)$$

and

$i = i + 1 = 3$. Go to the next iteration.

Iteration No. 4

Step 1 Determine the direction of improvement

a) Calculate the weights.

At the neighborhood of $\underline{f}^3 = (-2.91,\ -76.7,\ -236.0)$, both $f_1$ and $f_2$ go parallel (see the table in Step 2, Iteration No. 3); hence reference objective is moved from $f_2$ to $f_3$. The DM gives the following trade - offs at $\underline{f}^3$.

For $f_3$ and $f_1$:

$$(-2.91,\ -76.7,\ -236.0) \sim (-2.91-0.3,\ -76.7,\ -236.0+15.)$$

For $f_3$ and $f_2$:

$$(-2.91,\ -76.7,\ -236.) \sim (-2.91,\ -76.7-5.,\ -236.+15.)$$

That is,

$$w_1^4 = -\frac{\Delta f_3}{\Delta f_1} = -\frac{15}{-0.3} = 50$$

$$w_3^4 = -\frac{\Delta f_3}{\Delta f_2} = -\frac{15}{-5} = 3$$

$$w_3^4 = 1$$

The weight vector is equivalent to:

$$\underline{w}^4 = (1,\ 0.06,\ 0.02).$$

b) Calculate $\underline{y}^4$ and $\underline{z}^4$.

$\underline{y}^4$ is obtained by solving the following LP problem.

$$\max \quad f_1(\underline{y}^4) + 0.06\, f_2(\underline{y}^4) + 0.02\, f_3(\underline{y}^4)$$
$$\text{s.t.} \quad \underline{y}^4 \in X$$

The solution is:

$$\underline{y}^4 = (4.11,\ 0.14,\ 0.10,\ 10.0,\ 10.0,\ 0.)$$

and

$$\underline{z}^4 = \underline{y}^4 - \underline{x}^4 = (-0.05,\ -0.23,\ -0.13,\ 5.04,\ 4.96,\ -0.89)$$

Step 2 Determine $t^4$

The value of $\underline{f}(\underline{x}^4 + t\underline{z}^4)$ is given below for 0.2 interval of t.

| t | 0 | 0.2 | 0.4 | 0.6 | 0.8 | 1.0 |
|---|---|---|---|---|---|---|
| $f_1$ | -2.91 | -2.89 | -2.87 | -2.85 | -2.83 | -2.80 |
| $f_2$ | -76.7 | -72.5 | -68.3 | -64.2 | -60.0 | -55.5 |
| $f_3$ | -236.0 | -241.5 | -247.0 | -252.5 | -258.0 | -263.2 |

The DM chooses $\underline{f}^4 = (-2.89, -72.5, -241.5)$, then $t^4 = 0.2$.

The ratio of improvement on the 4th iteration is,

$$\frac{\Delta^4}{\Delta^1} = \frac{(1,\ w_2^4,\ w_3^4)\ (\underline{f}^4 - \underline{f}^3)}{(1,\ w_2^1,\ w_3^1)\ (\underline{f}^1 - \underline{f}^0)}$$

$$= .128$$

which satisfies the given criterion $\alpha = 0.15$. We terminate the iteration and have the final solution:

$$\underline{x} = (4.15,\ 0.32,\ 0.20,\ 6.0,\ 6.03,\ 0.71)$$

$$\underline{f} = (-2.89,\ -72.5,\ -241.5).$$

Note

The DM usually experiences difficulty in providing the interactive information for the analyst. To help the DM estimate trade-offs and step-size, Dyer [92] proposed a trade-off estimation routine which creates a dialogue between man and machine. It is a computerized assessment procedure using a series of simple, ordinal comparisons. Still, the lack of a systematic assessment procedure for trade-offs is a drawback of this method. Sometimes it is not easy to choose the reference objective when the number of objectives becomes larger than three.

The reasons for selecting the Frank - Wolfe algorithm in this interactive programming are its ultimate convergence properties and its rapid initial convergence rate [91] as well as its simplicity. This method can treat VMP problems with a nonlinear constraint set; but a problem with a linear constraint set, which will be an LP problem in Step 1 of the algorithm, always generates a corner point solution, hence a set of trade-offs which are close to each other. The implied direction remains unchanged; i.e., if $\underline{w}^i$ and $\underline{w}^{i+1}$ are close, then $\underline{y}^i = \underline{y}^{i+1}$ in Step 2. This method can solve problems of nonlinear objectives, but the concavity of the objectives is prerequisite to this algorithm as it is to the Frank - Wolfe algorithm.

This method is used to find the better point for each iteration by following the improved direction of the utility function; the DM's desires, unlike STEM or the method of constraints, are not actively expressed in the final compromised solution.

### 3.1.1b INTERACTIVE GOAL PROGRAMMING (IGP)

This method is another mathematical expression of the concept of the Geoffrion method, and the computational procedures are the same.

#### The method

Dyer [89] considers an extension of goal programming with interactive strategies to solve MODM problems by using the Frank - Wolfe alogorithm. We first present a special kind of GP model which works the same as the optimization of the overall utility function in the Geoffrion method.

We consider the following GP model (which is (3.23) of nonlinear goal programming (see Sec. 2.2.2b)).

$$\left.\begin{array}{ll} \min \underline{a} = \{a_1(\underline{d}^-, \underline{d}^+), a_2(\underline{d}^-, \underline{d}^+), \ldots, a_\ell(\underline{d}^-, \underline{d}^+)\} & \\ \text{s.t.} \quad g_i(\underline{x}) + d_i^- - d_i^+ = c_i, \; i = 1, \ldots, m & \\ \qquad f_i(\underline{x}) + d_{m+i}^- - d_{m+i}^+ = b_i, \; i = 1,2, \ldots, k & \\ \qquad \underline{d}^-, \underline{d}^+ \geq 0, \; d_i^- \cdot d_i^+ = 0 \; \forall_i & \end{array}\right\} \quad (3.38)$$

Let $\underline{x} \in X$ denote the permissive region formed by the absolute m objectives (constraints).

Under the assumption that the DM's preference for each objective is nondecreasing (i.e., the minimization of the overachievement $\underline{d}^+$ is not needed), (3.38) can be written as follows provided that the absolute objectives (constraints) are satisfied:

$$\left.\begin{array}{ll} \min & \underline{a} = \{h_1(\underline{d}^-), h_2(\underline{d}^-), \ldots, h_{\ell-1}(\underline{d}^-)\} \\ \text{s.t.} & \underline{x} \in X \\ & f_i(\underline{x}) + d_i^- - d_i^+ = b_i, \; i = 1,2, \ldots, k \\ & \underline{d}^-, \underline{d}^+ \geq 0, \; d_i^- \cdot d_i^+ = 0 \; \forall_i \end{array}\right\} \quad (3.39)$$

If the concept of priority levels among the nonabsolute objectives is replaced by specifying a "weight" for each of the objectives to represent the measure of relative importance, (3.39) can be rewritten as:

$$\left.\begin{array}{ll} \min & \sum_{i=1}^{k} w_i d_i^- \\ \text{s.t.} & \underline{x} \in X \\ & f_i(\underline{x}) + d_i^- - d_i^+ = b_i, \; i = 1,2, \ldots, k \\ & \underline{d}^-, \underline{d}^+ \geq 0, \; d_i^- \cdot d_i^+ = 0 \;\forall_i \end{array}\right\} \quad (3.40)$$

where $w_i$ is the weight for the ith objective. This particular GP formulation is called "one-sided" GP because only negative deviations are minimized.

The relationship between (3.31) and (3.40) can be clarified by noting that $\underline{d}^- = \underline{b} - \underline{f}(\underline{x}) + \underline{d}^+$. The vector of constants, $\underline{b}$, can be ignored in minimizing $\underline{d}^-$. The objective function of (3.40) becomes

$$\min \; \underline{w} \cdot (-\underline{f}(\underline{x}) + \underline{d}^+)$$

which is equivalent to

$$\max \; \underline{w} \cdot (\underline{f}(\underline{x}) - \underline{d}^+)$$

which is also equivalent to

$$\max \; U[\underline{f}(\underline{x})]$$

in the sense that U is an additive separable utility function, i.e., $U[\underline{f}(\underline{x})] = U_1[f_1(\underline{x})] + \ldots + U_k[f_k(\underline{x})]$, and that the marginal increase in utility associated with additional units of $f_j$ above $b_j$ is equal to zero; i.e., $\partial U/\partial f_j = 0$ for $f_j \geq b_j$.

Now it is easily recognizable that the one-sided GP is another mathematical expression of (3.31). The IGP simply follows the Geoffrion algorithm with the modification that (3.34) is replaced by (3.40). Other steps of the IGP algorithm are the same as that of the Geoffrion method.

For the IGP method, $U(\underline{f})$ should be an additive separable utility function, all the conditions postulated in the Geoffrion method must be satisfied, and each $b_j$ must be chosen to satisfy the condition of $\partial U/\partial f_j = 0$ for $f_j \geq b_j$. If the DM finds it difficult or impossible to identify such a point for all or some objective j, the corresponding $b_j$ should be set arbitrarily high so that $f_j < b_j$ for every $\underline{x} \in X$.

NUMERICLA EXAMPLE (The nutrition problem)

The nutrition problem is again considered. The three objectives of the GP problem are:

$$f_i(\underline{x}) + d_i^- - d_i^+ = b_i, \quad i = 1, 2, 3$$

where the goals are given as $\underline{b} = (b_1, b_2, b_3) = (-2.2, -17., -150)$. These goals are slightly larger than the ideal solutions of the VMP problem.

The solution steps are equivalent to those of the Geoffrion method. The difference appears in Step 2b, the computation of the direction of improvement $\underline{y}^i$. However, the results of $\underline{y}^i$ come out to be the same. We will illustrate the first iteration here.

Iteration No. 1:

Step 0 Choose an initial point $\underline{x}^1$

(It is exactly the same as that of the Geoffrion method.)

Step 1 Determine the direction of improvement

a) Calculate the weights.

(Same as that of the Geoffrion method.)

b) Compute an optimal solution $\underline{y}^1$ and $\underline{z}^1$.

The following LP problem of (3.40) is solved. It is to find $\underline{d}^-$ and $\underline{x}$ so as to:

$$\min \quad w_1^1 d_1^- + w_2^1 d_2^- + w_3^1 d_3^-$$

$$\text{s.t.} \quad \underline{x} \varepsilon X$$

$$f_1(\underline{x}) + d_1^- - d_1^+ = b_1$$

$$f_2(\underline{x}) + d_2^- - d_2^+ = b_2$$

$$f_3(\underline{x}) + d_3^- - d_3^+ = b_3$$

where $\underline{w}^1 = (w_1^1, w_2^1, w_3^1) = (1, 0.025, 0.017)$ and $\underline{b} = (b_1, b_2, b_3) = (-2.2, -17.0, -150.)$. Note that the constraints of $f_i(\underline{x}) + d_i^- - d_i^+ = b_i \ \forall_i$ are simplified to $f_i(\underline{x}) + d_i^- \geq b_i \ \forall_i$ in the computation.

The solution is:

$$\underline{d}^- = (d_1^-, d_2^-, d_3^-) = (1.11, 77.44, 1.77)$$

$$\underline{x} = (5.12, 0.66, 0.25, 0., 10., 0.)$$

Note that the solution vector $\underline{x}$ in (3.40) is equivalent to $\underline{y}^i$ in (3.34). (Why so?). Then the direction of improvement $z^1$ is:

$$\underline{z}^1 = \underline{y}^1 - \underline{x}^1 = (2.12, 0.16, 0.1, -5., 5., -3.)$$

It is worth noting that the results of computing the optimal solution for $\underline{y}^1$ and the direction of improvement $\underline{z}^1$ are exactly the same as those obtained in the Geoffrion method, and therefore the calculation procedures are the same.

### 3.1.2 SURROGATE WORTH TRADE-OFF METHOD

The Surrogate Worth Trade-off Method (SWT) is proposed by Haimes, Hall, and Freedman [BM-8, 140]. It recognizes that given any current set of objective levels attained, it is much easier for the DM to assess the relative value of the trade-off of marginal increases and decreases between any two objectives than their absolute values.

The method consists of two phases: Phase 1- Identification and generation of non-dominated solutions which form the trade-off functions in the objective surface. Phase 2- The search for a preferred solution in the non-dominated solutions. The preferred decision is located by interaction with the DM to assess the indifference band by the use of the newly introduced surrogate worth function.

<u>The Trade-off Functions</u>

The trade-off functions can be found from the values of the dual variables associated with the constraints in a reformulated problem. Problem (1.1) is reformulated as follows:

$$\left.\begin{aligned} &\max \quad f_1(\underline{x}) \\ &\text{s.t.} \quad f_j(\underline{x}) \geq \varepsilon_j, \qquad j = 2, 3, \ldots, k \\ &\qquad\; g_i(x) \leq 0, \qquad i = 1, 2, \ldots, m \end{aligned}\right\} \tag{3.41}$$

$$\text{where } \varepsilon_j = \bar{f}_j - \bar{\varepsilon}, \qquad j = 2, 3, \ldots, k$$

$$\bar{\varepsilon}_j > 0, \qquad j = 2, 3, \ldots, k$$

$\bar{f}_j$ are the feasible ideal solutions of the following problems:

$$\left.\begin{aligned} &\max \quad f_j \\ &\text{s.t.} \quad g_i(\underline{x}) \leq 0, \qquad i = 1, 2, \ldots, m \end{aligned}\right\} \tag{3.42}$$

$$j = 1, 2, \ldots, k$$

and $\bar{\varepsilon}_j$ are the deviations from the ideal values and will be varied parametrically in the process of constructing the trade-off functions.

The generalized Lagrangian, L, to (3.41) is:

$$L = f_1(\underline{x}) + \sum_{i=1}^{m} \mu_i g_i(\underline{x}) + \sum_{j=2}^{k} \lambda_{1j} \left(f_j(\underline{x}) - \varepsilon_j\right) \tag{3.43}$$

where $\mu_i$, $i = 1, 2, \ldots, m$, and $\lambda_{1j}$, $j = 2, 3, \ldots, k$ are generalized Lagrange multipliers. The subscript 1j in $\lambda$ denotes that $\lambda$ is the Lagrange multiplier associated (in the $\varepsilon$-constraint vector optimization problem, see Sec. 4.1.1.) with the first objective, $f_1(\underline{x})$, and the jth constraint. The Lagrange multiplier $\lambda_{1j}$ will be subsequently generalized to be $\lambda_{\ell j}$ associated with the $\ell$th objective function and the jth constraint. Let $\hat{X}$ be the set of all $\underline{x}$ and $\Omega$ be the set of all $\lambda_{\ell j}$ that satisfy the Kuhn-Tucker conditions [200] for (3.43). The conditions of interest to our analysis are:

$$\lambda_{1j} \left(f_j(\underline{x}) - \varepsilon_j\right) = 0, \qquad j = 2, 3, \ldots, k$$

$$\lambda_{1j} \geq 0, \qquad j = 2, 3, \ldots, k$$

Note that if $f_j(\underline{x}) > \varepsilon_j$ for any $j = 2, 3, \ldots, k$ (i.e., the constraint is not binding),then the corresponding Lagrange multiplier $\lambda_{1j} = 0$. The value of $\lambda_{1j}$, $j = 2, 3, \ldots, k$ corresponding to the binding constraints $(f_j(\underline{x}) - \varepsilon_j = 0)$ is of special interest since it indicates the marginal benefit (cost) of the objective function $f_1(\underline{x})$ due to reduction of a unit of $\varepsilon_j$. From (3.43), assuming that the solution is global, we derive:

$$\lambda_{1j}(\varepsilon_j) = -\frac{\partial L}{\partial \varepsilon_j}, \qquad j = 2, 3, \ldots, k$$

However, for $\underline{x} \in X$, $\underline{x} \in \hat{X}$, $\lambda_{1j} \in \Omega$ for all j,

$$f_1(\underline{x}) = L$$

thus

$$\lambda_{1j}(\varepsilon_j) = - \frac{\partial f_1(\cdot)}{\partial \varepsilon_j} , \qquad j = 2, 3, \ldots, k \tag{3.44}$$

In the derivation of the trade-off functions in the SWT method, only these $\lambda_{\ell j} > 0$ corresponding to $f_j(\underline{x}) - \varepsilon_j = 0$ are of interest, since they correspond to the non-dominated solutions. Thus, for $f_j(\underline{x}) = \varepsilon_j$, (3.44) can be written as:

$$\lambda_{1j}(\varepsilon_j) = - \frac{\partial f_1(\cdot)}{\partial f_j(\cdot)} , \qquad j = 2, 3, \ldots, k \tag{3.45}$$

(3.45) can be generalized where the index of performance is the $\ell$th objective function of problem (1.1) rather than the first one. Accordingly,

$$\lambda_{\ell j}(\varepsilon_j) = - \frac{\partial f_\ell(\cdot)}{\partial f_j(\cdot)} ; \; \ell \neq j; \; \ell, j = 1, 2, \ldots, k$$

It is shown [BM-8] that the following relationships hold:

$$\lambda_{\ell j} = \lambda_{\ell i} \cdot \lambda_{ij}; \; \ell \neq j; \quad \ell, j = 1, 2, \ldots, k$$

$$\lambda_{\ell j} = \frac{1}{\lambda_{j\ell}} \quad \text{for } \lambda_{j\ell} \neq 0$$

Several variational approaches for the determination of $\lambda_{\ell j}(\cdot)$ are discussed in [BM-8]. Two approaches will be presented later. Note that the trade-off rate function $\lambda_{\ell j}(\cdot)$ is applicable to any noncommensurable functions.

The Surrogate Worth Function

The surrogate worth function $W_{\ell j}$ provides the interface between the DM and the mathematical model. The value of $W_{\ell j}$ is the DM's assessment of how much (on an ordinal scale, say of from -10 to +10 with zero signifying equal preference) he/she prefers trading $\lambda_{\ell j}$ marginal units of the $\ell$th objective $f_\ell$ for one marginal unit of the jth objective $f_j$, given the other objectives remaining at their current values. Thus $w_{\ell j}$ may be expressed as a function of the trade-off rates, decision variables, or the objectives. Note that $w_{\ell j} > 0$ means the DM does prefer making such a trade, $w_{\ell j} < 0$ means he/she does not, and $w_{\ell j} = 0$ implies indifference. It can be defined as:

$$w_{\ell j} \begin{cases} > 0 & \text{when } \lambda_{\ell j} \text{ marginal units of } f_\ell(\underline{x}) \text{ are preferred over one marginal unit of } f_j(\underline{x}) \text{ given the satisfaction of all objectives at level } \varepsilon_i,\ i = 1, 2, \ldots, k. \\ = 0 & \text{when } \lambda_{\ell j} \text{ marginal units of } f_\ell(\underline{x}) \text{ are equivalent to one marginal unit of } f_j(\underline{x}) \text{ given the satisfaction of all objectives at level } \varepsilon_i,\ i = 1, 2, \ldots, k. \\ < 0 & \text{when } \lambda_{\ell j} \text{ marginal units of } f_\ell(\underline{x}) \text{ are not preferred over one marginal unit of } f_j(\underline{x}) \text{ given the satisfaction of all objectives at level } \varepsilon_i,\ i = 1, 2, \ldots, k. \end{cases}$$

It is worth noting that the DM is provided with the trade-off value (via the trade-off function) of any two objective functions at a given level of attainment of the other objective functions. Furthermore, all trade-off values generated from the trade-off function are associated with the non-dominated solution set. The band of indifference can be determined in the following way. The DM is asked whether $\lambda_{\ell j}$ units of $f_\ell(\underline{x})$ are greater, equal, or less desirable than one unit of $f_j(\underline{x})$ for two distinct values of $\lambda_{\ell j}$. A linear combination of the corresponding two answers $w_{\ell j}(\lambda_{\ell j})$ obtained from the DM in ordinal scale can be made as shown in Fig. 3.17. Then the value of $\lambda^*_{\ell j}$ is chosen so that $w_{\ell j}(\lambda^*_{\ell j}) = 0$. The DM can be asked additional questions in the neighborhood of $\lambda^*_{\ell j}$ to improve the accuracy of $w_{\ell j}(\lambda_{\ell j})$

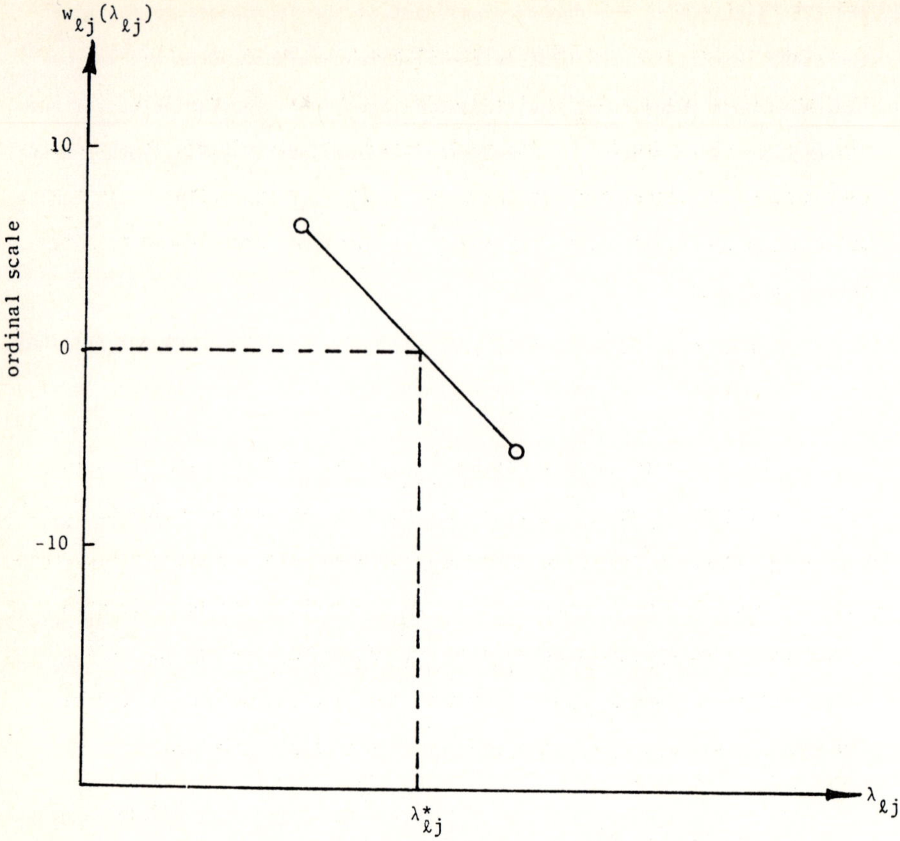


Fig. 3.17 Determination of the indifference band [BM-8].

and the indifference band.

Interaction with the DM should continue until a unique solution $\underline{f}^*$ is found for which all $w_{\ell j}(\lambda^*_{\ell j})$ are zero. This may not be possible in a finite number of solutions. An approximation of this process is to develop approximate functional relationships for $\hat{w}_{\ell j}(\underline{f})$ (by regression or interpolation) and determine the solution $\underline{f}^*$ ($f^*$ does not contain $f_\ell$) from the set of equations

$$\hat{w}_{\ell j}(\underline{f}^*) = 0 \qquad j = 1, \ldots, k$$
$$j \neq \ell.$$

If the surrogate worth function $w_{\ell j}$ is evaluated at a set of known non-dominated solutions, $\underline{f}^*$ will give rise to a feasible solution to (3.42). But, if $\underline{f}^*$ is estimated by regression or interpolation, there is no guarantee that $w_{\ell j}(f^*) = 0$; $f^*$ may not lead to a feasible solution. In such situations, the approximation $\hat{w}_{\ell j}$ for $w_{\ell j}$ can be improved by generating more solutions around $\hat{w}_{\ell j}(\underline{f}) = 0$, and an improved estimate of $\underline{f}^*$ can be found to satisfy $w_{\ell j}(f) = 0$ and to lead to a feasible solution.

Determination of Optimal Decision Vector

In general, the surrogate worth function assigns a scalar value to any given nondominated solution in objective function space. Once the indifference bands have been determined for $\lambda^*_{\ell j}$, the next and final step in the SWT method is to determine an $\underline{x}^*$ that corresponds to all $\lambda^*_{\ell j}$. To each $\lambda^*_{\ell j}$ which is determined from the surrogate worth function via the interaction with the DM, there corresponds $f_j^*(\underline{x})$, $j = 1, 2, \ldots, k$, $j \neq \ell$. These $f_j^*(\underline{x})$ are the values of $f_j(\underline{x})$ at the equality constraints $\varepsilon_j$ so that $\lambda_{\ell j}^* \, (f_j^*(\underline{x}) - \varepsilon_j) = 0$. The optimal decision vector $\underline{x}^*$ can be obtained by solving (3.46):

$$\left.\begin{array}{lll} \max & f_1(\underline{x}) & \\ \text{s.t.} & f_j(\underline{x}) \geq f_j^*(\underline{x}), & j = 2, 3, \ldots, k \\ & g_i(\underline{x}) \leq 0, & i = 1, 2, \ldots, m \end{array}\right\} \quad (3.46)$$

The solution of (3.46) yields the desired $\underline{x}^*$ for the total vector optimization problem of (1.1).

The Algorithm for the SWT Method

The five major steps in the SWT method are:

Step 1. Set up the multiple objective problem in the form of problem (1.1). Determine the ideal solution for each of the objectives in the problem. Select a primary objective $f_\ell$ arbitrarily.

Step 2. Identify and generate a set of non-dominated solutions by varying $\varepsilon$'s parametrically in problem (3.41). The non-dominated solutions are the ones which have non-zero values for the trade-off functions, $\lambda_{\ell j} = -\dfrac{\partial f_\ell}{\partial f_j}$.

Step 3. Interact with the DM to assess the surrogate worth function $w_{\ell j}$, provided that the values of $\underline{f}$ and $\lambda_{\ell j}$ are presented to the DM.

Step 4. Isolate the indifference solutions. The solutions, which have $w_{\ell j} = 0$ for all j, are said to be indifference solutions. Any one of such solutions is a preferred solution to the DM and hence the optimal solution to the multiple objective problem.

However, if there exists no indifference solution, develop approximate relations for all worth functions $w_{\ell j} = \hat{w}_{\ell j}(f_j, \forall_j, j \neq \ell)$. Solve the simultaneous equations $\hat{w}_{\ell j}(\underline{f}) = 0$ for all j to obtain $\underline{f}^*$ ($\underline{f}^*$ does not contain $f_\ell^*$). This would possibly form an indifference solution. Solve problem (3.46) with $\underline{f}^*$ for $\varepsilon$'s to obtain $f_\ell^*$, $\underline{x}^*$ and $\lambda_{\ell j}^*$ for all j. Present this solution to the DM, and ask if this is an indifference solution. If yes, it is a preferred solution; proceed to Step 5. Otherwise, repeat the process of generating more non-dominated solutions around $\hat{w}_{\ell j} = 0$ and refining the estimated $\underline{f}^*$ until it results in an indifference solution.

Step 5. If the solution in the decision space $\underline{x}$ corresponding to the preferred solution of Step 4 is not obtained already, solve problem (3.46) with $\underline{\varepsilon} = \underline{f}^*$ (note that $\underline{f}^*$ does not contain $f_\ell^*$). The optimal solution $f_\ell^*$ along with $\underline{f}^*$ and $\underline{x}^*$ would be the optimal solution to the multiple objective problem.

NUMERICAL EXAMPLE

Two examples will be presented to illustrate the method. The first is a simple one with two objective functions and two decision variables. It will show the procedural steps of the method without the computational complexities. The second example consists of three objectives, three decision variables and four constraints in addition to the bounds on the decision variables. It is not a real-world problem, but will demonstrate the computational requirements for the method.

Example 1.

The ABC company produces two similar products A and B. Both products are equally important. The total profit, in hundreds of dollars, can be approximated by the mathematical product of the two products in tons ($x_1x_2$), where $x_1$ and $x_2$ are daily production in tons of A and B, respectively. The inprocess inventory costs of each product, in hundreds of dollars per ton, are $(x_1 - 4)^2$ and $(x_2)^2$ for products A and B, respectively. Assume that the combined production of A and B cannot be greater than 25 tons/day.

Solution.

Step 1. Ideal solutions: The multiple objective problem is:

$$\max \quad f_1 = x_1x_2 \qquad \text{(profit, \$100/day)}$$

$$\min \quad f_2 = (x_1 - 4)^2 + x_2^2 \qquad \text{(inventory cost, \$100/day)}$$

$$\text{or} \quad \max \quad f_2' = -(x_1 - 4)^2 - x_2^2$$

$$\text{s.t.} \quad g_1(\underline{x}) = x_1 + x_2 \leq 25$$

$$x_1, x_2 \geq 0$$

The ideal solution of $f_1$ is $\overline{f}_1 = 156.25$ at $x_1 = x_2 = 12.5$. The ideal solution of $f_2$ is $f_2 = 0$ at $x_1 = 4$ and $x_2 = 0$.

Step 2. Non-dominated solutions: The problem in the form required by the SWT method is:

$$\max \quad f_1 = x_1x_2$$

$$\text{s.t.} \quad -(x_1 - 4)^2 - x_2^2 \geq -c$$

$$x_1 + x_2 \leq 25$$

$$x_1, x_2 \geq 0$$

where $c \geq 0$ is the inprocess inventory cost. The Lagrangian of this problem is:

$$L = x_1x_2 + \mu_1(x_1 + x_2 - 25) + \lambda_{12}[-(x_1 - 4)^2 - x_2^2 + c]$$

Since there is only one trade-off ratio $\lambda_{12}$, we will drop the subscript for simplicity. The Kuhn-Tucker conditions are:

$$\frac{\partial L}{\partial x_1} = x_2 - 2\lambda(x_1 - 4) + \mu_1 \leq 0$$

$$\frac{\partial L}{\partial x_2} = x_1 - 2\lambda x_2 + \mu_1 \leq 0$$

$$\frac{\partial L}{\partial \lambda} = [-(x_1 - 4)^2 - x_2^2 + c] \geq 0$$

$$\frac{\partial L}{\partial \mu_1} = x_1 + x_2 - 25 \leq 0$$

$$\mu_1(x_1 + x_2 - 25) = 0$$

$$\lambda[-(x_1 - 4)^2 - x_2^2 + c] = 0$$

From the above relationships, it is obvious that when $x_1 + x_2 \leq 25$, $\mu_1 = 0$; and $x_1$, $x_2 > 0$ implies $\frac{\partial L}{\partial x_1} = \frac{\partial L}{\partial x_2} = 0$, then we have

$$\lambda = \frac{x_2}{2(x_1 - 4)} = \frac{x_1}{2x_2}$$

or

$$x_2 = \sqrt{x_1(x_1 - 4)}$$

and

$$(x_1 - 4)^2 + x_2^2 = c$$

for all $\lambda > 0$. It implies that $x_1 > 4$ and $x_2 > 0$. The relation $x_2 = \sqrt{x_1(x_1 - 4)}$

defines the entire nondominated solution set. Table 3.5 shows a set of nondominated solutions generated using this relationship.

Step 3. Surrogate worth function: Table 3.5 also shows the DM's preference among the presented solutions. For example, the entry implies that given the net profit of 11.18 units (\$100/day) and the inventory cost of 6 units (\$100/day), the DM greatly prefers $w = +10$ on $-10$ to $+10$ scale to trade 1.118 units of increased profit for 1 unit increase in inventory cost. Note that $\lambda = -\partial f_1/\partial f_2 = + \partial f_1/\partial f_2 = 1.118$. Similarly, when $f_1 = 77.46$ units and $f_2 = 96$ units, the DM is completely indifferent ($w = 0$) to a trading of 0.645 units increased profit for one unit increased inventory cost.

Step 4. The indifference solution(s): Any two or more solutions from Table 3.5 can be used to estimate $\lambda^*$ at which $w(\lambda^*) = 0$ as described in Fig. 3.17. An alternate approach is $\lambda^* = 0.645$ for which $w = 0$ (in Table 3.5). Assuming that the DM's assessment is consistent and accurate, we take this solution as the preferred solution.

Step 5. Transformation to decision space:

From Table 3.5, we note that the solution in decision space is $\underline{x} = (10., 7.75)$.

Example 2. (The modified Bow River Valley water quality management problem)

The Bow River Valley water quality management problem (see Sec 3.2.2) is considered here with minor modifications. Both objectives corresponding to DO levels at Bowville and Plymton are changed to

Table 3.5. Nondominated soltuions for Example 1.

| $x_1$ | $x_2$ | $\lambda$ | $f_1$ profit | $f_2$ cost | w |
|---|---|---|---|---|---|
| 4 | 0 | $\infty$ | 0 | 0 | - |
| 5 | 2.24 | 1.118 | 11.18 | 6 | +10 |
| 6 | 3.46 | 0.866 | 20.78 | 16 | +8 |
| 7 | 4.58 | 0.764 | 32.08 | 30 | +7 |
| 8 | 5.66 | 0.707 | 45.26 | 48 | +3 |
| 9 | 6.71 | 0.670 | 60.37 | 70 | +1 |
| 10 | 7.75 | 0.645 | 77.46 | 96 | 0 |
| 11 | 8.78 | 0.626 | 96.53 | 126 | -3 |
| 12 | 9.80 | 0.612 | 117.58 | 160 | -7 |
| 13 | 10.82 | 0.601 | 140.61 | 198 | -10 |
| 14 | 11.83 | 0.592 | 165.65 | 240 | -10 |

constraints for $\leq 6.0$. The tax rate increase at Plympton is to be $\leq 1.50$.

The modified problem is :

$$\max \quad f_1(\underline{x}) = 2.0 + 0.524(x_1 - 0.3) + 2.79(x_2 - 0.3)$$

$$+ 0.882(w_1 - 0.3) + 2.65(w_2 - 0.3) \quad \text{(mg/ℓ DO, at state park)}$$

$$\max \quad f_2(\underline{x}) = 7.5 - 0.012\left(\frac{59}{1.09 - x_1^2} - 59\right) \quad \text{(\% earning, for cannery)}$$

$$\min \quad f_3(\underline{x}) = 1.80 * 10^{-3}\left(\frac{532}{1.09 - x_2^2} - 532\right) \quad \text{(\$/\$1000 additional tax at Bowville)}$$

$$\text{s.t.} \quad g_1(\underline{x}) = 4.75 + 2.27\ (x_1 - 0.3) \geq 6.0$$

$$g_2(\underline{x}) = 5.1 + 0.177(x_1 - 0.3) + 0.978(x_2 - 0.3)$$

$$+ 0.216(w_1 - 0.3) + 0.768(w_2 - 0.3) \geq 6.0$$

$$g_3(\underline{x}) = 2.50 * 10^{-3}\left(\frac{450}{1.09 - x_3^2} - 450\right) \leq 1.5$$

$$g_4(\underline{x}) = 1.0 + 0.0332(x_1 - 0.3) + 0.0186\ (x_2 - 0.3)$$

$$+ 3.34(x_3 - 0.3) + 0.0204(w_1 - 0.3)$$

$$+ 0.7\ 8(w_2 - 0.3) + 2.62(w_3 - 0.3) \geq 3.5$$

$$0.3 \leq x_i \leq 1.0, \qquad i = 1, 2, 3$$

Let the above constraints be denoted by $\underline{x} \in X$.

$w_i$ is related to $x_i$ by:

$$w_i = \frac{0.39}{1.39 - x_1^2}, \qquad i = 1, 2, 3$$

Solution.

Step 1. Ideal solutions: The ideal solutions are obtained by solving the following nonlinear programming problems:

$$\left.\begin{array}{ll} \max & f_i(\underline{x}) \\ \text{s.t.} & \underline{x} \in X \\ & i = 1, 2 \end{array}\right\} \quad \text{and} \quad \left.\begin{array}{l} \min f_3(\underline{x}) \\ \text{s.t. } \underline{x} \in X \end{array}\right\}$$

They are:

$$\bar{f}_1 = 6.79 \quad \text{at} \quad \underline{x} = (1.0, 1.0, 0.742)$$

$$\bar{f}_2 = 6.28 \quad \text{at} \quad \underline{x} = (0.851, 0.845, 0.811)$$

$$\bar{f}_3 = 0.00 \quad \text{at} \quad \underline{x} = (0.3, 0.3, 0.3)$$

Step 2. Nondominated solutions: The single objective optimization problem for generating a set of nondominated solutions can be formulated as:

$$\left.\begin{array}{ll} \max & f_1(\underline{x}) = 2.0 + 0.524(x_1 - 0.3) + 2.79(x_2 - 0.3) \\ & \qquad + 0.882(w_1 - 0.3) + 2.65(w_2 - 0.3) \\ \text{s.t.} & f_2(\underline{x}) = 7.5 - 0.012\left(\dfrac{59}{1.09 - x_1^2} - 59\right) \geq \varepsilon_2 \\ & f_3'(\underline{x}) = -1.80 * 10^{-3}\left(\dfrac{532}{1.09 - x_2^2} - 532\right) \geq \varepsilon_3 \\ & \underline{x} \in X. \end{array}\right\} \qquad (3.47)$$

Objective $f_1$ is chosen arbitrarily as the primary objective. $\varepsilon_2$ and $\varepsilon_3$ are bounds on $f_2$ and $f_3'$, respectively. The Kuhn-Tucker conditions of the above problem are too complex to be used for deriving all the trade-off ratios (Lagrange multipliers) as explicit functions of the decision variables. However, the solution of the above problem by a suitable nonlinear programming technique (here we use the GRG method) can be used to derive the trade-off ratios. $\varepsilon_2$ and $\varepsilon_3$ are varied parametrically to obtain several solutions, and all dominated solutions are to be discarded. The nondominated solutions are those with nonzero Lagrange multipliers. Table 3.6 summarizes a set of nondominated solutions for the present problem.

Step 3. Surrogate worth function: The values of the surrogate worth function assessed by the DM for the trade-off ratios $\lambda_{12}$ and $\lambda_{13}$ are tabulated in columns 5 and 7 of Table 3.6. Note that there exists a solution $\underline{f} = (5.01, 6.0, 1.9)$ for which both $w_{12}$ and $w_{13}$ are zero; hence this solution belongs to the indifference band.

Step 4. The indifference solution(s): As already mentioned, $\underline{f} = (5.01, 6.0, 1.9)$ is a nondominated solution in the indifference band. The corresponding trade-off ratios are $\lambda_{12} = 0.173$ and $\lambda_{13} = -0.489$. The corresponding solution in the decision space is $\underline{x} = (0.877, 0.869, 0.796)$.

However, we will describe a method to obtain an indifference solution when none is apparent, which is usually the case, in the set of nondominated solutions generated.

Multiple regressions may be performed to approximate $w_{12}\ (f_2, f_3)$ and $w_{13}\ (f_2, f_3)$. Due to the relative and subjective nature of the DM's responses, it is felt that a linear approximation is as good as any.

Table 3.6. A set of nondominated soltuions for Example 2.

| $f_2$ % return | $f_3$ tax rate | $f_1^*$ DO at park | $\lambda_{12}$ | $w_{12}$ | $\lambda_{13}$ | $w_{13}$ |
|---|---|---|---|---|---|---|
| 4.00 | 1.30 | 4.89 | 0.074 | -9 | -0.691 | +3 |
| 3.00 | 1.30 | 4.95 | 0.542 | -10 | -0.691 | +3 |
| 6.00 | 1.50 | 4.79 | 0.173 | -2 | -0.609 | +7 |
| 5.75 | 1.50 | 4.83 | 0.151 | -3 | -0.609 | +5 |
| 5.50 | 1.50 | 4.87 | 0.133 | -4 | -0.609 | 0 |
| 5.00 | 1.50 | 4.93 | 0.107 | -5 | -0.609 | -2 |
| 6.25 | 1.70 | 3.86 | 0.202 | +3 | -0.543 | 0 |
| 6.00 | 1.70 | 4.91 | 0.173 | 0 | -0.543 | +5 |
| 5.75 | 1.70 | 4.95 | 0.151 | -2 | -0.543 | +3 |
| 5.50 | 1.70 | 4.98 | 0.133 | -4 | -0.543 | -2 |
| 5.00 | 1.70 | 5.04 | 0.107 | -5 | -0.543 | -3 |
| 6.25 | 1.90 | 4.97 | 0.202 | +5 | -0.489 | -5 |
| 6.00 | 1.90 | 5.01 | 0.173 | 0 | -0.489 | 0 |
| 5.75 | 1.90 | 5.05 | 0.151 | -1 | -0.489 | +1 |
| 5.50 | 1.90 | 5.09 | 0.133 | -7 | -0.489 | -3 |
| 5.00 | 1.90 | 5.15 | 0.107 | -9 | -0.489 | -5 |
| 6.25 | 2.10 | 5.06 | 0.202 | -2 | -0.444 | -7 |
| 6.00 | 2.10 | 5.11 | 0.173 | -2 | -0.444 | -3 |
| 5.75 | 2.10 | 5.15 | 0.151 | -3 | -0.444 | -3 |
| 5.50 | 2.10 | 5.18 | 0.133 | -10 | -0.444 | -5 |
| 5.00 | 2.10 | 5.24 | 0.107 | -9 | -0.444 | -6 |

The approximated worth functions are (by using the data in Table 3.6):

$$\hat{w}_{12}(f_2, f_3) = -20.9535 + 5.0873f_2 - 6.0039f_3$$

$$\hat{w}_{13}(f_2, f_3) = 13.6840 + 1.8625f_2 - 13.9645f_3$$

with correlation coefficients of $R^2 = 0.83$ and 0.79, respectively (When quadratic terms were included $R^2 = 0.93$ and 0.82, respectively.) These two functions are set equal to zero; the corresponding equations are solved simultaneously to give an estimate of the preferred values $f_2^* = 6.26$ and $f_3^* = 1.82$ for which $w_{12} = w_{13} = 0$. The solution corresponding to these values, if feasible, is an indifference solution, but this must be validated by the DM since the worth functions developed are approximations of the DM's actual preference (which is, of course, not known explicitly).

Problem (3.47) is solved with $\varepsilon_2 = f_2^* = 6.26$ and $\varepsilon_3 = -f_3^* = 1.82$, which yields the following solution:

$$\underline{x} = (0.852, 0.863, 0.797)$$

$$\underline{f} = (4.92, 6.26, 1.82)$$

$$\lambda_{12}^* = 0.203 \quad \text{and} \quad \lambda_{13}^* = 0.509$$

When these trade-off ratios and the solution $\underline{f}^*$ are presented for validation, the DM has assigned values $w_{12} = 0$ and $w_{13} = 0$. Note that if the DM does not indicate this as an indifference solution, more solutions have to be generated around $w_{12} = 0$ and $w_{13} = 0$; the DM assesses the new solutions for $w_{12}$ and $w_{13}$ until an indifference solution (preferred solution) is reached.

Step 5. Transformation to decision space: Problem (3.47) is already solved in Step 4 for the indifference vector $\underline{f}$ = (4.92, 6.26, 1.82); the solution in terms of the decision variables is

$$\underline{x} = (0.852, 0.863, 0.797)$$

Discussion of the Results. The solution procedure utilized in solving problem (3.47) is the generalized reduced gradient (GRG) algorithm for nonlinear optimization. The FORTRAN IV computer code GREG is implemented on ITEL AS/5 system [1a, 167a]. More than 45 values of $\varepsilon_2$ and $\varepsilon_3$ were used as input, however, only the 21 solutions presented in Table 3.5 were useful. The remaining solutions were discarded, either because they were dominated solutions or did not converge in 5 sec of computer time. Each of the solutions in Table 3.5 were obtained in less than 1 sec computer time by an IBM 370/175 requiring less than 30 iterations.

The SWT method is moderately suitable for this problem. Recall that the mathematical model has only 3 decision variables, 3 objectives and four constraints. Though the solution algorithms (such as GREG used here) can handle larger problems efficiently, note that the set of nondominated solutions required increases enormously with the increased number of objectives so as to cover an acceptable range for all the objective values.

Interaction with the DM is moderate in this example also. However, as the solution set increases because of an increased number of objectives, the assessment required from the DM may become excessive. The approximations of the worth functions, if required, may not be at an acceptable level to generate indifference solutions. The effort needed for obtaining worth functions by multiple regression is minimal. However, note that while an increased $R^2$ value for the regression would not guarantee an indifference solution, the DM's validation is required.

Other disadvantages with the SWT method are: 1) the arbitrary change of $\varepsilon_j$'s may leave out some possible nondominated solutions which could be the final preferred solution; 2) $\lambda_{\ell j}$ indicate the marginal trade-off in a very small region around the current solution, but the DM may not properly perceive this limitation when providing $w_{\ell j}$ values.

The major advantages of the SWT method are: 1) the method requires the DM to consider only two objectives at a time while assessing the worth function, even if there are many objectives in the problem; 2) both linear and nonlinear models can be exercised; 3) the method is applicable to both static and dynamic problems; and 4) preference information from multiple decision makers with varied opinions can be processed.

### 3.1.3 METHOD OF SATISFACTORY GOALS

This method, proposed by Benson [19a], uses the "Bounded Objective Method" (see 2.1.2) interactively to determine a satisfactory solution. In this method the DM specifies a set of acceptable initial goal levels $L_j$, $j = 1,2, \ldots, k$ (which must be feasible) and then identifies one objective function whose goal level is the least satisfactory (LS). The LS objective is maximized subject to the original constraints and to additional constraints formed by the rest of the objective functions. The analyst, who works iteratively and interactively with the DM, can tighten one or more goal attainments until the best or most favorable solution is reached.

<u>The Algorithm</u>

<u>Step 0. Initialization</u>:

The DM is asked to state a set of minimally acceptable goal levels, $\underline{L}^1$, which will serve as a starting point for later goal revisions. The set of $\underline{L}^1$ and constraints of the problem should form a feasible region in Step 2; otherwise revisions in goals $\underline{L}^1$ are requested from the DM. Set $q = 1$.

<u>Step 1. Select the least satisfactory (LS) objective</u>:

The DM is asked to identify one objective whose goal level is LS among $\underline{L}^q$.

<u>Step 2. Optimize the LS objective:</u>

The LS objective is maximized subject to the original constraints and additional constraints formed by the rest of the objective functions:

$$\left.\begin{aligned} \max \quad & f_{LS}(\underline{x}) \\ \text{s.t.} \quad & g_i(\underline{x}) \leq 0, \quad i = 1,2, \ldots, m \\ & f_j(\underline{x}) \geq L_j^q, \quad j = 1,2, \ldots, k, \text{ and } j \neq LS \end{aligned}\right\} \qquad (3.48)$$

Step 3. Decision phase:

The DM is to indicate whether the attainment of $f_{LS}(\underline{x})$ in Step 2 is satisfactory.

a) If not, he/she revises some goals and sets new goals, $\underline{L}^{q+1}$ ($\leq \underline{L}^q$), with the help of the dual variables associated with the binding $f_j(\underline{x})$'s of (3.48). These dual variables indicate the trade-offs between $f_{LS}(\underline{x})$ and the binding $f_j(\underline{x})$'s. Set q = q+1 and return to Step 2.

b) If satisfactory, the DM is asked if the attained value of $f_{LS}(\underline{x})$ can be relaxed somewhat to improve other objectives. If it cannot be relaxed, then the $\underline{L}^q$ (except the current LS) and optimized $f_{LS}(\underline{x})$ are the best attained goals to the problem. Otherwise go to Step 4.

Step 4. Select the new goal level:

The DM specifies the amount of relaxation, $\Delta f_{LS}(\underline{x})$, which is acceptable. Set q = q+1 and return to Step 1.

NUMERICAL EXAMPLE (The nutrition problem).

The VMP problem is given by:

$$\max\ f_1(\underline{x}) = -0.225x_1 - 2.2x_2 - 0.8x_3 - 0.1x_4 - 0.05x_5 - 0.26x_6$$

$$\max\ f_2(\underline{x}) = -10x_1 - 20x_2 - 120x_3$$

$$\max\ f_3(\underline{x}) = -24x_1 - 27x_2 - 15x_4 - 1.1x_5 - 52x_6$$

$$\text{s.t. } g_1(\underline{x}) = 720x_1 + 107x_2 + 7080x_3 + 134x_5 + 1000x_6 \geq 5000$$

$$g_2(\underline{x}) = 0.2x_1 + 10.1x_2 + 13.2x_3 + 0.75x_4 + 0.15x_5 + 1.2x_6 \geq 12.5$$

$$g_3(\underline{x}) = 344x_1 + 460x_2 + 1040x_3 + 75x_4 + 17.4x_5 + 240x_6 \geq 2500$$

$$g_4(\underline{x}) = 18x_1 + 151x_2 + 78x_3 + 2.5x_4 + 0.2x_5 + 4x_6 \geq 63$$

$$g_5(\underline{x}) = x_1 \leq 6.0$$

$$g_6(\underline{x}) = x_2 \leq 1.0$$

$$g_7(\underline{x}) = x_3 \leq 0.25$$

$$g_8(\underline{x}) = x_4 \leq 10.0$$

$$g_9(\underline{x}) = x_5 \leq 10.0$$

$$g_{10}(\underline{x}) = x_6 \leq 4.0$$

$$x_i \geq 0, \quad i = 1,2, \ldots, 6$$

Let this constraint set be denoted by $\underline{x} \in X$.

Iteration No. 1:

Step 0. Initialization:

An initial set of acceptable goal levels, $\underline{L}^1 = (L_1^1, L_2^1, L_3^1) = (-3., -60., -300.)$, is given by the DM. Set q = 1.

Step 1. Select the LS objective:

The DM chooses $f_1$ from $\underline{L}^1$ as the least satisfactory objective, $f_{LS}$.

Step 2. Optimize the LS objective:

The LS objective $f_1$ is maximized subject to the original constraints and additional two constraints formed by $f_2$ and $f_3$.

$$\max \; f_1(\underline{x})$$

$$\text{s.t. } \underline{x} \in X$$

$$f_2(\underline{x}) \geq -60.$$

$$f_3(\underline{x}) \geq -300.$$

The solution to the LP problem for $f_1(\underline{x})$ is -2.34.

Step 3. Decision phase:

The DM indicates the attained value of $f_1$ is satisfactory and that it can be relaxed. Go to Step 4.

<u>Step 4. Select the new goal level</u>:

The DM specifies $\Delta f_1 = -0.36$ (i.e., $f_1$ can be relaxed up to -2.7); the new set of goals is $\underline{L}^2 = (-2.7, -60., -300)$. Set $q = q+1 = 2$ and return to Step 1.

<u>Iteration No. 2.</u>:

<u>Step 1. Select the LS objective</u>:

The DM selects $f_3$ from $\underline{L}^2$ as $f_{LS}$.

<u>Step 2. Optimzie the LS objective</u>:

$$\max \; f_3(\underline{x})$$
$$\text{s.t.} \; \underline{x} \in X$$
$$f_1(\underline{x}) \geq -2.7$$
$$f_2(\underline{x}) \geq -60.$$

The optimzied $f_3(\underline{x})$ is -258.3 and the dual values of $f_1$ and $f_2$ against $f_3$ are 49.5 and 2.2, respectively.

<u>Step 3. Decision phase</u>:

The DM is not satisfied with the value of -258.3 for $f_3$ and wants $f_3$ be at least -250. Knowing that both dual variables in Step 2 are greater than those in Step 1, the DM agrees to the degradation of $f_1$ and $f_2$ simultaneously so as to increase the value of $f_3$. The approaching goal of 8.3 (=-250. + 258.3) is divided in two and distributed for $f_1$, $\Delta f_1 = 0.08$ ($\simeq \frac{4.15}{49.5}$) and for $f_2$, $\Delta f_2 = 2.0$ ($\simeq \frac{4.15}{2.22}$). The new set of goals is: $\underline{L}^3 = (-2.7 - 0.08, -60. -2., -258.3) = (-2.78, -62., -258.3)$. Set $q = q+1 = 3$ and return to Step 2.

Iteration No. 3:

Step 2. Optimize the LS objective:

$$\max \; f_3(x)$$
$$\text{s.t. } \underline{x} \in X$$
$$f_1(\underline{x}) \geq -2.78$$
$$f_2(\underline{x}) \geq -62.$$

The optimized $f_3(\underline{x})$ is -249.9.

Step 3. Decision phase:

The DM is satisfied with the value of $f_3$ and does not want to relax $f_3$ from -249.9. Hence we terminate the procedure and take (-2.78, -62., -249.9) as our best attained goals. The final compromised solution is:

$$\underline{x} = (4.16, 0.15, 0.15, 9.0, 10., 0.)$$

and

$$\underline{f} = (-2.78, -62., -249.9).$$

Note

This method removes the LS objectives iteratively and interactively. The choice of the LS objective is not very difficult to make; however, the determination of a set of initial feasible goals may be time consuming as it is in the 'Bounded Objective Method'. Linear or non-linear models can be solved by this method, but the dual variable values from non-linear models are not easy to obtain, unlike those of LP solutions from the simplex method. Note that the trade-off information provided by the dual variable values is valid only in a local region.

### 3.1.4 METHOD OF ZIONTS-WALLENIUS

The method is proposed by Zionts and Wallenius [BM-19, 386]. It is assumed that all the objective functions are concave (to be maximized) and the constraints form a convex set; nonlinear functions are linearized. The overall utility function is assumed to be unknown explicitly to the DM, but is implicitly a linear function and, more generally, a concave function of the objective functions. The method makes use of such an implicit function on an interactive basis.

The first step of the method is to choose an arbitrary set of positive multipliers or weights and generate a composite objective function or utility function using these multipliers. The composite objective function is then optimized to produce a non-dominated solution to the problem. From the set of nonbasic variables, a subset of efficient variables is selected. (An efficient variable is one which, when introduced into the basis, cannot increase one objective without decreasing at least one other objective.) For each efficient variable a set of trade-offs is defined by which some objectives are increased and others reduced. A number of such trade-offs are presented to the DM, who is requested to state whether the trade-offs are desirable, undesirable or neither. From his/her answers a new set of consistent multipliers is constructed and the associated non-dominated solution is found. The process is then repeated, and a new set of trade-offs is presented to the DM at the current solution; convergence to an overall optimal solution with respect to the DM's (implicit) utility function is assured.

The Algorithm

Step 0. Initialization:

Choose an arbitrary set of positive multipliers or weights $\underline{\lambda}^1$ initially. Set $q = 1$.

Step 1. Generate and solve the composite objective function:

Generate a composite objective function or utility function using the multipliers $\underline{\lambda}^q$; a non-dominated solution is obtained by solving the following LP problem:

$$\left.\begin{aligned} \max \quad & \sum_{i=1}^{k} \lambda_i^q f_i(\underline{x}), \qquad \sum_{i=1}^{k} \lambda_i^q = 1 \\ \text{s.t.} \quad & g_j(\underline{x}) \leq 0, \; j = 1, 2, \ldots, m \\ & \underline{x} \geq 0 \end{aligned}\right\} \tag{3.49}$$

where $f_i(\underline{x})$ and $g_j(\underline{x})$ are linearized if they are originally nonlinear. A set of nonbasic variables is identified.

Step 2. Find a set of efficient variables:

In the process of finding a subset of efficient variables from the set of nonbasic variables, a set of $w_{ij}$, which is a decrease in objective function $f_i$ due to introducing a unit of the nonbasic variable, $x_j$, into the solution, must be estimated around the solution point obtained in Step 1.

For each nonbasic variable, $x_\ell$, $\ell \in N$, the following LP problem is solved:

$$\left.\begin{aligned} \min \quad & \sum_{i=1}^{k} w_{i\ell} \lambda_i \\ \text{s.t.} \quad & \sum_{i=1}^{k} w_{ij} \lambda_i \geq 0, \quad j \in N; \quad j \neq \ell \\ & \sum_{i=1}^{k} \lambda_i = 1 \end{aligned}\right\} \tag{3.50}$$

$$\underline{\lambda} \geq \underline{0}$$

where N is the set of nonbasic variables.

Then:

Test 1: If the minimum value of the objective function in (3.50) is negative, the variable $x_\ell$ is efficient.

Test 2: If the minumum value of the objective function in (3.50) is non-negative, the variable $x_\ell$ is not efficient.

Test 3: There will be at least one positive $w_{ij}$ and at least one negative $w_{ij}$ for any efficient variable $x_j$. If all values of $w_{ij}$ for the variable $x_j$ are positive, it indicates that $x_j$ is not an efficient variable; hence it is not necessary to solve (3.50) for $x_j$.

Step 3. Decision phase:

For each of the efficient variables ($x_\ell$, $\ell \in N$), the DM is asked: "Are you willing to accept a decrease in objective 1 of $w_{1\ell}$, a decrease in objective 2 of $w_{2\ell}$, ..., and a decrease in objective k of $w_{k\ell}$? Respond yes, no, or indifferent to the trade."

If the responses are all no for all efficient variables, terminate the procedures, and take $\underline{\lambda}^q$ as the best set of weights. Otherwise $x_\ell$ is classified in the following way:

For each yes response, construct an inequality of the form

$$\sum_{i=1}^{k} w_{i\ell}\,\lambda_i \leq -\,\varepsilon \qquad (3.51)$$

where $\varepsilon$ is a sufficiently small positive number. This is because the greatest value of $\sum_{i=1}^{k} w_{i\ell}\,\lambda_i$ is always less than zero in the case of an attractive trade.

For each no response, construct an inequality of the form

$$\sum_{i=1}^{k} w_{i\ell}\,\lambda_i \geq \varepsilon \qquad (3.52)$$

For each response of indifference, construct an inequality of the form

$$\sum_{i=1}^{k} w_{i\ell}\, \lambda_i = 0 \qquad (3.53)$$

and go to step 4.

Step 4. Find the new set of weights:

A feasible solution to the following set of constraints is found. The constraints are of (3.51), (3.52), (3.53), and

$$\sum_{i=1}^{k} \lambda_i = 1$$

$$\lambda_i \geq \varepsilon, \quad i = 1, 2, \ldots, k$$

The resulting set of $\lambda_i$'s is the new $\lambda_i$'s for (3.49).

Set $q = q + 1$ and return to Step 1.

<u>NUMERICAL EXAMPLE</u> (The nutrition problem)

The VMP problem is given by:

$$\max \ f_1(\underline{x}) = -0.225\,x_1 - 2.2x_2 - 0.8x_3 - 0.1x_4 - 0.05x_5 - 0.26x_6$$

$$\max \ f_2(\underline{x}) = -10x_1 - 20x_2 - 120x_3$$

$$\max \ f_3(\underline{x}) = -24x_1 - 27x_2 - 15x_4 - 1.1x_5 - 52x_6$$

$$\text{s.t.} \ g_1(\underline{x}) = 720x_1 + 107x_2 + 7080x_3 + 134x_5 + 1000x_6 \geq 5000$$

$$g_2(\underline{x}) = 0.2x_1 + 10.1x_2 + 13.2x_3 + 0.75x_4 + 0.15x_5 + 1.2x_6 \geq 12.5$$

$$g_3(\underline{x}) = 344x_1 + 460x_2 + 1040x_3 + 75x_4 + 17.4x_5 + 240x_6 \geq 2500$$

$$g_4(\underline{x}) = 18x_1 + 151x_2 + 78x_3 + 2.5x_4 + 0.2x_5 + 4x_6 \geq 63$$

$$g_5(\underline{x}) = x_1 \leq 6.0$$

$$g_6(\underline{x}) = x_2 \leq 1.0$$

$$g_7(\underline{x}) = x_3 \leq 0.25$$

$$g_8(\underline{x}) = x_4 \leq 10.0$$

$$g_9(\underline{x}) = x_5 \leq 10.0$$

$$g_{10}(\underline{x}) = x_6 \leq 4.0$$

$$x_i \geq 0, \quad i = 1, 2, \ldots, 6$$

Let this constraint set be denoted by $\underline{x} \in X$.

All inequality constraints are converted into equality constraints by adding slack/surplus variables:

$$\text{s.t.}\quad g_1(\underline{x}) = 720x_1 + 107x_2 + 7080x_3 + 134x_5 + 1000x_6 - x_7 = 5000$$

$$g_2(\underline{x}) = 0.2x_1 + 10.1x_2 + 13.2x_3 + 0.75x_4 + 0.15x_5 + 1.2x_6 - x_8 = 12.5$$

$$g_3(\underline{x}) = 344x_1 + 460x_2 + 1040x_3 + 75x_4 + 17.4x_5 + 240x_6 - x_9 = 2500$$

$$g_4(\underline{x}) = 18x_1 + 151x_2 + 78x_3 + 2.5x_4 + 0.2x_5 + 4x_6 - x_{10} = 63$$

$$g_5(\underline{x}) = x_1 + x_{11} = 6.0$$

$$g_6(\underline{x}) = x_2 + x_{12} = 1.0$$

$$g_7(\underline{x}) = x_3 + x_{13} = 0.25$$

$$g_8(\underline{x}) = x_4 + x_{14} = 10.0$$

$$g_9(\underline{x}) = x_5 + x_{15} = 10.0$$

$$g_{10}(\underline{x}) = x_6 + x_{16} = 4.0$$

$$x_i \geq 0, \quad i = 1, 2, \ldots, 6$$

Let this converted constraint set be denoted by $\underline{x} \in X'$.

Iteration No. 1:

Step 0. Initialization:

We arbitrarily chose a set of weights $\underline{\lambda}^1 = (0.333, 0.333, 0.333)$ for the composite objective function. Set $q = 1$.

Step 1. Generate and solve the composite objective function:

The composite objective function using $\underline{\lambda}^1$ as the multipliers is formulated in the following LP problem.

$$\max\ 0.333f_1(\underline{x}) + 0.333f_2(\underline{x}) + 0.333f_3(\underline{x})$$

$$\text{s.t.}\quad \underline{x} \in X'$$

The solution to the problem is:

$$\underline{x}^1 = (x_1^1, x_2^1, \ldots, x_{16}^1)$$

$$= (5.45, 0.98, 0., 0., 10., 0., 368.7, 0., 0., 185.3, 0.55, 0.02, 0.25, 10., 0., 4.)$$

and

$$\underline{f}^1 = (f_1(\underline{x}^1), f_2(\underline{x}^1), f_3(\underline{x}^1)) = (-3.88, -74.12, -168.3)$$

The set of nonbasic variables is $\{x_3, x_4, x_6, x_8, x_9, x_{15}\}$.

Step 2. Find a set of efficient variables:

The set of $w_{ij}$ is the decrease in objective function $f_i$ due to introducing a unit of the nonbasic variable $x_j$ into the solution. In the process of finding a set of effecient variables from the set of nonbasic variables, $w_{ij}$ must be estimated around the solution point obtained in Step 1. Since the extreme points of the problem are not identified, to find $w_{ij}$ the following LP problems are solved:

$$\max \; x_j$$

$$\text{s.t.} \quad \underline{x} \in X'$$

$$j = 3, 4, 6, 8, 9, 15.$$

The solutions and objective function values are presented in Table 3.7.

The vector of $\underline{w}^3 = (w_{13}, w_{23}, w_{33})$ is obtained (using the results of Table 3.7):

$$\underline{w}^3 = (w_{13}, w_{23}, w_{33}) = \frac{\underline{f}^1 - \underline{f}'^3}{x_3}$$

$$= \left(\frac{-3.88 + 2.26}{0.25}, \frac{-74.12 + 67.83}{0.25}, \frac{-168.3 + 281.7}{0.25}\right)$$

$$= ( -6.48, -25.2, 453.6)$$

Similarly, $\underline{w}^4$, $\underline{w}^6$, $\underline{w}^8$, $\underline{w}^9$, and $\underline{w}^{15}$ are obtained and presented in Table 3.8.

Table 3.7 The results of converting nonbasic variables into basic variables

| nonbasic variables | solution $x_1$ | $x_2$ | $x_3$ | $x_4$ | $x_5$ | $x_6$ | $x_8$ | $x_9$ | $x_{15}$ | solution $f'_1$ | $f'_2$ | $f'_3$ |
|---|---|---|---|---|---|---|---|---|---|---|---|---|
| $x_3$ | 3.78 | 0 | 0.25 | 10. | 0 | 0.79 | -* | - | - | -2.26 | -67.83 | -281.7 |
| $x_4$ | 2.47 | 0 | 0 | 10. | 0 | 3.76 | - | - | - | -2.53 | -24.67 | -404.5 |
| $x_6$ | 2.30 | 0 | 0 | 10. | 0 | 4. | - | - | - | -2.56 | -22.97 | -413.1 |
| $x_8$ | 6. | 1. | 0.25 | 10. | 10. | 4. | 15.9 | - | - | -6.29 | -110. | -540. |
| $x_9$ | 6. | 1. | 0.25 | 10. | 10. | 4. | - | 2168. | - | -6.29 | -110. | -540. |
| $x_{15}$ | 2.47 | 0 | 0 | 10. | 0 | 3.76 | - | - | 10. | -2.53 | -24.67 | -404.5 |

* the value for "_" sign $\geq$ 0, but not identified.

Table 3.8 The reduced cost for each objective due to introducing a unit of the nonbasic variable into the basic variable

| nonbasic variable | $w_{1i}$ | $w_{2i}$ | $w_{3i}$ |
|---|---|---|---|
| $x_3$ | -6.48 | -25.2 | 453.6 |
| $x_4$ | -0.14 | -4.95 | 23.6 |
| $x_6$ | -0.33 | -12.8 | 61.2 |
| $x_8$ | 0.15 | 2.26 | 23.4 |
| $x_9$ | 0.001 | 0.02 | 0.17 |
| $x_{15}$ | -0.14 | -4.95 | 23.6 |

We see (referring to Table 3.8) that nonbasic variables $x_8$ and $x_9$ cannot be efficient variables because all the components of $\underline{w}^8$ and $\underline{w}^9$ are positive; also that $\underline{w}^4$ is equal to $\underline{w}^{15}$. Hence $x_3$, $x_4$ and $x_6$ will be tested.

For $x_3$, the following LP problem of (3.50) is solved:

$$\min \quad -6.48\lambda_1 - 25.2\lambda_2 + 453.6\lambda_3$$

$$\text{s.t.} \quad -0.14\lambda_1 - 4.95\lambda_2 + 23.6\lambda_3 \geq 0$$

$$-0.33\lambda_1 - 12.8\lambda_2 + 61.2\lambda_3 \geq 0$$

$$\lambda_1 + \lambda_2 + \lambda_3 = 1$$

$$\lambda_1, \lambda_2, \lambda_3 \geq 0$$

The solution is:

$$(\lambda_1, \lambda_2, \lambda_3) = (0.994, 0., 0.006)$$

and the minimum value is -3.77; hence $x_3$ is an efficient variable.

Similarly, the corresponding LP problems for $x_4$ and $x_6$ are solved. Their solutions are:

For $x_4$:

$$(\lambda_1, \lambda_2, \lambda_3) = (0.930, 0.054, 0.016)$$

and the minimum value is -0.13 ; hence $x_4$ is an efficient variable.

For $x_6$:

$$(\lambda_1, \lambda_2, \lambda_3) = (0., 0.827, 0.173)$$

and the minimum value is 0.03 ; hence $x_6$ is not an efficient variable.

Step 3. Decision phase:

For each of the efficient variables, $x_3$ and $x_4$, the DM is asked to indicate the acceptability of the trade-offs represented by $\underline{w}^3$ and $\underline{w}^4$, respectively. The DM's response may be yes, no, or indifferent. For the example, we assume that the (implicit) utility function is $0.959f_1 + 0.029f_2 + 0.012f_3$, but we will use the knowledge of this function only in simulating the DM's responses.

For $\underline{w}^3$ the DM's implicit utility function gives the value of -1.502 ( = 0.959(-6.48) + 0.029(-25.2) + 0.012(453.6)), which indicates the trade-off by $\underline{w}^3$ results in decrease of -1.502 (actually increase of 1.502). Hence $\underline{w}^3$ is an attractive trade-off (i.e., yes response); therefore we have

$$-6.48\lambda_1 - 25.2\lambda_2 + 453.6\lambda_3 \leq -\varepsilon$$

Similarly, for $\underline{w}^4$ the implicit utility function gives the value of 0.006, which indicates that the trade-off of $\underline{w}^4$ is not attractive (i.e., response of no); therefore we have

$$-0.14\lambda_1 - 4.95\lambda_2 + 23.6\lambda_3 \geq \varepsilon$$

Step 4. Find the new set of weights:

With the two inequalities obtained in Step 3 we can find a feasible solution to the following set of constraints (arbitrarily setting $\varepsilon$ = 0.001).

$$-6.48\lambda_1 - 25.2\lambda_2 + 453.6\lambda_3 \leq -0.001$$

$$-0.14\lambda_1 - 4.95\lambda_2 + 23.6\lambda_3 \geq 0.001$$

$$\lambda_1 + \lambda_2 + \lambda_3 = 1$$

$$\lambda_1, \lambda_2, \lambda_3 \geq 0.001$$

A basic feasible solution of this constraint set is obtained by solving the following LP problem :

$$\max \quad -0.14\lambda_1 - 4.95\lambda_2 + 23.6\lambda_3$$

$$\text{s.t.} \quad -6.48\lambda_1 - 25.2\lambda_2 + 453.6\lambda_3 \leq -0.001$$

$$-0.14\lambda_1 - 4.95\lambda_2 + 23.6\lambda_3 \geq 0.001$$

$$\lambda_1 + \lambda_2 + \lambda_3 = 1$$

$$\lambda_1, \lambda_2, \lambda_3 \geq 0.001$$

A solution to the problem is:

$$\underline{\lambda}^2 = (0.985, 0.001, 0.014)$$

Set $q = q + 1 = 2$, and return to Step 1.

Iteration No. 2:

Step 1. Generate the composite objective function:

We form the composite objective function with $\underline{\lambda}^2$, then solve the following LP problem :

$$\max \quad 0.985f_1(\underline{x}) + 0.001f_2(\underline{x}) + 0.014f_3(\underline{x})$$

$$\text{s.t.} \quad \underline{x} \in X'$$

The solution is:

$$\underline{x}^2 = (x_1^2, x_2^2, \ldots, x_{16}^2)$$

$$= (5.44, 0.80, 0.25, 0., 0., 0., 771., 0., 0., 175.7, 0.56, 0.20, 0., 10., 10., 4.)$$

$$\underline{f}^2 = (-3.19, -100.4, -152.2).$$

The set of nonbasic variables is $\{x_4, x_5, x_6, x_8, x_9, x_{13}\}$.

Step 2. Find a set of efficient variables:

The values of $w_{ij}$ are obtained and presented in Table 3.9. $x_8$ and $x_9$ cannot be efficient variables (since all $w_{j8}$ and $w_{j9}$ are positive). Other variables, $x_4$, $x_5$, $x_6$ and $x_{13}$, are to be tested.

For $x_4$, the following LP problem is solved:

$$
\begin{aligned}
\min \quad & -0.066\lambda_1 - 7.56\lambda_2 + 25.23\lambda_3 \\
\text{s.t.} \quad & -0.041\lambda_1 - 7.16\lambda_2 + 20.47\lambda_3 \geq 0 \\
& -0.158\lambda_1 - 19.37\lambda_2 + 65.23\lambda_3 \geq 0 \\
& -2.64\lambda_1 - 303.1\lambda_2 + 1009.\lambda_3 \geq 0 \\
& \lambda_1 + \lambda_2 + \lambda_3 + 1 \\
& \lambda_1, \lambda_2, \lambda_3 \geq 0
\end{aligned}
$$

The solution is:

$$(\lambda_1, \lambda_2, \lambda_3) = (0.9974,\ 0.,\ 0.00261)$$

and the minimum value is -0.00000, hence $x_4$ is an efficient variable.

Similarly, the corresponding LP problems for $x_5$, $x_6$, and $x_{13}$ are solved. Their solutions give the minimum values of - 0.779 for $x_5$, 0.126 for $x_6$, and -0.0079 for $x_{13}$. Therefore $x_5$ and $x_{13}$ are efficient variables, but $x_6$ is not.

The efficient variables set is $\{x_4, x_5, x_{13}\}$.

Step 3. Decision phase:

For $\underline{w}^4$ the DM's implicit utility function gives the value of 0.02 (=0.959(-0.066) + 0.029 (-7.56) + 0.012 (25.23)); hence, the trade-off

Table 3.9 The $w_{ij}$ for iteration 2

| nonbasic variables | $w_{1i}$ | $w_{2i}$ | $w_{3i}$ |
|---|---|---|---|
| $x_4$ | -0.066 | -7.56 | 25.23 |
| $x_5$ | -0.041 | -7.16 | 20.47 |
| $x_6$ | -0.158 | -19.37 | 65.23 |
| $x_8$ | 0.195 | 0.601 | 24.39 |
| $x_9$ | 0.001 | 0.004 | 0.179 |
| $x_{13}$ | -2.64 | -303.1 | 1009. |

is not attractive (i.e., response of no), and we have

$$-0.066\lambda_1 - 7.56\lambda_2 + 25.23\lambda_3 \geq \varepsilon$$

Similarly, for $\underline{w}^5$ the value of implicit utility function is -0.001, which indicates that the trade-off of $\underline{w}^5$ is attractive (i.e., response yes), and we have

$$-0.041\lambda_1 - 7.16\lambda_2 + 20.47\lambda_3 \leq -\varepsilon$$

Step 4 Find the new set of weights:

The three inequalities generated in Step 3 are added to the constraint set in Step 4 of Iteration No. 1. That is,

$$\begin{aligned}
-6.48\,\lambda_1 - 25.2\,\lambda_2 + 453.6\,\lambda_3 &\leq -0.001 \\
-0.14\,\lambda_1 - 4.95\lambda_2 + 23.6\,\lambda_3 &\geq 0.001 \\
-0.066\lambda_1 - 7.56\lambda_2 + 25.23\lambda_3 &\geq 0.001 \\
-0.041\lambda_1 - 7.16\lambda_2 + 20.47\lambda_3 &\leq -0.001 \\
-2.64\,\lambda_1 - 303.1\lambda_2 + 1009.\lambda_3 &\geq 0.001 \\
\lambda_1 + \lambda_2 + \lambda_3 &= 1. \\
\lambda_1,\ \lambda_2,\ \lambda_3 &\geq 0.001
\end{aligned}$$

A basic feasible solution of the above constraint set is $\underline{\lambda}^3 = (0.945, 0.040, 0.015)$. Set $q = q + 1 = 3$, return to Step 1.

Iteration No. 3:

Step 1. Generate the composite objective function:

We form the composite objective function with $\underline{\lambda}^3$, then solve the following LP problem:

$$\begin{aligned}
\max \quad & 0.945f_1(\underline{x}) + 0.040f_2(\underline{x}) + 0.015f_3(\underline{x}) \\
\text{s.t.} \quad & \underline{x} \in X'
\end{aligned}$$

The solution is:

$$\underline{x}^3 = (x_1^3, x_2^3, \ldots, x_{16}^3)$$

$$= (4.10, 0.14, 0.10, 10., 10., 0., 0., 0., 0., 66.23, 1.90, 0.86, 0.15, 0., 0., 4.)$$

$$\underline{f}^3 = (-2.80, -55.0, -263.2)$$

The set of nonbasic variables is $\{x_6, x_7, x_8, x_9, x_{14}, x_{15}\}$.

Step 2. Find a set of efficient variable:

The calculated $\underline{w}^j$, j = 6, 7, 8, 9, 14, 15 are presented in Table 3.10. $x_7$, $x_8$, and $x_9$ are not efficient variables since all $w_{ij}$ for these variables are positive. $x_6$, $x_{14}$, and $x_{15}$ are tested and $x_{15}$ is found to be an efficient variable.

Step 3. Decision phase:

For $\underline{w}^{15}$ the utility function value is 0.054 ( = .959(-0.027) + 0.029(-3.083) + 0.012(14.13)), which indicates the trade-off is not attractive. Hence we terminate the procedure, and take $\underline{\lambda}^3$ = (0.945, 0.040, 0.015) as our unknown set of weights. The final compromised solution is:

$$\underline{x}^3 = (4.10, 0.14, 0.10, 10., 10., 0.)$$

and

$$\underline{f}^3 = (-2.80, -55.0, -263.2).$$

Table 3.10 The $w_{ij}$ for iteration 3.

| nonbasic variables | $w_{1i}$ | $w_{2i}$ | $w_{3i}$ |
|---|---|---|---|
| $x_6$ | -0.06 | -8.13 | 37.49 |
| $x_7$ | 0. | 0.008 | 0.04 |
| $x_8$ | 0.22 | 3.42 | 17.41 |
| $x_9$ | 0.002 | 0.03 | 0.13 |
| $x_{14}$ | 0.056 | -0.615 | 4.88 |
| $x_{15}$ | -0.027 | -3.08 | 14.13 |

Notes

On the (implicit) utility function: The implicit utility function plays a central role in "Step 3. Decision phase" in deciding whether the given trade-offs are attractive to the DM. Usually the DM does not have a precise (implicit) utility function initially. However, the DM's implicit utility function can be determined iteratively.

As an example, the (implicit) utility function used in the example in Sec. 2 is assumed to be $0.8\ f_1 + 0.1\ f_2 + 0.1\ f_3$. The decision phase (Step 3) in Iteration No. 1 becomes:

for $\underline{w}^3$, $0.8\ (-6.48) + 0.1\ (-25.2) + 0.1\ (453.6) = 37.7$

which indicates that the trade-off by $\underline{w}^3$ is not attractive. Similarly for $\underline{w}^4$ the implicit utility function gives the value of 1.76, which indicates that trade-off of $\underline{w}^4$ is not attractive. The compromised solution is $\underline{f}^1 = (-3.88, -74.1, -168.3)$. However, the DM feels that both $f_1^1 = -3.88$ and $f_2^1 = -74.1$ are lower than expected (especially $f_1^1$); the DM's implicit utility function is modified to $0.95f_1 + 0.03f_2 + 0.02f_3$. The decision phase (Step 3) in Iteration 1 is repeated. The DM's implicit utility function gives the values of 2.16 and 0.19 for $\underline{w}^3$ and $\underline{w}^4$, respectively. Both still have positive values; that is, the implicit utility function should be modified. It becomes $0.959f_1 + 0.029f_2 + 0.012f_3$, which is used in the example.

Scale each set of trade-offs: In presenting the trade-off questions to the DM, the units in which the variables are measured affect the relative scale of the trade-offs posed. Therefore, it is useful to scale each set of trade-offs so that the magnitudes are of the same order.

<u>The advantages of the method</u>: It guarantees a convergence in a finite number of iterations, since each trade-off which is attractive to the DM increases the DM's implicit utility functional value at each iteration. Also the demand on the DM is less as compared to other methods.

<u>The disadvantage of the method</u>: The method requires that all the constraint set and objective functions must be linear or feasible for linear approximation. It is very difficult to require the DM to have a reasonable (implicit) utility function. The linear utility function assumption is quite a sever one; it may be relaxed to an assumption of an additive separable utility function of the objectives. When it is relaxed to concave utility function, the number of questions and iterations are significantly increased.

## 3.2. Methods for Implicit Trade-Off Information Given

The methods in this section do not require explict information from the DM; the trade-off information is implicit. These methods have two important advantages over the methods of Sec. 3.1: (1) the DM is more confident in indicating acceptable achievement levels of objectives than in indicating preferred trade-offs as was necessary for Sec. 3.1 methods; (2) the trade-offs presented for the methods in Sec. 3.1 are generally valid over a narrow range of objective values not discussed or indicated clearly to the DM; thus without the range of validity presented it leads to improper trade-off selections; there is no problem here of improper trade-off selections resulting from the lack of a clearly defined range of validity.

### 3.2.1 STEM AND RELATED METHODS

A series of similar and inter-related methods have been proposed by Benayoun, Larichev, de Montoglfier, Tergny, and Keuneman [17-19]. The STEP-method (STEM), the progressive orientation procedure (POP), and the method of constraints are for solution of multiple objective linear programming (MOLP) problems. The STEM method is presented in this section.

The mathematical formulation of an MOLP problem (which is a special case of (1.1)) is:

$$\left.\begin{aligned} \max \quad & \left[\sum_{i=1}^{n} c_{1i}x_i, \ \sum_{i=1}^{n} c_{2i}x_i, \ldots, \ \sum_{i=1}^{n} c_{ki}x_i\right] \\ \text{s.t.} \quad & \sum_{i=1}^{n} a_{ij}x_j \leq b_i, \qquad i = 1,2, \ldots, m \\ & x_i \geq 0, \qquad i = 1,2, \ldots, n \end{aligned}\right\} \tag{3.54}$$

or in a vector form:

$$\left.\begin{aligned} \max \quad & [\underline{c}_1^T\underline{x}, \ \underline{c}_2^T\underline{x}, \ \ldots, \ \underline{c}_k^T\underline{x}] \\ \text{s.t.} \quad & A\underline{x} \leq \underline{b} \\ & \underline{x} \geq \underline{0} \end{aligned}\right\} \tag{3.54a}$$

#### The STEM Method

STEM allows the DM to learn to recognize good solutions and the relative importance of the objectives. In the method, phases of computation alternate (interactively) with phases of decision.

The STEM process follows these steps:

Step 0. Construction of a pay-off table:

A pay-off table (see Table 3.11) is constructed before the first interactive cycle. Let $f_j^*$, j = 1,2, ..., k, be feasible ideal solutions of the following k problems:

$$\left.\begin{array}{lll} \max & f_j(\underline{x}) = \underline{c}_j^T \underline{x} & \\ \text{s.t.} & A\,\underline{x} \leq b, & \underline{x} \geq 0 \\ & j = 1,2,\ldots,k & \end{array}\right\} \qquad (3.55)$$

In Table 3.11, row j corresponds to the solution vector $\underline{x}^*$ which maximizes the objective function $f_j$. A $z_{ij}$ is the value taken on by the ith objective $f_i$ when the jth objective $f_j$ reaches its maximum $f_j^*$.

Step 1. Calculation phase:

At the mth cycle, the feasible solution to LP of (3.56) is sought which is the 'nearest', in the MINIMAX sense, to the ideal solution $f_j^*$:

$$\left.\begin{array}{ll} \min\limits_{\{\underline{x},\lambda\}} & \lambda \\ \text{s.t.} & \lambda \geq \{f_j^* - f_j(\underline{x})\} * \pi_j, \qquad j = 1,2,\ldots,k \\ & \underline{x} \in X^m \\ & \lambda \geq 0 \end{array}\right\} \qquad (3.56)$$

where $X^m$ includes $A\underline{x} \leq \underline{b}$, $\underline{x} \geq \underline{0}$ plus any constraint added in the previous (m-1) cycles; $\pi_j$ give the relative importance of the distances to the optima, but it must be noted that they are only locally effective and are not of overriding importance as the weights are in the utility method.

Let us consider the jth column in the pay-off table (Table 3.11). $f_j^*$ is the maximum value of the column. Let $f_j^{min}$ be the minimum value; then $\pi_j$ are chosen such that

Table 3.11 A pay-off table of STEM

| | $f_1$ | $f_2$ | ... | $f_j$ | ... | $f_k$ |
|---|---|---|---|---|---|---|
| $f_1$ | | | | $z_{j1}$ | | |
| $f_2$ | | | | $z_{j2}$ | | |
| $\vdots$ | | | | $\vdots$ | | |
| $f_j$ | $z_{1j}$ | $z_{2j}$ | ... | $f_j^*$ | | $z_{kj}$ |
| $\vdots$ | | | | | | |
| $f_k$ | | | | $z_{jk}$ | | |

$$\pi_j = \frac{\alpha_j}{\sum_i \alpha_i}$$

where
$$\alpha_j = \frac{f_j^* - f_j^{min}}{f_j^*} \left[ \frac{1}{\sqrt{\sum_{i=1}^{n} (c_{ji})^2}} \right] \quad \text{if } f_j^* > 0$$

$$\alpha_j = \frac{f_j^{min} - f_j^*}{f_j^{min}} \cdot \left[ \frac{1}{\sqrt{\sum_{i=1}^{n} (c_{ji})^2}} \right] \quad \text{if } f_i^* \leq 0$$

where $c_{ji}$ are the coefficients of the jth objective. The value of $\alpha_j$ consists of two terms:

$$\frac{f_j^* - f_j^{min}}{f_j^*} \quad \text{or} \quad \frac{f_j^{min} - f_j^*}{f_j^{min}}, \quad \text{and} \quad \left[ 1 \Big/ \sqrt{\sum_{i=1}^{n} (c_{ji})^2} \right].$$

From the first term we can make the following assertion: if the value of $f_j$ does not vary much from the optimum solution by varying $\underline{x}$, the corresponding objective is not sensitive to a variation in the weighting values; therefore, a small weight $\pi_j$ can be assigned to this objective function. As the variation gets larger, the weight $\pi_j$ will become correspondingly bigger. The second term normalizes the values taken by the objective functions. The $\alpha_j$ are used to define the weights $\pi_j$ in such a way that the sum of $\pi_j$ is 1. This means that different solutions obtained from different weighting strategies can be easily compared.

Step 2. Decision phase:

The compromise solution $\underline{x}^m$ is presented to the DM, who compares its objective vector $\underline{f}^m$ with $\underline{f}^*$, the ideal one. If some of the objectives are satisfactory and others are not, the DM must relax a satisfactory objective $f_j^m$ enough to allow an improvement of the unsatisfactory objectives in the next iterative cycle. The DM gives $\Delta f_j$ as the amount of acceptable relaxation.

Then, for the next cycle the feasible region is modified as:

$$X^{m+1} = \begin{cases} X^m \\ f_j(\underline{x}) \geq f_j(\underline{x}^m) - \Delta f_j \\ f_i(\underline{x}) \geq f_i(\underline{x}^m); \; i \neq j, \; i = 1,2, \ldots, k \end{cases}$$

The weight $\pi_j$ is set to zero and the calculation phase of cycle m+1 begins.

The flow-chart of STEM is given in Fig. 3.18.

NUMERICAL EXAMPLE (Production scheduling of the Hardee toy company)

The VMP problem is given by:

$$\max \quad f_1(\underline{x}) = 0.4x_1 + 0.3x_2$$

$$\max \quad f_2(\underline{x}) = x_1$$

$$\text{s.t.} \quad \left.\begin{aligned} g_1(\underline{x}) &= x_1 + x_2 \leq 400 \\ g_2(\underline{x}) &= 2x_1 + x_2 \leq 500 \\ x_1, x_2 &\geq 0 \end{aligned}\right\} \text{Let these constraints by denoted by } \underline{x} \in X$$

Step 0. Construction of a pay-off table

The ideal solution for $f_1(\underline{x})$ is obtained by solving the following L P problem:

$$\max \quad f_1(\underline{x}) = 0.4x_1 + 0.3x_2$$

$$\text{s.t.} \quad \underline{x} \in X$$

The solution is: $x_1 = 100$, $x_2 = 300$, $f_1(\underline{x}^*) = 130$, and $f_2(100,300) = 100$.

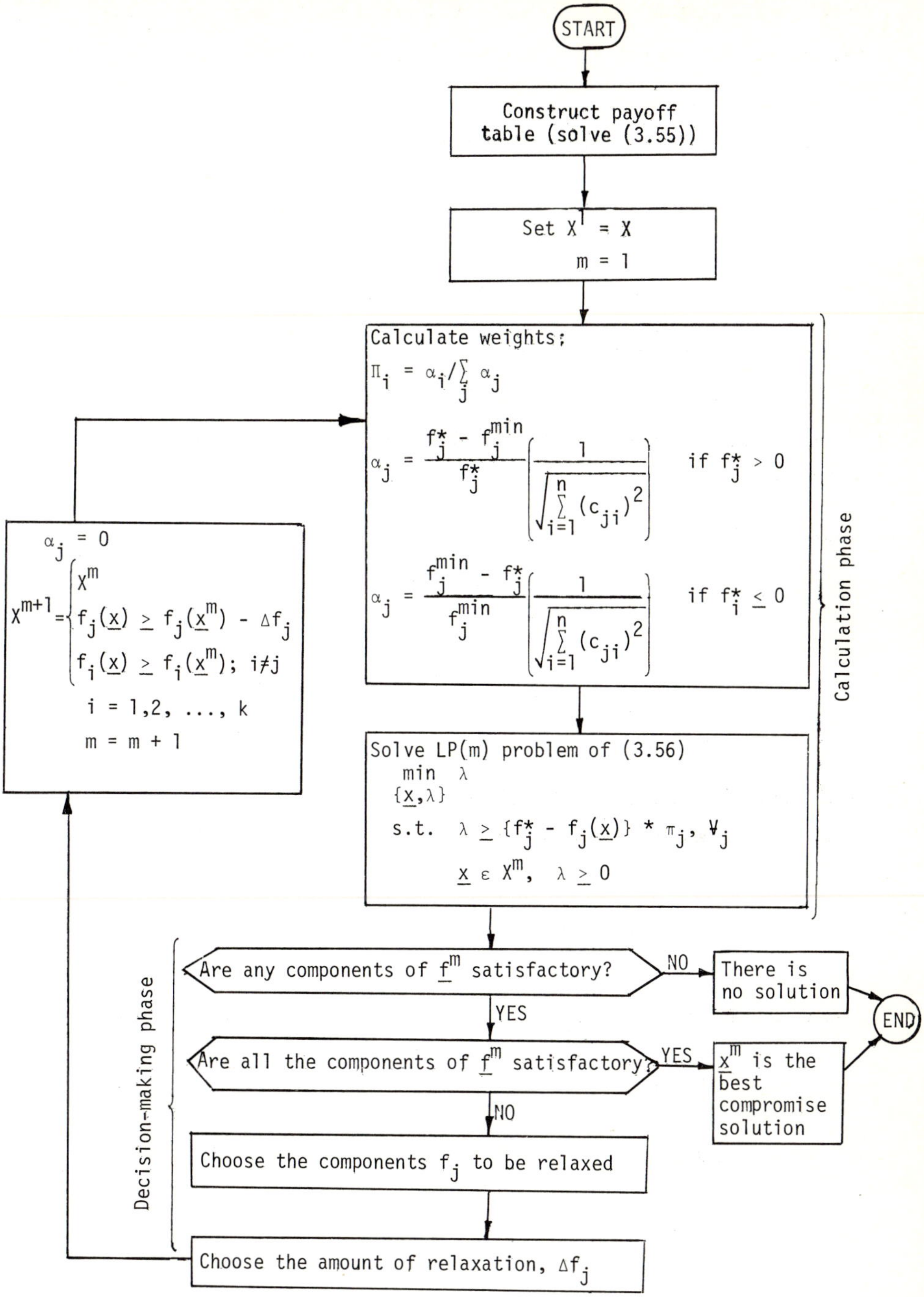


Fig. 3.18 Flow-chart of STEM [18].

Similarly, the ideal solution for $f_2(\underline{x})$ is obtained by solving the L P problem:

$$\max \quad f_2(\underline{x}) = x_1$$

$$\text{s.t.} \quad \underline{x} \in X$$

The solution is: $x_1 = 250$, $x_2 = 0$, $f_2(\underline{x}^*) = 250$, and $f_1(250,0) = 100$.

The results of the above solutions are summarized in the pay-off table.

| | $f_1$ | $f_2$ | $x_1$ | $x_2$ |
|---|---|---|---|---|
| $f_1$ | 130 | 100 | 100 | 300 |
| $f_2$ | 100 | 250 | 250 | 0 |

Iteration No. 1:

Step 1. Calculation phase

a) Calculate weights.

$$\alpha_1 = \frac{f_1 - f_1^{min}}{f_1^*}\left(\frac{1}{\sqrt{c_{11}^2 + c_{12}^2}}\right)$$

$$= \frac{130 - 100}{130}\left(\frac{1}{\sqrt{0.4^2 + 0.3^2}}\right)$$

$$= 0.4615$$

$$\alpha_2 = \frac{f_2^* - f_2^{min}}{f_2^*}\left(\frac{1}{\sqrt{c_{21}^2 + c_{22}^2}}\right)$$

$$= \frac{250 - 100}{250}\left(\frac{1}{\sqrt{1^2 + 0^2}}\right)$$

$$= 0.60$$

$$\pi_1 = \frac{\alpha_1}{\alpha_1 + \alpha_2} = 0.4348$$

$$\pi_2 = \frac{\alpha_2}{\alpha_1 + \alpha_2} = 0.5652$$

b) Solve the LP problem of (3.56):

$$\min_{\{\underline{x}, \lambda\}} \lambda$$

$$\text{s.t. } \underline{x} \in X, \lambda \geq 0$$

$$\lambda + 0.4348(0.4x_1 + 0.3x_2) \geq 0.4348(130)$$

$$\lambda + 0.5652x_1 \geq 0.5652(250)$$

The solution is:

$$\underline{x}^1 = (x_1^1, x_2^1) = (230, 40)$$

$$\underline{f}^1 = (f_1^1, f_2^1) = (104, 230)$$

Step 2. Decision phase

The compromise solution $\underline{x}^1$ (see Figs. 3.19 and 3.20) is presented to the DM, who compares its objective vector $\underline{f}^1 = (f_1^1, f_2^1) = (104, 230)$ with the ideal one, $\underline{f}^* = (f_1^*, f_2^*) = (130, 250)$. If $f_2^1$ is satisfactory, but $f_1^1$ is not, the DM must relax the satisfactory objective $f_2^1$ enough to allow an improvement of the unsatisfactory $f_1^1$. If $\Delta f_2 = 30$ is the acceptable amount of relaxation, the feasible region is modified as follows in the next iteration cycle:

$$X^2 = \begin{cases} X^1 \\ f_2(\underline{x}) \geq f_2(\underline{x}^1) - \Delta f_2 = 230 - 30 = 200 \\ f_1(\underline{x}) \geq f_1(\underline{x}^1) = 104 \end{cases}$$

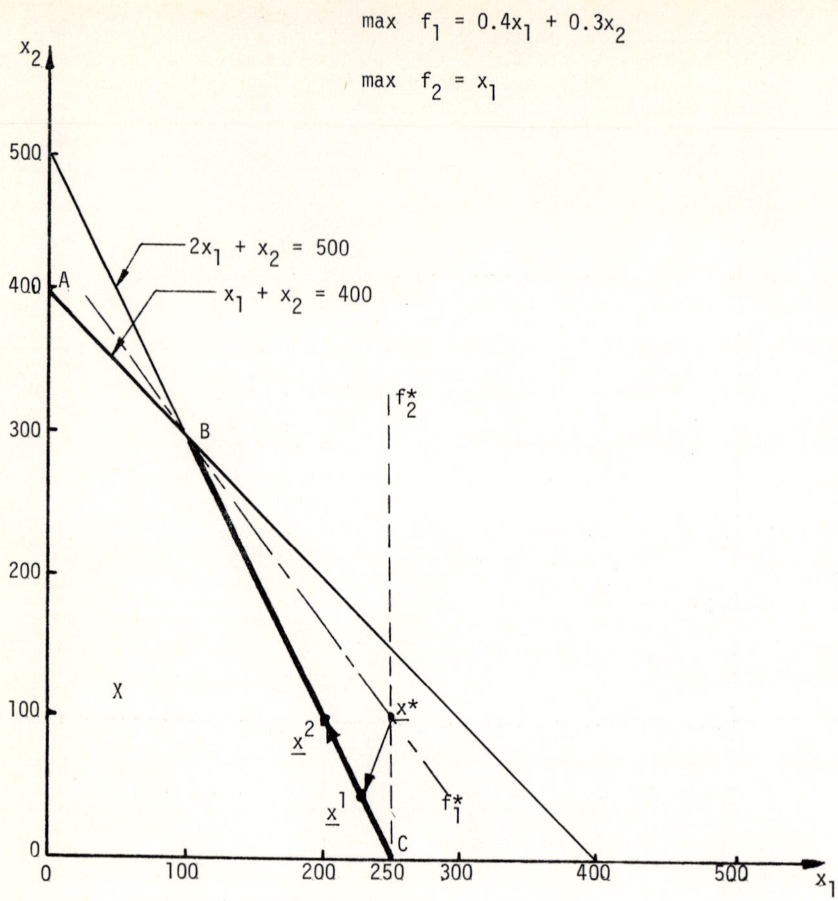


Fig. 3.19 Decision variable space representation of the feasible area of the example.

$$\max \ f_1 = 0.4x_1 + 0.3x_2$$

$$\max \ f_2 = x_1$$

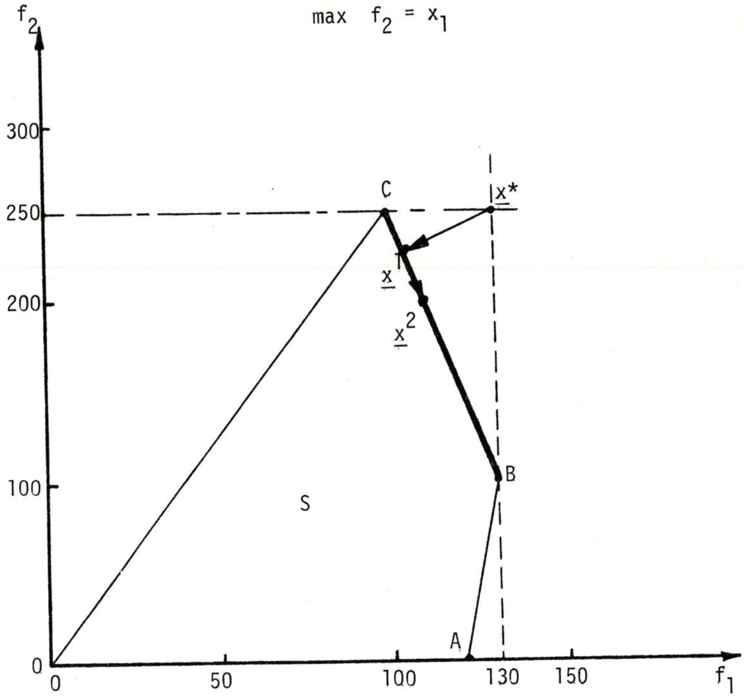


Fig. 3.20 Objective function space representation of feasible area of the example.

Iteration No. 2:

Step 1. Calculation phase

a) Calculate weights.

$\pi_1 = 1$

$\pi_2 = 0$

b) Solve the following LP problem of (3.56):

$$\min_{\{\underline{x},\ \lambda\}} \lambda$$

$$\text{s.t.}\quad \underline{x} \in X^2,\ \lambda \geq 0$$

$$\lambda + (0.4x_1 + 0.3x_2) \geq 130$$

where

$$X^2 = \begin{cases} \underline{x} \in X \\ x_1 \geq 200 \\ 0.4x_1 + 0.3x_2 \geq 104 \end{cases}$$

The solution is:

$$\underline{x}^2 = (x_1^2,\ x_2^2) = (200,\ 100)$$

$$\underline{f}^2 = (f_1^2,\ f_2^2) = (110,\ 200)$$

Step 2. Decision phase

The compromise solution $\underline{x}^2$ (see Figs. 3.19 and 3.20) is presented to the DM, who compares its objective vector $\underline{f}^2 = (f_1^2, f_2^2) = (110, 200)$ with the ideal one, $\underline{f}^* = (f_1^*, f_2^*) = (130, 250)$. If both objectives of the vector $\underline{f}^2$ are satisfactory, $\underline{f}^2$ is the final solution.

It is worth noting that both $\underline{x}^1$ and $\underline{x}^2$ (see Figs. 3.19 and 3.20) are non-dominated solutions on the segment of straight line BC (all points on the segment of straight line BC are non-dominated solutions).

<u>A sensitivity analysis</u>

To help the DM determine satisfactory objectives and amounts of relaxation in the decision phase, the analyst can carry out a standard sensitivity analysis to give the behavior of the different objectives in the neighborhood of the optimal solution $\underline{x}^m$ (at the mth iteration of the LP problem).

One simple way the analyst can help is by solving, during the calculation phase of the mth iteration (cycle), several LP problems with feasible regions $X^m$ corresponding to several thresholds $\Delta f_j$ such that $0 < \Delta f_j^1 < \Delta f_j^2 < \ldots < \Delta f_j^m$ ($\Delta f_j^m$ is the maximum acceptable relaxation). Then the DM can choose from the different LP solutions corresponding to each $\Delta f_j$; for example, the solution giving the best improvement ratio for the other objectives.

In the example, the analyst carries out a sensitivity analysis at Iteration No. 2 before Step 2, decision phase.

Let $\Delta f_2^1 = 10$, $\Delta f_2^2 = 20$, $\Delta f_2^3 = 30$, $\Delta f_2^4 = 40$. Then these 4 LP problems are to be solved:

$$\min_{\{\underline{x},\lambda\}} \quad \lambda$$

$$\text{s.t.} \quad \left. \begin{array}{l} \underline{x} \in X, \ \lambda \geq 0 \\ \lambda + (0.4x_1 + 0.3x_2) \geq 130 \\ 0.4x_1 + 0.3x_2 \geq 104 \\ f_2(\underline{x}) \geq f_2(\underline{x}^1) - \Delta f_2^\ell \end{array} \right\}$$

$$\ell = 1, 2, 3, 4$$

where $f_2(\underline{x}) = x_1$, $f_2(\underline{x}^1) = 230$.

The solutions for these 4 LP problems are summarized in the table:

| | $f_1$ | $f_2$ | $x_1$ | $x_2$ |
|---|---|---|---|---|
| $\Delta f_2^0 = 0$ | 104 | 230 | 230 | 40 |
| $\Delta f_2^1 = 10$ | 106 | 220 | 220 | 60 |
| $\Delta f_2^2 = 20$ | 108 | 210 | 210 | 80 |
| $\Delta f_2^3 = 30$ | 110 | 200 | 200 | 100 |
| $\Delta f_2^4 = 40$ | 112 | 190 | 190 | 120 |
| | $f_1^* = 130$ | $f_2^* = 250$ | | |

From this table the DM can see the trade-off between objectives $f_1$ and $f_2$ and decide which set of solutions is the best compromised one.

We may observe from this table that the trade-off of objectives has a simple linear relation since the example is a linear model.

<u>Note</u>

The progressive orientation procedure, a method similar to STEM, was developed by Benayoun et al. [19]. In this method the DM is presented with a subset of non-dominated extreme points. If the subset contains an acceptable solution, the procedure is terminated; otherwise the DM chooses a best subset of solutions, which is then used to determine a new set of non-dominated extreme points, and the process is repeated.

Benayoun et al. [17] suggest methods, also similar to STEM, for solving MOLP problems: (1) the weights of the objectives are known; (2) the relative importance of the objectives is known; (3) there is no information on the importance of the objectives.

### 3.2.2. SEMOPS AND SIGMOP METHODS

A Sequential Multiobjective Problem Solving technique (SEMOPS) is an interactive programming technique that dynamically involves the DM in a search process to locate a satisfactory course of action.
The method proposed by Monarchi, Kisiel, and Duckstein [247-248] allows the DM to trade off one objective vs another in an interactive manner. SEMOPS cyclically uses a surrogate objective function based on goals and the DM's aspirations toward achieving the objectives. The goal levels are conditions imposed on the DM by external forces, and the aspiration levels are attainment levels of the objectives which the DM personally desires to achieve. (Goals do not change, but aspiration levels change as each iterative cycle goes.)

The algorithm

Let $\underline{AL} = (AL_1, AL_2, \ldots, AL_T)$ be the DM's aspiration levels, and $\underline{f}(\underline{x}) = (f_1(\underline{x}), f_2(\underline{x}), \ldots, f_T(\underline{x}))$ be the multiple objective functions. A relevant range of $\underline{f}(\underline{x})$ for each objective is chosen as $[f_{iL}, f_{iU}]$. The relevant range for each objective is not necessarily the maximum and minimum of the function; rather it is the range given by the constraint set and bounds on the policy variables. By transforming the original response surface $f_i(\underline{x})$ to $y_i(x)$, where $y_i(\underline{x})$ is defined in the interval [0,1], we have:

$$y_i(\underline{x}) = \frac{f_i(\underline{x}) - f_{iL}}{f_{iU} - f_{iL}} + \varepsilon \tag{3.57}$$

where $\varepsilon$ is a small positive value (such as $10^{-20}$) added to circumvent the division by zero while defining the dimensionless indicator of attainment.

The DM's aspiration levels $\underline{AL}$ may be transformed into $\underline{A}$ by the same procedure as follows:

$$A_i = \frac{AL_i - f_{iL}}{f_{iU} - f_{iL}} + \varepsilon$$

Then $\underline{A}$ is in [0,1].

Five types of objectives and the corresponding dimensionless indicator of attainment, $\underline{d}$, are [248, BM-11]:

(1) at most:

$$f_i(\underline{x}) \leq AL_i;\ d_i = \frac{f_i(\underline{x})}{AL_i} = \frac{y_i(\underline{x})}{A_i}$$

(2) at least:

$$f_i(\underline{x}) \geq AL_i;\ d_i = \frac{AL_i}{f_i(\underline{x})} = \frac{A_i}{y_i(\underline{x})}$$

(3) equals:

$$f_i(\underline{x}) = AL_i;\ d_i = \frac{1}{2}\left(\frac{AL_i}{f_i(\underline{x})} + \frac{f_i(\underline{x})}{AL_i}\right) = \frac{1}{2}\left(\frac{A_i}{y_i(\underline{x})} + \frac{y_i(\underline{x})}{A_i}\right)$$

(4) within an interval:

$$AL_{iL} \leq f_i(\underline{x}) \leq AL_{iU};\ d_i = \left(\frac{AL_{iU}}{AL_{iL} + AL_{iU}}\right)\left(\frac{AL_{iL}}{f_i(\underline{x})} + \frac{f_i(\underline{x})}{AL_{iU}}\right)$$

$$= \left(\frac{A_{iU}}{A_{iL} + A_{iU}}\right)\left(\frac{A_{iL}}{y_i(\underline{x})} + \frac{y_i(\underline{x})}{A_{iU}}\right)$$

(5) outside an interval:

$$f_i(\underline{x}) \leq AL_{iL} \text{ or } f_i(\underline{x}) \geq AL_{iU};\ d_i = \left(\frac{AL_{iL} + AL_{iU}}{AL_{iU}}\right)\left(\frac{1}{\frac{AL_{iL}}{f_i(\underline{x})} + \frac{f_i(\underline{x})}{AL_{iU}}}\right)$$

$$= \left(\frac{A_{iL} + A_{iU}}{A_{iU}}\right)\left(\frac{1}{\frac{A_{iL}}{y_i(\underline{x})} + \frac{y_i(\underline{x})}{A_{iU}}}\right)$$

Types (1), (2) and (4) are the most common. In each instance, values of $d_i \leq 1$ imply that the objective is satisfied. Except for the first type (at most), the $d_i$ are all nonlinear functions of an objective function that may itself be nonlinear.

The algorithm generates information under the guidance of the DM so that he/she can make a decision. Information concerning the interrelationships between objectives is in terms of how achievement or non-achievement of one objective affects the aspiration levels of other objectives.

The cyclical optimization of a surrogate objective functions (3.58) is the mechanism by which information is generated for the DM. The word surrogate is used in recognition of the fact that the true preference function of the individual is unknown. Let T' be the subset of the set of T objectives, those objectives making up s at a given iteration of the decision-making process. Thus,

$$s \equiv \sum_{t \in T'} d_t \tag{3.58}$$

is defined as the surrogate objective function. The value of each $d_t$ in s reflects whether the t-th objective has been satisfied; unsatisfied objectives have values > 1.

Operationally, SEMOPS is a three-step algorithm involving setup, iteration, and termination. Setup involves transforming the original problem into a principal problem and a set of auxiliary problems with surrogate objective functions. The iteration step is the interactive segment of the algorithm and involves a cycling between an optimization phase (by analyst) and an evaluation phase (by the DM) until a preferred solution is reached, which terminates the algorithm.

The first iteration, i=1, solves the principal problem and a set of T auxiliary problems. The auxiliary problems are formed in which the aspiration level of each objective is given as the goal of each objective, i.e., $AL_i = b_i$, i = 1,2, ..., T.

The principal problem:

$$\left.\begin{array}{ll} \min & s_1 = \sum_{t=1}^{T} d_t \\ \text{s.t.} & \underline{x} \in X \end{array}\right\} \quad (3.59)$$

The set of auxiliary problems, $\ell$ = 1, 2, ..., T:

$$\left.\begin{array}{ll} \min & s_{1\ell} = \sum_{\substack{t=1 \\ t \neq \ell}}^{T} d_t \\ \text{s.t.} & \underline{x} \in X \\ & f_\ell(\underline{x}) \geq AL_\ell \end{array}\right\} \quad (3.60)$$

Solving (3.59) and (3.60) forms the optimization phase. The resulting policy vector and objectives for the principal problem and the set of auxiliary problems are presented to the DM for use in the evaluation phase. The impact of an action on the attainment of the other objectives is assessed, and a new aspiration level for an objective is set.

In general, the ith iteration solves the following principal problem and a set of auxiliary problems:

The principal problem:

$$\left.\begin{array}{ll} \min & s_i = \sum_{t \in T'} d_t \\ \text{s.t.} & \underline{x} \in X \\ & f_j(\underline{x}) \geq AL_j, \; j \in (T-T') \end{array}\right\} \quad (3.61)$$

The set of auxiliary problems, $\ell \in T'$ (the number of $T' = T - i+1$):

$$\left.\begin{aligned} &\min \quad s_{i\ell} = \sum_{\substack{t \in T' \\ t \neq \ell}} d_t \\ &\text{s.t.} \quad \underline{x} \in X \\ &\qquad f_j(\underline{x}) \geq AL_j \quad \text{for } \forall_j, \qquad j \in (T-T') \\ &\qquad f_\ell(\underline{x}) \geq AL_\ell, \text{ for one } \ell, \qquad \ell \in T' \end{aligned}\right\} \tag{3.62}$$

The optimization phase solves (3.61) and (3.62). The resulting solutions are used in the evaluation phase, and the DM gives direction for the next iteration cycle.

NUMERICAL EXAMPLE (The Bow River Valley water quality management)

This problem is based on a hypothetical case developed by Dorfman and Jacoby [88a] and modified by Monarchi et al. [247-249]. It concerns with the pollution problems of an artificial river basin, the Bow River Valley, whose main features are shown in Fig. 3.21. Industrial pollution originates from the Pierce-Hall Cannery, located near the head of the valley, and municipal waste pollutions come from two outlets at Bowville and Plympton. A state part is located between the cities, and the lower end of the valley is part of the state boundary line.

The specification of water quality has been reduced to a single dimension: dissolved oxygen concentration (DO). The waste content of the

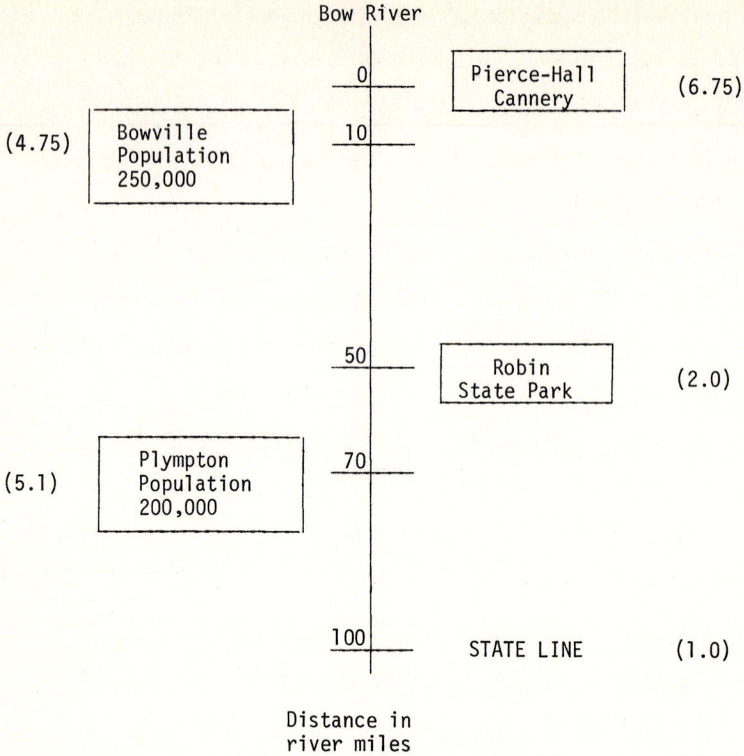


(Values in parentheses at the sides are current DO levels in milligrams per liter.)

Fig. 3.21 Main features of the Bow River Valley [248]

municipal and industrial effluent is described here by the number of pounds of biochemical oxygen demanding material (BOD) the effluents carry, which is identified as carbonaceous ($BOD_c$) and nitrogenous ($BOD_n$) material.

The cannery and the two cities already have primary treatment facilities which reduce BOD by 30% of their gross discharge. To reduce waste further, additional treatment facilities would have to be installed. The costs of the additional treatment facilities will reduce the investment return from the cannery and increase the tax rate in Bowville and Plympton.

The Bow Valley Water Pollution Control Commission is made up of representatives from all three waste dischargers and members of the state and federal government. It is responsible for maintaining river water quality by setting the waste reduction requirements at the three sources of pollution, but it must act with an awareness of the effect of any additional effluent treatment costs on the economy of the valley.

The Commission (the DM) is concerned with the following six objectives: the DO levels at Bowville, Robin State Park, and Plympton (objectives 1, 2, and 3, respectively); the percent return on investment at the Pierce-Hall Cannery (objective 4); and the addition to the tax rate for Bowville and Plympton (objectives 5 and 6, respectively). The first problem of the DM is to determine a waste treatment policy which satisfies the constraint that the DO level at the state line is above 3.5 mg/ℓ. Initially, the DM would like to raise the DO level at all of the above locations to at least 6.0 mg/ℓ, to maintain the rate of return on investment at Pierce-Hall above 6.5%, and to hold the tax rate at both Bowville and Plympton below \$1.5/\$1000 of assessed valuation.

The treatment levels of waste discharges at the Pierce-Hall Cannery, Bowville, and Plympton ($x_1$, $x_2$, and $x_3$, respectively) are the decision variables to be determined.

The Streeter-Phelps model [325a], that the decomposition of organic waste in a stream reduces the DO level at a rate proportional to the concentration of the waste in the stream, is used. The treatment levels are specified in terms of the carbonaceous $BOD_c$ by the relation:

$$w_i = 0.39/(1.39 - x_i^2) \tag{3.63}$$

where $x_i$ is the proportionate amount of gross $BOD_c$ removed at source i and $w_i$ is the corresponding value for $BOD_n$.

On the basis of the additivity assumptions, the water quality $q_j$ (the DO level) at a point j is calculated from

$$q_j = - \sum_i [d_{ij}^c \; L_i^c \; (x_i - 0.3) + d_{ij}^n \; L_i^n \; (w_i - 0.3)] + \bar{q}_j \tag{3.64}$$

where

$d_{ij}^c$ carbonaceous transfer coefficient between points i and j;

$d_{ij}^n$ nitrogenous transfer coefficient between points i and j;

$L_i^c$ carbonaceous BOD load for source i;

$L_i^n$ nitrogenous BOD load for source i;

$x_i$ proportionate reduction in $L_i^c$;

$w_i$ proportionate reduction in $L_i^n$;

$\bar{q}_j$ current DO level at point j;

i,j points (point i = 1, 2, or 3 represents Pierce-Hall Cannery, Bowville, or Plympton, respectively, and point j = 1,2,3, or 4 represents Bowville, Robin State Part, Plympton, or the state line).

The transfer coefficients ($d^c_{ij}$ and $d^n_{ij}$) for the points of interest are presented in Table 3.12. The waste levels are shown in Table 3.13.

A consulting firm has developed relationships between the proportionate reduction in $BOD_c$ above 30 percent and the incremental costs for each of the three sites. The respective gross additional annual cost in thousands of dollars are:

for Pierce-Hall Cannery

$$C_1 = [59/(109 - x_1^2)] - 59 \qquad 1000\$/year$$

for Bowville

$$C_2 = [532/(1.09-x_2^2)] - 532 \qquad 1000\$/year$$

for Plympton

$$C_3 = [450/(1.09 - x_3^2)] - 450 \qquad 1000\$/year$$

However, there are mitigating factors that reduce the gross cost for each institution. The federal corporation tax reduces the cannery's cost by 40%. The gross costs to Bowville and Plympton are reduced because the Federal Water Pollution Control Act provides a grant to municipalities that covers 50% of the construction costs, which are about one-half the total costs; so that each city pays about 75% of the total cost.

The cannery's average net profit has been \$375,000 per year, which is a return of 7.5% on the stockholders' equity of \$5 million. It is assumed

Table 3.12 Carbonaceous (C) and nitrogenous (N) transfer coefficients ($d_{ij}$)

| | Bowville | | Robin State Park | | Plympton | | State Line | |
|---|---|---|---|---|---|---|---|---|
| | C | N | C | N | C | N | C | N |
| Pierce-Hall Cannery | -5.68 | - | -1.31 | -3.15 | -0.442 | -0.771 | -0.083 | -0.073 |
| Bowville | 0 | 0 | -2.18 | -5.53 | -0.764 | -1.60 | -0.0145 | -0.162 |
| Plympton | - | - | - | - | 0 | 0 | -3.49 | -7.33 |

All values are times $10^{-5}$; i.e., the carbonaceous coefficient for Pierce-Hall Cannery to Bowville is $-5.68 \times 10^{-5}$ (mg/ℓ)(lb/day).

Table 3.13. BOD waste levels in pounds per day

| | Gross | | After Preliminary Treatment | |
|---|---|---|---|---|
| | $BOD_c$ | $BOD_n$ | $BOD_c$ | $BOD_n$ |
| Pierce-Hall Cannery | 40,000 | 28,000 | 28,000 | 19,000 |
| Bowville | 128,000 | 48,000 | 89,600 | 33,600 |
| Plympton | 95,700 | 35,700 | 67,000 | 25,000 |

that sales will remain stable over the foreseeable future, production costs will not change, and prices will not be raised because of the pressures of competition. Consequently, any increase in treatment costs will reduce net profit. The relationship between costs $C_1$ and percent return on investment r is

$$r = \frac{100}{5,000,000}(375,000 - 0.6C_1)$$

Additional waste treatment costs at Bowville will affect the city's tax rate. The city planning division has developed a relationship between the change in the tax rate $\Delta t$ and costs C:

$$\Delta t_2 = (2.4*10^{-3})(0.75C_2)$$

where $\Delta t$ is the change per thousand dollars assessed valuation. Similarly the relationship for plympton is:

$$\Delta t_3 = (3.33* \, 10^{-3})(0.75C_3)$$

<u>Objectives and Constraints</u>:

Objective 1: DO level at Bowville ($f_1 \geq AL_1 = 6$ mg/ℓ)

$$f_1 = q_1 = \bar{q}_1 - [d^c_{12} \, L^c_1 \, (x_1 - 0.3) + d^n_{12} \, L^n_1 \, (w_1 - 0.3)]$$

$$= 4.75 + (5.68 * 10^{-5}) \, (4.0 * 10^4) \, (x_1 - 0.3)$$

$$(\because d^n_{12} = 0)$$

Objective 2: DO level at Robin State Park ($f_2 \geq AL_2 = 6$ mg/ℓ):

$$f_2 = q_2 = 2.0 + (1.31 * 10^{-5})\ (4.0 * 10^4)\ (x_1 - 0.3)$$
$$+ (2.18 * 10^{-5})\ (1.28 * 10^5)\ (x_2 - 0.3)$$
$$+ (3.15 * 10^{-5})\ (2.8 * 10^4)\ (w_1 - 0.3)$$
$$+ (5.53 * 10^{-5})\ (4.8 * 10^4)\ (w_2 - 0.3)$$

Objective 3: DO level at Plympton ($f_3 \geq AL_3 = 6$ mg/ℓ):

$$f_3 = q_3 = 5.1 + (0.442 * 10^{-5})\ (4.0 * 10^4)\ (x_1 - 0.3)$$
$$+ (0.764 * 10^{-5})\ (1.28 * 10^5)\ (x_2 - 0.3)$$
$$+ (0.771 * 10^{-5})\ (2.8 * 10^4)\ (w_1 - 0.3)$$
$$+ (1.60 * 10^{-5})\ (4.8 * 10^4)\ (w_2 - 0.3)$$

Objective 4: percentage return on equity at Pierce-Hall Cannery ($f_4 \geq AL_4 = 6.5\%$):

$$f_4 = r = \frac{10^2}{5 * 10^6} [(3.75 * 10^5) - 0.6 (\frac{59}{1.09 - x_1^2} - 59) * 10^3]$$

Objective 5: addition to the tax rate at Bowville ($f_5 \leq AL_5 = 1.5$)

$$f_5 = \Delta t_2 = (2.4 * 10^{-3})\ (0.75)\ (\frac{532}{1.09 - x_2^2} - 532)$$

Objective 6: addition to the tax rate at Plympton ($f_6 \leq AL_6 = 1.5$):

$$f_6 = \Delta t_3 = (3.33 * 10^{-3})\ (0.75)\ (\frac{450}{1.09 - x_3^2} - 450)$$

Constraint: DO level at the state line ($q_4 \geq 3.5$ mg/ℓ):

$$q_4 = 1.0 + (8.3 * 10^{-7})\ (4.0 * 10^4)\ (x_1 - 0.3) + (1.45 * 10^{-7})$$

$$(1.28 * 10^5)\ (x_2 - 0.3) + (3.49 * 10^{-5})\ (9.57 * 10^4)$$

$$(x_3 - 0.3) + (7.3 * 10^{-7})\ (2.8 * 10^4)\ (w_1 - 0.3)$$

$$+ (1.62 * 10^{-6})\ (4.8 * 10^4)\ (w_2 - 0.3)$$

$$+ (7.33 * 10^{-5})\ (3.57 * 10^4)\ (w_3 - 0.3) \geq 3.5$$

Bounds: $0.3 \leq x_i \leq 1.0, \quad i = 1,2,3$

$$w_i = \frac{0.39}{1.39 - x_i^2}, \quad i = 1,2,3$$

The problem is summarized as follows: it is to determine $x_1$, $x_2$, and $x_3$ so as to satisfy the following objectives, constraints and goals. The six objectives are:

$$f_1 = 4.75 + 2.27\ (x_1 - 0.3) \qquad \text{(in mg/ℓ DO)}$$

$$f_2 = 2.0 + 0.524(x_1-0.3) + 2.79(x_2-0.3)$$

$$+ 0.882(w_1-0.3) + 2.65(w_2-0.3) \qquad \text{(in mg/ℓ DO)}$$

$$f_3 = 5.1 + 0.177\ (x_1 - 0.3) + 0.978\ (x_2-0.3)$$

$$+ 0.216\ (w_1-0.3) + 0.768\ (w_2 - 0.3) \qquad \text{(in mg/ℓ DO)}$$

$$f_4 = 7.5 - 0.012\left(\frac{59}{1.09 - x_1^2} - 59\right) \quad \text{(in \% earning)}$$

$$f_5 = 1.80 * 10^{-3}\left(\frac{532}{1.09 - x_2^2} - 532\right) \quad \text{(in \% additional tax rate)}$$

$$f_6 = 2.50 * 10^{-3}\left(\frac{450}{1.09 - x_3^2} - 450\right) \quad \text{(in \% additional tax rate)}$$

$$\text{s.t. } g_1 = 1.0 + 0.0332(x_1 - 0.3) + 0.0186(x_2 - 0.3)$$

$$+ 3.34(x_3 - 0.3) + 0.0204(w_1 - 0.3)$$

$$+ 0.778(w_2 - 0.3) + 2.62(w_3 - 0.3) \geq 3.5$$

$$0.3 \leq x_i \leq 1.0, \qquad i = 1, 2, 3$$

Let the above constraints be denoted by $\underline{x} \varepsilon X$.

$w_i$ is related to $x_i$ by:

$$w_i = \frac{0.39}{1.39 - x_i^2}, \qquad i = 1, 2, 3$$

The relevant range for each objective is:

$$0 \leq f_i \leq 8.5, \text{ i.e., } f_{iL} = 0,\ f_{iU} = 8.5, \quad i = 1, 2, 3$$

$$0 \leq f_4 \leq 7.5$$

$$0 \leq f_5 \leq 10$$

$$0 \leq f_6 \leq 12$$

The six goals are:

$$f_i \geq 6.0, \qquad i = 1, 2, 3$$

$$f_4 \geq 6.5$$

$$f_5 \leq 1.5$$

$$f_6 \leq 1.5$$

The initial aspiration levels of the DM are the same as the goals, that is,

$$AL_i = 6.0, \qquad i = 1, 2, 3$$

$AL_4 = 6.5$

$AL_5 = 1.5$

$AL_6 = 1.5$

The objectives and the corresponding dimensionless indicator of attainment, $\underline{d}$, are:

$$f_i \geq AL_i; \quad d_i = \frac{AL_i}{f_i(\underline{x})}, \qquad i = 1, 2, 3, 4$$

$$f_i \leq AL_i; \quad d_i = \frac{f_i(\underline{x})}{AL_i}, \qquad i = 5, 6$$

Cycle No. 1:

The principal problem is:

$$\min \quad s_1 = \sum_{t=1}^{6} d_t$$

$$\text{s.t.} \quad \underline{x} \in X$$

The six auxiliary problems, $\ell = 1, 2, \ldots, 6$ are:

$$\left.\begin{array}{ll} \min & s_{1\ell} = \sum\limits_{\substack{t=1 \\ t\neq\ell}}^{6} d_t \\ \text{s.t.} & \underline{x} \in X \\ & f_\ell(\underline{x}) \geq AL_\ell \qquad (\text{if } \ell = 1,2,3, \text{ or } 4) \\ \text{or} & \\ & f_\ell(\underline{x}) \leq AL_\ell \qquad (\text{if } \ell = 5 \text{ or } 6) \end{array}\right\}$$

The vector of the initial aspiration levels is:

$\underline{AL} = (6.0, 6.0, 6.0, 6.5, 1.5, 1.5).$

The above problems are nonlinear programming problems. Any nonlinear programming methods (e.g. SUMT, GRG) can be used to obtain solutions.

Here, we use the iterative nonlinear goal programming (INGP) approach (see Sec. 2.2.2b). The results of these optimizations are presented in Table 3.14. On examination of these numbers it is apparent that the change in the tax rate of the sixth objective $f_6$ is relatively independent of attainment or non-attainment of the other goals because the necessary reduction in $BOD_c$ at Plympton is heavily influenced by the DO constraint at the state line. Therefore, it seems reasonable to choose an aspiration level for the sixth objective and enter it as a constraint.

The DM can assess the impact of such an action on the attainment of the other objectives by using Table 3.14. The results of the principal problem and the sixth auxiliary problem are:

| | $f_1$ | $f_2$ | $f_3$ | $f_4$ | $f_5$ | $f_6$ |
|---|---|---|---|---|---|---|
| Principal problem | 5.96 | 3.83 | 5.70 | 6.44 | 0.53 | 1.55 |
| The 6th auxiliary problem | 6.03 | 4.19 | 5.81 | 6.17 | 0.77 | 1.50 |

Table 3.14 Results of the first cycle for the Bow River Valley problem

$\underline{AL}$ = (6.0, 6.0, 6.0, 6.5, 1.5, 1.5)

| s | $\underline{x}$ | $\underline{d}$ | $\underline{f}$ |
|---|---|---|---|
| $s_1$ = 6.02 | (0.830, 0.668, 0.818) | (1.01, 1.57, 1.05, 1.01, 0.35, 1.03) | (5.96, 3.83, 5.70, 6.44, 0.53, 1.55) |
| $s_{1.1}$ = 5.01 | (0.853, 0.666, 0.816) | (1.00, 1.55, 1.05, 1.04, 0.35, 1.02) | ($\underline{6.00}$, 3.86, 5.70, 6.25, 0.52, 1.53) |
| $s_{1.2}$ = 7.36 | (0.926, 0.963, 0.797) | (0.97, 1.00, 0.94, 1.26, 3.29, 0.90) | (6.17, $\underline{6.00}$, 6.37, 5.17, 4.93, 1.35) |
| $s_{1.3}$ = 6.21 | (0.963, 0.894, 0.797) | (0.96, 1.10, 0.97, 1.69, 1.56, 0.90) | (6.25, 5.44, $\underline{6.19}$, 3.85, 2.34, 1.35) |
| $s_{1.4}$ = 5.02 | (0.824, 0.667, 0.815) | (1.01, 1.57, 1.05, 1.00, 0.35, 0.99) | (5.94, 3.82, 5.69, $\underline{6.50}$, 0.53, 1.49) |
| $s_{1.5}$ = 5.66 | (0.762, 0.793, 0.847) | (1.03, 1.38, 1.02, 0.95, 0.75, 1.26) | (5.80, 4.34, 5.87, 6.82, $\underline{1.12}$, 1.90) |
| $s_{1.6}$ = 5.03 | (0.862, 0.732, 0.813) | (0.99, 1.43, 1.03, 1.05, 0.51, 1.00) | (6.03, 4.19, 5.81, 6.17, 0.77, $\underline{1.50}$) |

The new aspiration level for $f_6$ on the next cycle is assumed to be $A_6'$. Let $\alpha$ be the proportion:

$$\alpha = \frac{A_6' - 1.50}{1.55 - 1.50}$$

Adding the sixth objective as the constraint, the estimated objectives for the principal problem of the next cycle are:

$$f_1 = \alpha(5.96 - 6.03) + 6.03$$

$$f_2 = \alpha(3.83 - 4.19) + 4.19$$

$$f_3 = \alpha(5.70 - 5.81) + 5.81$$

$$f_4 = \alpha(6.44 - 6.17) + 6.17$$

$$f_5 = \alpha(0.53 - 0.77) + 0.77$$

The DM can try out values of $A_6'$ until the estimated objectives are acceptable. Finally the DM sets a new aspiration level of 1.55 for the sixth objective, and estimates the other objectives for the principal problem of the next cycle as follows:

| $f_1$ | $f_2$ | $f_3$ | $f_4$ | $f_5$ |
|---|---|---|---|---|
| 5.96 | 3.83 | 5.70 | 6.44 | 0.53 |

where $f_1$,$f_2$,$f_3$ are DO concentrations in milligrams per liter, $f_4$ is the percent return on investment, and $f_5$ is the increase in the tax rate in dollars per $1000 of assessed valuation. The DM argues that the increase to 1.55 is not greatly different from the original goal of 1.5.

Cycle No. 2:

The principal problem is:

$$\min \quad s_{2.6} = \sum_{t=1}^{5} d_t$$

$$\text{s.t.} \quad \underline{x} \in X$$

$$f_6(\underline{x}) \leq 1.55$$

The five auxiliary problems, $\ell = 1,2, \ldots, 5$ are:

$$\min \quad s_{2.6\ell} = \sum_{\substack{t=1 \\ t \neq \ell}}^{5} d_t$$

$$\text{s.t.} \quad \underline{x} \in X$$

$$f_6(\underline{x}) \leq 1.55$$

$$f_\ell(\underline{x}) \geq AL_\ell \quad (\text{if } \ell = 1,2,3 \text{ or } 4)$$

or

$$f_\ell(\underline{x}) < AL_\ell \quad (\text{if } \ell = 5)$$

The vector of the aspiration levels is:

$$\underline{AL} = (6.0,\ 6.0,\ 6.0,\ 6.5,\ 1.5,\ \underline{1.55})$$

The problems are again solved by the INGP method. The results are shown in Table 3.15. On observation of these results it is apparent that values for $f_2$ (4.19, 4.19, 6.10, 4.77, 3.85, 4.67) are significantly lower than the DM's aspiration level of 6.0 mg/$\ell$, except in the case of Auxiliary Problem 2 which has $f_2 \geq 6.0$ as the constraint of the problem. From the results of Auxiliary problem 2, it is apparent that the tax rate at Bowville, $f_5$ = 6.65,

Table 3.15 Results of the second cycle for the Bow River Valley problem

$\underline{AL} = (6.0, 6.0, 6.0, 6.5, 1.5, \underline{1.55})$

| s | $\underline{x}$ | $\underline{d}$ | $\underline{f}$ |
|---|---|---|---|
| $s_{2.6} = 5.03$ | (0.862, 0.732, 0.813) | (1.00, 1.43, 1.03, 1.05, 0.51, 0.97) | (6.03, 4.19, 5.81, 6.17, 0.77, 1.50) |
| $s_{2.61} = 4.04$ | (0.862, 0.732, 0.813) | (1.00, 1.43, 1.03, 1.05, 0.51, 0.97) | ($\underline{6.03}$, 4.19, 5.81, 6.17, 0.77, 1.50) |
| $s_{2.62} = 7.42$ | (0.862, 0.982, 0.813) | (1.00, 0.98, 0.94, 1.05, 4.43, 0.97) | (6.03, $\underline{6.10}$, 6.40, 6.17, 6.65, 1.50) |
| $s_{2.63} = 4.39$ | (0.795, 0.855, 0.817) | (1.02, 1.26, 1.00, 0.98, 1.14, 0.99) | (5.87, 4.77, $\underline{6.00}$, 6.66, 1.71, 1.54) |
| $s_{2.64} = 3.99$ | (0.821, 0.675, 0.817) | (1.01, 1.56, 1.05, 1.00, 0.37, 0.99) | (5.94, 3.85, 5.70, $\underline{6.50}$, 0.55, 1.54) |
| $s_{2.65} = 4.29$ | (0.807, 0.837, 0.817) | (1.02, 1.29, 1.01, 0.99, 1.00, 0.99) | (5.80, 4.67, 5.97, 6.60, $\underline{1.50}$, 1.54) |

is going to be affected drastically if a DO level of $f_2 \geq 6$ mg/ℓ is set. The state standards (a slight modification of the Massachusetts standards) indicate that water with â 5 mg/ℓ DO concentration is suitable for recreational purposes (including water contact sports), provides an excellent fish and wildlife habitat, and is esthetically pleasing [88a]. Therefore, the DM agrees to set the aspiration level of the second objective as 5.0 mg/ℓ and enter it as a constraint in the next cycle. Table 3.15 enables the DM to project the effect of satisfying objective 2 at a level of 5 mg/ℓ in the same manner as in the previous cycle.

Cycle No. 3:

The principal problem is:

$$\min \quad s_{3.62} = \sum_{\substack{t=1 \\ t\neq 2}}^{5} d_t$$

$$\text{s.t.} \quad \underline{x} \in X$$

$$f_6(\underline{x}) \leq 1.55$$

$$f_2(\underline{x}) \geq 5.0$$

The four auxiliary problems, $\ell = 1,3,4,5$ are:

$$\min \quad s_{3.62\ell} = \sum_{\substack{t=1 \\ t\neq 2 \\ t\neq \ell}}^{5} d_t$$

$$\text{s.t.} \quad \underline{x} \in X$$

$$f_6(\underline{x}) \leq 1.55$$

$$f_2(\underline{x}) \geq 5.0$$

$$f_\ell(\underline{x}) \geq AL_\ell \quad (\text{if } \ell = 1,3,4)$$

or

$$f_\ell(\underline{x}) \leq AL_\ell \quad (\text{if } \ell = 5)$$

The vector of the aspiration level is:

$$\underline{AL} = (6.0, \underline{5.0}, 6.0, 6.5, 1.5, \underline{1.55})$$

The results of the third cycle are contained in Table 3.16. They indicate that the values of $f_4$ are quite low except for Auxiliary Problem 3 which set $f_4 \geq 6.50$ as its constraint. The continued economic existence of the Pierce-Hall Cannery is important to the welfare of the whole valley and particularly to Bowville, since the entire work force of 800 people lives in Bowville. The DM recognizes this situation and decides that a firm bound on the cannery's investment return must be entered as a constraint. The examination of Table 3.16 enables the DM to adopt 6.0% as an acceptable level of return. This constraint is added to the principal problem for the next cycle (Cycle No. 4).

<u>Cycle No. 4</u>:

The vector of the aspiration level for this cycle is:

$$\underline{AL} = (6.0, \underline{5.0}, 6.0, \underline{6.0}, 1.5, \underline{1.55})$$

The results of cycle No. 4 are presented in Table 3.17. On examination of these results, the DM is informed by the results of Auxiliary problem 3 that it forms an inconsistent constraint set ($f_2 \geq 5.0$, and $f_5 \leq 1.5$ are violated). The DM finds that the aspiration of objective 5, $AL_5$, needs to be modified, or the previously fixed aspirations ($AL_2 = 5.0$, $AL_4 = 6.0$, $AL_6 = 1.55$) should be revised. Fortunately, raising $AL_5$ is not logically at odds with the development up to this point.

Table 3.16 Results of the third cycle for the Bow River Valley problem

$\underline{AL} = (6.0, \underline{5.0}, 6.0, 6.5, 1.5, \underline{1.55})$

| s | $\underline{x}$ | $\underline{d}$ | $\underline{f}$ |
|---|---|---|---|
| $s_{3.62} = 4.58$ | (0.961, 0.835, 0.808) | (0.96, 1.00, 0.99, 1.65, 0.99, 0.94) | (6.25, 5.01, 6.06, 3.94, 1.48, 1.45) |
| $s_{3.621} = 3.34$ | (0.855, 0.873, 0.818) | (1.00, 1.00, 0.99, 1.04, 1.31, 1.00) | ($\underline{6.01}$, 5.00, 6.07, 6.23, 1.96, 1.55) |
| $s_{3.623} = 3.35$ | (0.898, 0.866, 0.811) | (0.98, 0.99, 0.99, 1.14, 1.23, 0.95) | (6.11, 5.03, $\underline{6.08}$, 5.72, 1.85, 1.47) |
| $s_{3,624} = 3.46$ | (0.819, 0.887, 0.813) | (1.01, 0.99, 0.99, 1.00, 1.46, 0.97) | (5.93, 5.04, 6.08, $\underline{6.52}$, 2.19, 1.50) |
| $s_{3.625} = 3.50$ | (0.956, 0.836, 0.811) | (0.96, 1.00, 0.99, 1.55, 1.00, 0.95) | (6.24, 5.00, 6.06, 4.19, $\underline{1.49}$, 1.48) |

Table 3.17 Results of the fourth cycle for the Bow River Valley problem

$\underline{AL} = (6.0, \underline{5.0}, 6.0, \underline{6.0}, 1.5, \underline{1.55})$

| s | $\underline{x}$ | $\underline{d}$ | $\underline{f}$ |
|---|---|---|---|
| $s_{4.624} = 3.23$ | (0.877, 0.867, 0.818) | (0.99, 1.00, 0.99, 1.00, 1.25, 1.00) | (6.06, 5.00, 6.07, 6.00, 1.88, 1.55) |
| $s_{4.6241} = 2.24$ | (0.877, 0.867, 0.816) | (0.99, 1.00, 0.99, 1.00, 1.25, 0.99) | ($\underline{6.06}$, 5.00, 6.07, 6.00, 1.88, 1.53) |
| $s_{4.6243} = 2.78$ | (0.870, 0.909, 0.809) | (0.99, 0.94, 0.97, 0.99, 1.79, 0.94) | (6.04, 5.32, $\underline{6.17}$, 6.09, 2.68, 1.46) |
| $s_{4.6245} = 1.99$ | (0.877, 0.837, 0.809) | (0.99, 1.04, 1.00, 1.00, 1.00, 0.94) | (6.06, $\underline{4.80}$, 6.00, 6.00, $\underline{1.51}$, 1.46) (infeasible solution) |

Noting that Bowville already has an advantage over Plympton in the realm of tax rates, the DM decides to modify the aspirations regarding $f_5$. Examining the results of Table 3.17 on the values of $f_5$ (1.88, 1.88, 2.68, 1.51), the DM decides to raise $AL_5$ to be 1.95 and enter into the next cycle.

Cycle No. 5:

The results of this cycle are shown in Table 3.18. From this information the DM decides that all three solutions are the same and are satisfactory. The DM's policy decision is to impose waste reduction requirements of 88% on the cannery, 87% on Bowville, and 81% on Plympton. The values of objective functions are $\underline{f}$ = (6.06, 5.04, 6.08, 6.00, 1.95, 1.46).

Note

The upper and lower bounds on the objective function values should be carefully selected because they are given in information void.

Unless mathematical simplification are made (as shown in [238a]), this method may convert a linear problem into a nonlinear problem.

The computer program given in Monarchi [247] needs too much computer time to solve a moderate size linear problem. For the numerical example with 104 variables, 80 constraints and 4 objectives, it needs more than 10 minutes of CPU time in an IBM 370/158 to give a solution for just the principal problem in the first cycle.

A very undesirable aspect of this approach is the possibility of finding inconsistent constraint sets when solving auxiliary problems. In such a situation, the determination of a consistent set of aspiration levels becomes random and unsystematic.

Table 3.18 Results of the fifth cycle for the Bow River Valley problem

$\underline{AL} = (6.0, \underline{5.0}, 6.0, \underline{6.0}, \underline{1.95}, \underline{1.55})$

| s | $\underline{x}$ | $\underline{d}$ | $\underline{f}$ |
|---|---|---|---|
| $s_{5.6425} = 1.98$ | (0.877), 0.872, 0.809) | (0.99, 0.99, 0.99, 1.00, 1.00, 0.94) | (6.06, 5.04, 6.08, 6.00, 1.95, 1.46) |
| $s_{5.64251} = 0.99$ | (0.877, 0.872, 0.809) | (0.99, 0.99, 0.99, 1.00, 1.00, 0.94) | ($\underline{6.06}$, 5.04, 6.08, 6.00, 1.95, 1.46) |
| $s_{5,64253} = 0.99$ | (0.877, 0.872, 0.809) | (0.99, 0.99, 0.99, 1.00, 1.00, 0.94) | (6.06, 5.04, $\underline{6.08}$ 6.00, 1.95 1.46) |

It is possible to get a dominated solution when solving the auxiliary problem if the aspirations are set in such a way that one or more of them become nonconflicting.

The advantages of SEMOPS are: (1) it can be used to solve nonlinear problems; (2) the DM can reevaluate the desirable achievement levels at each cycle of calculation for the objectives.

The Sequential Information Generator for Multiple Objective Problems (SIGMOP) proposed by Monarchi, Weber, and Duekstein [249] enbeds a nonlinear goal programming approach within the principal problem and the set of auxiliary problems of the optimization phase to replace the surrogate objective functions in SEMOPS.

### 3.2.3 METHOD OF THE DISPLACED IDEAL

This method, proposed by Zeleny [BM22, 378-380], is for multiple objective linear programming (MOLP) problems. In MOLP problems, finding the set of nondominated solutions can be considered the second step of any decision making methodology. Such a solution set could, however, be too large to allow the DM to choose the final solution easily; the method of displaced ideal helps reduce this set. Several complementary ways of reducing the nondominated set (N) are described in [BM22]. We first summarize their main features and describe the $L_p$-metric method. We then illustrate the method by a numerical example.

<u>Methods to reduce the nondominated set N.</u>

The set of nondominated solutions, N or the nondominated extreme points $N_{ex}$ can be generated by any of the MOLP algorithms (see Sec. 4.1.3. MOLP Methods). Zeleny suggests the following five methods for reducing N to a compromise set $C^i$:

(i) If the decision maker can express reliably a strict preference between any two elements of N, then the "unpreferred" solution can be removed.

(ii) In the framework of linear programming the decomposition of the parametric space of weights is available. Fuzzy assessment of possible weight intervals then leads to reduction of N.

(iii) We can transform outcomes into degrees of closeness to the ideal solution with respect to a single criterion and then retain only those solutions with the degree of closeness with respect to all criteria exceeding predetermined aspiration level.

(iv) Find a compromise set C which is the subset of N of all solutions closest to the ideal solution with respect to one or more $L_p$- metric.

(v) Using the entropy measure of importance we can discard those criteria which manifest low contrast intensity and therefore receive low weight of importance. Corresponding decrease in the number of criteria considered could lead to the reduction of N.

An algorithm for the method of displaced ideal.

The net result of discarding some elements of N using any of the above approaches is the corresponding displacement of the ideal point. The basic steps in the solution algorithm are:

Step 1. Generate the set of nondominated solutions by using any of the MOLP algorithms (See Sec. 4.1.3). Let this set be N. Step 2. Obtain the ideal solutions by solving (3.1). Step 3. Find a compromise set $C^i$ which is the subset of N of all solutions closest to the ideal point by some criteria. Step 4. Is $C^i$ small enough so that the DM can choose a satisfactory solution? If yes, stop; otherwise, define a new ideal solution and go back to Step 3.

The method of displaced ideal for two objectives is illustrated in Fig. 3.22. The nondominated solutions of the problem are represented by $N = C^o$ (the point set between point A and point B of upper northeast part). The initial ideal solution is $\underline{f}(\underline{x}^*)$, which is not a feasible solution, i.e.,$\underline{x}^* \notin X$. Applying some criteria (which will be presented later), the set of nondominated solutions is reduced by eliminating some obviously bad solutions. The successive compromise sets are represented by $C^1$ and $C^2$. The path of displacement of ideal solutions is also indicated.

The use of $L_p$- metric method for determining the compromise set $C^i$ in Step 3 of the algorithm is:

Let $f_j(\underline{x}^*) = f_j^*$, j = 1,2, ..., k be the ideal solutions of (3.1).

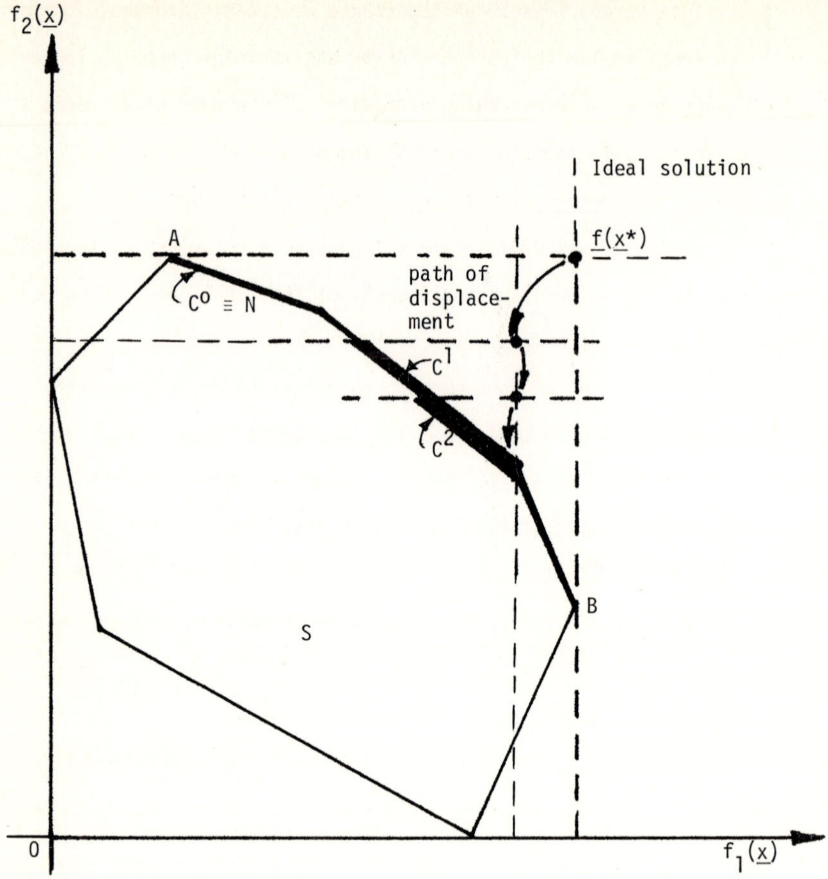


Fig. 3.22. Illustration of the method of the displaced ideal for two objectives [378].

Then $\underline{f}^* = (f_1^*, f_2^*, \ldots, f_k^*)$ can be defined as the ideal point. If there existed $\underline{x}^* \in X$ such that $\underline{f}(\underline{x}^*) = \underline{f}^*$, then such solution $\underline{x}^*$ would be the optimal solution, and there would be no decision problem. But such an ideal solution is generally infeasible; $\underline{x}^* \notin X$. The DM is trying to find a solution which would be as close as possible to the ideal point.

Let the degree of closeness of an $\underline{x}^i \in N$ to $\underline{x}^*$ with respect to objective j be designated as $d_j(\underline{x}^i)$, which has the properties:

$$d_j(\underline{x}^i) = 1 \text{ if } f_j(\underline{x}^i) = f_j^*;\ 0 \leq d_j(\underline{x}^i) \leq 1,\ j = 1, 2, \ldots, k,$$
$$i = 1, 2, \ldots, \ell$$

That is, for $\underline{x}^i = \underline{x}^*$ we have $d_j(\underline{x}^i) = 1$, the highest degree of closeness. As the difference $f_j^* - f_j(\underline{x}^i)$ increases for different $\underline{x}^i \in N$, the corresponding $d_j(\underline{x}^i)$ decrease toward zero. The assignment of $d_j(\underline{x}^i)$ can be given by

$$d_j(\underline{x}^i) = \frac{f_j(\underline{x}^i) - f_{jL}}{f_j^* - f_{jL}} \qquad (3.65a)$$

where $f_{jL}$ is $\min_{i=1,2,\ldots,\ell} f_j(\underline{x}^i)$. Let us define the distance between $\underline{x}^i$ and $\underline{x}^*$ as:

$$\bar{d}_j(\underline{x}^i) = 1 - d_j(\underline{x}^i) \equiv \bar{d}_{ji} \qquad (3.65b)$$

and use a family of $L_p$ - metrics which provides a wide range of geometric measures of closeness possessing many desirable properties. They are defined as

$$L_p(\underline{x}^i) = \left[\sum_{j=1}^{k} (\bar{d}_{ji})^p\right]^{\frac{1}{p}}, \qquad 1 \leq p < \infty \qquad (3.65c)$$

where $(\bar{d}_{ji})^p$ indicates the pth exponent of $\bar{d}_{ji}$.

$$\text{If} \min_{\underline{x}^i \in X} L_p(\underline{x}^i) = S_p(\tilde{\underline{x}}^p)$$

then $\tilde{\underline{x}}^p \in X$ is called a compromise solution with respect to p, and its objectives are $\underline{f}(\tilde{\underline{x}}^p)$.

Since all objectives cannot be assumed to be of equal importance, a more general form of (3.65c) is:

$$L_p(\underline{\lambda}, \underline{x}^i) = [\sum_{j=1}^{k} (\lambda_j)^p (\bar{d}_{ji})^p]^{\frac{1}{p}}, \quad 1 \leq p < \infty \qquad (3.66)$$

The power 1/p can be disregarded in (3.66) for $1 \leq p < \infty$, since the solutions $\tilde{\underline{x}}^p$ would not be affected. The choice of p reflects the strength of our concern about making such deviation from the ideal solution as small as possible.

NUMERICAL EXAMPLE. (The Ace Electronic Inc. production planning)

The MOLP problem is to find $x_i$, i = 1, 2, 3, 4, so as to:

$$\begin{aligned}
\max \quad & f_1(\underline{x}) = 10x_1 + 30x_2 + 50x_3 + 100x_4 \\
\max \quad & f_2(\underline{x}) = x_1 + x_2 \\
\max \quad & f_3(\underline{x}) = x_1 + 4x_2 + 6x_3 + 2x_4 \\
\text{s.t.} \quad & g_1(\underline{x}) = 5x_1 + 3x_2 + 2x_3 \leq 240 \\
& g_2(\underline{x}) = 3x_3 + 8x_4 \leq 320 \\
& g_3(\underline{x}) = 2x_1 + 3x_2 + 4x_3 + 6x_4 \leq 180 \\
& x_1, x_2, x_3, x_4 \geq 0
\end{aligned}$$

Step 1. The nondominated extreme point solutions for the above problem are shown in Table 3.19 (see Sec. 4.1.3. for details of obtaining these).

Step 2. The ideal solutions for each of the objectives, $f_j^*$, j = 1, 2, 3 are also shown in Table 3.19.

Table 3.19. Nondominated solutions.

| $f_j$ \ $\underline{x}$ | $\underline{x}^1$ | $\underline{x}^2$ | $\underline{x}^3$ | $\underline{x}^4$ | $f_j^*$ | $f_{jL}$ |
|---|---|---|---|---|---|---|
| $f_1$ | 3000 | 1800 | 2250 | 1600 | 3000 | 1600 |
| $f_2$ | 0 | 60 | 0 | 66.67 | 66.67 | 0 |
| $f_3$ | 60 | 240 | 270 | 20.67 | 270 | 20.67 |

Table 3.20 $L_p$-metric for the nondominated solutions

| $\overline{d}_j$ \ $\underline{x}^i$ | $\underline{x}^1$ | $\underline{x}^2$ | $\underline{x}^3$ | $\underline{x}^4$ |
|---|---|---|---|---|
| $\overline{d}_1$ | 0 | 0.857 | 0.536 | 1 |
| $\overline{d}_2$ | 1 | 0.10 | 1 | 0 |
| $\overline{d}_3$ | 0.842 | 0.12 | 0 | 1 |
| $L_1$ | 1.842 | <u>1.077</u> | 1.536 | 1 |
| $L_2$ | 1.307 | <u>0.871</u> | 1.135 | 1.414 |
| $L_\infty$ | 1 | <u>0.857</u> | 1 | 1 |

Step 3. Assume all objectives are of equal importance. Using (3.65a), (3.65b) and (3.65c) the $L_p$-metric can be computed for each of the nondominated solutions as shown in Table 3.20. As an approximation, it is suggested [378] that p = 1, 2 and ∞ are sufficient to define the set C. Note that for p = ∞.

$$L_\infty = \max_j \{\bar{d}_j(\underline{x}^i)\}$$

Step 4. $C^1 = \{\underline{x}^2\}$. Since $C^1$ is small enough (only one solution in this case), we present this solution to the DM. If he/she is not satisfied with this solution, we ask the DM to redefine the ideal point and return to Step 3. In this example we assume that the DM is satisfied with $\underline{x}^2$.

Note

The method of the displaced ideal does not require any "hard information" from the DM. The final decision is reached by an interactive process concentrating on sequential identification of "bad" solutions. Thus the DM has the opportunity to learn the objectives, their weight of importance, and the impact of his/her intermediate decisions. All decisions which the DM cannot make, does not want to make or does not know how to make are postponed or entrusted to the model for if-then analysis. It allows the analysis of multiple noncommensurable objectives which may be complex,ill-defined, fuzzy or conflicting.

### 3.2.4 GPSTEM METHOD

Goal Programming Step Method (GPSTEM), proposed by Fichefet [109], is a link between GP (see Sec. 2.2.2) and STEM (see Sec. 3.2.1). It is for multiobjective linear programming (MOLP) problems. In GP approach the DM ignores the ideal solutions of objectives $f_i(\underline{x})$ when $\underline{x} \in X$. In STEM, the compromise solution in the first iteration may be very far from the DM's satisfactory levels (goals). GPSTEM eliminates these disadvantages. GPSTEM explores the nondominated solutions that give the objective functional values close to goal levels imposed by the DMs; it also provides an equilibrium solution resulting from a bimatrix game (nonzero, non-cooperative, two-person) which can be useful in the case of complete disagreement among the DMs.

The Algorithm

Step 0. Construction of a payoff table (matrix A):

Find the feasible ideal solutions of the LP problems of

$$\max f_j(x)$$

$$\text{s.t. } \underline{x} \in X$$

$$j = 1,2,\ldots,k$$

and construct a payoff matrix A (see Table 3.11 of STEM).

Step 1. Find the initial compromise solution:

Ask the DMs to provide their best satisfactory levels (goals), $b_j$, $j = 1,2,\ldots,k$, for their respective objectives[1]. Solve the following GP problem for an initial compromise solution $\underline{x}^o$.

$$\left.\begin{aligned} &\min \sum_{j=1}^{k} (d_j^- + d_j^+) \\ &\text{s.t. } \underline{x} \in X \\ &\qquad f_j(x) + d_j^- - d_j^+ = b_j, \quad j = 1,2,\ldots,k \\ &\qquad \underline{d}^-, \underline{d}^+ \geq 0, \quad d_j^- \cdot d_j^+ = 0 \quad \forall_j \end{aligned}\right\} \qquad (3.67)$$

The $d_j^-$ and $d_j^+$ variables in the achievement function may eventually be weighted. It is expected that $\underline{d}^+$ have zero values.

If $d_j^- > 0$ for at least one j, set $E = \phi$ and go to Step 2. If $d_j^- = 0$ for all j, go to Step 5 with $\underline{x}^e = \underline{x}^o$.

---

[1]It is assumed that each DM represents one objective of the multiple objective decision making (MODM) problem.

Step 2. Find the parametric solutions:

For each $j \in \{1,2,\ldots,k\} \setminus E$, solve the parametric LP problem ($\theta_j \geq o$)

$$\left.\begin{aligned}
&\min\ y_j = \sum_{i=1}^{k} d_i^- \\
&\text{s.t. } \underline{x} \in X \\
&\qquad f_i(\underline{x}) + d_i^- = b_i - \theta_j \delta_{ij}, \quad i = 1,2,\ldots,k \\
&\qquad \delta_{ij} = 0 \qquad \text{for } i \neq j \\
&\qquad \delta_{ij} = 1 \qquad \text{for } i = j \\
&\qquad d_i^- \geq 0 \quad \forall_i
\end{aligned}\right\} \qquad (3.68)$$

to find the smallest value of $\theta_j$ for which $y_j = 0$ and let $\theta_{jm}$ be this value. Save the intervals of variation of $\theta_j$, $[0, \theta_{j1}]$, $[\theta_{j2}, \theta_{j3}], \ldots, [\theta_{jm-1}, \theta_{jm}]$, the end-points of which imply changes of basis, and save also the corresponding simplex tables.

Set $\ell = 1$. Let $\underline{x}^{\ell}$ be the optimal solution of the above LP problems for $\theta_j = 0$. Also let $\tilde{\underline{x}}^j$ be the solution corresponding to $\theta_j = \theta_{jm}$.

Step 3. Obtain equilibrium points for bimatrix game:

Form the matrix B in which the element in the jth column and the ith row is $f_j(\tilde{\underline{x}}^i) = z_{ji}$(refer to the payoff table of STEM). Then determine an equilibrium of the bimatrix game (A,B), i.e., a pair of mixed strategies $(\underline{u}^*, \underline{v}^*)$ such that, for any other mixed strategies, $\underline{u}$ and $\underline{v}$,

$$\underline{u}^T A \underline{v}^* \leq (\underline{u}^*)^T A \underline{v}^*$$

$$(\underline{u}^*)^T B \underline{v} \leq (\underline{u}^*)^T B \underline{v}^*$$

This can be carried out by means of Lemke and Howson's algorithm (257a).

Step 4. Find an equilibrium efficient solution:

Solve the LP problem for an equilibrium efficient solution, $\underline{x}^e$:

$$\max \sum_{i=1}^{k} u_i^* f_i(\underline{x})$$

$$\text{s.t.} \quad \underline{x} \in X$$

Step 5. Decision phase:

Propose $\underline{x}^\ell$ and $\underline{x}^e$ to the DMs. If $\underline{x}^\ell$ is satisfactory, stop. If not, there are three possibilities:

(i) All $d_j^-$ corresponding to $\underline{x}^\ell$ are zero. Explore the nondominated solutions "close to" $\underline{x}^\ell$ by determining, for each j and with the help of parametric LP, the maximum possible value of $\bar{b}_j$ for which $d_j^-$ still remains zero. If all these maximum values are equal to their respective $b_j$, then the DMs have to adopt $\underline{x}^e$ as a compromise solution. If not, set $E = \phi$ and $\ell = 0$, replace each $b_j$ by its possible maximum value, and go to Step 2.

(ii) If $d_j^- > 0$ for at least one j and if a DM (let the DM be q) agrees to relax goal $b_q$, go to Step 6.

(iii) If $d_j^- > 0$ for at least one j, and if no DM agrees to relax the goal, then the DMs have to adopt $\underline{x}^e$ as a compromise solution.

Step 6. Propose the amount of relaxation:

Let $\Delta b_q > b_q - f_q(\underline{x}^\ell)$ be the amount of relaxation of $b_q$. Find the interval, $I = [\theta_{qm-1}, \theta_{qm}]$, such that $\Delta b_q \varepsilon I$. To find the basic compromise solution of the next iteration, $\underline{x}^{\ell+1}$, replace $b_q$ by $b_q - \Delta b_q$, $\ell$ by $\ell+1$, and set $E = \{q\}$. Go to Step 2.

NUMERICAL EXAMPLE (Production scheduling of the Hardee toy company).

The VMP problem is given by:

$$\max \quad f_1(\underline{x}) = 0.4x_1 + 0.3x_2$$

$$\max \quad f_2(\underline{x}) = x_1$$

$$\text{s.t.} \quad \left.\begin{array}{l} g_1(\underline{x}) = x_1 + x_2 \leq 400 \\ g_2(\underline{x}) = 2x_1 + x_2 \leq 500 \\ x_1, x_2 \geq 0 \end{array}\right\} \text{ Let these constraints be denoted by } \underline{x} \in X$$

Iteration No. 1:

Step 0. Construction of a payoff table (matrix A):

The ideal solutions of the two LP problems are obtained by solving the following:

$$\max_{\underline{x} \in X} \quad f_1(\underline{x}) = 0.4x_1 + 0.3x_2$$

and

$$\max_{\underline{x} \in X} \quad f_2(\underline{x}) = x_1$$

The payoff table, matrix A is:

$$A = \begin{bmatrix} 130 & 100 \\ 100 & 250 \end{bmatrix}$$

Step 1. Find the initial compromise solution:

The best satisfactory levels $\underline{b} = (120, 200)$ are provided by the DMs.

The following GP problem with the given $\underline{b}$ is solved by the simplex method.

$$\min \quad (d_1^- + d_1^+ + d_2^- + d_2^+)$$

$$\text{s.t.} \quad \underline{x} \in X$$

$$f_1(\underline{x}) + d_1^- - d_1^+ = 120$$

$$f_2(\underline{x}) + d_2^- - d_2^- = 200$$

$$\underline{d}^-, \underline{d}^+ \geq 0$$

The solution is: $\underline{x}^o = (200, 100)$, $d_1^- = 10$ and $d_1^+ = d_2^+ = d_2^- = 0$. Hence set $E=\phi$ and go to Step 2.

Step 2. Find the parametric solutions:

As $E=\phi$, j= 1, 2, and the following parametric LP problems are solved.

a) For j=1

$$\min \quad y_1 = d_1^- + d_2^-$$

$$\text{s.t.} \quad \underline{x} \in X$$

$$f_1(\underline{x}) + d_1^- = 120 - \theta_1$$

$$f_2(\underline{x}) + d_2^- = 200$$

$$d_1^-, d_2^- \geq 0$$

The solution of the above problem is:

| $\theta_1$ | $x_1$ | $x_2$ | $d_1^-$ | $d_2^-$ | $y_1$ |
|---|---|---|---|---|---|
| $0 \leq \theta_1 \leq 10$ | 200 | 100 | 0 | $10 - \theta_1$ | $10 - \theta_1$ |
| $10 \leq \theta_1 \leq 40$ | 200 | $\frac{1}{3}(400-10\theta_1)$ | 0 | 0 | 0 |

Hence $\theta_{1m} = 10$ is the smallest value of $\theta_1$ which yields $y_1 = 0$; and the intervals of variation of $\theta_1$ is $[\theta_{1m-1}, \theta_{1m}] = [0, 10]$.

b) For j=2

$$\min \quad y_2 = d_1^- + d_2^-$$

$$\text{s.t.} \quad \underline{x} \in X$$

$$f_1(\underline{x}) + d_1^- = 120$$

$$f_2(\underline{x}) + d_2^- = 200 - \theta_2$$

$$d_1^-, d_2^- \geq 0$$

The solution of the above problem is:

| $\theta_2$ | $x_1$ | $x_2$ | $d_1^-$ | $d_2^-$ | $y_2$ |
|---|---|---|---|---|---|
| $50 \leq \theta_2 \leq 200$ | $200 - \theta_2$ | $\frac{1}{3}(400 + 4\theta_2)$ | 0 | 0 | 0 |

Hence $\theta_{2m} = 50$ is the smallest value of $\theta_2$ which gives $y_2 = 0$. The intervals of variation of $\theta_2$ are $[\theta_{2m-1}, \theta_{2m}] = [0, 50]$. Set $\ell=1$. We have the first compromise solution $\underline{x}^1 = (200, 100)$ by letting $\theta_1 = 0$ in the parametric solutions of $\theta_1$, and have $\tilde{\underline{x}}^1 = (200, 100)$ and $\tilde{\underline{x}}^2 = (150, 200)$ by substituting $\theta_1 = \theta_{1m} = 10$ and $\theta_2 = \theta_{2m} = 50$ in their parametric solution sets, respectively.

Step 3. Obtain equilibrium points for bimatrix game:

Matrix B is formed with $\tilde{\underline{x}}^1$ and $\tilde{\underline{x}}^2$, whose element in the $j^{th}$ column and the $i^{th}$ row is $f_j(\tilde{\underline{x}}^i)$. The two matrices A and B are:

$$A = \begin{bmatrix} 130 & 100 \\ 100 & 250 \end{bmatrix}, \qquad B = \begin{bmatrix} 110 & 120 \\ 200 & 150 \end{bmatrix}.$$

The equilibrium points obtained by Lemke and Howson's algorithm is:

$$\underline{u}^* = (0.8333, \quad 0.1667)$$

$$\underline{v}^* = (0.8334, \quad 0.1666).$$

Step 4. Find an equilibrium efficient solution:

Solve the following LP problem for an equilibrium efficient solution, $x^e$.

$$\begin{aligned} \max \quad & 0.8333 f_1(\underline{x}) + 0.1667 f_2(\underline{x}) \\ \text{s.t.} \quad & \underline{x} \in X \end{aligned}$$

or

$$\begin{aligned} \max \quad & 0.5\, x_1 + 0.25\, x_2 \\ \text{s.t.} \quad & x_1 + x_2 \le 400 \\ & 2x_1 + x_2 \le 500 \\ & x_1, x_2 \ge 0 \end{aligned}$$

The equilibrium efficient solution obtained is a multiple solution, which is:

$$\underline{x}^e = \{x_1, x_2 \mid 2x_1 + x_2 = 500, \ 100 \leq x_1 \leq 250\}.$$

Step 5. Decision phase:

The solution of $\underline{x}^1 = (200, 100)$ and the equilibrium solution of $\underline{x}^e$ are proposed to the DM. The solution of $\underline{x}^1$ is not satisfactory and this solution has $d_1^- = 10$. The DM-2, who has $f_2$ objective, agrees to relax the goal (i.e., q=2); hence go to Step 6.

Step 6. Propose the amount of relaxation:

The amount of relaxation of $b_2$ is $\Delta b_2 > b_2 - f_2(\underline{x}^1) = 200 - 200 = 0$, and $\Delta b_2 \in I$ where $I = [\theta_{2m-1}, \theta_{2m}] = [0, 50]$. The DM-2 chooses $\Delta b_2 = 10$. Replace $b_2 = b_2 - \Delta b_2 = 200 - 10 = 190$.

Set $\ell = \ell + 1 = 2$, $E = \{2\}$ and go to Step 2.

Iteration No. 2:

Step 2. Find the parametric solutions

$$j \in \{1, 2\} \backslash \{2\} = \{1\}$$

$$\min \ y_1 = d_1^- + d_2^-$$

$$f_1(\underline{x}) + d_1^- = 120 - \theta_1$$

$$f_2(\underline{x}) + d_2^- = 190$$

$$\underline{x} \in X$$

$$d_1, d_2 \geq 0$$

The solution of the above parametric LP problem is:

| $\theta_1$ | $x_1$ | $x_2$ | $d_1^-$ | $d_2^-$ | $y_1$ |
|---|---|---|---|---|---|
| $0 \leq \theta_1 \leq 8$ | 190 | 120 | $8 - \theta_1$ | 0 | $8 - \theta_1$ |
| $8 \leq \theta_1 \leq 44$ | 190 | $\frac{1}{3}(440-10\theta_1)$ | 0 | 0 | 0 |

Hence $\theta_{1m} = 8$ is the smallest value of $\theta_1$ for which $y_1 = 0$; and the intervals of variation of $\theta_1$ are [0, 8]. The value of $\underline{x}^2$ is obtained by solving the following LP problem:

$$\min \quad y_1 = d_1^- + d_2^-$$

$$f_1(\underline{x}) + d_1^- = 120$$

$$f_2(\underline{x}) + d_2^- = 190$$

$$\underline{x} \in X, \quad d_1^-, d_2^- \geq 0$$

The solution is $\underline{x}^2 = (190, 120)$. The value of $\underline{\tilde{x}}^1$ is (190, 120) which is obtained by lettering $\theta_1 = \theta_{1m} = 8$ in the parametric solution of $\theta_1$.

Step 3. Obtain equilibrium points for bimatrix game:

Form matrix B with $\underline{\tilde{x}}^1 = (190, 120)$ and $\underline{\tilde{x}}^2 = (150, 200)$. The two matrices A and B are:

$$A = \begin{bmatrix} 130 & 100 \\ 100 & 250 \end{bmatrix} \qquad B = \begin{bmatrix} 112 & 120 \\ 190 & 150 \end{bmatrix}$$

The equilibrium points obtained are:

$\underline{u}^* = (0.8333, 0.1667)$

$\underline{v}^* = (0.8334, 0.1666)$

which are the same values obtained in Iteration No. 1.

Step 4. Find an equilibrium efficient solution:

The equilibrium efficient solution is the same as that of Iteration No. 1. That is, $\underline{x}^e = \{x_1, x_2 | \; 2x_1 + x_2 = 500, \; 100 \leq x_1 \leq 250\}$

Step 5. Decision phase:

After reviewing $\underline{x}^1 = (190, 120)$ with $\underline{x}^e$, the DMs agree to take $\underline{x}^2$ as the final solution. That is, $\underline{f} = (112, 190)$.

Note: GPSTEM has not yet been tested with large real MODM problems. The Lemke and Howson algorithm in Step 3 for obtaining the equilibrium points involves a complex procedure. In this method, the DMs can set their initial goals properly by using the ideal solutions obtained at Step 0., and can relax their satisfactory levels (goals) systematically by using the parametric solution sets. Hence GPSTEM may give a compromised solution within fewer iterations than STEM does.

### 3.2.5. METHOD OF STEUER (INTERACTIVE MOLP METHOD)

The method, proposed by Steuer [323,324], is an extension of the MOLP method (see Sec. 4.1.3). MOLP problems, even moderately sized ones, often have an unworkably large number of nondominated extreme points. Steuer's interactive MOLP method presents to the DM 2k+1 nondominated extreme points at each iteration (k is the number of objectives); the DM has only to indicate the most preferable solution from this set. Once this solution is identified, the nondominated extreme points in the neighborhood are explored and a new set of 2k+1 nondominated solutions are identified and presented to the DM.

The advantages of this interactive procedure are: (1) the DM does not have to specify any weights or relaxation quantities; (2) no mathematical sophistication is required on the part of the DM; (3) a small number of candidate solutions is presented to the DM at each iteration; (4) the procedure can be operated so as to have error correcting capabilities (on the part of DM in earlier iterations); (5) the procedure converges in a finite number of iterations. The analyst's mathematical tools include (i) linear programming; (ii) an (objective function) gradient cone construction technique; (iii) a vector-maximum algorithm; (iv) a device for filtering extreme point solutions. It is the analyst's responsibility to develop each iteration's cluster of solutions appropriately.

The MOLP problem of (3.54a) is to

$$\left.\begin{array}{ll} \max & [\underline{c}_1^T\underline{x}, \underline{c}_2^T\underline{x}, \ldots, \underline{c}_k^T\underline{x}] \\ \text{s.t.} & A\underline{x} \leq \underline{b} \\ & \underline{x} \geq \underline{0} \end{array}\right\} \tag{3.69}$$

Let $X = \{\underline{x} \in R^n \mid A\underline{x} \leq \underline{b}, \underline{x} \geq \underline{0}, \underline{b} \in R^m\}$. Then (3.69) can be reexpressed in vector-maximum form:

$$\overline{\text{eff}}\ \{C\underline{x} = \underline{z} \mid \underline{x} \in X\} \tag{3.69a}$$

where criterion matrix C is k x n. The notation $\overline{\text{eff}}$ signifies that the purpose of the problem is to find all efficient points (nondominated solutions). The nondominated solutions are of interest because the DM's optimal point is nondominated (efficient). The contemplated purpose of the interactive MOLP approach is to present to the DM a set of nondominated solutions from which to identify a preferred solution in each iteration which would subsequently lead to a set of nondominated solutions in the neighborhood of the preferred solution.

It is beneficial to look at VMP problems from a weighted-sum point of view (see 4.1.1. parametric method or weighting method). Problem (3.69a) is equivalent to solving the family of weighted-sum problems:

$$\{\max \quad [\underline{\lambda}^T C\underline{x} \mid \underline{x} \in X]: \ \underline{\lambda} \in \Lambda^1\}$$
$$\text{where } \Lambda^1 = \{\underline{\lambda} \in R^k \mid \lambda_i \in (0,1), \ \sum_{i=1}^{k} \lambda_i = 1\} \tag{3.70}$$

for all maximizing extreme points. By allowing the criterion weights to come from anywhere in the open unit interval — that is, assuming no information about the DM's preferences — the number of nondominated extreme point solutions to (3.70) becomes very large. Therefore, it is necessary to have partial information about the DM's preferences, expressed in terms of subsets of the unit interval for each of the $\lambda_i$. If we let $\ell_i$ and $\mu_i$ specify the subinterval lower and upper bounds on the ith criterion weight, the following family of weighted-sums problems results:

$$\{\max \quad [\underline{\lambda}^T C\underline{x} \mid \underline{x} \in X]: \ \underline{\lambda} \in \Lambda^2\}$$
$$\text{where } \Lambda^2 = \{\underline{\lambda} \in R^k \mid \lambda_i \in (\ell_i,\mu_i), \ \sum_{i=1}^{k} \lambda_i = 1\} \tag{3.71}$$

In its present form, (3.71) cannot be solved for all maximizing extreme points, but it can be translated into an equivalent VMP problem by examining the effects of the subinterval criterion weights upon the gradient cone.

Gradient Cone Analysis of Efficiency:

The concept of the gradient cone is applied to study the question of what makes so many extreme points efficient. The gradient cone is defined to be the convex cone generated by the gradients of the different objectives (i.e., by the k rows of C). The larger the gradient cone the larger the number of nondominated (efficient) extreme points, and the smaller the gradient cone the smaller the number of nondominated extreme points. The cause of this can be seen in the following Lemma:

Lemma Let $\underline{x}^o \in X$ and let M be an n x n diagonal matrix with

$$m_{jj} = \begin{cases} 1 & \text{if } x_j^o = 0 \\ 0 & \text{otherwise} \end{cases}$$

Then $\underline{x}^o$ is nondominated if and only if there exists $\underline{\lambda} \in R^k$, $\underline{y} \in R^n$, $\underline{w} \in R^m$ such that

$$\underline{\lambda}^T C = -\underline{y}^T M - \underline{w}^T A$$

where $\underline{\lambda} > 0$, $\underline{y} \geq 0$, $\underline{w}$ unrestricted.

It is assumed that the gradients of the original k objectives form a linearly independent set of n-vectors. This is because a set of linearly dependent original gradients would introduce complexities into the following analysis which have not yet been completely resolved.

By converting (3.71) to an equivalent VMP problem

$$\overline{\text{eff}}\ \{D\underline{x} = z_d \mid \underline{x} \in X\} \qquad (3.72)$$

an algorithm of the multicriteria simplex method (see Sec. 4.1.3 MOLP methods) can be used for solving the problem. Problem (3.72) is equivalent to (3.71) in the sense that each nondominated extreme solution of (3.72) is a maximizing extreme point of (3.71) and vice versa. In (3.72) the vertical dimension and the contents of the q x n "criterion" matrix D requires special calculation.

The motivation for constructing D is to isolate the subset of the gradient cone of (3.69a) associated with the pre-specified interval criterion weights. By considering the extreme rays (whose number is q) of the subset cone as gradients of the equivalent VMP problem (3.72), the rows of D are determined.

The extreme rays of the subset gradient cone are calculated in accordance with

$$\{\underline{d}^1, \ldots, \underline{d}^q\} = \{\underline{d} \in R^n \mid \underline{d} = \sum_{i=1}^{k} \lambda^*_{ji} c^{ji};\ \lambda^*_{ji} \in \{\ell_{ji}, \mu_{ji}\}$$
$$\text{for } 1 \leq i \leq k-1;\ \ell_{jk} \leq \lambda^*_{jk} = 1 - \sum_{i=1}^{k-1} \lambda^*_{ji} \leq \mu_{jk}\} \qquad (3.73)$$

where the double subscripts allow for all possible renumbering schemes. (3.73) first tests for the q sets of critical weights $\lambda_{ji}^*$ formed from the feasible endpoint combinations of all but one of the intervals at a time. Then by forming a convex combination of the original objectives with each set of critical weights, the q rows of D are specified.

As an example of the first stage of (3.73), consider the critical weights intervals

$$0.2 < \lambda_1 < 0.7,\ 0.3 < \lambda_2 < 0{,}6,\quad 0.1 < \lambda_3 < 0.4 \tag{3.74}$$

from which the q sets of critical weights will be determined. By testing the end point combinations of the first-second, first-third, and second-third criterion weight bounds, the following five sets of critical weights are found:

$$\begin{array}{ccc} & & \downarrow \\ \hline 0.2 & 0.3 & - \\ 0.2 & 0.6 & 0.2 \\ 0.7 & 0.3 & - \\ 0.7 & 0.6 & - \\ \hline \end{array}\ \begin{array}{c} \\ \\ 1 \\ \\ \\ \end{array} \qquad \begin{array}{ccc} & \downarrow & \\ \hline 0.2 & - & 0.1 \\ 0.2 & 0.4 & 0.4 \\ 0.7 & - & 0.1 \\ 0.7 & - & 0.4 \\ \hline \end{array}\ \begin{array}{c} \\ \\ 2 \\ \\ \\ \end{array} \qquad \begin{array}{ccc} \downarrow & & \\ \hline 0.6 & 0.3 & 0.1 \\ 0.3 & 0.3 & 0.4 \\ 0.3 & 0.6 & 0.1 \\ - & 0.6 & 0.4 \\ \hline \end{array}\ \begin{array}{c} \\ 3 \\ 4 \\ 5 \\ \\ \end{array} \tag{3.75}$$

Then by applying the sets of critical weights thus determined to the original objectives constructing D, (3.71) is ready for solution by means of an algorithm for the VMP problem. Thus the DM will receive only the cluster of nondominated extreme point solutions corresponding to his/her prespecified interval criterion weight bounds. For this example $q \geq k$ (where k is the number of original objectives). Since q rapidly increases above k as k increases, there is a computational need to reduce q which can be accomplished by the gradient cone modification technique.

Modification of Gradient Cone

A large gradient cone (in the same geometric proportions and orientation of the original gradient cone of (3.69a)) with only k defining extreme rays is used to enclose the contracted gradient cone defined by the given critical weights intervals and (3.73). Using these new gradients to form the rows of E, algorithms for the VMP problem can be used to solve

$$\overline{\text{eff}}\ \{E\underline{x} = z_e \mid \underline{x} \in X\} \tag{3.76}$$

instead of (3.72). Note that E is k x n.

The goal is to make the gradient cone generated by the k rows of E as small as possible while still containing the gradient cone generated by the q rows of D. It is expected that (3.76) generates a larger number of nondominated extreme point solutions than (3.72). Offsetting this should be possible reductions in computer execution time.

The procedure for calculation of E is as follows. First, consider the sets of critical weights used to construct the $d^j$ $(1 \leq j \leq q)$ in (3.73). Then corresponding to the ith $(1 \leq i \leq k)$ original objective, select the smallest critical weight and reset $\ell_i$ to this new value and $\mu_i$ to one. Finally, with the new set of updated lower and upper bounds, perform process (3.73) a second time. This will generate the k gradients used to form E.

The gradient cone modification technique will be illustrated by considering the interval criterion weights of (3.74). Scanning the first columns in (3.75) for the smallest critical weight, the new lower bound associated with the first objective is $\ell_1 = 0.2$; similarly scanning the second and third columns in (3.75) for the smallest criterial weights, the new $\ell_2$ and $\ell_3$ are $\ell_2 = 0.3$ and $\ell_3 = 0.1$, respectively. Now with the new intervals

$$0.2 < \lambda_1 < 1.0, \; 0.3 < \lambda_2 < 1.0, \quad 0.1 < \lambda_3 < 1.0 \tag{3.77}$$

procedure (3.73) produces the following tables:

| | | ↓ | |
|---|---|---|---|
| 0.2 | 0.1 | 0.7 | 1 |
| 0.2 | 1.0 | - | |
| 1.0 | 0.1 | - | |
| 1.0 | 1.0 | - | |

| | ↓ | | |
|---|---|---|---|
| 0.2 | 0.7 | 0.1 | 2 |
| 0.2 | - | 1.0 | |
| 1.0 | - | 0.1 | |
| 1.0 | - | 1.0 | |

| ↓ | | | |
|---|---|---|---|
| 0.6 | 0.3 | 0.1 | 3 |
| - | 0.3 | 1.0 | |
| - | 1.0 | 0.1 | |
| - | 1.0 | 1.0 | |

(3.78)

The three new sets of critical weights will generate E for problem (3.76).

<u>Trial Gradients of a Gradient Cone</u>

To produce a diversity of gradient cones over the current ones the 2k+1 convex combination trial gradients are employed. It is to obtain evenly dispersed extreme points over that portion of the surface of the feasible region defined as efficient with regard to the ith reduced gradient cone. By selecting one of these nondominated extreme points, that part of the nondominated solution surface is explored in more detail. In this way, the algorithm iteratively focuses in with greater powers of magnification on the corner points of the feasible region surrounding the nondominated extreme point of greatest utility.

The 2k+1 dispersed convex combination trial gradients are generated by the following sets of weights applied to the extreme ray gradients of the current reduced gradient cone:

$$\begin{aligned}
\underline{\lambda}^1 &= (1, 0, \ldots, 0) \\
\underline{\lambda}^2 &= (0, 1, \ldots, 0) \\
&\vdots \\
\underline{\lambda}^k &= (0, 0, \ldots, 1) \\
\underline{\lambda}^{k+1} &= (1/k^2, r, \ldots, r) \\
\underline{\lambda}^{k+2} &= (r, 1/k^2, \ldots, r) \\
&\vdots \\
\underline{\lambda}^{2k} &= (r, r, \ldots, 1/k^2) \\
\underline{\lambda}^{2k+1} &= (1/k, 1/k, \ldots, 1/k)
\end{aligned} \tag{3.79}$$

where $r = (k+1)/k^2$. In order to eliminate the possible generation of dominated extreme points by the first k weighting vectors of (3.79), the following vectors might be considered:

$\underline{\lambda}^j = (\varepsilon, \ldots, 1-(k-1)\varepsilon, \ldots, \varepsilon)$, $j \varepsilon 1, \ldots, k$, where $\varepsilon$ is a very small positive number. In situations where the coefficients of the different objective functions of (3.79) are out of scale, each of the objective function gradients should be normalized before using the convex combination weights of (3.79).

In (3.79), the first k weight vectors lead to the extreme rays of the current reduced cone; the next k weight vectors lead to the off-center internal points; and the last weight vector leads to the center point of the current gradient cone. As an illustration, consider $k = 3$; Fig. 3.23 depicts the location at which the trial gradient corresponding to the weighting vector $\underline{\lambda}^j$, $j = 1, 2, \ldots, 7$ penetrates a cut of the current reduced cone.

Each of the 2k+1 dispersed trail gradients leads to a single objective linear programming problem.

$$\max \quad \underline{\lambda}^{j^T} C\underline{x} \qquad (3.80)$$
$$\text{s.t.} \quad \underline{x} \in X$$

whose optimal solution is a nondominated extreme point solution of (3.69). From the set of 2k+1 nondominated extreme points generated, the DM is asked to select the most preferred solution. Around the trial gradient which produced the preferred extreme point, the gradient cone is contracted. The new reduced gradient cone is to be of the same geometric proportions and orientation as the previous reduced cone but of only 1/kth the cross sectional volume. This is to assure adequate overlap in the covering of the ith reduced gradient cone by the union of all possible (i+1)th reduced gradient cones. Note that over the course of the iterations, the sequence of reduced cones forms a series of nested subsets of the original gradient cone of (3.69a).

With reference to Fig. 3.23, if trial gradient 5 corresponded to the DM's preferred point, the next gradient cone would be contracted to one whose cut is indicated by the dashed lines in Fig. 3.24. If trial gradient 2 were selected by the DM, the new gradient cone would have the cut indicated by the dotted lines.

The new reduced gradient cone is computed from the current reduced gradient cone by using the set of interval criterion weights of Tables 3.21, 3.22, and 3.23 depending upon the particular trial gradient indicated by the selection of the most preferred point. When the selected trial gradient is an extreme ray of the current reduced gradient cone, Table 3.21 is used. Table 3.22 is for when the preferred gradient is one of the off-center interval trial gradients, and Table 3.23 is for when the preferred gradient is the center trial gradient. In these tables, $p = 1 - k^{-(1/(k-1))}$ and $h = k - 1$. The last term of p, $k^{-(1/(k-1))}$, is derived from

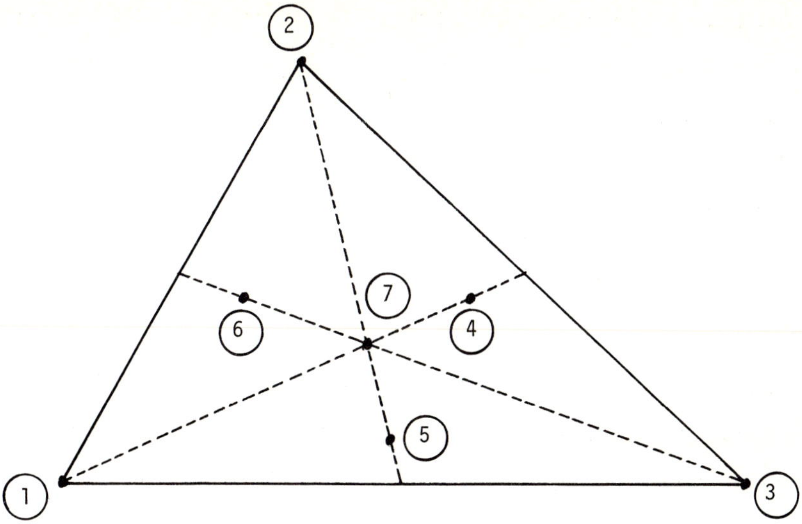


Fig. 3.23 Dispersion of convex combination trial gradients when k = 3.

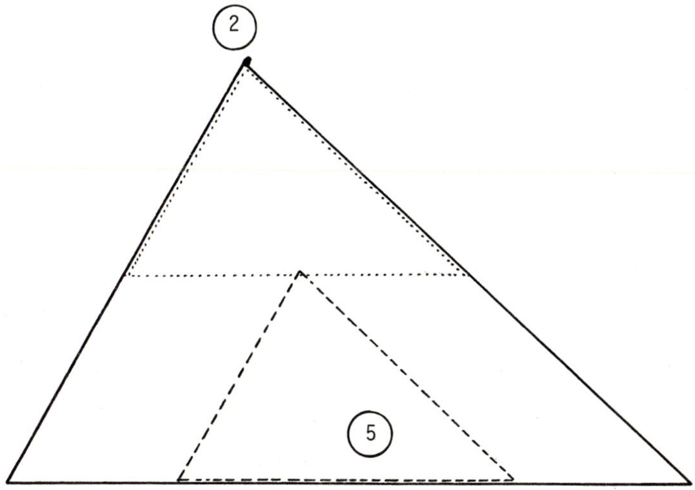


Fig. 3.24 Cuts of the new reduced gradient cone corresponding to trial gradients 2 and 5.

Table 3.21 Interval criterion weights $(\ell_i, \mu_i)$ for when preferred gradient is an extreme ray trial gradient

| i | Trial gradient | | | |
|---|---|---|---|---|
| | 1 | 2 | ... | k |
| 1 | (p,1) | (0,1) | | (0,1) |
| 2 | (0,1) | (p,1) | | (0,1) |
| ⋮ | ⋮ | ⋮ | | ⋮ |
| k | (0,1) | (0,1) | | (p,1) |

Table 3.22 Interval criterion weights $(\ell_i, \mu_i)$ for when preferred gradient is an off-center trial gradient

| i | Trial gradient | | |
|---|---|---|---|
| | k+1 | k+2 | 2k |
| 1 | (0,1) | (p/h,1) | (p/h,1) |
| 2 | (p/h,1) | (0,1) | (p/h,1) |
| ⋮ | | | |
| k | (p/h,1) | (p/h,1) | (0,1) |

Table 3.23 Interval criterion weights $(\ell_i, \mu_i)$ for when preferred gradient is center trial gradient

| i | Trial gradient |
|---|---|
| | 2k+1 |
| 1 | (p/k,1) |
| 2 | (p/k,1) |
| ⋮ | |
| k | (p/k,1) |

the relationship that the volume of a (k-1) dimensional simplicial solid (properly oriented) can be computed as a constant times the multiplication of its projections onto the coordinate axes. As an example, with k=4, a cut of the gradient cone will yield a 3-dimensional tetrahedron. The volume of a tetrahedron is given by one-third the area of the base, $A_b$, times its height a. With the area of $A_b$ given by $\frac{1}{2}$ bh, $V = \frac{1}{6}$ bha.

To proportionally reduce the size of the tetrahedron to $(1/k = \frac{1}{4})$th its volume, each dimension would have to be reduced by the proportionality factor v where

$$\frac{1}{6} \text{vbvhva} = \frac{1}{4} V \quad \text{or} \quad \frac{1}{6} v^3 \text{ bha} = \frac{1}{4} V$$

$$v = 4^{-1/3} = k^{-(1/(k-1))}$$

<u>The Interactive MOLP Procedure [323]</u>

The strategy of the proposed MOLP interactive procedure is to gradually contract and shift the gradient cone until it focuses (in the far side of the moon sense) upon a small portion of the surface of the feasible region containing the DM's nondominated extreme point of greatest utility. Step by step the procedure is as follows:

Step 1. Set i = 0.

Step 2. Is it desired to determine all extreme points efficient with respect to the current gradient cone?

- Step 2.1. If "yes" solve full vector-maximum problem associated with the original gradient cone, select most preferred nondominated extreme point, and then go to Step 11.
- Step 2.2. If "no" go to Step 3.

Step 3. Dispersed over the ith gradient cone, determine 2k+1 convex combination trial gradients.

Step 4. Maximize each of the 2k+1 convex combination trial gradients to yield 2k+1 associatedly dispersed nondominated extreme points.

Step 5. Select most preferred nondominated extreme point.

Step 6. Is it desired to terminate with present most preferred extreme point?

Step 6.1. If "yes" go to Step 11.

Step 6.2. If "no" go to Step 7.

Step 7. Is it desired to determine all extreme points efficient with respect to the ith gradient cone?

Step 7.1. If "yes" solve vector-maximum problem associated with ith gradient cone, select most preferred nondominated extreme point, and then go to Step 11.

Step 7.2. If "no" go to Step 8.

Step 8. Set i = i + 1.

Step 9. About the trial gradient generating the most preferred extreme point, construct the ith successively smaller gradient cone containing the trial gradient. The ith gradient cone is to be of the same relative proportions as the (i - 1)th gradient cone but of only 1/kth the cross-sectional volume.

Step 10. Go to Step 2.

Step 11. STOP.

NUMERICAL EXAMPLE (The nutrition problem)

For the nutrition problem (see Sec. 3.1.1 for problem statement), there exist 20 nondominated extreme point solutions as presented in Table 3.24. Generation of nondominated solutions for a VMP problem by the multicriteria simplex method is discussed in Sec. 4.1.3. Twenty nondominated solutions are more than one would normally prefer to see during decision making. The interactive MOLP algorithm generates only a subset of these efficient solutions for the DM.

Step 1. Set i=0.

Step 2. Assume that the determination of all nondominated extreme points is not desirable.

Table 3.24 Nondominated extreme points of the nutrition problem

| Extreme point number | Objective function values | | |
|---|---|---|---|
| | 1 | 2 | 3 |
| 1 | -3.88 | -74.1 | -168.3 |
| 2 | -3.31 | -94.4 | -151.8 |
| 3 | -3.56 | -63.7 | -207.4 |
| 4 | -3.95 | -96.7 | -150.0 |
| 5 | -3.19 | -100.4 | -152.2 |
| 6 | -2.52 | -70.0 | -245.0 |
| 7 | -2.80 | -55.5 | -263.2 |
| 8 | -2.93 | -39.9 | -305.2 |
| 9 | -2.50 | -79.0 | -234.0 |
| 10 | -2.56 | -64.2 | -256.1 |
| 11 | -2.41 | -70.3 | -253.2 |
| 12 | -2.78 | -28.8 | -356.9 |
| 13 | -2.36 | -72.9 | -253.5 |
| 14 | -2.26 | -67.8 | -281.7 |
| 15 | -2.82 | -23.0 | -389.0 |
| 16 | -2.94 | -17.9 | -412.0 |
| 17 | -2.53 | -24.7 | -404.5 |
| 18 | -2.30 | -71.5 | -264.7 |
| 19 | -2.54 | -23.8 | -409.5 |
| 20 | -2.56 | -23.0 | -413.1 |

Step 3. Dispersed over the original gradient cone, the 2k+1 = 7 convex combination trial gradient weighting vectors from (3.79) are

| $j$ | $\underline{\lambda}^j$ |
|---|---|
| 1 | (1, 0, 0) |
| 2 | (0, 1, 0) |
| 3 | (0, 0, 1) |
| 4 | (1/9, 4/9, 4/9) |
| 5 | (4/9, 1/9, 4/9) |
| 6 | (4/9, 4/9, 1/9) |
| 7 | (1/3, 1/3, 1/3) |

The first three weight vectors, representing the k extreme ray trial gradients, imply the maximization of each of the objectives separately, i.e., the ideal solutions of each objective.

Step 4. Maximize the seven trial objective linear programming problems formed by the above weight vectors. The resulting dispersed nondominated extreme points, in terms of the objective functions, would be

| extreme point number | $z_1$ | $z_2$ | $z_3$ |
|---|---|---|---|
| 14 | -2.26 | -67.8 | -281.7 |
| 16 | -2.94 | -17.9 | -412.0 |
| 4 | -3.95 | -96.6 | -150.0 |
| 1 | -3.89 | -74.1 | -168.3 |
| 4 | -3.95 | -96.6 | -150.0 |
| 8 | -2.93 | -39.9 | -305.2 |
| 1 | -3.89 | -74.1 | -168.3 |

Note that the above set contains only five extreme solutions. This indicates that a change in the weighting vector does not necessarily lead to a different extreme point. Recall that such behaviour was noted in Fig. 3.3.

Step 5. Assume that the DM has selected the efficient extreme point 8 as the most preferred among the five solutions generated. Note that this solution corresponds to the third off-center trial gradient.

Step 6 & 7. Assume that the selected efficient point is not the final desired solution and reduction of the gradient cone is desired.

Step 8. $i = i+1 = 1$.

Step 9. Since the preferred nondominated point (of Step 5) corresponds to the third off-center trial gradient, the interval criterion weights from Table 3.22 are:

$$(p/h,\ 1),\quad (p/h,\ 1),\quad \text{and } (0,\ 1)$$

respectively for the three objectives. Since k=3.

$$p = 1-k^{-(1/(k-1))} = 0.42265$$

$$h = k-1 = 2$$

$$p/h = 0.21$$

Thus,

$$0.21 \leq \lambda_1 \leq 1.0,\quad 0.21 \leq \lambda_2 \leq 1.0,\quad 0.0 \leq \lambda_3 \leq 1.0$$

The procedure of (3.73) results in the following three sets of critical weights:

$$(0.21,\ 0.21,\ 0.58)$$

$$(0.21,\ 0.00,\ 0.79)$$

$$(1.00,\ 0.00,\ 0.00)$$

Using these critical weights, the extreme ray gradients of the first gradient cone are:

$$\nabla_1 = (-16.06725,\ -20.32199,\ -25.368,\ -8.721,\ -0.64850,\ -30.21458)$$

$$\nabla_2 = (-19.00723,\ -21.79198,\ -0.168,\ -11.871,\ -0.8795,\ -41.13458)$$

$$\nabla_3 = (\ -0.225,\ -2.2,\ -0.8,\ -0.1,\ -0.05,\ -0.26)$$

Step 2. At this point let us assume that the DM does not wish to iterate further and requests an explosion for all extreme points efficient with regard to his first reduced gradient cone. The VMP problem to be solved is (3.76) where the rows of E are the gradients $\nabla_j$, j = 1, 2, 3. The resulting seven nondominated extreme points are:

| extreme point number | Objective function vector, $\underline{f}$ | | |
|---|---|---|---|
| 4 | -3.95 | -96.7 | -150.0 |
| 2 | -3.30 | -94.4 | -151.8 |
| 5 | -3.19 | -100.4 | -152.2 |
| 9 | -2.50 | -79.0 | -234.0 |
| 13 | -2.35 | -72.9 | -253.5 |
| 18 | -2.30 | -71.5 | -264.7 |
| 16 | -2.94 | -17.9 | -412.1 |

From this selected list, the DM should be able to locate the efficient extreme point of greatest utility. Recall that in the solution of this problem by the Zionts-Wallenius method (see Sec. 3.1.4), the final solution was (-2.8, -55.5, -263.2). However, since the assessment of the DM's preference is done in an entirely different manner, the solutions from different methods obviously may not lead to a unique solution.

<u>A Filtering Technique [324]</u>

Even though the subinterval criterion weights enable the vector-maximum approach to focus in on only the most relevant portion of the nondominated surface as indicated by the pre-specified criterion weight intervals, on larger problems the number of nondominated extreme points generated from this region may still be too large. Additional assistance may be needed to further reduce the list of candidate solutions before presentation to the DM. A filtering technique might be applied in such cases.

To the set of nondominated extreme points produced by the subinterval criterion weights vector-maximum formulations (3.72) or (3.76), the following filtering technique can be applied to operate on the principle of discarding solutions not sufficiently "dissimilar" from those already retained by the filter. Its purposes are: (a) to reduce an undesirably large set of nondominated extreme points to a more workable size, and (b) to characterize the portion of the nondominated surface of the feasible region indicated by the subinterval criterion weights with a relatively evenly dispersed collection of extreme points.

With regard to a metric parameter p and a "distance" parameter d, a filtering rule that will accomplish either one or both of these objectives is given by

$$\{\sum_{i=1}^{k} k\bar{\lambda}_i |z_i^{h} - z_i^{l}|^p\}^{1/p} \geq d \qquad (3.81)$$

where: k is the number of objectives

$\bar{\lambda}_i$ is the mid-point (or some such central point) of the ith criterion interval such that $\sum_{i=1}^{k} \bar{\lambda}_i = 1$

$z_i$ is the ith criterion value

$h$ is the extreme point number assigned to the nondominated extreme point undergoing the dissimilarity test

$l$ is the extreme point number of a nondominated extreme point previously retained by the filtering rule for inclusion in the shortened list

For a nondominated extreme point to be retained by the filter, relationship (3.80) must individually hold for each extreme point previously retained by the filter. Any violation with respect to a point already held by the filter establishes "similarity" and will cause the point in question to pass through the filter and be disregarded from further consideration.

For a given p, it is to be noted that when d is small the shortened list will be longer than when d is large. Thus by manipulating d, a shortened list of any reduced length can be obtained.

## A Five Phase Vector-Maximum Procedure [324]

Considering the three phase vector-maximum strategy described in conjunction with the subinterval criterion weights modification and the filtering technique, an expanded vector-maximum procedure for solving MOLP problems can be devised. Five phases are distinguished.

Phase 0: (Optional) Specify subinterval criterion weight bounds. If specified, indicate which vector-maximum formulation, (3.72) or (3.76), is to be applicable. If subinterval criterion weights are not specified, vector-maximum formulation (3.69a) is to be employed.

Phase I: Find an initial feasible extreme point.

Phase II: With regard to the vector-maximum problem indicated in Phase 0, find an initial nondominated extreme point.

Phase III: Find all remaining nondominated extreme points of the prevailing vector-maximum formulation.

Phase IV: (Optional) Apply a filtering technique to the generated efficient extreme points.

In this way the three phase vector-maximum algorithms presented in this section can be more flexibly utilized, enabling the DM to more readily adapt the vector-maximum approach to the particular MOLP purposes at hand. (See [324] for detail).

## 4. Methods for 'A Posteriori' Articulation of Preference Information Given

The methods of this class determine a subset of the complete set of nondominated solutions to the VMP. From this subset the DM chooses the most satisfactory solution, making implicit trade-offs between objectives based upon some previously unindicated or nonquantifiable criteria. In any case, the trade-off information (which remains implicit) is received from the DM after the method has terminated and the subset of nondominated solutions has been generated.

This class of methods does not require any assumption or information regarding the DM's utility function. One disadvantage which has severely limited these methods' practical applicability is that they usually generate a large number of nondominated solutions; it becomes almost impossible for the DM to choose one which is the most satisfactory. Therefore, the methods are generally incorporated into some of the interactive methods: e.g. the method of Zionts-Wallenius (see Sec. 3.1.4), the method of the displaced ideal (see Sec. 3.2.3), and the method of Steuer (see Sec. 3.2.5).

### 4.1.1. PARAMETRIC METHOD (WEIGHTING METHOD)

Suppose that the relative importance of the k objectives is known and constant. Then the preferred solution, which is a nondominated solution of the VMP, is obtained by solving [123, 200, 374]:

$$\left.\begin{aligned} &\max \sum_{j=1}^{k} w_j f_j(\underline{x}) \\ &\text{s.t. } \underline{x} \in X \end{aligned}\right\} \qquad (3.82)$$

where $w_j \geq 0$ are the weighting coefficients representing the relative importance of the objectives. The $w_j$ are usually normalized so that

$$\sum_{j=1}^{k} w_j = 1.$$

Although this assumption of additive and linear utilities is not easily satisfied, this method can be used to generate nondominated solutions by utilizing various values of $\underline{w}$. In other words, the weighting coefficients $\underline{w}$ do not reflect the relative importance of the objectives in the proportional sense, but are only parameters varied to locate the nondominated solution points [9]. If the feasible region is a convex set, then a systematic variation of $w_j$'s will result in the generation of a complete nondominated solution set.

The parametric method can be interpreted geometrically. The set $L = \{\underline{f}(\underline{x}) \mid \underline{w}^T\underline{f}(\underline{x}) = c\}$ (where c is a constant), defines a hyperplane in $R^k$ with inward normal $\underline{w}$. The maximization of $\underline{w}^T\underline{f}(\underline{x})$ can be seen as moving this hyperplane L with fixed $\underline{w}$ on a negative direction as far as possible from the origin but keeping the intersection of L and S, $L \cap S$, nonnull. This maximum will be the point where L is tangent to S (as the feasible region is a convex set). The method for two objectives is illustrated in Fig. 3.25; L is a line with slope $- w_1/w_2$; the maximum (the preferred solution for the given set of $w_1$ and $w_2$) occurs at point A. Point A is a point in the nondominated set illustrated by heavy line in Fig. 3.25.

For a nonconvex set, some points in the nondominated set cannot be found for any set of $\underline{w}$. Consider the point A in Fig. 3.26. The line L

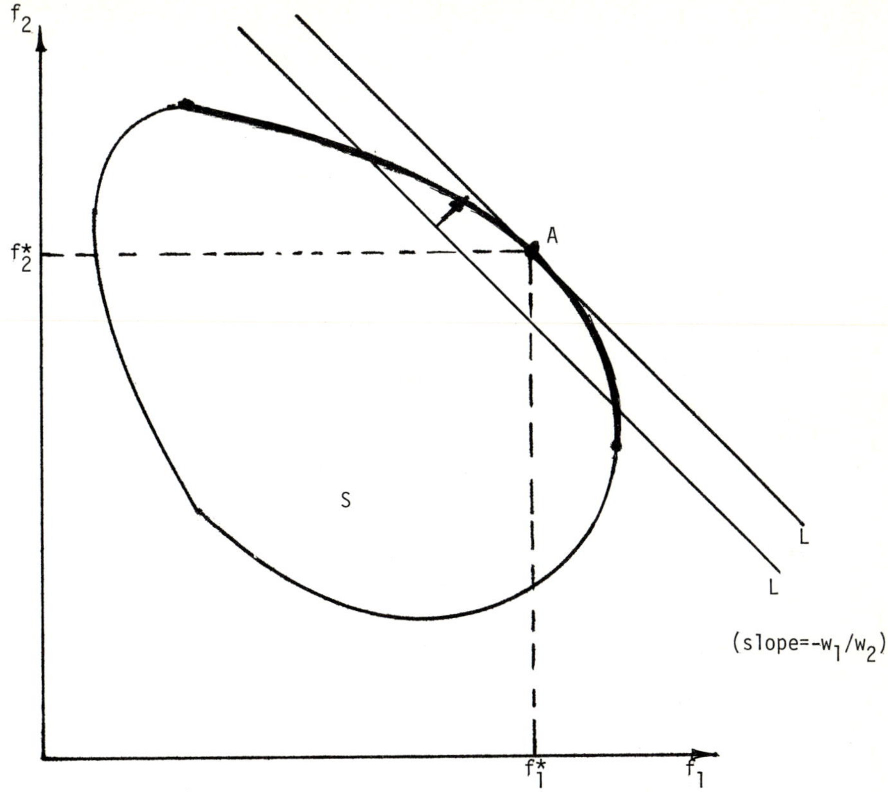


Fig. 3.25 Parametric method of two objectives with convext set.

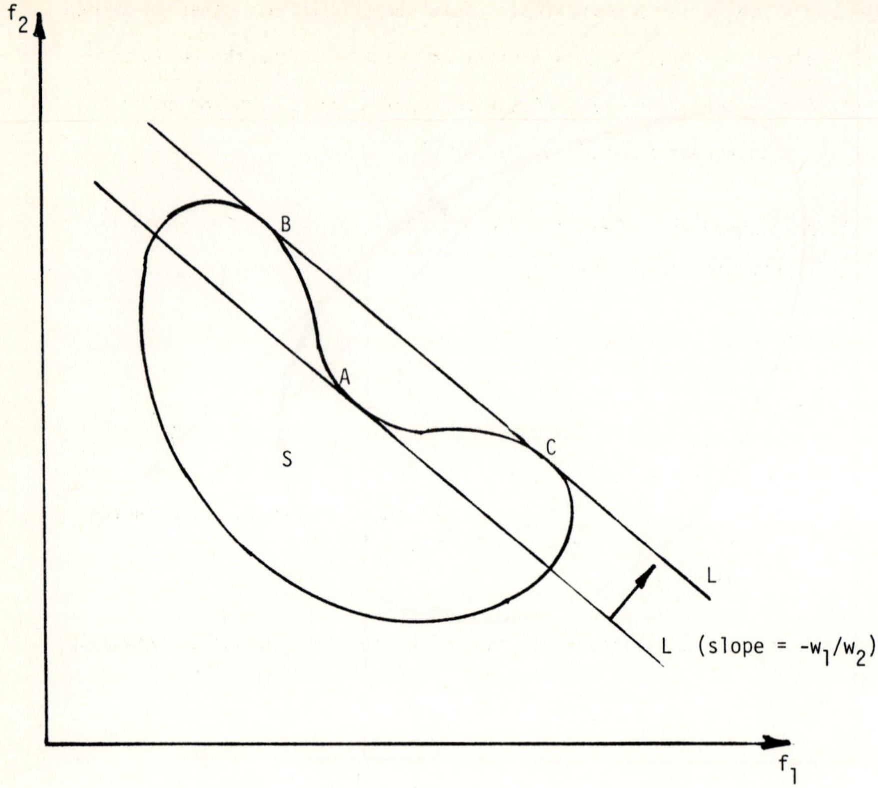


Fig. 3.26 Parametric method of two objectives with non-convex set.

which is tangent at A with slope $-w_1/w_2$ can be moved further in a negative direction until it is a tangent at point B. Thus the parametric method with this value of $\underline{w}$ will find point B and C, but not point A (even it is a nondominated point) [BM-8].

<u>NUMBERICAL EXAMPLE</u> (Production scheduling of the Hardee toy company)

The VMP problem is given by:

$$\max \quad f_1(\underline{x}) = 0.4x_1 + 0.3x_2$$

$$\max \quad f_2(\underline{x}) = x_1$$

$$\text{s.t.} \quad \left.\begin{aligned} g_1(\underline{x}) &= x_1 + x_2 \leq 400 \\ g_2(\underline{x}) &= 2x_1 + x_2 \leq 500 \\ x_1, x_2 &\geq 0 \end{aligned}\right\} \text{Let these constraints be denoted by } \underline{x} \in X$$

The composite objective function with the given constraint set is:

$$\max \quad w_1 f_1(x) + w_2 f_2(x)$$

$$\text{s.t.} \quad \underline{x} \in X$$

The nondominated solutions from the varied set of $\underline{w}$ are obtained and given in Table 3.25. All the generated nondominated points are located in the line segment of BC, which is recognized intuitively as the nondominated set in Fig. 3.27. Since the feasible region of the problem forms a convex set, the generated points are the complete set of the nondominated set.

Table 3.25 The nondominated solution set

| $w_1$ | $w_2$ | $-w_1/w_2$ | $x_1$ | $x_2$ | $f_1$ | $f_2$ | Location* of $\underline{f}$ |
|---|---|---|---|---|---|---|---|
| 0. | 1.0 | 0. | 250 | 0 | 100 | 250 | C |
| 0.2 | 0.8 | -0.25 | 250 | 0 | 100 | 250 | C |
| 0.4 | 0.6 | -0.67 | 250 | 0 | 100 | 250 | C |
| 0.6 | 0.4 | -1.5 | 250 | 0 | 100 | 250 | C |
| 0.8 | 0.2 | -4. | 250 | 0 | 100 | 250 | C |
| 0.833 | 0.167 | -5.** | — | — | — | — | Segment BC |
| 1.0 | 0. | | 100 | 300 | 130 | 100 | B |

* Locations in Fig. 3.27

** It is equal to the slope of BC in Fig. 3.27, hence the solution set has infinite points.

Note

For multiple objective linear programming (MOLP) problems the convexity requirement is satisfied; hence this approach can be used to find the complete nondominated set in all MOLP problems [BM-22] (see Sec. 4.1.3). Even with a convex set, the nonlinear cases are incomparably more difficult to solve. All difficulties of the nonlinear programming theory are compounded here together with complex characterization of the nondominated set in nonlinear cases. Geoffrion developed a parametric procedure for finding a complete nondominated set for the case of maximizing two concave functions with a convex set of constraints [126, 127].

In most cases the complete nondominated solution set has a large number of solutions which make it hard for the DM to reach the final compromised solution. One example of generating a small number of nondominated solu-

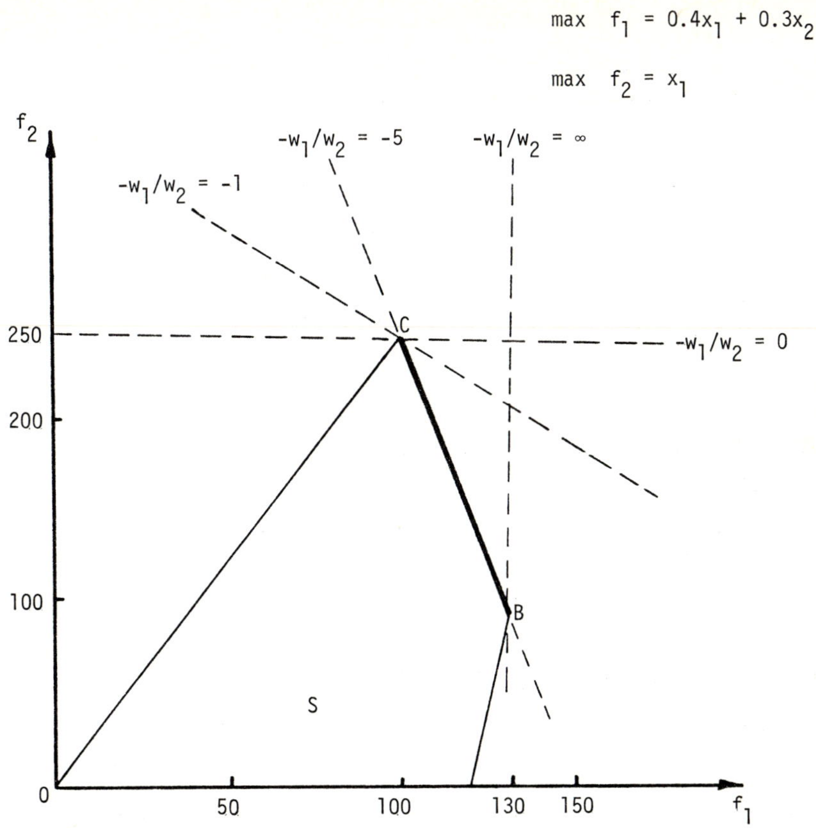


Fig. 3.27 Generation of nondominated set of two objectives.

tions is found in the method of Zionts-Wallenius (see Sec. 3.1.4): the parametric method is used interactively and $w_j$'s are varied systematically to lead to a preferred solution without generating all the nondominated solutions.

### 4.1.2 THE ε-CONSTRAINT METHOD

If the minimum allowable levels $(\varepsilon_1, \varepsilon_2, \ldots, \varepsilon_{i-1}, \varepsilon_{i+1}, \ldots, \varepsilon_k)$ for the k-1 objectives $(f_1, f_2, \ldots, f_{i-1}, f_{i+1}, \ldots, f_k)$ are specified, a preferred solution is the one which solves the following problem [68]:

$$\left.\begin{aligned} &\max && f_1(\underline{x}) \\ &\text{s.t.} && \underline{x} \in X \\ & && f_j(\underline{x}) \geq \varepsilon_j,\ j = 1, 2, \ldots, k,\ j \neq i \end{aligned}\right\} \qquad (3.83)$$

This preferred solution is a nondominated one. A systematic variation of $\varepsilon_j$'s will yield a set of nondominated solutions. However, the determination of the minimum level and the assumption about this form of preference in finding the preferred decision are often questionable in real problems. The ε-constraint method is applicable to a nonconvex feasible region problem.

The ε-constraint method has been incorporated into the surrogate worth trade-off method (see Sec. 3.1.2), an interactive decision making method. The bounded objective methods (see Sec. 2.1.2) are another variation of this approach.

The ε-constraint method for two objectives is illustrated in Fig. 3.28 (for a convex problem) and in Fig. 3.29 (for a nonconvex problem) for the following problem:

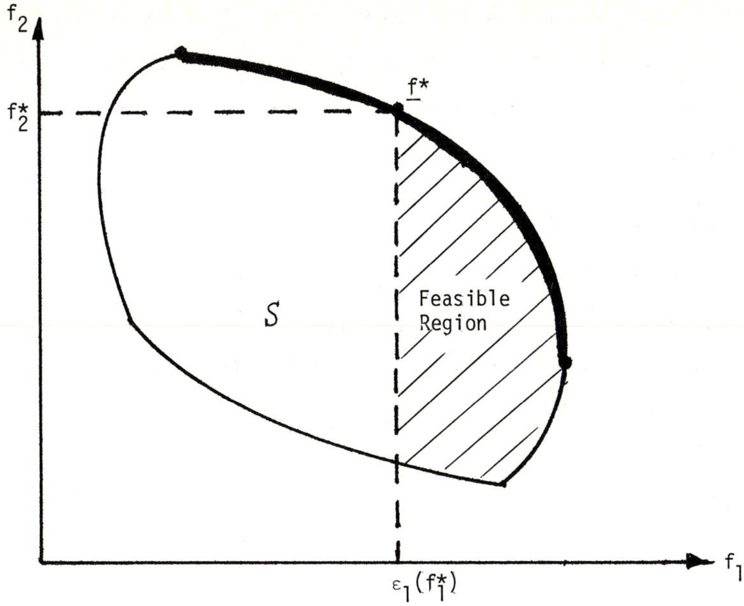


Fig. 3.28 ε-constraint method for a convex problem of two objectives.

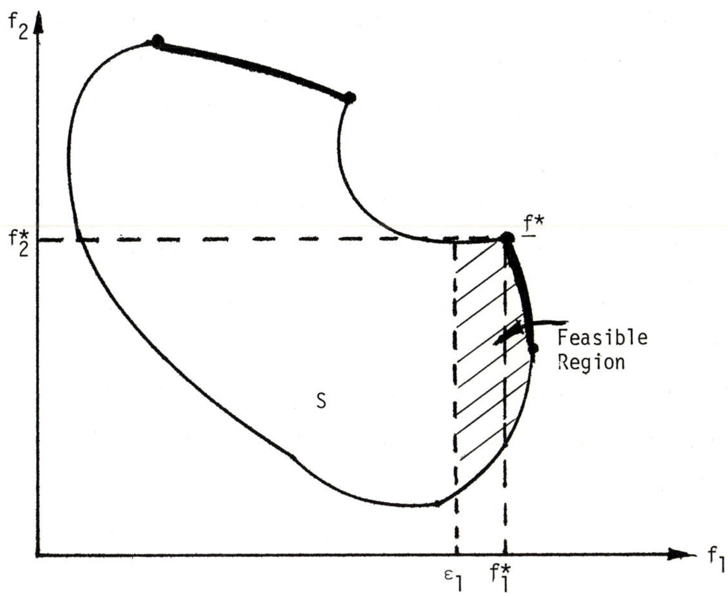


Fig. 3.29 ε-constraint method for a nonconvex problem of two objectives.

$$\max \quad f_2(\underline{x})$$

$$\text{s.t.} \quad \underline{x} \in X$$

$$f_1(\underline{x}) \geq \varepsilon_1$$

The preferred solution, $\underline{f}^*$, is a point of the nondominated solution set (indicated by the heavy solid lines).

NUMERICAL EXAMPLE

The method is illustrated by Step 2 of Example 2 in Sec. 3.1.2. the surrogate worth trade-off method.

### 4.1.3. MULTIPLE OBJECTIVE LINEAR PROGRAMMING (MOLP) METHODS

For a VMP where all the functions are linear, the complete set of nondominated extreme points, which are also the extreme points of the convex set formed by the linear constraints, are generated by multiple objective linear programming (MOLP) methods. For MOLP problems, the set of nondominated extreme points is a connected set and any nondominated point can be expressed as a convex combination of the set of nondominated extreme points [BM-22]. Thus the usual approach is to determine one nondominated extreme point first and then find all other nondominated extreme points by pivoting from basis to basis or extreme point to extreme point.

The MOLP problem is restated below:

$$\left.\begin{array}{ll} \max & C\underline{x} \\ \text{s.t.} & A\underline{x} = \underline{b} \\ & \underline{x} \geq \underline{0} \end{array}\right\} \qquad (3.84)$$

where C is a kxn objective function coefficient matrix, A is an mxn constraint function coefficient matrix, $\underline{x}$ is an nx1 decision variable vector, $\underline{b}$ is an mx1 constant vector, and $\underline{0}$ is an nx1 null vector. For simplicity it has been assumed that all the constraints have been converted to the equality form with the addition of slack and artificial variables.

Most MOLP algorithms consist of three basic steps:

Step 1. Find an initial feasible extreme point.

This step is treated in a manner similar to that for single objective linear programming; a new objective function consisting of artificial variables is formed and optimized. A successful completion of this step indicates a consistent problem.

Step 2. Find an initial nondominated extreme point.

This step consists of moving from the feasible extreme point, found in Step 1, to a nondominated extreme point, if any exist. This is possible because if the constraint set has a nondominated point, then at least one extreme point is nondominated [320]. There are various approaches to finding the initial nondominated extreme point; see [199, 320, BM-22] for a discussion of this. Steuer [320] has listed the following five approaches for finding the initial nondominated extreme point.

a. perform sequential maximization;

b. perform sequential maximization with testing for extreme point nondominance (the test will be explained later) after each maximization stage;

c. perform sequential maximization with testing for extreme point nondominance at each extreme point encountered;

d. maximize a single objective function formed by equally weighing the different original objectives; and

e. maximize the objective as formed above but with testing for extreme point nondominance at each extreme point encountered.

The sequential maximization is carried out in a recursively defined set as follows:

$$\left.\begin{array}{l} X_0 = \{\underline{x} \geq \underline{0} \mid A\underline{x} = \underline{b}\} \\ X_1 = \{f_1^* = \max f_1(\underline{x}) \mid x \in X_0\} \\ \vdots \qquad\qquad \vdots \qquad\qquad \vdots \\ X_k = \{f_k^* = \max f_k(\underline{x}) \mid \underline{x} \in X_{k-1},\ f_{k-1}(\underline{x}) = f_{k-1}^*\} \end{array}\right\} \quad (3.85)$$

However, if the problem is bounded with respect to at least one objective function $f_j$, then the initial nondominated extreme point can be found by maximizing $f_j$. Zeleny [BM-22] has incorporated this approach into his computer program for MOLP.

Step 3. Find all nondominated extreme points.

Once an initial nondominated extreme point has been determined, this step generates all the nondominated extreme points. The three approaches to accomplish this are:

a. Parametric approach: this approach has been fully discussed (see Sec. 4.1.1).

b. Adjacent nondominated basis approach: this approach involves pivoting among all nondominated bases. From each existing nondominated basis, new bases, which can be arrived at in one pivot, are determined and tested for nondominance. See Yu and Zeleny [372] and Steuer [320] for more detailed discussion of this approach. In case of degeneracy, two or more bases can be associated with one nondominated extreme point; in such instances the adjacent basis approach will result in unnecessary pivoting.

c. Adjacent nondominated extreme point approach: this approach involves the pursuit of all nondominated edges emanating from an existing nondominated extreme point as a strategy for locating all nondominated extreme points. The main premise is that since all points on the nondominated edge are nondominated and all nondominated extreme points are connected, this approach can be used to generate all the nondominated extreme points.

Note that in the absence of degeneracy, approaches b and c result in the same procedure. See Evans and Steuer [100] and Steuer [320] for further details of approach c.

Details of Step 3 of MOLP

Let $A_B$ denote the columns of A in basis (i.e., the basis matrix), $A_N$ denote the columns not in basis, and W the reduced cost matrix.

The nondominance of a basis is established if the following sub-problem has a bounded optimum objective function value (i.e., zero) while an unbounded value indicates dominance.

$$\left.\begin{array}{ll} \max & \underline{e}^T\underline{v} \\ \text{s.t.} & W\underline{y} + I\underline{v} = \underline{0} \\ & \underline{y},\ \underline{v} \geq \underline{0} \end{array}\right\} \quad (3.86)$$

where $\underline{e} = \{1, 1, \ldots, 1\}^T$, I is an identity matrix, and $\underline{y}$ and $\underline{v}$ are vectors of dummy variables.

If $x_j$ is nonbasic, i.e., $x_j \in A_N$, then an attempt to bring $x_j$ in basis will result in a nondominated basis if the following sub-problem has a bounded optimum objective function value.

$$\left.\begin{array}{ll} \max & \underline{e}^T\underline{v} \\ \text{s.t.} & W\underline{y} - \underline{w}_j\underline{r} + I\underline{v} = \underline{0} \\ & \underline{r},\ \underline{y},\ \underline{v} \geq \underline{0} \end{array}\right\} \quad (3.87)$$

where $\underline{w}_j$ is the column in W associated with $x_j$.

The nondominance of an extreme point is established if the following sub-problem has a bounded optimum value of the objective function.

$$\left.\begin{aligned} \max \quad & \underline{e}^T \underline{v} \\ \text{s.t.} \quad & W\underline{y} + I\underline{v} = \underline{0} \\ & (A_B^{-1} A_N)_D \underline{y} + I\underline{r} = \underline{0} \\ & \underline{r},\ \underline{v},\ \underline{y} \geq \underline{0} \end{aligned}\right\} \qquad (3.88)$$

where D refers to the degenerate rows. Notice that in case of nondegeneracy, (3.86) and (3.88) result in the same problem.

Once a nondominated extreme point has been found, the nondominance of an edge (or direction) is established if the following subproblem has a bounded optimum objective function value.

$$\left.\begin{aligned} \max \quad & \underline{e}^T \underline{v} \\ \text{s.t.} \quad & W\underline{y} + (-W\underline{\mu}_{Nj})\underline{s} + I\underline{v} = \underline{0} \\ & (A_B^{-1} A_N)_D \underline{y} \qquad\quad + I\underline{r} = \underline{0} \\ & \underline{r},\ \underline{v},\ \underline{s},\ \underline{y} \geq \underline{0} \end{aligned}\right\} \qquad (3.89)$$

where $\underline{\mu}_{Nj}$ is the edge being tested which is determined from the lower part of the jth column of the terminal Chernikova matrix; for further details see Steuer [320].

The adjacent nondominated extreme point approach has been used in the MOLP computer program ADEX by Steuer [322a]. The adjacent nondominated basis approach has been programmed by Steuer in ADBASE [322b] and by Yu and Zeleny [372, BM-22].

SOLUTION BY ADBASE

The adjacent nondominated basis approach as implemented in ADBASE will now be explained through a numerical example. The production scheduling of the Hardee toy company problem is given by:

$$\left.\begin{aligned} \max \quad & f_1 = 0.4x_1 + 0.3x_2 \\ \max \quad & f_2 = x_1 \\ \text{s.t.} \quad & x_1 + x_2 \leq 400 \\ & 2x_1 + x_2 \leq 500 \\ & x_1, x_2 \geq 0 \end{aligned}\right\} \tag{3.90}$$

In the notation of MOLP, the problem can be rewritten as

$$C = \begin{pmatrix} 0.4 & 0.3 & 0 & 0 \\ 1.0 & 0 & 0 & 0 \end{pmatrix}$$

$$A = \begin{pmatrix} 1.0 & 1.0 & 1.0 & 0 \\ 2.0 & 1.0 & 0 & 1.0 \end{pmatrix}$$

$$\underline{b} = \begin{pmatrix} 400 \\ 500 \end{pmatrix}$$

$$\underline{x} = \begin{pmatrix} x_1 \\ x_2 \\ x_3 \\ x_4 \end{pmatrix}$$

where $x_3$ and $x_4$ are slack variables. The problem is written in the simplex tableau after including two additional slack variables $x_5$ and $x_6$ for objective function values.

Initial tableau

| Variables in basis | $x_1$ | $x_2$ | $x_3$ | $x_4$ | $x_5$ | $x_6$ | RHS |
|---|---|---|---|---|---|---|---|
| $x_3$ | 1. | 1. | 1. | 0 | 0 | 0 | 400 |
| $x_4$ | 2. | 1. | 0 | 1. | 0 | 0 | 500 |
| $x_5$ | -.4 | -.3 | 0 | 0 | 1. | 0 | 0 |
| $x_6$ | -1. | 0 | 0 | 0 | 0 | 1. | 0 |

Step 1. Find an initial feasible extreme point.

Since the problem does not have any artificial variable, the initial feasible extreme point is the same as given in initial tableau, i.e., $(x_1, x_2, x_3, x_4) = (0, 0, 400, 500)$ and $(f_1, f_2) = (x_5, x_6) = (0, 0)$.

Step 2. Find an initial nondominated extreme point.

Of the 5 approaches suggested by Steuer, approach b will be used here. Approach b consists of sequential maximization with testing for nondominance at the end of each maximization stage. First, maximize $f_1$ with respect to the original constraints. The results of two iterations needed are shown in tableau 1 and 2.

Tableau 1

| basis | $x_1$ | $x_2$ | $x_3$ | $x_4$ | $x_5$ | $x_6$ | RHS |
|---|---|---|---|---|---|---|---|
| $x_3$ | 0 | .5 | 1. | -.5 | 0 | 0 | 150 |
| $x_1$ | 1. | .5 | 0 | .5 | 0 | 0 | 250 |
| $x_5$ | 0 | -.1 | 0 | .2 | 1. | 0 | 100 |
| $x_6$ | 0 | .5 | 0 | .5 | 0 | 1. | 250 |

Tableau 2

| basis | $x_1$ | $x_2$ | $x_3$ | $x_4$ | $x_5$ | $x_6$ | RHS |
|---|---|---|---|---|---|---|---|
| $x_2$ | 0 | 1. | 2. | -1. | 0 | 0 | 300 |
| $x_1$ | 1. | 0 | -1. | 1. | 0 | 0 | 100 |
| $x_5$ | 0 | 0 | .2 | .1 | 1. | 0 | 130 |
| $x_6$ | 0 | 0 | -1. | 1. | 0 | 1. | 100 |

The solution in tableau 2 will now be tested for nondominance by using problem (3.88). However, in the sequential maximization case this test problem is modified slightly. In the first constraint, only the reduced costs associated with unmaximized objectives are used. The objectives that have been maximized as converted to equality constraints and the slack variables associated with these objectives are held at zero levels. Hence these rows become the degenerate rows. For this example, the third row is modified as

$$.2x_3 + .1x_4 = -130$$

$$\text{or} \quad .2x_3 + .1x_4 + x_5(=0) = -130$$

Thus row 3, associated with $x_5$, is considered as the degenerate row.

Step 2a. Test for nondominance of an extreme point.

$$\begin{aligned} \max \quad & v_1 \\ \text{s.t.} \quad & -y_1 + y_2 + v_1 = 0 \\ & 2y_1 + y_2 + r_1 = 0 \\ & y_1, y_2, v_1, r_1 \geq 0 \end{aligned}$$

The solution is bounded, i.e., max $v_1 = 0$. So the extreme point of tableau 2 is nondominated. This brings Step 2 to its completion. The current point is point B in Figs. 3.19 and 3.20. Note that the solution in tableau 1 is point C and is the maximum value of $f_2$. If approach c were followed where testing for nondominance is done at each extreme point encountered, this point would have been found as the initial nondominated extreme point.

Step 3. Find all nondominated extreme points.

From the current nondominated basis, two new bases can be obtained in one pivot by introducing either $x_3$ or $x_4$ into the basis. If this results in a nondominated basis, test must be made, by using problem (3.87).

Step 3a. Test if introduction of $x_3$ into basis results in a nondominated basis.

Solve the problem:

$$\max \quad z_1 = v_1 + v_2$$

$$\text{s.t.} \quad .2y_1 + .1y_2 - .2r_1 + v_1 = 0$$

$$-y_1 + y_2 + r_1 + v_2 = 0$$

$$y_1, y_2, r_1, v_1, v_2 \geq 0$$

This problem has a bounded optimum value for the objective function (i.e., max $z_1 = 0$), so if $x_3$ is brought into the basis then the resulting basis will be nondominated.

Step 3b. Test if the introduction of $x_4$ into basis will result in a nondominated basis.

Solve the following problem:

$$\max \quad z_1 = v_1 + v_2$$

$$\text{s.t.} \quad .2y_1 + y_2 - .1r_1 + v_1 = 0$$

$$-y_1 + y_2 - r_1 + v_2 = 0$$

$$y_1, y_2, r_1, v_1, v_2 \geq 0$$

This problem does not have a bounded optimum objective function value, hence, introduction of $x_4$ into the basis will not result in a nondominated basis.

Step 3c. Find all the nondominated extreme points resulting in one pivot from the current extreme point. From Steps 3a and 3b we obtain only one nondominated extreme point from the current nondominated extreme point. Determine this new nondominated extreme point by introducing $x_3$ into the basis; the result is given in tableau 3.

Tableau 3

| basis | $x_1$ | $x_2$ | $x_3$ | $x_4$ | $x_5$ | $x_6$ | RHS |
|---|---|---|---|---|---|---|---|
| $x_3$ | 0 | .5 | 1. | -.5 | 0 | 0 | 150 |
| $x_1$ | 1. | .5 | 0 | .5 | 0 | 0 | 250 |
| $x_5$ | 0 | -.1 | 0 | .2 | 1 | 0 | 100 |
| $x_6$ | 0 | .5 | 0 | .5 | 0 | 1 | 250 |

This is the same as in tableau 1, i.e., point C in Figs. 3.19 and 3.20.

Now, tests must be made if introduction of $x_2$ or $x_4$ will result in a new nondominated basis. If $x_2$ is introduced into the basis then a point in tableau 2 will be obtained, which has already been found. Introduction of $x_4$ will not result in a nondominated basis. Interested readers may confirm this by performing a subproblem test by using problem (3.87).

The two nondominated extreme points for this problem are:

B: $(x_1, x_2) = (100, 300)$; $(f_1, f_2) = (130, 100)$

C: $(x_1, x_2) = (250, 0)$; $(f_1, f_2) = (100, 250)$

Since there is no degeneracy in this problem, the use of the adjacent extreme point approach would have resulted in the same procedure as described above.

SOLUTION BY MULTICRITERIA SIMPLEX METHOD

In this section we present another multicriteria simplex method, which is also based on the adjacent nondominated basis approach as implemented by Yu and Zeleny [372, BM-22].

Let N denote a set of all nondominated solutions of a MOLP problem, and D = X-N the set of all dominated solutions. Also let $N_{ex}$ denote the set of all nondominated basic solutions (or extreme points of X). For MOLP problems, the set of nondominated extreme points is a connected set and any nondominated point can be expressed as a convex combination of a subset of the set of nondominated extreme points. Hence we can concentrate on exploring $N_{ex}$ only.

Let X be the polyhedron of all feasible solutions, adding slack and surplus variables when necessary. Then for a basic solution $\underline{x}^o \in X$ a general simplex tableau is as shown in Table 3.26. Notice that the components of $C\underline{x}$ are now appended as k criteria rows (or objective rows). A composite function $\sum_{i=1}^{k} \underline{c}^i \underline{x}$ has also been added as the (k+1)st criteria row. The purpose of this row will be explained later.

With each basic solution, there are now associated k objective rows of $z_j^i$, i = 1,2, ..., k and j = 1,2, ..., n. Let J denote the index set of the basic variables, while $\bar{J}$ will indicate the index of currently nonbasic variables. Note $J \cup \bar{J} = \{1,2, ..., n\}$, but let $J = \{1,2, ..., m\}$ for simplicity.

Table 3.26 A general simplex tableau

| r | Basis | Basic Variables | | Nonbasic Variables | | | b |
|---|---|---|---|---|---|---|---|
| | | $x_1$ ... | $x_m$ | $x_{m+1}$ | ... $x_j$ | ... $x_n$ | |
| 1 | $x_1$ | 1 ... | 0 | $y_{1(m+1)}$ | ... $y_{1j}$ | ... $y_{1n}$ | $b_1$ |
| ⋮ | ⋮ | ⋮ | ⋮ | ⋮ | ⋮ | ⋮ | ⋮ |
| m | $x_m$ | 0 ... | 1 | $y_{m(m+1)}$ | ... $y_{mj}$ | ... $y_{mn}$ | $b_m$ |
| m+1 | $\underline{C}_1$ | 0 ... | 0 | $z_{m+1}^1$ | ... $z_j^1$ | ... $z_n^1$ | $z_0^1$ |
| ⋮ | | ⋮ | ⋮ | ⋮ | ⋮ | ⋮ | ⋮ |
| m+k | $\underline{C}_2$ | 0 ... | 0 | $z_{m+1}^k$ | ... $z_j^k$ | ... $z_n^k$ | $z_0^k$ |
| | $\sum$ | 0 ... | 0 | $z_{m+1}^{k+1}$ | ... $z_j^{k+1}$ | ... $z_n^{k+1}$ | $z_0^{k+1}$ |

If $\underline{x}^0$ is nondegenerate, then $\underline{x}^0 = \{x_1, ..., x_m, 0, ..., 0\}$, where $x_j = b_j > 0$ for $j \in J$ and $x_j = 0$ for $j \in \bar{J}$. Note that for all $j \in J$ all $z_j^i = 0$.

Then

$$z_j^i = \sum_{r=1}^{m} c_r^i y_{rj} - c_j^i$$

and the corresponding value of the ith objective function is given by $z_0^i = \sum_{r=1}^{m} c_r^i b_r$, i = 1, ..., k. Corresponding to each nonbasic column of Table 3.26 there is a column vector

$$\underline{z}_j \equiv \begin{pmatrix} z_j^1 \\ \vdots \\ z_j^k \end{pmatrix}$$

and with each basic solution (and its tableau), say $x^0$, there is an associated vector of value of k objectives:

$$\underline{z}_0 \equiv \begin{pmatrix} z_0^1 \\ \vdots \\ z_0^k \end{pmatrix} .$$

Other characteristics of this simplex tableau which will be used in exploring the nondominated extreme points are summarized in the following remarks.

Remark 1. From the theory of simplex method, for $j \in \bar{J}$, if $y_{rj} > 0$, we define

$$\theta_j = \min_r \{b_r/y_{rj}\}$$

By introducing the jth column into the basis, we obtain a new basic solution, say $\underline{x}^1$, and also a new vector $\underline{z}_1$, for which the following relation holds:

$$\underline{z}_1 = \underline{z}_0 - \theta_j \underline{z}_j .$$

Remark 2. Given a basic feasible solution $\underline{x}^0$ and assuming $\theta_j > 0$ for $j \in \bar{J}$, then

(a) if $\underline{z}_j \leq \underline{0}$ (i.e., all $z_j^i \leq 0$ and at least one $z_j^i < 0$) then $\underline{x}^0 \notin N$.

(b) if $\underline{z}_j \geq \underline{0}$, then introducing the jth column into the basis will lead to a dominated solution.

Remark 3. Given a basic feasible solution $\underline{x}^0$, if there are columns j and k such that $\theta_j z_j \leq \theta_k z_k$ (i.e., for at least one i, $\theta_j z_j^i < \theta_k z_k^i$), $j \neq k$ and $j, k \in \bar{J}$, then the solution resulting from introducing the kth column is dominated by the solution resulting from introducing the jth column.

Remark 4. Notice that the jth column should never be introduced if $z_j \geq 0$ and $\theta_j > 0$ at $\underline{x}^0$. Looking at criteria rows at each iteration, if $z_j^i \geq 0$ for all $j \in \bar{J}$ then the ith objective function is at its maximum. If there is also no column $k \in \bar{J}$ with $z_k^i = 0$ (i.e., no alternate optimal solution), then the corresponding basic solution is nondominated.

Remark 5. Consider $\theta_j, \theta_k > 0$. Given a basic feasible solution $\underline{x}^0$, if there are columns $j, k \in J$ such that we can find $0 < \bar{\theta}_j \leq \theta_j$, $0 < \bar{\theta}_k \leq \theta_k$ for which $\bar{\theta}_j z_j \leq \bar{\theta}_k z_k$, $j \neq k$, $j, k \in \bar{J}$, then the solution resulting from introducing the kth column is dominated. Observe also that $z_j \leq z_k$ implies that by introducing the kth column we obtain a dominated solution if $\theta_j, \theta_k > 0$.

These remarks considerably limit the number of bases which must be explored in search for nondominated solutions. A nondominance test is designed for cases where the presented remarks are still inconclusive.

When the nondominance of a basic solution cannot be established from Remark 4, a "nondominance subroutine" is used. The nondominance test problem is a linear programming problem in which the maximum value of its objective function $\underline{e}^T\underline{v}$ indicates whether the current basis $\underline{x}^i$ is a nondominated solution ($\underline{x}^i \in N$ if $\max \underline{e}^T\underline{v} = 0$ and $\underline{x}^i \in D$ if $\max \underline{e}^T\underline{v} > 0$).

To simplify the description here, we present only the procedural details of formulating and solving the nondominance test problem. For complete details of this and the multicriteria simplex method, see [372, 373, BM22].

Algorithm of Multicriteria Simplex Method.

Step 1. For some basic solution $\underline{x}^i \in X$, check if any objective function is maximized. This assures that $\underline{x}^i$ or some alternate solution will be nondominated (Remark 4).

Step 2. If $\underline{x}^i$ uniquely maximizes at least one objective function then $\underline{x}^i \in N$, and go to Step 5.

Step 3. If $\underline{z}_j \leq 0$ for at least one $j \in \bar{J}$, then $\underline{x}^i \in D$ if $\theta_j > 0$, and if the corresponding jth column leads to an unexplored basis, make the transformation and return to Step 1; if it leads to an already explored basis go to Step 8. If there exists no j with all $z^i_j \leq 0$, go to Step 4.

Step 4. Test if the current basis is a nondominated solution using the nondominance subroutine as described in the next section.

Step 5. Select the variable which would give a solution dominating all other points reachable from $\underline{x}^i$ (Remarks 3 and 5). If there is one yet unexplored, make the transformation and go to Step 1. Otherwise, go to Step 6.

Step 6. Select columns which would lead to solutions noncomparable to $\underline{x}^i$. If there are none, go to Step 8. If there are some, but $\underline{x}^i \in D$, go to Step 8.

Step 7. Select and store all columns (and their bases) which would lead to an unexplored solution. These are bases which might potentially be nondominated.

Step 8. Whenever there are no bases stored in Step 7 for the current $\underline{x}^i$, terminate the procedure.

Algorithm for Nondominance Subroutine

Step ND1. Check the composite objective row. If there is no negative element $\underline{x}^i \in N$, return to Step 5 (of multicriteria simplex method).

Step ND2. If there is at least one negative element in the composite objective row, say $z_j^{(k+1)}$, check $z_j$. If all $z_j^i \leq 0$, go to Step ND3. If there is at least one $z_j^i > 0$, go to Step ND4.

Step ND3. If $\theta_j = 0$ go to Step ND6. If $\theta_j > 0$ then $\underline{x}^i \in D$ and return to Step 5.

Step ND4. Form the nondominance test problem from the criterial parts of Table 3.26. The test is to include all objective rows and columns of nonbasis variables only. If $\theta_j > 0$, go to Step ND5. If $\theta_j = 0$, for all $j \in \overline{J}$, add the corresponding row(s) to the nondominance problem to keep track of any change in $\theta_j$. The composite objective row is used as the criteria row for simplex iteration of this problem.

Step ND5. Perform the simplex iteration with $z_j^i > 0$ as key element. Note that j and i were selected in Steps ND1 and ND2. Go to Step ND1.

Step ND6. If any rows giving $\theta_j = 0$ were added to the nondominance test problem, explore them after each step for any $y_{rj} > 0$. If there is none, then $\theta_j > 0$ since a bounded solution is assumed. If there is $y_{rj} > 0$, then $\theta_j = 0$; hence perform the next iteration around $y_{rj}$ and go to Step ND1.

In the above description, the step numbers are prefixed with 'ND' to distinguish between the steps in the nondominance routine and those in the multicriteria simplex procedure.

NUMERICAL EXAMPLE

Example 1 (Production scheduling of the Hardee toy company)

We again consider the production scheduling of the Hardee toy company as presented by (3.90) and plotted in Figs. 3.19 and 3.20.

From Fig. 3.20, it is bovious that point B, $(f_1, f_2) = (130, 100)$, and point C, $(f_1, f_2) = (100, 250)$ are nondominated extreme points, $N_{ex}$.

The initial tableau for this multicriteria simplex method is:

Initial tableau

| Basis | $x_1$ | $x_2$ | $y_1$ | $y_2$ | b |
|---|---|---|---|---|---|
| $y_1$ | 1 | 1 | 1 | 0 | 400 |
| $y_2$ | 2 | 1 | 0 | 1 | 500 |
| $\underline{c}_1$ | -0.4 | -0.3 | 0 | 0 | 0 |
| $\underline{c}_2$ | -1.0 | 0 | 0 | 0 | 0 |
| Σ | -1.4 | -0.3 | 0 | 0 | 0 |

The steps in generating $N_{ex}$ are:

Step 1. $\underline{x}^0 = (0, 0)$. In the initial tableau, no objective row has all the coefficients nonnegative, hence no objective is at its maximum.

Step 2. Not applicable.

Step 3. Since $\underline{z}_1 = (-0.4, -1.0) \leq \underline{0}$, $\underline{x}^0 = (0,0)$ is a dominated solution (Remark 2a). For column 1 in the initial tableau, $\theta_1 = \min_r (b_r/y_{rj}) =$ min (400/1, 500/2) = 250. Similarly, for column 2, $\theta_2$ = min (400/1, 400/1) = 400. $\theta_1\underline{z}_1 = (-100, -250)$ and $\theta_2\underline{z}_2 = (-120, 0)$. From Remark 3 we note that neither of these vectors dominate the other. We introduce $x_1$ into solution (since $z_1^3 = -1.4$ is the least among all possible for nonbasic variables). The transformation results in Tableau 1. Go to Step 1.

Tableau 1

| Basis | $x_1$ | $x_2$ | $y_1$ | $y_2$ | b |
|---|---|---|---|---|---|
| $y_1$ | 0 | 0.5 | 1 | -0.5 | 150 |
| $x_1$ | 1 | 0.5 | 0 | 0.5 | 250 |
| $\underline{c}_1$ | 0 | -0.1 | 0 | 0.2 | 100 |
| $\underline{c}_2$ | 0 | 0.5 | 0 | 0.5 | 250 |
| $\Sigma$ | 0 | 0.4 | 0 | 0.7 | 350 |

Step 1. In the objective row 2, all the coefficients are nonnegative, hence $f_2$ has reached its maximum.

Step 2. $\underline{x}^1 = (250, 0)$ maximizes $f_2$ and there is no alternate optimal solution. Hence $\underline{x}^1$ is a nondominated extreme point (Point C in Fig. 3.19 and 3.20). Go to Step 5.

Step 5. $\theta_2\underline{z}_2 = (-30, 150)$ and $\theta_4\underline{z}_4 = (100, 250)$. From Remark 3, $x_2$ dominates $y_2$ in the sense that $x_2$ should be preferred over $y_2$. The introduction of $x_2$ into solution results in Tableau 2. Go to Step 1.

Tableau 2

| Basis | $x_1$ | $x_2$ | $y_1$ | $y_2$ | b |
|---|---|---|---|---|---|
| $x_2$ | 0 | 1 | 2.0 | -1.0 | 300 |
| $x_1$ | 1 | 0 | -1.0 | 1.0 | 100 |
| $\underline{c}_1$ | 0 | 0 | 0.2 | 0.1 | 130 |
| $\underline{c}_2$ | 0 | 0 | -1.0 | 1.0 | 100 |
| $\Sigma$ | 0 | 0 | -0.8 | 1.1 | 230 |

Step 1. Objective 1 is at its maximum (Point B in Figs. 3.19 and 3.20).

Step 2. Since there is no alternative optimum for $f_2$, $\underline{x}^2 = (100, 300)$ is a nondominated extreme point. Go to Step 5.

Step 5. Neither of $y_1$ and $y_2$ dominate the other. However, the introduction of $y_1$ into solution would lead to an already explored basis (Tableau 1). Introducing $y_2$ into solution results in Tableau 3. Go to Step 1.

Tableau 3

| Basis | $x_1$ | $x_2$ | $y_1$ | $y_2$ | b |
|---|---|---|---|---|---|
| $x_2$ | 1 | 1 | 1 | 0 | 400 |
| $y_2$ | 1 | 0 | -1 | 1 | 100 |
| $\underline{c}_1$ | -0.1 | 0 | 0.3 | 0 | 120 |
| $\underline{c}_2$ | -1.0 | 0 | 0.0 | 0 | 0 |
| $\Sigma$ | -1.1 | 0 | 0.3 | 0 | 120 |

Step 1. No objective is at its maximum. $\underline{x}^3 = (0, 400)$.

Step 2. Go to Step 3.

Step 3. Since $\underline{z}_1 = (-0.1, -1.0) \leq 0$, $\underline{x}^3$ is a dominated solution (Remark 2a). Since $\underline{z}_3 = (0.3, 0.0) \geq 0$, introduction of $y_1$ leads to a dominated solution (Remark 2b). Furthermore, introduction of $x_1$ or $y_1$ leads to an already explored basis (Tableau 3 and the initial tableau, respectively). No other variable could be entered. Go to Step 8.

Step 8. Terminate the procedure.

In this simple example, we could generate all the nondominated extreme points (points B and C) by exploring four of the five corners of X. However, we did not have to use the nondominance subroutine' which we will illustrate by another example.

Example 2. (The Ace Electronic Inc. production planning)

Ace Electronic Inc. manufactures four types of calculators: D1 and D2 for domestic use, and S1 and S2 for scientific use. Its inputs are electronic components of three different solid-state circuits, called A, B and C, and labor. Circuits A and B are imported, but circuit C is produced within the company. Input-output relationships and daily available resources for imported items and labor are shown in the following table. The marketing department wants more production of the domestic calculators, because of its popularity among housewives. Now the production manager's duty is to plan the number of each calculator to be manufactured daily so as to

i) maximize the profit;

ii) maximize the production of domestic calculators:

iii) maximize the use of nonimported circuit C.

| | D1 | D2 | S1 | S2 | Resources available per day |
|---|---|---|---|---|---|
| Circuit A (unit) | 5 | 3 | 2 | 0 | 240 |
| Circuit B (unit) | 0 | 0 | 3 | 8 | 320 |
| Nonimported Circuit C (unit) | 1 | 4 | 6 | 2 | |
| Labor (hr) | 2 | 3 | 4 | 6 | 180 |
| Profit ($) | 10 | 30 | 50 | 100 | |

Let $x_1$, $x_2$, $x_3$ and $x_4$ be the number of calculators D1, D2, S1 and S2 to be produced daily, respectively. The problem is to find $x_i$, i = 1, 2, 3, 4, so as to:

$$\begin{aligned}
\max \quad & f_1(\underline{x}) = 10x_1 + 30x_2 + 50x_3 + 100x_4 \\
\max \quad & f_2(\underline{x}) = x_1 + x_2 \\
\max \quad & f_3(\underline{x}) = x_1 + 4x_2 + 6x_3 + 2x_4 \\
\text{s.t.} \quad & g_1(\underline{x}) = 5x_1 + 3x_2 + 2x_3 \leq 240 \\
& g_2(\underline{x}) = 3x_3 + 8x_4 \leq 320 \\
& g_3(\underline{x}) = 2x_1 + 3x_2 + 4x_3 + 6x_4 \leq 180 \\
& x_1, x_2, x_3, x_4 \geq 0
\end{aligned}$$

Solution. In this example, there are 3 objectives to be maximized subject to 3 constraints. There are 4 decision variables. The solution to the problem using the multicriteria simplex method indicates the following four nondominated extreme points:

1. $\underline{x} = (0, 0, 0, 30)$, $\underline{f} = (3000, 0, 60)$
2. $\underline{x} = (0, 60, 0, 0)$, $\underline{f} = (1800, 60, 240)$
3. $\underline{x} = (0, 0, 45, 0)$, $\underline{f} = (2250, 0, 270)$
4. $\underline{x} = (20, 46.67, 0, 0)$, $\underline{f} = (1600, 66.67, 20.67)$

The multicriteria simplex algorithm applied to this problem is described with the help of the simplex tableaus. $\underline{x}^0 = (0, 0, 0, 0)$. From the initial tableau note that no objective is at its maximum. Since $\underline{z}_4 = (-100, 0, -2) \leq \underline{0}$, $\underline{x}^0$ is (from Remark 2) a dominated solution. Introduce $x_4$ into solution ($y_3$ leaves). The transformation leads to Tableau 1. $\underline{x}^1 = (0, 0, 0, 30)$. In Tableau 1, objective 1 is at its maximum since all its coefficients are nonnegative. No alternate optimum exists. Hence $\underline{x}^1$ is a nondominated extreme point. Introducing $x_3$ into solution leads back to the initial tableau, so introduce $x_2$ into solution ($x_4$ leaves). The transformation results in Tableau 2. $\underline{x}^2 = (0, 60, 0, 0)$. No objective is at its maximum. To verify the nondominance of this solution, "nondominance subroutine" will be used.

In the composite objective row of Tableau 2, there are some negative elements. Since at least one $z_j^i$ is nonnegative, the nondominance tableau can be formed Tableau 2.1. Note that Tableau 2.1 is formed from "critical" parts of Tableau 2; specifically, only objective rows and nonbasis columns are selected. An identity matrix is added to correspond to the variables $\varepsilon_i$, i = 1, 2, 3, where

$$\underline{C}_i\underline{x} - \varepsilon_i = \underline{C}_i\underline{x}^k.$$

$\underline{x}^k$ is the current basis solution. The sum of all $\varepsilon_i$ is the objective function (of the test problem) to be maximized. In Tableau 2.1, column 3 corresponds to the smallest element of the composite objective row.

Initial Tableau

| Basis | $x_1$ | $x_2$ | $x_3$ | $x_4$ | $y_1$ | $y_2$ | $y_3$ | b |
|---|---|---|---|---|---|---|---|---|
| $y_1$ | 5 | 3 | 2 | 0 | 1 | 0 | 0 | 240 |
| $y_2$ | 0 | 0 | 3 | 8 | 0 | 1 | 0 | 320 |
| $y_3$ | 2 | 3 | 4 | 6 | 0 | 0 | 1 | 180 |
| $\underline{C}_1$ | -10 | -30 | -50 | -100 | 0 | 0 | 0 | 0 |
| $\underline{C}_2$ | -1 | -1 | 0 | 0 | 0 | 0 | 0 | 0 |
| $\underline{C}_3$ | -1 | -4 | -6 | -2 | 0 | 0 | 0 | 0 |
| $\sum$ | -12 | -35 | -56 | -102 | 0 | 0 | 0 | 0 |

Tableau 1

| Basis | $x_1$ | $x_2$ | $x_3$ | $x_4$ | $y_1$ | $y_2$ | $y_3$ | b |
|---|---|---|---|---|---|---|---|---|
| $y_1$ | 5 | 3 | 2 | 0 | 1 | 0 | 0 | 240 |
| $y_2$ | -8/3 | -4 | -7/3 | 0 | 0 | 1 | -4/3 | 80 |
| $x_4$ | 1/3 | 1/2 | 2/3 | 1 | 0 | 0 | 1/6 | 30 |
| $C_1$ | 70/3 | 20 | 50/3 | 0 | 0 | 0 | 50/3 | 3000 |
| $C_2$ | -1 | -1 | 0 | 0 | 0 | 0 | 0 | 0 |
| $C_3$ | -1/3 | -3 | -14/3 | 0 | 0 | 0 | 1/3 | 60 |
| $\sum$ | 22 | 16 | 12 | 0 | 0 | 0 | 17 | 3060 |

Tableau 2

| | $x_1$ | $x_2$ | $x_3$ | $x_4$ | $y_1$ | $y_2$ | $y_3$ | b |
|---|---|---|---|---|---|---|---|---|
| $y_1$ | 3 | 0 | -2 | -6 | 1 | 0 | -1 | 60 |
| $y_2$ | 0 | 0 | 3 | 8 | 0 | 1 | 0 | 320 |
| $x_2$ | 2/3 | 1 | 4/3 | 2 | 0 | 0 | 1/3 | 60 |
| $C_1$ | 10 | 0 | -10 | -40 | 0 | 0 | 10 | 1800 |
| $C_2$ | -1/3 | 0 | 4/3 | 2 | 0 | 0 | 1/3 | 60 |
| $C_3$ | 5/3 | 0 | -2/3 | 6 | 0 | 0 | 4/3 | 240 |
| $\sum$ | 34/3 | 0 | -28/3 | -32 | 0 | 0 | 35/3 | 2100 |

Tableau 2.1

| | $x_1$ | $x_3$ | $x_4$ | $y_3$ | $\varepsilon_1$ | $\varepsilon_2$ | $\varepsilon_3$ |
|---|---|---|---|---|---|---|---|
| $\varepsilon_1$ | 10 | -10 | -40 | 10 | 1 | 0 | 0 |
| $\varepsilon_2$ | -1/3 | 4/3 | 2 | 1/3 | 0 | 1 | 0 |
| $\varepsilon_3$ | 5/3 | -2/3 | 6 | 4/3 | 0 | 0 | 1 |
| $\sum$ | 34/3 | -28/3 | -32 | 35/3 | 0 | 0 | 0 |

Tableau 2.2

| | $x_1$ | $x_3$ | $x_4$ | $y_3$ | $\varepsilon_1$ | $\varepsilon_2$ | $\varepsilon_3$ |
|---|---|---|---|---|---|---|---|
| $\varepsilon_1$ | 190/9 | -130/9 | 0 | 170/9 | 1 | 0 | 20/3 |
| $\varepsilon_2$ | -8/9 | 14/9 | 0 | -1/9 | 0 | 1 | -1/3 |
| $x_4$ | 5/18 | -1/9 | 1 | 2/9 | 0 | 0 | 1/6 |
| $\sum$ | 182/9 | -116/9 | 0 | 169/9 | 0 | 0 | 16/3 |

Introduce $x_4$ into solution with $z_3^3$, the largest positive element in that column, as the key element. The transformation results in Tableau 2.2. Some negative elements still exist in the composite objective row. Introduce $x_3$ into solution, with $z_2^2$ as key element. The transformation results in Tableau 2.3. All elements of the composite objective row are nonnegative. Hence the test problem proves $\underline{x}^2$ of Tableau 2 is a nondominated extreme point.

Since introduction of $x_4$ into solution from Tableau 2 would lead to an already explored basis (Tableau 1), $x_3$ is introduced into solution ($x_4$ leaves). The resulting tableau is: $\underline{x}^3 = (0, 0, 45, 0)$. In Tableau 3, objective 3 is maximized and no alternate optimum exists. Hence $\underline{x}^3$ is a nondominated extreme point. Introduction of $x_4$ or $x_2$ into solution would lead back to Tableau 1 or 2, respectively. Hence, introduce $x_1$ into solution ($y_1$ leaves). Interested readers may verify that the resulting $\underline{x}^4$ is a dominated solution. However, $\underline{x}^5 = (20, 46.67, 0, 0)$ will be a nondominated extreme point.

Note: Computational experience reported in Evans and Steuer [100] and by us [238] utilizing ADBASE and ADEX verified one of the characteristics of MOLP problem: that is, even moderately sized problems often have an unworkably large number of nondominated extreme points. It also consumes substantial amounts of computer time and requires a large amount of core storage.

In order to reduce the number of nondominated extreme points produced by the MOLP methods, Steuer [322] has utilized the concept of gradient cone. The gradient cone is defined to be the convex cone generated by the gradients of the different objectives (i.e., by the k rows of C). The DM

Tableau 2.3

| | $x_1$ | $x_3$ | $x_4$ | $y_3$ | $\varepsilon_1$ | $\varepsilon_2$ | $\varepsilon_3$ |
|---|---|---|---|---|---|---|---|
| $\varepsilon_1$ | 810/63 | 0 | 0 | 1125/63 | 1 | 130/14 | 25/7 |
| $x_3$ | -4/7 | 1 | 0 | -1/14 | 0 | 9/14 | -3/14 |
| $x_4$ | 3/14 | 0 | 1 | 3/14 | 0 | 1/14 | 1/7 |
| $\sum$ | 810/63 | 0 | 0 | 1125/63 | 0 | 58/7 | 18/7 |

Tableau 3

| | $x_1$ | $x_2$ | $x_3$ | $x_4$ | $y_1$ | $y_2$ | $y_3$ | b |
|---|---|---|---|---|---|---|---|---|
| $y_1$ | 4 | 3/2 | 0 | -3 | 1 | 0 | -1/2 | 150 |
| $y_2$ | -3/2 | -9/4 | 0 | 7/2 | 0 | 1 | -3/4 | 185 |
| $x_3$ | 1/2 | 3/4 | 1 | 5/2 | 0 | 0 | 1/4 | 45 |
| $c_1$ | 15 | 15/2 | 0 | -25 | 0 | 0 | 25/2 | 2250 |
| $c_2$ | -1 | -1 | 0 | 0 | 0 | 0 | 0 | 0 |
| $c_3$ | 2 | 1/2 | 0 | 7 | 0 | 0 | 3/2 | 270 |
| $\sum$ | 16 | 7 | 0 | -18 | 0 | 0 | 14 | 2520 |

can, by specifying an interval of weights for each objective, control the size of the cone. The number of nondominated extreme points is directly related to the size of the gradient cone and hence depends indirectly upon the tightness of the weight interval of the objectives [100, 321, 322]. However, this process involves some 'a priori' articulation of preference information by the DM which is a combination of class 2 and class 4 methods. An interactive MOLP method presented by Steuer has been discussed (SEE Sec. 3.2.5).

### 4.1.4 ADAPTIVE SEARCH METHOD

This method, proposed by Beeson and Meisel [15], generates a set of representative nondominated solutions sufficiently distinct in objective function space or decision variable space to present true alternatives.

One of the properties of the set of nondominated solutions is that if $\underline{x}^i$ is the unique global optimum of $f_i(\underline{x})$, then $\underline{x}^i$ is a member of the nondominated solutions set. Hence the approach suggested here is to search for nondominated solutions by moving from one nondominated solution to another starting from $\underline{x}^i$, i = 1,2, ..., k. As an adaptive search procedure (based on the gradient method) is employed to obtain the nondominated solutions, this algorithm does not require any continuity in the objective functions on their derivatives, however, all the objective functions are to be differentiable.

There are three major facets of the algorithm. First the method of setting up a search algorithm; second, the method of adapting the parameters of the search algorithm; and third the method used for detecting, storing, and displaying the nondominated solutions.

The search algorithm: The algorithm first determines k starting points by maximizing each objective function individually. Let $\underline{x}^i$, i = 1, ..., k, be the starting point. At each starting point several searching problems are formed based on the following iterative technique:

$$\underline{x}(i+1) = \underline{x}(i) - \varepsilon(i)\ [J^T(\underline{x}(i))\underline{w}(i)] + \underline{\delta}(i)$$

where, i is the iteration number, $J(\underline{x}\ (i))$ is the kxn Jacobian matrix evaluated at $\underline{x}(i)$, $\underline{w}(i)$ is a k-dimensional weight vector, $\underline{\delta}(i)$ is an n dimensional penalty vector, and $\underline{x}(0) = \underline{x}^j$, where $\underline{x}^j$ is the jth starting point. The parameters $\varepsilon(i)$ and $\underline{w}(i)$ determine the step size and direction of movement, respectively. $\underline{\delta}(i)$ represents the penalty due to violation of any of the constraints.

Adaptation of parameters: The scalar $\varepsilon(i)$ controls the stepsize, and can be increased if the gradient is small and decreased if it is large. The value of $\varepsilon(i+1)$ is determined as follows:

$$\varepsilon(i+1) = \begin{cases} 0.9\ \varepsilon(i) & \text{for } K_M(i) = M \\ \varepsilon(i) & \text{for } 1 \leq K_M(i) \leq M \\ 1.1\ \varepsilon(i) & \text{for } K_M(i) = 0 \end{cases}$$

where $K_M(i)$ is the number of new solutions found in last M steps. The initial value of $\varepsilon(i)$ may be chosen by experimentation.

A series of problems are formulated at each starting point $\underline{x}^i$ by choosing the different initial value for the coefficient vector of the Jacobian matrix. Hence $\underline{w}(i+1)$ for the $\ell$th subproblem at the jth starting point are set in the following way:

$$w_p(i+1) = \gamma_p(i)\ w_p(i), \quad \text{for all } p = 1,\ldots,k, \quad p \neq j$$

where $\gamma_p(i)$ is a random number with a normal distribution around 1.0 and for $p \neq j$,

$$w_p(0) = \begin{cases} 1.0 & \text{for } p = \ell \\ \frac{0.5}{k-1} & \text{for al others} \end{cases}$$

$$w_p(i+1) = \begin{cases} 0.99\ w_p(i) & \text{if } \Delta(i) < \Delta(i-1) \\ w_p(i) & \text{if } \Delta(i) = \Delta(i-1) \\ 1.01\ w_p(i) & \text{if } \Delta(i) > \Delta(i-1) \end{cases}$$

where $\Delta(i) = |f_p(\underline{x}(i)) - f_p(\underline{x}(i-1))|$, and $w_p(0) = 0.1$. All components of $\underline{w}$ are limited to a maximum change of $\pm$ 50%.

Form a table of the representative nondominated solutions: Thus this algorithm solves k x(k-1) subproblems. Each subproblem is stopped if any one of three conditions are met:

1. A new step is within a given small distance of any starting location, or
2. No new solutions are found within the last 100 steps, or
3. A maximum of 5000 steps is taken.

After one problem is stopped, a new one is started by adjusting the $\underline{w}$ or selecting a new starting location.

Whenever a new point is found by the above method, the algorithm evaluates the new point first by checking the signs of the gradients. If any two of the gradients are of opposite sign and if the point is located on the boundary of the feasible set then the new point is considered as a candidate for nondominated solution. A candidate solution is stored if it is nondominated with respect to all other points already stored and the distance from the candidate point to any other stored point is greater than some threshold. After the number of stored nondominated solutions has increased above a maximum number of points, the threshold distances are increased and the table is purged.

NUMERICAL EXAMPLE

An example [15] in two dimensions, simple enough for analytic solution, is given. The VMP is:

$$\min \quad f_1(\underline{x}) = x_1^2 - x_2^2$$

$$\min \quad f_2(\underline{x}) = x_1/x_2$$

$$\text{s.t.} \quad -1 \leq x_1 \leq 2$$

$$1 \leq x_2 \leq 2$$

Figures 3.30 and 3.31 illustrate a representative set of nondominated solutions in decision variable and objective function space, respectively. This representative set has 30 nondominated solutions after 3000 steps were undertaken. Since solutions can be displayed graphically only for the two dimensional case, the most general form of display is tabular, as in Table 3.27 [15].

Note

The method generates a finite set of nondominated solutions for the study of trade-offs and alternatives, rather than determining the results by a fixed assignment of weights or fixed constraints. The method can be used for nonlinear model problems. However, the drawbacks of the method are: (1) the computational effort can become immense when there are many decisions; (2) no means are presented for choosing a preferred solution from the set of nondominated ones.

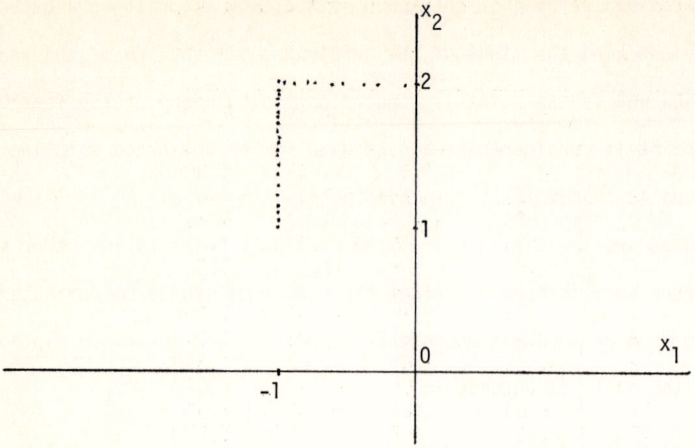


Fig. 3.30 Nondominated solutions in decision variable space [15]

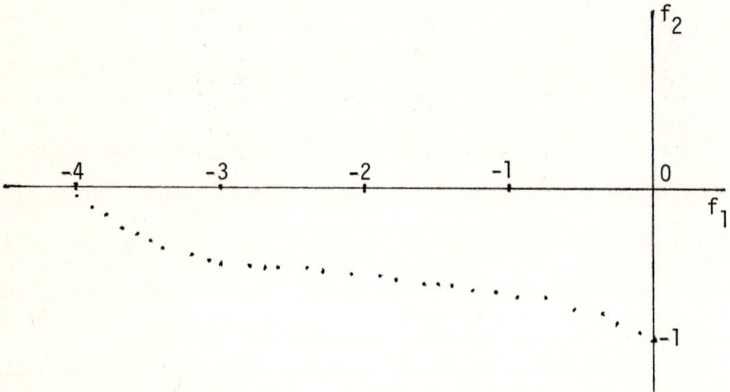


Fig. 3.31 Nondominated solutions in objective function space [15]

Table 3.27 A set of nondominated solutions [15]

| Solution No. | $f_1$ | $f_2$ | $x_1$ | $x_2$ |
|---|---|---|---|---|
| 1 | 0 | -1.0 | -1.00 | 1.00 |
| 2 | - .09 | - .96 | -1.00 | 1.04 |
| 3 | - .25 | - .90 | -1.00 | 1.12 |
| 4 | - .36 | - .86 | -1.00 | 1.17 |
| 5 | - .53 | - .81 | -1.00 | 1.24 |
| 6 | - .75 | - .74 | - .95 | 1.29 |
| 7 | - .93 | - .72 | -1.00 | 1.39 |
| 8 | -1.1 | - .69 | -1.00 | 1.44 |
| 9 | -1.25 | - .67 | -1.00 | 1.50 |
| 10 | -1.4 | - .65 | -1.00 | 1.54 |
| 11 | -1.5 | - .63 | -1.00 | 1.59 |
| 12 | -1.6 | - .62 | -1.00 | 1.61 |
| 13 | -1.8 | - .60 | -1.00 | 1.67 |
| 14 | -1.9 | - .58 | -1.00 | 1.71 |
| 15 | -2.1 | - .57 | -1.00 | 1.76 |
| 16 | -2.3 | - .55 | -1.00 | 1.81 |
| 17 | -2.4 | - .54 | -1.00 | 1.86 |
| 18 | -2.6 | - .53 | -1.00 | 1.90 |
| 19 | -2.7 | - .52 | -1.00 | 1.93 |
| 20 | -2.8 | - .51 | -1.00 | 1.96 |
| 21 | -3.0 | - .50 | -1.00 | 2.00 |
| 22 | -3.1 | - .47 | - .95 | 2.00 |
| 23 | -3.2 | - .44 | - .88 | 2.00 |
| 24 | -3.4 | - .40 | - .79 | 2.00 |
| 25 | -3.5 | - .35 | - .71 | 2.00 |
| 26 | -3.6 | - .30 | - .61 | 2.00 |
| 27 | -3.7 | - .26 | - .52 | 2.00 |
| 28 | -3.8 | - .19 | - .39 | 2.00 |
| 29 | -3.9 | - .14 | - .29 | 2.00 |
| 30 | -4.0 | - .05 | - .09 | 2.00 |

## IV. APPLICATIONS

The drive to have realistic models for management systems has been the impetus towards the development of many fine methods for MODM problems presented in the preceding section. However, few methods have yet been tested with large real-world problems. Table 4.1 shows a classification of references on applications. Many papers on the list present general discussion of MODM concepts applying to each class of applications, but reported examples of applications of MODM models to real-world problems seem to be rare.

The applications are classified into 12 categories as indicated in Table 4.1. We try to describe the problems briefly and indicate the MODM methods used in solving the problems in this section.

Table 4.1 Classification of references on applications

| Class | References |
|---|---|
| 1. Academic Planning | 105,130,134,149,213,254,255a,300,352, 353a |
| 2. Econometrics and Development Planning | 86a,225a,310,327a,333a,348,363-364 |
| 3. Financial Planning | |
| Capital Budgeting | 5,43-44,154,168,211,215,268,301a,351 |
| Working Capital Management | 190,294 |
| Portfolio Selection | 201,216 |
| Others | 150,349 |
| 4. Health Care Planning | BM-13,174,347,359 |
| 5. Land Use Planning for | |
| Community Development | 9-10,73 |
| 6. Manpower Planning | 58,269,271,279 |
| 7. Media Planning | BM-13,55,57 |
| 8. Production Planning | 137,166,173,209-210,214,314,349-350 |
| 9. Public Administration | BM-13,34a,115a,217,278,324 |
| 10. Systems Reliability | 167,204,211a |
| 11. Transportation Planning | |
| and Traffic Management | 1,59,69,218 |
| 12. Water Resources Management | BM-8,66-68,79,84,101,119,139,140,165,225, 225a,236,244,247-249,252,253,277,328,343 |
| 13. Miscellaneous | 46a,69,84a,134a,191,219a,304,326,356 |

1. Academic Planning

Efforts to develop and apply the methods of management science to higher education have increased. The rising cost of higher education has caused us to develop a keen and critical view of the operational efficiency of educational institutions.

University Admissions Planning: The problem of university admissions planning arises from the multiple objectives of the university. Okello, Kaufman, and Zionts [254] present the development of an interactive multiple objective decision procedure to assist the admissions director of a large public university in determining the number, quality and composition of new students to the university. The method of Wallenius-Zionts (see Sec. 3.1.4) was used.

The Allocation of Faculty Effort of an Academic Department: The method of Geoffrion (see Sec. 3.1.1) was used by Geoffrion, Dyer and Feinberg [105, 130] for the optimal allocation of faculty effort among three principal activities (formal teaching, departmental service duties, and other tasks such as research and student counseling), given an exogeneous budget for personnel in terms of full time equivalent positions.

The Establishment of Faculty Teaching Schedules: The faculty assignment problem is only one of many day-to-day situations which can be viewed as allocations of scarce resources. The problem was addressed by Harwood and Lawless [149] by using the linear goal programming approach (see Sec. 2.2.2).

University Budget Planning and Resources Allocation: Goal programming models of a university budget planning and resources allocation problem are presented by Lee and Clayton [213] for a single-period

(one-year) within a college, and by Schroeder [300] for a multiple period (long-range) with several academic units. The goals to be achieved are accreditation, salary increase, faculty/student ratios, faculty/staff ratio, faculty distribution by rank, faculty/graduate assistant ratio, and cost minimization. Walters, Mangold, and Haran [352] propose another goal programming model for long-range planning which includes faculty staffing goals, career constraints, teaching and course loads, tenure constraints and budget constraints.

Long-Range Planning of a University: A long-range planning procedure for administrators in private universities is presented by Wehrung, Hopkins, and Massy [353a] by using a modified Geoffrion method. The procedure generate a sequence of alternative future configurations of the university that satisfy several financial constraints. An administrator examines the configurations and makes a choice based on twelve key variables: regular faculty, auxilary faculty, undergraduate student enrollment, graduate student enrollment, tenured faculty/faculty ratio, staff/faculty ratio, tuition level, faculty leverage, new program and net improvements, tuition growth rate, faculty salary growth rate, and staff salary growth rate; these are variables over which the university had administrative control.

Others: A curriculum design problem concerning the upper grades of a combined elementary and junior high school is presented by Oppenheimer [255a] for resource allocation decisions. He introduces a proxy approach which is a modified Geoffrion method. Gibbs [134] proposes a goal programming model of the development of a training program for a group of systems analysts.

2. Econometrics and Development Planning

Economic policy planning is one of the emerging areas for the application of MODM methods. Economic policy making determines the means for attaining specified economic and social goals. The problems involve policy decisions for both short- and long-range economic planning.

KLEIN I- Econometric Model for the U.S. in Thirties: The model considered by Theil [333a] is an adaptation of the econometric model for the U.S. called KLEIN I. The model contains six goal (or endogenous) variables, and three instrument (or exogenous) variables. The goal variables are consumption, corporate profit, private wage, investment, national income, and capital stock. The instrument variables are government wages, tax revenue, and government expenditure. The DM has three targets: consumption, net investment and the ratio of profits to the private wage bill. Spivey and Tamura [310] use Goal Programming to solve this problem. Despontin and Vincke [86a] propose the use of a modified STEM method (see Sec. 3.2.1).

An Econometric Model for Finland: Wallenius et al. [348], use the method of Geoffrion (see Sec. 3.1.1), to solve the annual economic policy model which is an adaptation for Finland of the Dutch short-term annual model. The goal variables in the model consist of four traditional aggregate variables: percentage change in GDP, unemployment, rate of inflation, and the balance of trade. The exogeneous variables include indirect taxes, income transfers, public expenditure and changes in the exchange rate. Monetary policy instruments have not been incorporated in the model. There are 12 econometric (or behavioral) equations and

34 definitional equations. The model parameters have been estimated using the data for the years 1951-1970.

A Long-Range Comprehensive Economic Planning Model: Yoon [363-364] uses Goal Programming for a dynamic multi-sectoral comprehensive economic planning model for Korea. The economy has been divided into 16 aggregate sectors. There are 5 types of equations: distributional relationships, capacity relationships, capital accounting relationships, import ceiling, and savings relationships. Four objectives for each year of the planning period are consumption growth rate, capital stock growth rate, balance of payment, and GNP. Past Korean data (1970) is used to estimate the parameters, and policy decisions are obtained for the five-year planning period of 1977-1981. A similar goal programming model for Thailand is studied by Tantasuth [327a].

3. Financial Planning

Financial planning is one of the key areas of corporate management. This is also an area where multiple conflicting objectives are embedded in the problem. The financial planning problems can be divided into three broad categories: capital budgeting, working capital management, and portfolio selection.

Capital Budgeting: Capital budgeting problems involve mid- to long-range decisions regarding the selection of projects from a candidate set in which capital investments are to be made. General concepts of applying MODM approaches to capital budgeting have been presented in [43, 44, 154, 301a].

A Hypothetical Corporate Investment Planning: Linear goal programming has been used by Lee and Lerro [215] for solving the capital budgeting problem of a hypothetical company which has 15 investment opportunities over a four year period. The 8 distinguishable objectives (goals) for the planning are: capital expenditures constrained by budget allocations; interperiod transfer of funds; accept project 9 or 12 and 3 or 4; maximize net present value of the firm; keep 50% growth rate; maximize the cash flow in the third year; provide a minimum liquidity for each year; increase foreign investment; and maximize the total cash flow over 4-year planning horizon. Similar kind of problems are treated by Ashton et al. [5] using the interactive linear GP method (see Sec. 3.1.1); by Lawrence et al. [211] using the MOLP method (see Sec. 4.1.3); and by Powell and Vergin [268] using a heuristic simulation model.

Selection of a Research and Development (R & D) Program: Ignizio [168] uses the linear integer goal programming approach for selection of an R & D program. It is a simple example with 3 programs from which one must select none, one, two, or all programs so as to maximize two objectives while still satisfying all future year budgetary constraints.

A Long-Range Capital Investment in a Steel Corporation: An implementing the interactive MODM method (the method of Zionts-Wallenius; see Sec. 3.1.4) to a real-world problem (a Belgian steel corporation) for long-range capital investment decisions is reported by Wallenius and Zions [351]. Four objectives approximately measuring key criteria in the evaluation of corporate planning decisions are: (1) maximize cumulative cash flow at the end of the horizon; (2) minimize long-term loans taken during the horizon; (3) maximize net worth at the end of the horizon; (4) minimize short-term loans. Two versions of the model have been formulated: a small two-period model in which each period represents one year, and a larger four-period, ten-year model in which successive periods represent one, two, three, and four years.

Working Capital Management: Working capital management involves the short-term (usually a year) investment and financing decision of a firm; thus the firm's multiple objectives relate to its profitability, liquidity, and use of financial leverage. Keown and Martin [190] introduce uncertainty in the working capital management problems through a chance-constrained goal programming. The uncertainty is associated with expected cash balance, net cash flow, net change in inventory, net change in current assets and liabilities, and change in long-term debt. The objectives (goals) include profit, cash level, inventory level, current ratio, acid test ratio, debt to total asset ratio, and fixed charges coverage ratio. Sartoris and Spruill [294] use goal programming to solve a firm's one-period financial decision model that includes both the profitability and liquidity objectives.

Portfolio Selection: Portfolio analysis involves selection of a set of stocks from the candidate set for an investor with a specified amount of money to invest. Lee and Lerro [216] use goal programming for a problem in which the candidate stocks are from 61 companies in 10 industry groups. The objectives include expected return, growth, risk, and price variation. Kumar and Philippatos [201] consider the portfolio selection problem using goal programming for the Dual-Purpose Funds (DPF). DPF's are diversified closed-end investment companies that issue two types of securities in equal amounts - Income and Capital shares. DPF's attempt through the portfolio to maximize dividend income to the income shareholders and capital appreciation to the capital shareholders. The candidate stocks and securities considered consisted of 62 common stocks and 7 preferred stocks from 9 different industrial classifications. The goals consist of systematic and unsystematic risk, income return, and capital return.

4. Health Care Planning

Two basic factors, inefficient delivery of health services to the population and skyrocketing medical costs, challenge the health care planning in the United States. It is essential to apply modern scientific management techniques to assure an efficient delivery of health services at a reasonable cost.

A Resources Allocation Model for Hospital Administration: Lee [B-13] presents a linear goal programming model for administrating a hospital located in a small city (25,000 population). The administrators goals are: (1) secure the necessary manpower to provide adequate service; (2) replace and/or acquire equipment; (3) provide adequate pay increases to personnel; (4) achieve the desired personnel/patient ratio; (5) achieve the desired distribution of each personnel category; (6) achieve the desired nurse/staff, nurse/professional and professional/staff ratios; (7) minimize costs and break even in the operation. Wacht and Whitford [347] present a problem concerning capital investment analysis for hospitals; linear goal programming is used to obtain a rational allocation of resources.

Financing (Capital Budgeting) Public Hospitals in Ontario: Jackman [174] describes a model for the financing of over 200 active hospitals in the Province of Ontario - population approximately 8,000,000. The model is an integer programming algorithm leading to selection and financing of capital projects proposed by the hospitals.

Budget Planning for a Health Care Clinic: Goal programming approach is used by Lee [BM-13] for an aggregate budget planning for a health care clinic.

5. Land Use Planning for Community Development

In comprehensive land use planning for community development, an emerging trend is the use of analytical models as aids to decision making which systematically consider various planning aspects.

County-Wide Land Use Planning for an Urban Community Development: Bammi and Bammi [10] propose an optimization model for comprehensive land use planning (OPTPLAN) to arrive at optimal acreages of ten land use types in several regions within a county or city. They use a modified form of utility function approach (see Sec. 2.1.1). The objectives considered are: (1) minimization of conflict between different land uses; (2) minimization of travel distance of new trips to the existing transportation network; (3) generation of a fiscally sound plan; (4) minimization of environmental impact.

Small City Development Based on Municipal Cost-Revenue Analysis: Awerbuch and Wallace [9] applied cost-revenue analysis by incorporating socioeconomic and demographic factors to assisting municipal government in studying the impact of physical development on the fiscal well-being of the community. They used the parametric method (see Sec. 4.1.1). The objective functions (community goals) considered in their model are total tax rate, average family income, percent low income families, percent elderly households, total population, total retail sales, and job opportunity.

Urban-Suburban Population Location Preferences Problem:

Courtney, Klastorin and Ruefli [73] employ a goal programming formulation (see Sec. 2.2.2) to treat the problem of population location in a metropolitan area. They divide a target population into groups which then compete for a share of limited capacity in a number of urban sectors. The possible usefulness of this approach to urban planning, real estate development, and transportation systems design is illustrated.

6. Manpower Planning

A common problem of manpower planning within a hierarchy is devising a two- or three-year staffing plan (quotas for recruiting, training, promotion, etc.) which respects organizational constraints (e.g., financial constraints), permits the attainment of short-term organizational objectives, and does not prevent longer-term objectives from being reached. The objectives of the organization are often in conflict. The MODM methods are applied to solve these problems.

Planning Equal Employment Opportunities in the Navy: Charnes, Cooper, et al. [58] have utilized multi-period Markoff processes embedded in goal programming models for planning equal employment opportunities in the Navy. The plan is directed to changing the mix of employees (minorities, females, etc.) by recruitment, training and placement, and is also for altering present probabilities of promotion and transfer to new steady state values.

The Canadian Force Officers Promotion and Recruiting Planning: A goal programming model (see Sec. 2.2.2) of the manpower system for officers within the Canadian Forces has been constructed by Price [269] and Price and Piskor [271]. The model forms part of a control system for fixing promotion and recruiting quotas for a given planning horizon. The objective functions of the planning are budget, military effectiveness, promotion equitability and stability of rank structure.

The Postal Service Short-Term Manpower Scheduling Problem: Ritzman and Krajewski [279] consider a short-term manpower scheduling problem in a post office. The problem is to achieve a desirable balance between mail transit times and resource expenditures. They have used a super-objective function (a utility function) by weighting the individual objective functions.

7. Media Planning

The purpose of media planning is to allocate available advertising budget to selected media. All feasible media are considered in terms of maximizing their effectiveness for available resources or minimizing costs for a desired level of effectiveness.

Applications of goal programming models for selection of media mix and advertising scheduling are studied by Charnes, Cooper et al. [57,59]. The objectives considered include the percentage reach and frequency of appearance in different types of media aimed at different segments of the market at different time periods, and cost of the advertising. Lee [BM-13] considers a similar problem and also use the goal programming approach.

8. Production Planning

The difficult problem encountered in an aggregate production planning is the fluctuation in demand over time. Demand fluctuations can be absorbed by adjusting the size of work force, allowing overtime or idle time while maintaining a constant work force, and adjusting the inventory level. Production planning aims to achieve the most efficient utilization of available resources by organizational policies concerning employment, inventories, and production.

Aggregate Planning of Production and Work Force: The problem is to determine the scheduling of production, work force, and inventories to satisfy known demand requirements over a finite time horizon. The objectives include production cost minimization, balancing of labor force, and minimization of inventories or back-orders. A linear goal programming model for multiple product, multiple period aggregate production planning problems has been studied by Jaaskelainen [173] and Lee and Jaaskelainen [214]. Wallenius [349-350] uses the STEM method (see Sec. 3.2.1) and the method of Geoffrion (see Sec. 3.1.1) to solve a single product aggregate production planning problem. The classical Holt quadratic model of the problem of scheduling aggregate production and work force has been approximated by a linear goal programming model by Goodman [137]. The original Holt quadratic model has been modified to a multiple objective problem and solved by the iterative nonlinear goal programming by Raju [273a].

Coordinated Production and Logistics Planning: Lawrence and Burbridge [209] use the MOLP method (see Sec. 4.1.4) to decide what products should be produced, how much of each product to produce, and where production should take place. The decison-making process utilizes several key objectives: (1) maximizing total sales revenue for specific location and customer; (2) minimizing total cost of production and distribution; and (3) maximizing production of a particular item at a particular location.

The Blending of Materials Problem: The problem concerns the production process of blending several raw materials into a product conforming to given specifications. Multiple objectives of the problem are: (1) determining the least costly product; (2) minimizing the amount of imported raw materials used in a blend; (3) maximizing the ith property of the product blend; (4) minimizing the amount of impurities in the product blend; (5) minimizing the use of volatile materials. A modified goal programming and the MOLP method have been used for solving the problem by Lawrence and Burbridge [210].

Production Scheduling for a Large Food Manufacturer: A major food manufacturer is concerned with short term problems of the utilization of existing company resources of space, labor, raw materials, plant capacity and machine availability, none of which can be expressed in meaningful cost terms. Stainton [314] uses a heuristic approach to solve this MODM problem of the production scheduling in which modification to an existing plan is necessary when certain operating factors change drastically from those forecast at the time of original planning.

9. Public Administration

Two primary functions of administration of a governmental agency are: (1) allocating the scarce resources in the most efficient manner to the provision of services; (2) allocating equipment, supplies, and services to the various groups that constitute the system in the most equitable manner. A wide variety of MODM problems such as school busing, allocation of fire companies in a big city, economic planning of a small town, forest management, school allocation, planning the dimensions of a growing industrial town, etc., have been studied.

School Busing Model: Lee [217] reports on the application of goal programming (see Sec. 2.2.2) to the school busing problem. The model attempts to reflect such goals as providing educational opportunity to children, striving for a racial balance, balancing overcrowding among schools, permitting the community school concept, and minimizing total transportation costs.

Allocation of Fire Companies in New York City: The major objectives of a fire department are to reduce casualties and monetary loss caused by fire. A surrogate measure, strongly related to losses and fatalities, is the time it takes for a fire company, once it has been dispatched, to arrive at the scene of a fire. The parametric allocation model, proposed by Rider [278], uses travel time to fire to measure system performance and generate allocations satisfying criteria ranging from the minimization of city-wide travel time to the equalization of average travel in different regions in New York City.

Public Forest Resources Management: An interactive MOLP approach (see Sec. 3.2.5) has been applied by Steuer and Schuler [324] to prepare preliminary management plans for a 10,000 acre subunit of a national forest. The objectives for the subunit planning are timber production, dispersed recreation, hunting forest species, hunting open land species, and grazing; these are subject to three constraints: acreage limitations, budget constraint, timber harvesting restriction.

Economic Planning in a Small Rural Town: A model for the capital improvement requirements of a small rural town for a three-year planning horizon is presented by Lee and Sevebeck [BM-13] using goal programming approach.

School Allocation and Dimensioning of a Growing Industrial Town: Borreani-Ostaneilo and Capellaro [34a] present a multiobjective, linear, mixed integer model formulation of problems of allocating and dimensioning school services of a growing industrial town in Italy. Demographic situation and trends to the near future (5 to 8 years), structural and qualitative characteristic of the population, quality of school structures and estimates of need have been considered. Three criteria which must be minimized are investment costs, displacement time, and double-turns of students (i.e., the use of the same structure two different periods in a day). Zeleny's MOLP method (see Sec. 4.1.3) was used.

Resource Allocation in a Decentralized Organization: A government agency of the UK administers several autonomous regional offices to improve training and retraining opportunities for individuals. The agency's primary function is to ensure that a satisfactory allocation of funds is made to each region so that national targets of individuals trained can be achieved. Two mathematical models (one in deterministic and another in stochastic) for allocating funds are presented by Flavell and Salkin [115a]; they use interactive goal programming (see Sec. 3.1.1).

10. Systems Reliability and Maintenance Policy

Optimum Systems Reliability: A complex system reliability problem with two objectives (maximizing the system reliability and minimizing the system cost) is solved by an iterative nonlinear goal programming by Hwang et al. [167]. A system reliability problem with redundancy is formulated to have 4 objectives (system reliability, cost, weight, volume) and solved by Lee [211a] using nonlinear integer goal programming.

Maintenance Policy of Aircraft According to Multiple Criteria: Ladany and Aharoni [204] present a model for scheduled replacement maintenance policies for the critical parts of aircraft based on multiple criteria. The criteria are the lowest possible operating cost per unit of time, maximum mission reliability, and minimal expected inflight failure cost.

11. Transportation Planning and Traffic Management

Transportation Networks Design Problems: The design of transportation networks in the context of four objectives has been presented by Agarwal [1]. The objectives are: (1) minimize the total travel time; (2) minimize the total construction costs; (3) minimize the total vehicle miles; and (4) minimize the total number of dwelling units taken for rights-of-way. The method of Geoffrin (see Sec. 3.1.1) and the STEM method (see Sec. 3.2.1) are used.

Traffic Management for Air Pollution Episode Avoidance: Collins [69] suggests the adaptive search method for designing a feasible feedback control mechanism for the management of freeway traffic in order to abate or prevent air pollution episodes.

Transportation Problem: The analysis of transportation problems includes the determination of optimal shipping patterns, the analysis of production scheduling problems, transshipment problems, and assignment problems. Lee and Moore [218] use linear goal programming for optimizing transportation problems. Charnes, Cooper et al. [59] present an assignment problem which is a variant of the transportation model.

12. Water Resources Management

A review of MODM methods for water resources planning has been carried out by Cohon and Marks [68]. A bibliography of multiobjective water resources planning was presented by Loucks [225] in 1975. Many papers [101, 119, 139, 225a, 236, 252, 328] present general discussion of MODM concepts applying to water resources system planning, but reported examples of successful applications to real-world problems seem to be rare.

A Hypothetical Bow River Valley Water Quality Management: Monarchi et al. [247-249] present two interactive methods: SEMOPS and SIGMOP (see sec. 3.2.2), which are applied to the pollution control problems of an artificial river basin, the Bow River Valley. The multiple conflicting goals are to raise the dissolved oxygen (DO) levels (for higher water quality in the basin), to keep a high percentage return on industrial investment (by reducing expenditures for waste water treatment), and to retain low tax rates for cities (by not spending much on city's sewage treatment). A preferred solution has to be determined by the river basin management committee.

A Multiobjective Reservoir Management: A problem is introduced by Reid and Vemuri [277] with a dam of finite height impounds water in the reservoir and that water is required for various purposes such as flood control, irrigation, industrial and urban use, and power generation. Three objectives (the capital cost of the project, the water loss due to evaporation, and the total volume capacity of the reservoir) are considered. A modified parametric method (see Sec. 4.1.1) for generating non-dominated solutions is used by them. The same problem is treated by Haimes, Hall et al. [BM-8, 140] by using the surrogate worth trade-off method (see Sec. 3.1.2). Vemuri [343] also solves the problem by a modified geometric programming approach.

The Water Resources Development Problem in San Angelo, Texas: Dean and Shih [84] present the decision analysis solution to San Angelo's water resources development problem by using utility theory (see Sec. 2.1.1) with Monte-Carlo simulation. Six independent criteria of San Angelo's water resources development goals are: quantity, dependability, quality, cost, flexibility and social-economic impact.

A River Basin Planning: Cohon and Marks [66-67] present a hypothetical river basin planning problem concerned with allocation of water among several uses and development alternatives in terms of multiobjective water resource planning. A multiobjective screening model is used.

Alternative Long-Range Water Resource Systems in the Hungarian Great Plain of the Tisza River Basin: David and Duckstein [79] present a case study in Hungary of the definition and comparison of alternative water resources systems designed to meet long-range goals (say 60 years). A comprehensive cost-effectiveness approach is adapted to define goals of the system for meeting increasing economic and social requirements of water management.

A Water Quality Management for Miami River Basin in Ohio: Hwang and Paidy [165] have formulated a multiple objective water quality management model for Miami river basin in Ohio; they use a nonlinear goal programming approach (see Sec. 2.2.2) to obtain the preferred solution. The multiple conflicting objectives in the model are: (1) minimize the cost of treatment; (2) minimize the capital investments into treatment plants; (3) minimize the deviation of individual treatment levels from their mean; (4) meet the water quality standards

## V. CONCLUDING REMARKS

This survey of MODM methods and applications is a guided tour through the literature. It provides readers with a capsule look into the existing methods, their characteristics, and their applicability to analysis of MODM problems.

### On MODM Methods Classification:

We have proposed a system of classifying about two dozen MODM methods (see Fig. 1.1. A Taxonomy of methods for multiple objective decision making); most of these methods have been proposed by various researchers in the last few years, but here for the first time they are presented together. The literature of these methods is identified and classified systematically (see Table 1.3).

### On Applications of MODM:

MODM applications are classified into 12 categories. Each topic's references are identified (see Table 4.1), and a summary of each article is presented. Many papers on the list present general discussion of MODM concepts relating to each class of applications, but reported examples of applications of MODM methods to real-world problems seem to be rare.

### On Multiple Attribute Decision Making (MADM) Methods:

In the study of decision making in complex environments, such terms as "multiple objectives", "multiple attribute", "multiple criteria", or "multiple dimensional" are used to describe decision situations. Often these terms are used interchangeable [229], and there are no universal definitions of these terms [BM-12]. Multiple criteria decision making (MCDM) has become the accepted designation for all methodologies dealing with MODM and/or MADM. Our definitions distinguish between MODM and MADM (see II. Basic concepts and Terminology). In our survey the problems of MCDM are broadly classified into two categories - MADM and MODM. MADM methods are for selecting an alternative from a small, explicit list of alternatives, while MODM methods are used for an infinite set of alternatives implicitly defined by the constraints [229]. The procedure for MODM thus involves a design problem rather than a choice problem for MADM.

Literature on MADM methods has been reviewed extensively by MacCrimmon [227,229] and others (see Table 1.2), therefore, it is excluded from our survey. The MADM methods may be classified as follows:

1. Methods for full dimensional approach
   - 1.1 Dominance
   - 1.2 Disjunctive and conjunctive constraints
2. Methods for single dimensional approach
   - 2.1 Maximin
   - 2.2 Maximax
   - 2.3 Lexicography
   - 2.4 Elimination by aspects
   - 2.5 Effective index
3. Methods for single dimensional approach - with utility theory
   - 3.1 Unidimensional utility theory
   - 3.2 Additive utility model
   - 3.3 Additive expected utility model
   - 3.4 Quasi-additive utility model
   - 3.5 Hierarchical utility model
4. Methods for intermediate dimensional approach
   - 4.1 Trade-offs
   - 4.2 Nonmetric multidimensional scaling

The so-called "multiattribute utility theory" is applicable to both MADM and MODM problems, but few methods are applicable to both (as seen by comparing the MODM methods in Fig. 1.1 with the above MADM methods) if the characteristics of MODM and MADM problems are defined as we have distinguished them.

<u>On Illustration and Comparative Evaluation of MODM Methods</u>:

We have illustrated the procedure for each method by a simple numerical example in detail. This will help the reader comprehend the basic concept, the computational procedures, and the characteristics of each method. Since several simple common numerical examples are used through the illustration of the methods, it may serve for the comparative evaluation of the methods.

These examples and the methods they illustrate are:

(1) Numerical example of production scheduling of the Hardee Toy Company.

It is a linear model problem with 2 objectives, 2 decision variables, and 2 constraints. The problem is solved by:

1.1.1 The method of global criterion

2.1.1 Utility function methods

2.2.2a Linear goal programming

2.2.3 Goal attainment method

3.2.1 STEM method

3.2.4 GPSTEM

4.1.1 Parametric method

4.1.3 MOLP methods

(2) Numerical example of the nutrition problem.

This is a linear model problem with 3 objectives, 6 decision variables, and 10 constraints. It is solved by:

3.1.1a Method of Geoffrion

3.1.1b Iterative goal programming

3.1.3 Method of satisfactory goals

3.1.4 Method of Zionts-Wallenius

3.2.5 Method of Steuer (interactive MOLP method)

(3) Numerical example of Bow River Valley water quality management.

The original problem is a nonlinear model problem with 6 objectives, 3 decision variables, and 7 constraints. It is solved by:

3.2.2 SEMOPS method

The modified nonlinear model problem, with 3 objectives, 3 decision variables and 10 constraints is solved by:

3.1.2 Surrogate worth trade-off method

(4) Numerical example of the ABC company management problem.

It is a nonlinear model problem with 3 objectives, 2 decision variables, and 3 constraints. The problem is solved by:

2.2.2b Nonlinear goal programming

3.1.2 Surrogate worth trade-off method

(5) Numerical example of the Ace Electronic Inc. production planning problem.

This is a linear model problem with 3 objectives, 4 decision variables, and 3 constraints. It is solved by:

3.2.3 Method of the displaced ideal

4.1.3 MOLP methods

(6) Numerical example of optimal scheduled maintenance policy.

This nonlinear model problem has 4 objectives, and 1 decision variable. It is solved by:

2.2.1 Lexicographic method

Since most of the MODM methods have been developed only in recent years, comparative evaluation of them is scarce. Agarwal [1] employs Geoffrion's method (see Sec. 3.1.1) and STEM (see Sec. 3.2.1) to solve an urban transportation network design model. Criteria for rating performance of methods in the study are: 1) quality of results obtained; 2) the DM's like or dislike of the methods; 3) computational burden of each method. Dyer [90] tests Geoffrion's method (see Sec. 3.1.1) using 9 subjects (as the DMs) to rate the method in terms of 1) the difficulty of its use, and 2) the DM's confidence in the solution obtained. Masud [238a] uses linear goal programming (see Sec. 2.2.2a), STEM (see Sec. 3.2.1) and SEMOPS (see Sec. 3.2.2) solving an aggregate production planning problem with 4 objectives, 88 decision variables and 48 constraints on the linear model. The criteria for comparative evaluation of the methods are 1) quality of results obtained, and 2) ease of use.

Wallenius [350] presents probably the only systematic comparative evaluation of three interactive methods (Geoffrion method, STEM, and the structured approach- a simple trial-and-error procedure). These methods are applied to a problem of planning production, inventory and labor for a fictitious company; the problem has 3 objectives, 25 decision variables and 19 constraints. The methods are evaluated through the following measures of performance:

1) DM's confidence in the best compromise.
2) Ease of use of the method.
3) Ease of understanding the logic of the method.
4) Usefulness of the information provided to aid the DM.
5) Rapidity of convergence, measured by the number of cycles and the total time for solving the problem.
6) CPU-time on a computer.

The criteria for evaluating the performance of MODM methods are complex and have not been defined and discussed in literature. The six criteria used in Wallenius' paper listed above are the most extensive ones, yet they are by no means complete. It is interesting to compare these measures of performance with the criteria for evaluation of a nonlinear programming algorithm (a single objective decision making method). The question as to what is the best in a nonlinear programming algorithm encompasses the following criteria [157a]:

1) Time required in a series of tests (execution time and/or number of functional evaluations).
2) Size of the problem (dimensionality, number of inequality and equality constraints).
3) Accuracy of the solution with respect to the optimal decision variables and/or with respect to the objective function, inequality and equality constraints, and gradient.

4) Simplicity of use (time required to introduce data functions into the computer program).

5) Simplicity of computer program to execute the algorithm.

6) Applicability to real-world problems (large scale problems) most of the time.

It can be concluded that the comparative evaluation of MODM methods is almost nonexistent; the criteria for rating performance of each method are much more complex than those for a single objective decision making method (e.g., a nonlinear programming algorithm), and they are not yet established.

In selecting criteria for evaluating MODM methods, we must consider:

1) Characteristic of problems:
   a) linear vs nonlinear models;
   b) small-scale vs large-scale (real-world) problems in numbers of objectives, decision variables, and constraints;
   c) information availability.
2) Interface between DM-analyst and analyst-machine:
   a) Ease of understanding or complexity of the logic
   b) Ease of use
   c) Confidence in the compromised solutions
   d) Coding difficulty
   e) DM's acceptance
3) Implementation of compromised solutions obtained:
   a) DM's confidence in the solution
   b) Simplicity and usefulness of the information provided to aid DM

Advantages and disadvantages mentioned in our text come mainly from original sources by individual authors quoted. Since most methods have not been tested by real-world problems, we cannot yet discuss in depth the advantages, disadvantages, applicability, computational complexity, difficulty, etc., of each method. A large variety of problems approached by the various methods will provide a comparative analysis of the methods. This kind of activity should be carried out and continued for some time to come.

On Future Study:

It seems that MODM models, methods, and applications have already grown beyond infancy. A variety of fairly good methods for linear model problems are available as shown in Fig. 1.1 and Table 1.3. The MODM models are presented in a diversified field of applications as shown in Table 4.1. But few methods have been tested with large real-world problems, and reported examples of applications of MODM models to real-world problems seem to be rare. Much will be gained from applications. The skills for modeling, critical views of coding the methods (algorithms), the computational experiences on large real-world problems, and the implementation of the optimal solutions are urgently needed and beneficial to all.

Efficient computer codes for MODM nonlinear models are still lacking; the complexity of nonlinear models in general, and the unavailability of a general dependable code for nonlinear programming (single objective) problems hamper the progress of its development.

Two areas where there has been little progress, from a methodological point of view, are: MODM problems with uncertainty and stochastic process, and the area of MODM dynamic control problems. It is hoped these areas will receive attention from researchers in the future.

The development of methods for "fuzzy" area which combines MODM and MADM problems may be a topic for future research. Many multiple criteria decision making problems blend selection (multiple attribute decision making) and design (multiple objective decision making) of alternatives. Except for utility function methods which are used in both MODM and MADM, few applicable methods are available.

The importance of applying MODM methods to solving real-world problems cannot be over emphasized. As for the applicability of decision analysis by these methods, at the present stage of development it is probably more useful as a means of providing insight than analytical answers. It is hoped that the DM can and will make educated compromises and judgements based on insights generated by MODM approaches.

## VI. BIBLIOGRAPHY

Books, Monographs, and Conference Proceedings:


[BM-1] Barrett, J. H., Individual Goals and Organizational Objectives: A Study of Integration Mechanisms, University of Michigan Press, Ann Arbor, Michigan, 1970.

[BM-2] Cochrane, J. L., and M. Zeleny (eds.), Multiple Criteria Decision Making, University of South Carolina Press, Columbia, South Carolina, 1973.

[BM-3] Easton, A., Complex Managerial Decisions Involving Multiple Objectives, Wiley, New York, 1973.

[BM-4] Fishburn, P. C., Utility Theory for Decision Making, Wiley, New York, 1970.

[BM-5] Green, P. E. and F. J. Carmone, Multidimensional Scaling and Related Techniques in Marketing Analysis, Allyn and Bacon, Boston, Massachusetts, 1970.

[BM-6] Green, P. E. and V. R. Rao, Applied Multidimensional Scaling: A Comparison of Approaches and Algorithms, Holt, Rinehart and Winston, New York, 1972.

[BM-7] Green, P. E. and Y. Wind, Multiattribute Decisions in Marketing: A Measurement Approach, Dryden Press, Hinsdale, Illinois, 1973.

[BM-8] Haimes, Y. Y., W. A. Hall and H. T. Freedman, Multiobjective Optimization in Water Resources Systems, The Surrogate Worth Trade-off Method, Elsivier Scientific, New York, 1975.

[BM-9] Ignizio, J. P., Goal Programming and Extensions, Lexington Books, Massachusetts, 1976.

[BM-10] Ijiri, Y., Management Goals and Accounting for Control, North-Holland, Amsterdam, 1965.

[BM-11] Johnsen, E., Studies in Multiobjective Decision Models, Monograph No. 1, Economic Research Center in Lund, Sweden, 1968.

[BM-12] Keeney, R. L. and H. Raiffa, Decision with Multiple Objectives: Preferences and Value Tradeoffs, Wiley, New York, 1976.

[BM-13] Lee, S. M., Goal Programming for Decision Analysis, Auerbach Publishers, Philadelphia, Pennsylvania, 1972.

[BM-14] Leitmann, G. (ed.), Multicriteria Decision Making and Differential Games, Plenum Press, New York, 1976.

[BM-15] Leitmann, G. and A. Marzollo (eds.), Multicriteria Decision Making, Springer-Verlag, New York, 1975.

[BM-16] Miller, J. R. III, Professional Decision Making: A Procedure for Evaluating Complex Alternatives, Praeger, New York, 1970.

[BM-17] Starr, M. K. and M. Zeleny (eds.), Multiple Criteria Decision Making, North Holland, New York, 1977.

[BM-18] Thiriez, H. and S. Zionts, (eds.), Multiple Criteria Decision Making: Jouy-en-Josas, France, Springer-Verlag, New York, 1976.

[BM-19] Wallenius, J., Interactive Multiple Criteria Decision Methods: An Investigation and Approach, The Helsinki School of Economics, Helsinki, 1975.

[BM-20] Wendt, D. and C. Vlek (eds.), Utility, Probability, and Human Decision Making, D. Reidel Pub. Co., Boston, 1975.

[BM-21] Wilhelm, J., Objectives and Multi-objective Decision Making Under Uncertainty, Springer-Verlag, New York, 1975.

[BM-22] Zeleny, M., Linear Multiobjective Programming, Springer-Verlag, New York, 1974.

[BM-23] Zeleny, M. (ed.), Multiple Criteria Decision Making: Kyoto 1975, Springer-Verlag, New York, 1976.

[BM-24] Zionts, S. (ed.), Multiple Criteria Problem Solving: Proceedings, Buffalo, N. Y. (U.S.A.), 1977, Springer-Verlag, New York, 1978.

[BM-1a] Bell, D. E., R. L. Keeney and H. Raiffa (eds.), Conflicting Objectives in Decisions, Wiley, New York, 1977.

[BM-16a] Sfeir-Yonnis, A. and D. W. Bromley, Decision Making in Developing Countries-Multiobjective Formulation and Evaluation Methods, Prueger, New York, 1977.

Journal Articles, Technical Reports, Thesses:


1. Agarwal, S. K., "Optimizing Techniques for the Interactive Design of Transportation Networks under Multiple Objectives", Ph.D. Dissertation, Northwestern University, 1973.

2. Allesio, F. J., "Multiple Criteria in Environmental Control: Use of Economic Maximization Rules to Determine Relative Standards," in Ref. [BM-2], pp. 544-549, 1973.

3. Arrow, K., E. Barankin and D. Blackwell, "Admissible Points of Convex Sets", in H. W. Kuhn and A. W. Tucker (eds.), Contributions to the Theory of Games, pp. 87-91, Princeton University Press, 1953.

4. Ashour, S., Sequencing Theory, Springer-Verlag, New York, 1972. (Chap. 3 Measures of Performance.)

5. Ashton, D. J., and D. R. Atkins, "Multicriteria Programming for Financial Planning", Presented at the 23rd International Meeting of TIMS, Athens, Greece, July 1977.

6. Athans, M. and H. P. Geering, "Necessary and Sufficient Conditions for Differentiable Nonscalar-Valued Functions to Attain Extrema, "IEEE Trans. on Automatic Control, Vol AC-18, No. 2, pp. 132-139, 1973.

7. Aubin, J-P., "A Pareto Minimum Principle", in H. W. Kuhn and G. P. Szegö (eds.), Differential Games and Related Topics, pp. 147-175, North-Holland, Amsterdam, 1971.

8. Awerbuch, S., J. G. Ecker, and W. A. Wallace, "A Note: Hidden Nonlinearities in the Application of Goal Programming", Management Science, Vol. 22, No. 8, pp. 918-920, 1976.

9. Awerbuch, S. and W. Wallace, "A Goal-Setting and Evaluation Model for Community Development", IEEE Trans. of Systems, Man, and Cybernetics, Vol. SMC-7, No. 8, pp. 589-597, 1977.

10. Bammi, D. and D. Bammi, "Land Use Planning: An Optimizing Model", OMEGA*, Vol 3, No. 5, pp. 583-594, 1975.

11. Baron, D. P., "Stochastic Programming and Risk Aversion", in Ref. [BM-2], pp. 124-138, 1973.

12. Baum, S. and R. C. Carlson, "Multigoal Optimization in Managerial Science", OMEGA*, Vol. 2, No. 5, pp. 607-623, 1974.

13. Baumgarten, E. O., "An Investigation of the Goal Programming Method", M.S. Thesis, Kansas State University, 1973.

14. Baumol, W. J., "The Firm and its Objectives", in K. S. Palda (ed.), Readings in Managerial Economics, Prentice-Hall, New Jersey, 1973.

15. Beeson, R. M. and W. S. Meisel, "The Optimization of Complex Systems with Respect to Multiple Criteria", IEEE Systems, Man and Cybernetics Group Annual Symposium Record, IEEE, pp. 144-149, 1971.

16. Belenson, S. M. and K. C. Kapur, "An Algorithm for Solving Multicriterion Linear Programming Problems with Examples", Operational Reserach Quarterly, Vol. 24, No. 1, pp. 65-77, 1973.

17. Benayoun, R., O. Larichev, J. de Montgolfier, and J. Tergny, "Linear Programming with Multiple Objective Functions: The Method of Constraints", Automatic and Remote Control, Vol. 32, No. 8, pp. 1257-1264, 1971.

18. Benayoun, R., J. de Montgolfier, J. Tergny, and O. Larichev, "Linear Programming with Multiple Objective Functions: Step Method (STEM)", Mathematical Programming, Vol. 1, No. 3, pp. 366-375, 1971.

19. Benayoun, R., J. Tergny, and D. Keuneman, "Mathematical Programming with Multi-objective Function: A Solution by P.O.P. (Progressive Orientation Procedure)", METRA, Vol. 9, No. 2, pp. 279-299, 1970.

*OMEGA - The International Journal of Management Science

20. Benveniste, M., "Testing for Complete Efficiency in a Vector Maximization Problem", Mathematical Programming, Vol. 12, No. 2, pp. 285-288, 1977.

21. Bereanu, B., "Large Group Decision Making with Multiple Criteria", in Ref. [BM-18], pp. 87-102, 1976.

22. Bergstresser, K., A. Charnes, and P. L. Yu, "Generalization of Domination Structures and Nondominated Solutions in Multicriteria Decision Making", Journal of Optimization Theory and Applications, Vol. 18, No. 1, pp. 3-13, 1976.

23. Berhold, M., "Multiple Criteria Decision Making in Consumer Behavior", in Ref. [BM-2], pp. 570-576, 1973.

24. Bernardo, J. and H. Lanser, "A Capital Budgeting Decision Model with Subjective Criteria", Journal of Financial and Quantitative Analysis, Vol. 12, No. 2, pp. 261-275, 1977.

25. Bernstein, S. and W. Mellon, "Multidimensional Considerations in the Evaluation of Urban Policy", in Ref. [BM-2], pp. 530-543, 1973.

26. Bertier, P. and J. de Montgolfier, "On Multicriteria Analysis: An Application to a Forest Management Problem", METRA, Vol. 13, No. 1, pp. 33-45, 1974.

27. Bettman, J. R., "A Graph Theory Approach to Comparing Consumer Information Processing Models", Management Science, Vol. 18, No. 4 (Part II), pp. p114-p128, 1971.

28. Bilkey, W. J., "Empirical Evidence Regarding Business Goals", in Ref. [BM-2] pp. 613-634, 1973.

29. Birkin, S. J. and J. S. Ford, "The Quantity/Quality Dilemma: The Impact of a Zero Defects Program", in Ref. [BM-2], pp. 517-529, 1973.

30. Blackwell, D., "An Analog of the Minimax Theorem for Vector Payoffs", Pacific Journal of Mathematics, Vol. 6, No. 1, pp. 1-8, 1956.

31. Blaquiere, A., "Vector Valued Optimization in Multi-player Quantitative Games", in Ref. [BM-15], pp. 33-54, 1975.

32. Blin, J-M., "The General Concept of Multidimensional Consistency: Some Algebraic Aspects of the Aggregation Problem", in Ref. [BM-2], pp. 164-178, 1973.

33. Blin, J-M., "Fuzzy Sets in Multiple Criteria Decision-Making", in Ref. [BM-17], pp. 129-146, 1977.

34. Boebion, J. and L. Pun, "A Series-Parallel Multiple-Criteria Model for a Scheduling Problem in the Dress-Making Industry", in Ref. [BM-18], pp. 305-318, 1976.

35. Bowling, A. L. and J. F. Hair, Jr., "Optimal Decisions on Multiple Objectives Through Canonical Analysis", in Ref. [BM-2], pp. 729-731, 1973.

36. Bowman, V. J., Jr., "On the Relationship of the Tchebycheff Norm and the Efficient Frontier of Multiple-Criteria Objectives", in Ref. [BM-18], pp. 76-86, 1976,

37. Boychuk, L. M. and V. O. Ovchinnikov, "Principal Methods for Solution of Multicriterial Optimization Problems (Survey)", Soviet Automatic Control, Vol. 6, No. 3, pp. 1-4, 1973.

38. Brauers, W. K., "Multiple-Criteria Decision Making with a Special Application on Defense Problems", in Ref, [BM-18], pp. 199-200, 1976.

39. Briskin, L. E., "A Method of Unifying Multiple Objective Functions", Management Science, Vol. 12, No. 10, p. B406-B416, 1966.

40. Briskin, L. E., "Establishing a Generalized Multi-Attribute Utility Function", in Ref. [BM-2], pp. 236-245, 1973.

41. Buffa, E. S. and J. S. Dyer, Management Science/Operations Research, Wiley, New York, 1977, (Chap. 4 Evaluative Models for Multiple Criteria).

42. Bussey, L. E., The Economic Analysis of Industrial Projects, Prentice-Hall, New Jersey, 1978, (Chap. 9 Multiple Projects and Constraints II (Extended Deterministic Formulations).

43. Candler, W., "Linear Programming in Capital Budgeting with Multiple Goals", in Ref. [BM-2], pp. 416-428, 1973.

44. Candler, W. and M. Boehlje, "Use of Linear Programming in Capital Budgeting with Multiple Goals", American Journal of Agricultural Economics, Vol. 53, No. 2, pp. 325-330, 1971.

45. Cantley, M. F., "The Choice of Corporate Objectives", Long Range Planning, Vol. 3, No. 1, pp. 36-41, 1970.

46. Caplin, D. A. and J. S. H. Kornbluth, "Multiobjective Investment Planning Under Uncertainty", OMEGA, Vol. 3, No. 4, pp. 423-441, 1975.

47. Castellani, G., "Explicit Solution for a Class of Allocation Problems", in Ref. [BM-15], pp. 351-386, 1975.

48. Chang, S. S. L., "General Theory of Optimal Processes", Journal of SIAM Control, Vol. 4, No. 1, pp. 46-55, 1966.

49. Charnes, A., R. W. Clower, and K. O. Kortanek, "Effective Control Through Coherent Decentralization with Preemptive Goals", Econometrica, Vol. 35, No. 2, pp. 294-320, 1967.

50. Charnes, A. and W. W. Cooper, Management Models and Industrial Applications of Linear Programming, Vol. I, Wiley, New York, 1961. (Chap. 6, Appendix B, Basic Existence Theorems and Goal Programming).

51. Charnes, A. amd W. W. Cooper, "Some Network Charaterizations for Mathematical Programming and Accounting Approaches to Planning and Control", Accounting Review, Vol. 42, No. 1, pp. 24-52, 1967.

52. Charnes, A. and W. W. Cooper, "Deterministic Equivalents for Optimizing and Satisficing under Chance Constriants", Operations Research, Vol. 11, No. 1, pp. 18-39, 1963.

53. Charnes, A. and W. W. Cooper, "Goal Programming and Constained Regression - A Comment", OMEGA, Vol. 3, No. 4, pp. 403-409, 1975.

54. Charnes, A. and W. W. Cooper, "Goal Programming and Multiple Objective Optimization - Part 1", European Journal of Operational Research, Vol. 1, No. 1, pp. 39-54, 1977.

55. Charnes, A., W. W. Cooper, J. K. DeVoe, D. B. Learner, and W. Reinecke, "A Goal Programming Model for Media Planning", Management Science, Vol. 14, No. 8, pp. B423-B430, 1968.

56. Charnes, A., W. W. Cooper, D. Klingman, and R. J. Niehaus, "Explicit Solutions in Convex Goal Programming", Management Science, Vol. 22, No. 4, pp. 438-448, 1975.

57. Charnes, A., W. W. Cooper, D. B. Learner, and E. F. Snow, "Note on an Application of a Goal Programming Model for Media Planning", Management Science, Vol. 14, No. 8, pp. B431-B436, 1968.

58. Charnes, A., W. W. Cooper, K. A. Lewis, and R. J. Niehaus, "A Multi-Objective Model for Planning Equal Employment Opportunities", in Ref. [BM-23], pp. 111-134, 1976.

59. Charnes, A., W. W. Cooper, R. J. Niehaus, and A. Stedry, "Static and Dynamic Assignment Models with Multiple Objectives and Some Remarks on Organizational Design", Management Science, Vol 15, No. 8, pp. B365-B375, 1969.

60. Charnes, A., and A. C. Stedry, "Search-Theoretic Models of Organization Control by Budgeted Multiple Goals", Management Science, Vol. 12, No. 5, pp. 457-482, 1966.

61. Chu, K. C., "On the Noninferior Set for the Systems with Vecotr-valued Objective Function", IEEE Trans. on Automatic Cotnrol, Vol. AC-15, No. 5, pp. 591-593, 1970.

62. Churchman, C. W., "Morality as a Value Criterion", in Ref. [BM-2], pp. 3-8, 1973.

63. Churchman, C. W. and R. L. Ackoff, "An Approximate Measure of Value", Operations Research, Vol. 2, No. 2, pp. 172-187, 1954.

64. Chyung, D. H., "Optimal Systems with Multiple Cost Functionals", SIAM Journal of Control, Vol. 5, No. 3, pp. 345-351, 1967.

65. Cohon, J. L., "Applications of Multiple Objectives to Water Resources Problems", in Ref. [BM-23], pp. 255-270, 1976.

66. Cohon, J. L. and D. H. Marks, "Multiobjective Screening Models and Water Resource Investment", Water Resources Research, Vol. 9, No. 4, pp. 826-836, 1973.

67. Cohon, J. L. and D. H. Marks, "Multiobjective Analysis in Water Resources Planning", in R. de Neufville and D. Marks (eds.), Systems Planning and Design, pp. 304-321, Prentice-Hall, New Jersey, 1974.

68. Cohon, J. L. and D. H. Marks, "A Review and Evaluation of Multiobjective Programming Techniques", Water Resources Research, Vol, 11, No. 2, pp. 208-220, 1975.

69. Collins, D. C., "Applications of Multiple Criteria Evaluation to Decision Aiding", in Ref. [BM-2], pp. 477-505, 1973.

70. Contini, M. B., "A Decision Model Under Uncertainty with Multiple Payoffs", in A. Mensch (ed.), Theory of Games: Techniques and Applications, pp. 50-63, English Univeristy Press, London, 1966.

71. Contini, B., "A Stochastic Approach to Goal Programming", Operations Research, Vol. 16, No. 3, pp. 576-856, 1968.

72. Contini, B. and S. Zionts, "Restricted Bargaining for Orgamizations with Multiple Objectives", Econometrica, Vol. 36, No. 2, pp. 397-414, 1968.

73. Courtney, Jr., J. F., T. H. Klastorin, and T. W. Ruefli, "A Goal Programming Approach to Urban-Suburban Location Preferences", Management Science, Vol. 18, No. 6, pp. B258-B268, 1972.

74. Crawford, A. B., "Impact Analysis Using Differentially Weighted Evaluative Criteria", in Ref. [BM-2], pp. 732-735, 1973.

75. Crowston, W. B. and P. R. Kleindorfer, "Coordinating Multi-Project Networks", in Ref. [BM-2], pp. 668-685, 1973.

76. Da Cunha, N. O., and E. Polak, "Constrained Minimization under Vector-Valued Criteria in Finite Dimensional Spaces", Journal of Math. Anal. and Appl., Vol. 19, No. 1, pp. 103-124, 1967.

77. Dalkey, N. C., "Group Decision Analysis", in Ref. [BM-23], pp. 45-74, 1976.

78. Dauer, J. P. and R. J. Krueger, "An Iterative Approach to Goal Programming", Operational Research Quarterly, Vol. 28, No. 3ii, pp. 671-681, 1977.

79. David, L. and L. Duckstein, "Multicriterion Ranking of Alternative Long-range Water Resources Systems", Water Resources Bulletin, Vol. 12, No. 4, pp. 731-754, 1976.

80. Dawes, R. M., "A Case Study of Graduate Admissions: Applications of Three Principles of Human Decision Making", American Psychologist, Vol 26, No. 2, pp. 180-188, 1971.

81. Dawes, R. M., "Objective Optimization Under Multiple Subjective Functions", in Ref. [BM-2], pp. 9-17, 1973.

82. Dawes, R. M. and J. Eagle, "Multivariate Selection of Students in a Racist Society: A Systematically unfair Approach", in Ref. [BM-23], pp. 97-110, 1976.

83. Day, R. H. and S. M. Robinson, "Economic Decisions with L** Utility", in Ref. [BM-2], pp. 84-92, 1973.

84. Dean, J. H. and C. S. Shih, "Multiattribute Water Resources Decision Making", AIIE Trans., Vol. 7, No. 4, pp. 408-413, 1975.

85. De Neufville, R. and R. L. Keeney, "Use of Decision Analysis in Airport Development for Mexico City", in A. Drake, R. L. Keeney and P. Morse (eds.) Analysis of Public Systems, pp. 497-519, MIT Press, Cambridge, Massachusetts, 1972.

86. De Neufville, R. and R. L. Keeney, "Multiattribute Preference Analysis for Transportation Systems Evaluation", Transportaiton Research, Vol. 7, No. 1, pp. 63-76, 1973.

87. Dinkelbach, W. and H. Isermann, "On Decision Making Under Multiple Criteria and Under Incomplete Information", in Ref. [BM-2], pp. 302-312, 1973.

88. diRoccaferrera, G. M. F., "Behavioral Aspects of Decision Making Under Multiple Goals", in Ref. [BM-2], pp. 635-656, 1973.

89. Dyer, J. S., "Interactive Goal Programming", Management Science, Vol. 19, No. 1, pp. 62-70, 1972.

90. Dyer, J. S., "An Empirical Investigation of a Man-Machine Interactive Approach to the Solution of Multiple Criteria Problem", in Ref. [BM-2], pp. 202-216, 1973.

91. Dyer J. S., "The Effect of Error in the Estimation of the Gradient on the Frank-Wolfe Algorithm, with Implications for Interactive Programming", Operations Research, Vol 22, No. 1, pp. 160-174, 1974.

92. Dyer, J. S., "A Time-Sharing Computer Program for the Solution of the Multiple Criteria Problem", Management Science, Vol. 19, No. 12, pp. 1379-1383, 1973.

93. Easton, A., "One-of-a-Kind Decisions Involving Weighted Multiple Objectives and Disparate Alternatives", in Ref. [BM-2], pp. 657-667, 1973.

94. Eckenrode, R. T., "Weighing Multiple Criteria", Management Science, Vol. 12, No. 3, pp. 180-192, 1965.

95. Ecker, J. G. amd I. A. Kouada, "Finding Efficient Points for Linear Multiple Objective Programs", Mathematical Programming, Vol. 8, No. 3, pp. 375-377, 1975.

96. Edwards, W., "How to use Multiattribute Utility Measurement for Social Decisionmaking", IEEE Trans. on Systems, Man, and Cybernetics, Vol. SMC-7, No. 5, pp. 326-340, 1977.

97. Eilon, S., "Goals and Constraints in Decision-Making", Operational Research Quarterly, Vol 23, No. 1, pp. 3-15, 1972.

98. Elayat, H. and S. Jaisingh, "Multiple Objective Linear Programming Model for Decision Analysis", Presented at the 4th International Conference on Production Reserach, Pre-print 11.2, Tokyo, 1977.

99. Evans, J. P. and R. E. Steuer, "A Revised Simplex Method for Linear Multiple Objective Programs", Mathematical Programming, Vol. 5, No. 1, pp. 54-72, 1973.

100. Evans, J. P. and R. E. Steuer, "Generating Efficient Extreme Points in Linear Multiple Objective Programming: Two Algorithms and Computing Experience", in Ref. [BM-2], pp. 349-365, 1973.

101. Falkson, L. M., "Discussion: 'Approaches to Multi-objective Planning in Water Resources Projects', by B. W. Taylor III, R. Davis, and R. M. North", Water Resources Bulletin, Vol. 12, No. 5, pp. 1071-1077, 1976.

102. Fandel, G. and J. Wilhelm, "Rational Solution Principles and Information Requirements as Elements of a Theory of Multiple Criteria Decision Making", in Ref. [BM-18], pp. 215-231, 1976.

103. Farquhar, P. H., "A Survey of Multiattribute Utiliity Theory and Applications", in Ref. [BM-17], pp. 59-90, 1977.

104. Farquhar, P. H. and V. R. Rao, "A Balance Model for Evaluating Subsets of Multiattributed Items", Management Science, Vol. 22, No. 5, pp. 528-539, 1976.

105. Feinberg, A., "An Experimental Investigation of an Interactive Approach for Multi-criterion Optimization, with an Application to Academic Resource Allocation", Ph.D. Dissertation, University of California, Los Angeles, 1972.

106. Feinberg, A., "Incorporation of Political Objectives in Multi-criteria Decision Making Involving Multiple Constituencies", Presented at the 23rd International Meeting of TIMS, Athens, Greece, July 25-27, 1977.

107. Ferguson, C. E., "The Thoery of Multidimensional Utility Analysis in Relation to Multiple-Goal Business Behavior: A Synthesis", The Southern Economic Journal, Vol. 32, No. 2, pp. 169-175, 1965.

108. Ferguson, C. E. and R. Blair, "Inferior Factors, Externalities and Pareto Optimality", Quarterly Review of Economics and Business, Vol. 11, No. 3, pp. 17-25, 1971.

109. Fichefet, J., "GPSTEM: An Interactive Multiobjective Optimization Method", in A. Prekopa (ed.), Progress in Operations Research, Vol. 1, pp. 317-332, North Holland, Amsterdam, 1976.

110. Firstman, S. I. and D. S. Stoller, "Establishing Objectives, Measures, and Criteria for Multi-Phase Complementary Activities," Operations Research, Vol. 14, No. 1, pp. 84-99, 1966.

111. Fischer, G. W., "Experimental Applications of Multi-attribute Utility Models", in Ref. [BM-20], pp. 7-45, 1975.

112. Fishburn, P. C., "Additive Utilities with Finite Sets: Applications in the Management Sciences", Naval Research Logistics Quarterly, Vol. 14, No. 1, pp. 1-10, 1967.

113. Fishburn, P. C. , "Lexicographic Orders, Utilities and Decision Rules: A Survey", Management Science, Vol. 20, No. 11, pp. 1442-1471, 1974.

114. Fishburn, P. C., "Bernoullian Utilities for Multiple-Factor Situations", in Ref. [BM-2], pp. 47-61, 1973.

115. Fishburn, P. C. and R. L. Keeney, "Seven Independence Concepts and Continuous Multiattribute Utility Functions", Journal of Mathematical Psychology, Vol. 11, No. 3, pp. 294-327, 1974.

116. Forsyth, J. D., "Utilization and Goal Programming in Production and Capital Expenditure Planning", CORS Journal*, Vol. 7, No. 2, pp. 136-140, 1969.

117. Forsyth, J. D. and D. J. Laughhunn, "Capital Rationing in the Face of Multiple Organizational Objectives", in Ref. [BM-2], pp. 439-446, 1973.

118. Frederick, D. G., "Multiple Objectives in Bayesian Analysis: An Applied Case", in Ref. [BM-2], pp. 736-737, 1973.

119. Freeman, A. M. III and R. H. Haveman, "Benefit-Cost Analysis and Multiple Objectives: Current Issues in Water Resources Planning", Water Resources Research, Vol. 6, No. 6, pp. 1533-1539, 1970.

*CORS Journal — Canadian Operations Research Society (later renamed as INFOR)

120. Freimer, M. and P. L. Yu, "An Approach Toward Decision Problems with Multiobjectives", Center for System Sciences, CSS No. 72-03, University of Rochester, New York, 1972.

121. Freimer, M. and P. L. Yu, "The Applications of Compromise Solutions to Reporting Games", in A. Rapoport (ed.), Games Theory as a Theory of Conflict Resolution, pp. 235-260, D. Reidel Publishing Co., Boston, 1974.

122. Freimer, M. and P. L. Yu, "Some New Results on Compromise Solutions for Group Decision Problems", Management Science, Vol. 22, No. 6, pp. 688-693, 1976.

123. Gal, T. and J. Nedoma, "Multiparametric Linear Programming", Management Science, Vol. 18, No. 7, pp. 406-421, 1972.

124. Gardiner, P. C. and W. Edwards, "Public Values: Multiattribute Utility Measurement for Social Decision Making", in M. F. Kaplan and S. Schwartz (eds.), Human Judgement and Decision Processes, pp. 1-37, Academic Press, New York, 1975.

125. Gembicki, F., "Performance and Sensitivity Optimization: A Vector Index Approach", Ph.D. Dissertation, Case Western Reserach University, 1974.

126. Geoffrion, A. M., "Strictly Concave Parametric Programming, Part I: Basic Theory", Management Science, Vol. 13, No. 3, pp. 244-253, 1966.

127. Geoffrion, A. M., "Strictly Concave Parametric Programming, Part II: Additional Theory and Computational Considerations", Management Science, Vol. 13, No. 5, pp. 359-370, 1967.

128. Geoffrion, A. M., "Solving Bicriterion Mathematical Programs", Operations Research, Vol. 15, No. 1, pp. 39-54, 1967.

129. Geoffrion, A. M., "Proper Efficiency and the Theory of Vector Maximization", Journal of Mathematical Analysis and Applications, Vol. 22, No. 3, pp. 618-630, 1968.

130. Geoffrion, A. M., J. S. Dyer, and A. Feinberg, "An Interactive Approach for Multi-Criterion Optimization, with an Application to the Operation of an Academic Department", Management Science, Vol. 19, No. 4(Part I), pp. 357-368, 1972.

131. Geoffrion, A. M. and W. Hogan, "Coordination of Two-level Organizations with Multiple Objectives". in A. Balakrishnan (ed.), Techniques of Optimization, pp. 455-466, Academic Press, New York, 1972.

132. Geogescu-Roegen, N., "Choice, Expectations and Measurability," Quarterly Journal of Economics, Vol. 68, No. 4, pp. 503-541, 1954.

133. Giauque, W. C. and T. C. Peebles, "Application of Multidimensional Utility Theory in Determining Optimal Test-Treatment Strategies for Streptococcal Sore Throat and Rheumatic Fever", Operations Research, Vol. 24, No. 5, p. 933-950, 1976.

134. Gibbs, T. E., "Goal Programming", Journal of Systems Management, Vol. 24, No. 5, pp. 38-41, 1973.

135. Goffin, J-L. and A. Haurie, "Necessary Conditions and Sufficient Conditions for Pareto Optimality in a Multicriterion Perturbed System", in R. Contini and A. Ruberti (eds.), 5th Conference on Optimization Techniques, Part I, pp. 184-193, Springer-Verlag, New York, 1973.

136. Goffin, J-L. and A. Haurie, "Pareto Optimality with Nondifferentiable Cost Functions", in Ref. [BM-18], pp. 232-246, 1976.

137. Goodman, D. A., "A Goal Programming Approach to Aggregate Planning of Production and Work Force", Management Science, Vol. 20, No. 12, pp. 1569-1575, 1974.

138. Green, P. E., "Multidimensional Scaling and Conjoint Measurement in the Study of Choice Among Multiattribute Alternatives", in Ref. [BM-2], pp. 577-609, 1973.

139. Gum, R. L., T. G. Roefs and D. B. Kimball, "Quantifying Societal Goals: Development of a Weighting Methodology", Water Resources Research, Vol. 12, No. 4, pp. 612-622, 1976.

140. Haimes, Y. Y. and W. A. Hall, "Multiobjectives in Water Resources Systems Analysis: The Surrogate Worth Trade Off Method", Water Resources Research, Vol. 10, No. 4, pp. 615-623, 1974.

141. Haimes, Y. Y., L. S. Lasdon and D. A. Wismer, "On a Bicriterion Formulation of the Problems of Integrated System Identification and System Optimization," IEEE Trans. on Systems, Man, and Cybernetics, Vol. SMC-1, No. 3, pp. 296-297, 1971.

142. Haimes, Y. Y., and D. A. Wismer, "A Computational Approach to the Combined Problem of Optimization and Parameter Identification," Automatica, Vol. 8, No. 3, pp. 337-347, 1972.

143. Hall, W. A. and Y. Y. Haimes, "The Surrogate Worth Trade-off Method with Multiple Decision-makers", in Ref. [BM-23], pp. 207-234, 1976.

144. Hammond, K. R., "Externalizing the Parameters of Quasirational Thought", in Ref. [BM-23], pp. 75-96, 1976.

145. Hanieski, J. F., "Technological Change as the Optimization of a Multidimensional Product", in Ref. [BM-2], pp. 550-569, 1973.

146. Hannan, E. L., "Effects of Substituting a Linear Goal for a Fractional Goal in the Goal Programming Problem", Presented at the Joint TIMS/ORSA National Meeting, San Fransisco, May 9-11, 1977.

147. Hansen, P., M. Anciaux-Mundeleer and P. Vincke, "Quasi-Kernels of Outranking Relations", in Ref. [BM-18], pp. 53-63, 1976.

148. Harnett, R. M. and J. P. Ignizio, "A Heuristic Program for the Covering Problem with Multiple Objectives", in Ref. [BM-2], pp. 738-740, 1973.

149. Harwood, G. B. and R. W. Lawless, "Optimizing Organization Goals in Assigning Faculty Teaching Schedules", Decision Sciences, Vol. 6, No. 3, pp. 513-524, 1975.

150. Hasenauer, R., "Theoretical Analysis and Empirical Application of Goal Programming with Preemptive Priority Structures", in Ref. [BM-18], pp. 120-135, 1976.

151. Hatry, H. P., "Measuring the Effectiveness of Non-Defense Public Programs," Operations Research, Vol. 18, No. 5, pp. 772-784, 1970.

152. Haurie, A., "On Pareto Optimal Decisions for a Coalition of a Subset of Players," IEEE Trans. on Automatic Control, Vol. AC-18, No. 2, pp. 144-149, 1973.

153. Haurie, A. and M. C. Delfour, "Individual and Collective Rationality in a Dynamic Pareto Equilibrium", in Ref. [BM-14], pp. 149-162, 1976.

154. Hawkins, C. A. and R. A. Adams, "A Goal Programming Model for Capital Budgeting", Financial Management, Vol. 3, No. 1, pp. 52-57, 1974.

155. Heenan, D. A. and R. B. Addleman, "Quantitative Techniques for Today's Decision Makers", Harvard Business Review, Vol. 54, No. 3, pp. 32-62, 1976.

156. Hemming, T., "A New Method for Interactive Multiobjective Optimization: A Boundary Point Ranking Method", in Ref. [BM-18], pp. 333-340, 1976.

157. Hill, M., "Goals-Achievement Matrix for Evaluating Alternative Plans," Journal of the American Institute of Planners, Vol. 34, No. 1, pp. 19-28, 1968.

158. Hirsch, G., "The Notion of Characteristic Set and Its Implication for the Analysis and Development of Multicriterion Methods", in Ref. [BM-18], pp. 247-262, 1976.

159. Hopkins, D. S. P., J.-C. Larréché, and W. F. Massy, "Multiattribute Reference Functions of University Administrators", in Ref. [BM-23], pp. 287-290, 1976.

160. House, P. W., "How Do You Know Where You're Going?", in Ref. [BM-2], pp. 741-744, 1973.

161. Huang, S. C., "Note on the Mean-Square Strategy of Vector Values Objective Function," Journal of Optimization Theory and Applications, Vol. 9, No. 5, pp. 364-366, 1972.

162. Huber, G. P., "Multi-Attribute Utility Models: A Review of Field and Field-Like Studies", Management Science, Vol. 20, No. 10, pp. 1393-1402, 1974.

163. Hughes, A. and D. Grawiog, Linear Programming: An Emphasis on Decision Making, Addison-Wesley, Reading, Massachusetts, 1973, (Chap. 15).

164. Humphreys, P. and A. Humphreys, "An Investigation of Subjective Preference Orderings for Multiattributed Alternatives", in Ref. [BM-20], pp. 119-133, 1975.

165. Hwang, C. L. and S. Paidy, "Regional Water Quality Management by Nonlinear Goal Programming", to be published.

166. Hwang, C. L., S. Paidy, K. Raju, and A. Masud, "Nonlinear Goal Programming Method - An Iterative Approach", to be published.

167. Hwang, C. L., F. A. Tillman, K. Yoon, and A. Masud, "Optimum System Reliability by Nonlinear Goal Programming", to be published.

168. Ignizio, J. P., "An Approach to the Capital Budgeting Problem with Multiple Objectives", The Engineering Economist, Vol. 21, No. 4, pp. 259-272, 1976.

169. Ijiri, Y., "A Historical Cost Approach to Aggregation of Multiple Goals", in Ref. [BM-2], pp. 395-405, 1973.

170. Isermann, H., "Existence and Duality in Multiple Objective Linear Programming", in Ref. [BM-18], pp. 64-75, 1976.

171. Isermann, H., "The Enumeration of the Set of All Efficient Solutions for a Linear Multiple Objective Programs", Operational Research Quarterly, Vol. 28, No. 3ii, pp. 711-725, 1977.

172. Isermann, H., "The Relevance of Duality in Multiple Objective Linear Programming", in Ref. [BM-17], pp. 241-262, 1977.

173. Jaaskelainen, V., "A Goal Programming Model of Aggregate Production Planning", The Swedish Journal of Economics, Vol. 71, No. 1, pp. 14-29, 1969.

174. Jackman, H. W., "Financing Public Hospitals in Ontario: A Case Study in Rationing of Capital Budgets", Management Science, Vol. 20, No. 4 (Part 2), pp. 645-655, 1973.

175 Jacquet-Lagreze, E., "How we can use the Notion of Semi-Orders to Build Outranking Relations in Multi-Criteria Decision Making", in Ref. [BM-20], pp. 87-111, 1975.

176. Jaikumar, R., "A Heuristic 0-1 Algorithm with Multiple Objectives and Constraints", in Ref. [BM-2], pp. 745-748, 1973.

177. Johnsen, E., "Experiences in Multiobjective Management Processes", in Ref. [BM-23], pp. 135-152, 1976.

178. Juralewicz, R. S., "Interpersonal Dimensions of Decision Making in a Cross-Cultural Setting", in Ref. [BM-2], pp. 749-752, 1973.

179. Kafarov, V. V., G. B. Lazarev, and V. I. Avdeev, "Multicriterial Problems in the Control of Complex Chemical-Engineering Systems", Soviet Physics-Doklady, Vol. 16, No. 5, pp. 344-345, 1971.

180. Kapur, K. C., "Mathematical Methods of Optimization for Multi-objective Transportation Systems", Socio-Economic Planning Science, Vol. 4, No. 4 pp. 451-467, 1970.

181. Keen, P. G. W., "The Evolving Concept of Optimality", in Ref. [BM-17], pp. 31-58, 1977.

182. Keeney, R. L., "Utility Independence and Preferences for Multiattributed Consequences", Operations Research, Vol. 19, No. 4, pp. 875-893, 1971.

183. Keeney, R. L., "An Illustrated Procedure for Assessing Multiattributed Utility Functions", Sloan Management Review, Vol. 14, No. 1, pp. 37-50, 1972.

184. Keeney, R. L., "Evaluating Multidimensional Situations Using a Quasi-Separable Utility Function," IEEE Trans. on Man-Machine Systems, Vol. MMS-9, No. 2, pp. 25-28, 1968.

185. Keeney, R. L., "Risk Independence and Multiattributed Utility Functions", Econometrica, Vol. 41, No. 1, pp. 27-39, 1973.

186. Keeney, R. L., "Examining Corporate Policy Using Multiattribute Utility Analysis", Sloan Management Review, Vol. 17, No. 1, pp. 63-76, 1975.

187. Keeney, R. L., "Utility Functions for Multiattributed Consequences," Management Science, Vol. 18, No. 5 (Part I), pp. 276-287, 1972.

188. Keeney, R. L., "Quantifying Corporate Preferences for Policy Analysis", in Ref. [BM-18], pp. 293-304, 1976.

189. Keeney, R. L., "Concepts of Independence in Multiattribute Utility Theory", in Ref. [BM-2], pp. 62-71, 1973.

190. Keown, A. J. and J. D. Martin, "A Chance Constrained Goal Programming Model for Working Capital Management", The Engineering Economist, Vol. 22, No. 3, pp. 153-174, 1977.

191. Killough, L. N. and T. L. Souders, "A Goal Programming Model for Public Accounting Firms", Accounting Review, Vol. 48, No. 2, pp. 268-279, 1973.

192. Kirkwood, C. W., "Superiority Conditions in Decision Problems with Multiple Objectives", IEEE Trans. on Systems, Man, and Cybernetics, Vol. SMC-7, No. 7, pp. 542-544, 1977.

193. Klahr, C. N., "Multiple Objectives in Mathematical Programming", Operations Research, Vol. 6, No. 6, pp. 849-855, 1958.

194. Klahr, D., "Decision Making in a Complex Environment: The Use of Similarity Judgements to Predict Preferences", Management Science, Vol. 15, No. 11, pp. 595-617, 1969.

195. Klinger, A., "Improper Solutions of the Vector Maximum Problem," Operations Research, Vol. 15, No. 3, pp. 570-572, 1967.

196. Klinger, A., "Vector-Valued Performance Criteria," IEEE Trans. on Automatic Control, Vol. AC-9, No. 1, pp. 117-118, 1964.

197. Kolesar, P. and W. E. Walker, "An Algorithm for the Dynamic Relocation of Fire Companies", Operations Research, Vol. 22, No. 2, pp. 249-274. 1974.

198. Kornbluth, J. S. H., "Duality, Indifference and Sensitivity Analysis in Multiple Objective Linear Programming", Operational Research Quarterly, Vol. 25, No. 4, pp. 599-614, 1974.

199. Kouada, I. A., "Linear Vector Maximization", Ph.D. Dissertation, Rensselaer Polytechnic Institute, New York, 1975.

200. Kuhn, H. W., and A. W. Tucker, "Nonlinear Programming", in J. Neyman (ed.), Proceedings Second Berkeley Symposium on Mathematical Statistics and Probability, pp. 481-491, University of California Press, Berkeley, California, 1951.

201. Kumar, P. C. and G. C. Philippatos, "A Goal Programming Formulation to the Selection of Portfolios by Dual-Purpose Funds", Presented at the 23rd International Meeting of TIMS, Athens, Greece, July 25-27, 1977.

202. Kumbaraci, T. E., "The Judgment of Improvement--Choice for Decisions Relating to Medical Efficacy", in Ref. [BM-2], pp. 753-754, 1973.

203. Kunreuther, H., "Extensions of Bowman's Theory on Managerial Decision-Making", Management Science, Vol. 15, No. 8, pp. B415-B439, 1969.

204. Ladany, S. P. and M. Aharoni, "Maintenance Policy of Aircraft According to Multiple Criteria", International Journal of Systems Science, Vol. 6, No. 11, pp. 1093-1101, 1975.

205. Landsberger, M. and A. Subotnik, "Optimal Behavior of a Monopolist Facing A Bicriteria Objective Function", Internatioanl Economic Review, Vol. 17, No. 3, pp. 581-600, 1976.

206. Larichev, O. I., "Man-Machine Procedures for Decision Making (Review)," Automation and Remote Control, Vol. 32, No. 12, (part 2) pp. 1973-1983, 1971.

207. Lasdon, L. S., "Duality and Decomposition in Mathematical Programming" IEEE Trans. on System Science and Cybernetics, Vol. SSC-4, No. 2, p. 86-100, 1968.

208. LaValle, I. H., "On Admissibility and Bayesness When Risk Attitutde But Not the Preference Ranking Is Permitted to Vary", in Ref. [BM-2], pp. 72-83, 1973.

209. Lawrence, K. D. and J. J. Burbridge, "A Multiple Goal Linear Programmming Model for Coordinated Production and Logistics Planning", International Journal of Production Research, Vol. 14, No. 2, March 1976.

210. Lawrence, K. D. and J. J. Burbridge, "Multiobjective Linear Programming Models for the Blending of Materials Problem", Presented at the Fourth International Conference on Production Research, Pre-print 11.1, Tokyo, 1977.

211. Lawrence, K. D., S. M. Lawrence, and R. Berger, "Multiple Objective Linear Programming Models for Large-Scale Capital Expenditures", Presented at the Joint TIMS/ORSA National Meeting, San Fransisco, May 9-11, 1977.

212. Lee, S. M., "Goal Programming for Decision Analysis of Multiple Objectives", Sloan Management Review, Vol. 14, No. 2, pp. 11-24, 1973.

213. Lee, S. M. and E. R. Clayton, "A Goal Programming Model for Academic Resource Allocation", Management Science, Vol. 18, No. 8, pp. B395-B408, 1972.

214. Lee, S. M. and V. Jaaskelainen, "Goal Programming: Management's Math Model", Industrial Engineering, Vol. 3, No. 2, pp. 30-35, 1971.

215. Lee, S. M. and A. J. Lerro, "Capital Budgeting for Multiple Objectives", Financial Management, Vol. 3, No. 1, pp. 58-66, 1974.

216. Lee, S. M. and A. J. Lerro, "Optimizing the Portfolio Selection for Mutual Funds", The Journal of Finance, Vol. 28, No. 5, pp. 1087-1101, 1973.

217. Lee, S. M. and L. J. Moore, "Multi-Criteria School Busing Models", Management Science, Vol. 23, No. 7, pp. 703-715, 1977.

218. Lee, S. M. and L. J. Moore, "Optimizing Transportation Problems with Multiple Objectives", AIIE Transactions, Vol. 5, No. 4, pp. 333-338, 1973.

219. Lee, S. M. and R. L. Morris, "Integer Goal Programming Methods", in Ref. [BM-17], pp. 273-289, 1977.

220. Lin, J. G., "Maximal Vectors and Multi-objective Optimization", Journal of Optimization Theory and Applications, Vol. 18, No. 1, pp. 41-64, 1976.

221. Lin, J. G., "Three Methods for Determining Pareto-Optimal Solutions of Multiple-Objective Problems", in Y. Ho and S. Mitter (eds.), Directions in Large-Scale Systems, pp. 117-138, Plenum Press, New York, 1976.

222. Lin, J. G., "Multiple Objective Optimization: Proper Equality Constraints (PEC) and Maximization of Index Vectors", in Ref. [BM-14], pp. 103-128, 1975.

223. Lin, J. G., G. Katopis, S. Patellis, and H. Shen, "On Relatively Optimal Controls of Dynamic Systems with Vector Performance Indices", Proceedings: 7th Annual Princeton Conference on Information Sciences and Systems, pp. 579-584, 1973.

224. Lin, S. A. Y., "Dynamic Growth of the Firm Under Uncertainty with Multiple Goals", in Ref. [BM-2], pp. 755-759, 1973.

225. Loucks, D. P. (ed.), "Multiobjective Water Resources Planning - A Bibliography", Report No. OWRT/WRSIC 75-206, Water Resource Scientific Information Center, Office of Water Research and Technology, U. S. Department of the interior, Washington, D. C., 1975.

226. Lucas, H. C., Jr., and J. R. Moore, Jr., "A Multiple-Criterion Scoring Approach to Information System Project Selection", INFOR, Vol. 14, No. 1, pp 1-12, 1976.

227. MacCrimmon, K. R., "Decision Making Among Multiple-Attribute Alternatives: A Survey and Consolidated Approach", RAND Memorandum, RM-4823-ARPA, 1968.

228. MacCrimmon, K. R., "Improving the System Design and Evaluation Process by the Use of Trade-off Information: An Application to Northeast Corridor Transportation Planning", RAND Memorandum, RM-5877-DOT, 1969.

229. MacCrimmon, K. R., "An Overview of Multiple Objective Decision Making", in Ref. [BM-2], pp. 18-44, 1973.

230. MacCrimmon, K. R. and M. Toda, "The Experimental Determination of Indifference Curves", The Review of Economic Studies, Vol. 36, No. 4, pp. 433-450, 1969.

231. Mahoney, F. J. III, "The Design of Regression Experiments with Multiple Objectives", in Ref. [BM-2], pp. 760-763, 1973.

232. Major, D. C., "Benefit-Cost Ratios for Projects in Multiple Objective Investment Programs", Water Resources Research, Vol. 5, No. 6, pp. 1174-1178, 1969.

233. Major, D. C., "Multiobjective Redesign of the Big Walnut Project", in R. De Neufville and D. Marks (eds.), Systems Planning and Design, pp. 322-337, Prentice-Hall, New York, 1974.

234. Marks, D. H., "Water Quality Management", in A. Drake, R. Keeney, and P. Morse (eds.), Analysis of Public Systems, p. 356-375, MIT Press, 1972.

235. Marschak, J., "Guided Soul-Searching for Multi-Criterion Decisions", in Ref. [BM-23], pp. 1-16, 1976.

236. Marshall, H. E., "Cost Sharing and Multiobjectives in Water Resource Development", Water Resources Research, Vol. 9, No. 1, pp. 1-10, 1973.

237. Marzollo, A. and W. Ukovich, "On Some Broad Classes of Vector Optimal Decisions and their Characterization", in Ref. [BM-15], pp. 281-324, 1975.

238. Masud, A. and C. L. Hwang, "A Multiple Objective Energy Planning and Allocation Model", to be published.

239. McGrew, D. R., and Y. Y. Haimes, "Parametric Solution to the Joint System Identification and Optimization Problem," Journal of Optimization Theory and Applications, Vol. 13, No. 5, pp. 582-605, 1974.

240. Medanic, J., "Minimax Pareto Optimal Solutions with Application to Linear Quadratic Problems", in Ref. [BM-15], pp. 55-124, 1975.

241. Meisel, W. S., "Tradeoff Decisions in Multiple Criteria Decision Making", in Ref. [BM-2], pp. 461-476, 1973.

242. Miller, J. R. III, "Assessing Alternative Transportation Systems", RAND Memorandum, RM-5865-DOT, 1969.

243. Miller, W. L., and D. M. Byers, "Development and Display of Multiple Objective Project Impacts," Water Resources Research, Vol. 9, No. 1, pp. 11-20, 1973.

244. Miller, W. L. and S. P. Erickson, "The Impact of High Interest Rates on Optimum Multiple Objective Design of Surface Runoff Urban Drainage Systems", Water Resources Bulletin, Vol. 11, No. 1, pp. 49-59, 1975.

245. Minnehan, R. F., "Multiple Objectives and Multigroup Decisions Making in Physical Design Situations", in Ref. [BM-2], pp. 506-516, 1973.

246. Mitroff, I. I., "On Being Consistent: The Management of Inquiry as a Multi-Criteria Decision Problems", in Ref. [BM-17], pp. 291-300, 1977.

247. Monarchi, D. E., "Interactive Algorithm for Multiple Objective Decision Making", Technical Reports on Hydrology and Water Resources, (No. 6), University of Arizona, 1972.

248. Monarchi, D. E., C. C. Kisiel, and L. Duckstein, "Interactive Multi-objective Programming in Water Resources: A Case Study", Water Resources Research, Vol. 9, No. 4, pp. 837-850, 1973.

249. Monarchi, D. E., J. E. Weber, and L. Duckstein, "An Iteractive Multiple Objective Decision-Making Aid Using Nonlinear Goal Programming", in Ref. [BM-23], pp. 235-253, 1976.

250. Morris, W. T., Engineering Economic Analysis, Reston Publishing Co., Reston, Virginia, 1976, (Chap. 7 Evaluating Outcomes - Multiple Criteria).

251. Narasimhan, S. L., "A Survey of Business Applications of Multiple Criteria Decision Making Techniques", Presented at the Joint TIMS/ORSA National Meeting, San Fransisco, May 9-11, 1977.

252. Neely, W.P., R.M. North, and J.C. Fortson, "Planning and Selecting Multi-objective Projects by Goal Programming" Water Resources Bulletin, Vol. 12, No. 1, pp. 19-25, 1976.

253. Nijkamp, P. and J. B. Vos, "A Multicriteria Analysis for Water Resource and Land Use Development", Water Resources Research, Vol. 13, No. 3, pp. 513-518, 1977.

254. Okello, R.M., S. Kaufman, and S. Zionts, "A Multiple Objective Decision Procedure for University Admissions Planning", presented at the Joint TIMS/ORSA National Meeting, San Fransisco, May 9-11, 1977.

255. Ölander, F., "Search Behavior in Non-Simultaneous Choice Situations: Satisficing or Maximizing?", in Ref. [BM-20], pp. 297-320, 1975.

256. Ören, T. I. and C. Y. Ören, "Solution Selection Techniques for Decision Making in Complex Systems", in Ref. [BM-2], pp. 764-767, 1973.

257. Osteryoung, J. S., "Multiple Goals in the Capital Budgeting Decision", in Ref. [BM-2], pp. 447-457, 1973.

258. Pascual, L. D. and A. Ben-Israel, "Vector-Valued Criteria in Geometric Programming," Operations Research, Vol. 19, No. 1, pp. 98-104, 1971.

259. Pasternak, H. and U. Passy, "Bicriterion Mathematical Programs with Boolean Variables," in Ref. [BM-2], pp. 327-348, 1973.

260. Pau, L. F., "Two-Level Planning with Conflicting Goals", in Ref. [BM-18], pp. 263-273, 1976.

261. Philip, J., "Algorithms for the Vector Maximization Problem," Mathematical Programming, Vol. 2, No. 2, pp. 207-229, 1972.

262. Philip, J., "An Algorithm for Combined Quadratic and Multiobjective Programming", Ref. [BM-18], pp. 35-51, 1976.

263. Philippatos, G. C., "On the Specification of Viable Financial Goals", Managerial Planning, Vol. 20, No. 1, p. 11-16, 1971.

264. Philippatos, G. C., "Behavioral Implications of Discrepancies in Expectations Between the Firm and Its Stockholders with an Application to Dividend Policies", in Ref. [BM-2], pp. 768-770, 1973.

265. Podrebarae, M. L. and S. S. Sengupta, " Parametric Linear Programming: Some Extensions", INFOR, Vol. 9, No. 3, pp. 305-319, 1971.

266. Polak, E., "On the Approximation of Solutions to Multiple Criteria Decision Making Problems", in Ref. [BM-23], pp. 271-282, 1976.

267. Polak, E. and A. N. Payne, "On Multicriteria Optimization", in Y. C. Ho and S. K. Mitter (eds.), Directions in Large-Scale Systems, pp. 77-94, Plenum Press, New York, 1976.

268. Powell, J. and R. Vergin, "A Heuristic Model for Planning Corporate Financing", Financial Management, Vol. 4, No. 2, p. 13-20, 1975.

269. Price, W. L., "Goal Programming and a Manpower Problem", in P. L. Hammer and G. Zoutendijk (eds.), Mathematical Programming in Theory and Practice, pp. 395-416, North-Holland, New York, 1974.

270. Price, W. L., "An Interactive Objective Function Generator for Goal Programmes", Ref. [BM-18], pp. 147-158, 1976.

271. Price, W. L. and W. G. Piskor, "The Application of Goal Programming to Manpower Planning," INFOR, Vol. 10, No. 3, p. 221-231, 1972.

272. Radner, R., "Satisficing", in G. Marchuk (ed.), Optimization Techniques: IFIP Technical Conference, pp. 252-263, Springer-Verlag, New York, 1975.

273. Raiffa, H., Decision Analysis, Addison-Wesley, Reading, Mass, 1968.

274. Rapoport, A., "Interpersonal Comparison of Utilities", in Ref. [BM-23], pp. 17-43, 1976.

275. Reeves, G., "Quadratic Goal Programming", presented at the Joint TIMS/ORSA National Meeting, San Fransisco, May 9-11, 1977.

276. Reid, R. W., and S. J. Citron, "On Noninferior Performance Index Vectors," Journal of Optimization Theory and Applications, Vol. 7, No. 1, pp. 11-28, 1971.

277. Reid, R. W., and V. Vemuri, "On the Noninferior Index Approach to Large Scale Multi-Criteria Systems," Journal of the Franklin Institute, Vol. 291, No. 4, pp. 241-254, 1971.

278. Rider, K. L., "A Parametric Model for the Allocation of Fire Companies in New York City", Management Science, Vol. 23, No. 2, pp. 146-158, 1976.

279. Ritzman, L. P. and L. J. Karjewski, "Multiple Objectives in Linear Programming - An Example in Scheduling Postal Resources", Decision Sciences, Vol. 4, No. 3, pp. 364-378, 1973.

280. Roy, B., "Problems and Methods with Multiple Objective Functions", Mathematical Programming, Vol. 1, No. 2, pp. 239-266, 1971.

281. Roy, B., "From Optimization to Multi-Criteria Decision Aid: Three Main Operational Attitudes", in Ref. [BM-18], pp. 1-34, 1976.

282. Roy, B., "A Conceptual Framework for a Prescriptive Theory of 'Decision-Aid'", in Ref. [BM-17], pp. 179-210, 1977.

283. Roy, B., "How Outranking Relation Helps Multiple Criteria Decision Making", in Ref. [BM-2], pp. 179-201, 1973.

284. Roy, B., "Why Multicriteria Decision Aid may not Fit in with the Assessment of a Unique Criterion", in Ref. [BM-23], pp. 283-286, 1976.

285. Ruefli, T. W., "A Generalized Goal Decomposition Model," Management Science, Vol. 17, No. 8, pp. B505-B518, 1971.

286. Ruefli, T. W., "Linked Multi-Criteria Decision Models", in Ref. [BM-2], pp. 406-415, 1973.

287. Salama, A. I. A. and V. Gourishankar, "Optimal Control of Systems with a Single Control and Several Cost Functionals," International Journal of Control, Vol. 14, No. 4, pp. 705-725, 1971.

288. Salama, A. I. A. and M. H. Hamza, "On the Optimization of Static Systems with Several Cost Measures," IEEE Trans. on Automatic Control, Vol. AC-17, No. 1, pp. 170-172, 1972

289. Salukvadze, M. E., "Linear Programming Problem with a Vector-Valued Performance Criterion," Automation and Remote Control, Vol. 33, No. 5, (Part 1) pp. 794-799, 1972.

290. Salukvadze, M. E., "Optimization of Vector Functionals. I. The Programming of Optimal Trajectories," Automation and Remote Control, Vol. 32, No. 8, pp. 1169-1178, 1971.

291. Salukvadze, M. E., "Optimization of Vector Functionals II. The Analytic Construction of Optimal Controls", Automation and Remote Control, Vol. 32, No. 9, (part 1) pp. 1347-1357, 1971.

292. Salukvadze, M. "On the Existence of Solutions in Problems of Optimization under Vector Valued Criteria," Journal of Optimization Theory and Application, Vol. 13, No. 2, pp. 203-217, 1974.

293. Sarin, R. K., "Interactive Evaluation and Bound Procedure for Selecting Multi-Attributed Alternatives", in Ref. [BM-17], pp. 211-224, 1977.

294. Sartoris, W. L. and M. L. Spruill, "Goal Programming and Working Capital Management", Financial Management, Vol. 3, No. 1, pp. 67-74, 1974.

295. Sayeki, Y. and K. H. Vespers, "Allocation of Importance in a Hierarchial Goal Structure," Management Science, Vol. 19, No. 6, pp. 667-675, 1973.

296. Schiemenz, B., "Possibilities to Consider Multiple Criteria in Decision Situations" in Ref. [BM-18], pp. 274-292,1976.

297. Schmidt, J. W. and G. K. Bennett, "Economic Multiattribute Acceptance Sampling," AIIE Trans., Vol. 4, No. 3, pp. 194-199, 1972.

298. Schmitendorf, W. E., "Cooperative Games and Vector-Valued Criteria Problems," IEEE Trans. on Automatic Control, Vol. AC-18, No. 2, pp. 139-144, 1973.

299. Schmitendorf, W. E. and G. Moriarty, "A Sufficiency Condition for Coalitive Pareto-Optimal Solutions" in Ref. [BM-14], pp. 163-172,1976

300. Schroeder, R. G., "Resource Planning in University Management by Goal Programming", Operations Research, Vol. 22, No. 4, pp. 700-710, 1974.

301. Schwartz, L. E., "Uncertainty Reduction Over Time in the Theory of Multiattributed Utility", in Ref. [BM-2], pp. 108-123 1973.

302. Schwartz, S. L., I. Vertinsky and W. T. Ziemba, "R&D Project Selection Behavior: Study Designs and Some Pilot Results", in Ref. [BM-18], pp. 136-146, 1976.

303. Schwartz, S. L., I. Vertinsky, W. T. Ziemba and M. Bernstein, "Some Behavioural Aspects of Information Use in Decision Making: A Study of Clinical Judgements", in Ref. [BM-18], pp. 378-391, 1976.

304. Seinfeld, J. H. and W. Z. McBridge, "Optimization with Multiple Performance Criteria," I & EC Process Design and Development, Vol. 9, No. 1, pp. 53-58, 1970.

305. Sengupta, S. S., M. L. Podrebarac and T. D. H. Fernando, "Probabilities of Optima in Multi-Objective Linear Programmes," in Ref. [BM-2], pp. 217-235, 1973.

306. Shapiro, J. F., "Multiple Criteria Public Investment Decision Making by Mixed Integer Programming", in Ref. [BM-18], pp. 170-182, 1976.

307. Shepard, R. N., "On Subjectively Optimum Selection Among Multiattribute Alternatives," in M. W. Shelly and G. L. Bryan (eds.), Human Judgments and Optimality, pp. 257-281, Wiley, New York, 1964.

308. Slovic, P., "Analyzing the Expert Judge: A Discriptive Study of a Stockbroker's Decision Processes", Journal of Applied Psychology, Vol. 53, No. 4, pp. 255-263, 1969.

309. Smith, R. D. and P. S. Greenlaw, "Simulation of a Psychological Decision Process in Personnel Selection", Management Science, Vol. 13, No. 8, pp. B409-B419, 1967.

310. Spivey, W. A. and H. Tamura, "Goal Programming in Econometrics", Naval Research Logistics Quarterly, Vol. 17, No. 2, pp. 183-192, 1970.

311. Srinivasan, V. and A. Shocker, "MUMP--Multidimensional Unfolding via Mathematical Programming", Working paper No. 7108, Graduate School of Management, University of Rochester, New York, 1971.

312. Stadler, W., "Sufficient Conditions for Preference Optimality", in Ref. [BM-14], pp. 129-148, 1976.

313. Stadler, W., "Preference Optimality and Applications of Pareto Optimality", in Ref. [BM-15], pp. 125-226, 1975.

314. Stainton, R. S., "Production Scheduling with Multiple Criteria Objectives", Operational Research Quarterly, Vol. 28, No. 2i, pp. 285-292, 1977.

315. Starr, M. K. and I. Stein, The Practice of Management Science, Prentice-Hall, New Jersey, 1976 (Unit 5 Decisions with Multiple Criteria).

316. Starr M. K. and L. H. Greenwood, "Normative Generation of Alternatives with Multiple Criteria Evaluation", in Ref. [BM-17], pp. 111-128, 1977.

317. Starr, M. K. and M. Zeleny, "MCDM-State and Future of the Arts", in Ref. [BM-17], pp. 5-29, 1977.

318. Stedry, A. C. and A. Charnes, "Investigation in the Theory of Multiple Budgeted Goals," in C. P. Bonini, R. K. Jaedicke and H. M. Wagner, (eds.), Management Controls: New Directions in Basic Research, pp. 186-204, McGraw-Hill, New York, 1964.

319. Stern, R. J. and A. Ben-Israel, "On Linear Optimal Control Problems with Multiple Quadratic Criteria", in Ref. [BM-2], pp. 366-372, 1973.

320. Steuer, R. E., "Linear Multiple Objective Programming: Theory and Computational Experience", Ph.D. Dissertation, University of North Carolina, 1973.

321. Steuer, R. E., "Multiple Objective Linear Programming with Interval Criterion Weights", Management Science, Vol. 23, No. 3, pp. 305-316, 1976.

322. Steuer, R. E., "A Five Phase Procedure for Implementing a Vector-Maximum Algorithm for Multiple Objective Linear Programming Problems" in Ref. [BM-18], pp. 159-169, 1976.

323. Steuer, R. E., "An Interactive Multiple Objective Linear Programming Procedure", in Ref. [BM-17], pp. 225-239, 1977.

324. Steuer, R. E. and A. T. Schuler, "An Interactive Multiple Objective Linear Programming Approach to a Problem in Forest Management", Operations Research, Vol.26, No.2, pp. 254-269, 1978.

325. Snyder, W. W., "Economic Policy and Multiple Objective Decision Making Lessons from the Postwar Period", in Ref. [BM-2], pp. 771-733, 1973.

326. Taft, M. I. and A. Reisman, "A Proposed Generalized Heuristic Algorithm for Scheduling with Respect to n-Interrelated Criterion Functions," International Journal of Production Research, Vol. 5, No. 2, pp. 155-162, 1966.

327. Tamura, K., "A Method for Constructing the Polar Cone of a Polyhedral Cone, with Applications to Linear Multicriteria Decision Problems", Journal of Optimization Theory and Applications, Vol. 19, No. 4, pp. 547-564, 1976.

328. Taylor, B. W. III, K. R. Davis and R. M. North, "Approaches to Multiobjective Planning in Water Resources Projects", Water Resources Bulletin, Vol. 11, No. 5, pp. 999-1008, 1975.

329. Taylor, R. L., "Consistent Multiattributed Decision Procedures", in Ref. [BM-2], pp. 774-778, 1973.

330. Tell, B., "A Comparative Study of Four Multiple-Criteria Methods", in Ref. [BM-18], pp. 183-197, 1976.

331. Terry, H., "Comparative Evaluation of Performance Using Multiple Criteria", Management Science, Vol. 9, No. 3, pp. 431-442, 1963.

332. Tersine, R. J., "Organizational Objectives and Goal Programming: A Convergence", Managerial Planning, Vol. 25, No. 2, pp. 27-40, 1976.

333. Theil, H., "On the Symmetry Approach to the Committee Decision Problem", Management Science, Vol. 9, No. 3, pp. 380-393, 1963.

334. Thiriez, H. and D. Houri, "Multi-Person Multi-Criteria Decision-Making: A Sample Approach", in Ref. [BM-18], pp. 103-119, 1976.

335. Togsverd, T., "Multi-Level Planning in the Public Sector", in Ref. [BM-18], pp. 201-214, 1976.

336. Tomlinson, J. W. C. and I. Vertinsky, "Selecting a Strategy for Joint Venture in Fisheries: A First Approximation", in REf. [BM-18], pp. 351-363, 1976.

337. Trippi, R. R., "On the Evaluation of Investment Proposals Having Multiple Attributes", Naval Research Logistics Quarterly, Vol. 21, No. 2, pp. 327-332, 1974.

338. Turk, D. R., "Priorities Modeling Using Goal Growth Programming", Report No. JCAP-DM-T701, Joint Conventional Ammunition Program Coordinating Group, Decision Models Directorate, Rock Island, Illinois, 1977.

339. Van De Panne, C., "A Node Method for Multiparametric Linear Programming", Management Science, Vol. 21, No. 9, pp. 1014-1020, 1975.

340. Vedder, J., "Planning Problems with Multidimensional Consequences," Journal of the American Institute of Planners, Vol. 36, No. 2, pp. 112-119, 1970.

341. Vedder, J. N., "Multiattribute Decision Making Under Uncertainty Using Bounded Intervals", in Ref. [BM-2], pp. 93-107, 1973.

342. Velichenko, V. V., "Sufficient Conditions for Absolute Minimum of the Maximal Functional in the Multi-Criteria Problem of Optimal Control", in G. Marchuk (ed.), Optimization Techniques: IFIP Technical Conference, pp. 220-225, Springer-Verlag, New York, 1975.

343. Vemuri, V., "Multiple Objective Optimization in Water Resource Systems", Water Resources Research, Vol. 10, No. 1, pp. 44-48, 1974.

344. Vincke, P., "A New Approach to Multiple Criteria Decision-Making", in Ref. [BM-18], pp. 341-350, 1976.

345. Viswanathan, B., V. V. Aggarwal, K. P. K. Nair, "Multiple Criteria Markov Decision Processes", in Ref. [BM-17], pp. 263-272, 1977.

346. Volpato, M., "Estimating the Common Cost of a Good When the Local Costs are Known in the Countries of a Community," in Ref. [BM-15], pp . 325-350, 1975.

347. Wacht, R. F. and D. T. Whitford, "A Goal Programming Model for Capital Investment Analysis in Nonprofit Hospitals", Financial Management, Vol. 5, No. 2, pp. 37-47, 1976.

348. Wallenius, H., J. Wallenius, and P. Varita, "An Approach to Solving Multiple Criteria Macroeconomic Policy Problems and an Application", Working Paper 76-54, European Institute for Advanced Studies in Management, 1976.

349. Wallenius, J., "Interactive Multiple Criteria Decision Methods: An Investigation and an Approach", Acta Academiae Oeconomicae Helsingiensis, Series A:14, Helsinki School of Economics, Finalnd, 1975.

350. Wallenius, J., "Comparative Evaluation of Some Interactive Approaches to Multicriterion Optimization", Management Science, Vol. 21, No. 12, pp. 1387-1396, 1975.

351. Wallenius, J. and S. Zionts, "Some Tests of an Interactive Programming Method for Multicriterion Optimization and Attempt at Implementation", in Ref. [BM-18], pp. 319-331, 1976.

352. Walters, A., J. Mangold, and E. Haran, "A Comprehensive Planning Model for Long-range Academic Strategies", Management Science, Vol. 22, No. 7, pp. 727-738, 1976.

353. Waltz, F. M., "An Engineering Approach: Hierarchical Optimization Criteria," IEEE Trans. on Automatic Control, Vol. AC-12, No. 2, pp. 179-180, 1967.

354. Welam, U. P., "Comments on Goal Programming for Aggregate Planning", Management Science, Vol. 22, No. 6, pp. 708-712, 1976.

355. Wendell, R. E. and D. N. Lee, "Efficiency in Multiple Objective Optimization Problems", Mathematical Programming, Vol. 12, No. 3, pp. 406-414, 1977.

356. Wheeler, B. M. and J. R. M. Russell, "Goal Programming and Agricultural Planning", Operational Research Quarterly, Vol. 28, No. 1i, pp. 21-32, 1977.

357. White, C. M., "Multiple Goals in the Theory of the Firm," in K. E. Boulding and W. A. Spivey (eds.), Linear Programming and the Theory of the Firm, pp. 181-201, Macmillan, New York, 1960.

358. Williams, F. E., "On the Evaluation of Intertemporal Outcomes", in Ref. [BM-2], pp. 429-438, 1973.

359. Wind, Y. and L. Spitz, "Analytical Approach to Marketing Decisions in Health-Care Organizations," Operations Research, Vol. 24, No. 5, pp. 973-990, 1976.

360. Winterfeldt, D. V., "Multi-Criteria Decision Making: Comments on Jacquet-Lagreze's Paper", in Ref. [BM-20], pp. 113-117, 1975.

361. Winterfeldt, D. V. and G. W. Fischer, "Multiattribute Utility Theory: Models and Assessment Procedures", in Ref. [BM-20], pp. 47-85, 1975.

362. Wright, P. L. and F. Barbour, "Phased Decision Strategies: Sequels to an Initial Screening", in Ref. [BM-17], pp. 91-110, 1977.

363. Yoon, K., "A Goal Programming Model for Korea Economic Planning", M.S. Thesis, Kansas State University, 1977.

364. Yoon, K. and C. L. Hwang, "A Goal Programming Model for Development Planning: A Case of Korea", to be published.

365. Young, D. R., "Choosing Among Alternative Complex Systems When Input Characteristics are Uncertain", IEEE Trans. on Systems, Man, and Cybernetics, Vol. SMC-1, No. 1, pp. 77-82, 1971.

366. Yu, P. L., "Cone Convexity, Cone Extreme Points, and Nondominated Solutions in Decision Problems with Multiobjectives", Journal of Optimization Theory and Applications, Vol. 14, No. 3, pp. 319-376, 1974.

367. Yu, P. L., "Decision Dynamics with an Application to Persuasion and Negotiation", in Ref. [BM-17], pp. 159-178, 1977.

368. Yu, P. L., "Introduction to Domination Structures in Multicriteria Decision Problems", in REf. [BM-2], pp. 249-261, 1973.

369. Yu, P. L., "Domination Structures and Nondominated Solutions", in Ref. [BM-15], pp. 227-280, 1975.

370. Yu, P. L. and G. Leitmann, "Compromise Solutions, Domination Structures, and Salukvadze's Solution," Journal of Optimization Theory and Applications, Vol. 13, No. 3, pp. 362-378, 1974.

371. Yu, P. L. and G. Leitmann, "Nondominated Decisions and Cone Convexity in Dynamic Multicriteria Decision Problems", in Ref. [BM-14], pp. 61-72, 1976.

372. Yu, P. L., and M. Zeleny, "The Set of all Non-Dominated Solutions in Linear Cases and a Multicriteria Simplex Method," Journal of Mathematical Analysis and Applications, Vol. 49, No. 2, pp. 430-368, 1975.

373. Yu, P. L. and M. Zeleny, "Linear Multiparametric Programming by Multicriteria Simplex Method", Management Science, Vol. 23, No. 2, pp. 159-170, 1976.

374. Zadeh, L. A., "Optimality and Nonscalar-Valued Performance Criteria," IEEE Trans. on Automatic Control, Vol. AC-8, No. 1, pp. 59-60, 1963.

375. Zadeh, L. A., "Outline of a New Approach to the Analysis of Complex Systems and Decision Processes", in Ref. [BM-2], pp. 686-725, 1973.

376. Zeleny, M., "A Selected Bibliography of Works Related to Multiple Criteria Decision Making", in Ref. [BM-2], pp. 779-796, 1973.

377. Zeleny, M., "The Attribute-Dynamic Attitude Model (ADAM)", Management Science, Vol. 23, No. 1, pp. 12-26, 1976.

378. Zeleny, M., "A Concept of Compromise Solutions and the Method of the Displaced Ideal", Computers and Operations Research, Vol. 1, No. 4, pp. 479-496, 1974.

379. Zeleny, M., "Compromise Programming", in Ref. [BM-2], pp. 262-30, 1973.

380. Zeleny, M., "The Theory of the Displaced Ideal", in Ref. [BM-23], pp. 153-206, 1976.

381. Zeleny, M., "MCDM Bibliography - 1975", in Ref. [BM-23], pp. 291-321, 1976.

382. Zeleny, M., "Adaptive Displacement of Preferences in Decision Making", in Ref. [BM-17], pp. 147-158, 1977.

383. Zeleny, M., "Multicriteria Simplex Method: A Fortran Routine", in Ref. [BM-23], pp. 323-345, 1975.

384. Zeleny, M. and J. L. Cochrane, "A Priori and A Posteriori Goals in Macroeconomic Policy Making", in Ref. [BM-2], pp. 373-391, 1973.

385. Zionts, S., "Integer Linear Programming with Multiple Objectives", Working Paper No. 229, School of Management, State University of New York at Buffalo, 1976.

386. Zionts, S. and J. Wallenius, "An Interactive Programming Method for Solving the Multiple Criteria Problem", Management Science, Vol. 22, No. 6, pp. 652-663, 1976.

Supplement

1a. Abadie, J., and J. Carpenter, "Generalization of the Wolfe Reduced Gradient Method to the Case of Nonlinear Constraints", in Optimization, R. Fletcher (editor), Academic Press, N. Y., 1969.

19a. Benson, R. G., "Interactive Multiple Criteria Optimization Using Satisfactory Goals", Ph. D. Thesis, University of Iowa, 1975.

34a. Borreani-Ostanello, A. and P. Capillaro, "Efficient Solutions of a Multiple-Objective Programming Method, for a Problem of School Allocation and Dimensioning," in M. Roubens (ed.), Advances in Operations Research, pp. 55-60, North-Holland, Amsterdam, 1977.

42a. Buyanov, B. B. and V. M. Ozernoy, "A Decision Method Using Vector Criterion", Engineering Cybernetics, Vol. 12, No. 3, pp. 49-54, 1974.

46a. Carlson, R. C. and H. H. Therp, "A Multicriteria Approach to Strategic Planning: An Application in Inventory Control", in M. Roubens (ed.), Advances in Operations Research, pp. 75-83, North-Holland, Amsterdam, 1977.

46b. Carlsson, C., "An Approach to Adaptive Multigoal Control using Fuzzy Automata", in M. Roubens (ed.), Advances in Operations Research, pp. 85-93, North-Holland, Amsterdam, 1977.

64a. Clarke, D. and B. H. P. Rivett, "A Structural Mapping Approach to Complex Decision-Making", Journal of Operational Research Society, Vol. 29, No. 2, pp. 113-128, 1978.

78a. Dauer, J. P. and R. J. Krueaer, "An Iterative Approach to Goal Programming", Report no. T. R. 76-1, Department of Mathematics, University of Nebraska-Lincoln, 1976.

84a. Deckro, R. F., "Multiple Objective Districting: A General Heuristic Approach Using Multiple Criteria", Operational Research Quarterly, Vol. 1, No. 4ii, pp. 953-961, 1977.

86a. Despontin, M. and P. Vincke, "Multiple Criteria Economic Policy", in M. Roubens (ed.), Advances in Operations Research, pp. 119-128, North-Holland, Amsterdam, 1977.

86b. DiGuglielmo, F., "Nonconvex Duality in Multiobjective Optimization", Mathematics of Operations Research, Vol. 2, No. 3, pp. 285-291, 1977.

88a. Dorfman, R., and H. Jacoby, "A Model fo Public Decision Illustrated by a Water Pollution Policy Problem, The Analysis and Evaluation of Public Expenditures: The PPB System", pp. 226-276, Joint Economic Committee, 91st Congress, 1st Session, 1969.

97a. Einhorn, H. J. and W. McCoach, "A Simple Multiattribute Utility Procedure for Evaluation", Behavioral Sciences, Vol. 22, No. 4, pp. 270-282, 1977.

115a. Flavell, R. B. and G. R. Salkin, "Resource Allocation in a Decentralized Organisation", in M. Roubens (ed.), Advances in Operations Research, pp. 169-175, North-Holland, Amsterdam, 1977.

117a. Frank, M. and P. Wolfe, "An Algorithm for Quadratic Programming", Naval Research Logistics Quarterly, Vol. 3, No. 1 and 2, pp. 95-110, 1956.

122a. Gal, T., "A General Method for Determining the Set of All Efficient Solutions to a Linear Vectormaximum Problem", European Journal of Operational Research, Vol. 1, No. 5, pp. 307-322, 1977.

122b. Gal, T. and H. Leberling, "Redundant Objective Functions in Linear Vector Maximum Problems and Their Determination", European Journal of Operational Research, Vol. 1, No. 3, pp. 176-184, 1977.

122c. Gal, T. and H. Leberling, "Relaxation Analysis in Multi-Criteria Linear Programming: An Introduction", in M. Roubens (ed.), Advances in Operations Research, pp. 177-180, North-Holland, Amsterdam, 1977.

126a. Geoffrion, A. M., "Vector Maximal Decomposition Programming", Working paper No. 164, Western Management Science Institute, University of California, Los Angeles, September 1970.

134a. Giordano, J.-L. and J. -C. Suquet, "On Multicriteria Decision Making: An Application to a Work-Shop Organization Problem", in M. Roubens (ed.), Advances in Operations Research, pp. 181-192, North Holland, Amsterdam, 1977.

138a. Griffith, R. E., and P. A. Stewart, "A Nonlinear Programming Technique for the Optimization of Continuous Processing Systems," Management Science Vol. 7, No. 4, pp. 379-392, 1961.

165a. Hwang, C. L., K. C. Lai, F. A. Tillman, and L. T. Fan, "Optimization of Systems Reliability by the Sequential Unconstrained Minimization Technique", IEEE Trans. on Reliability, Vol. R-24, pp. 133-135 (1975).

165b. Hwang, C. L., J. L. Williams, and L. T. Fan, "Introduction to the Generalized Reduced Gradient Method", Institute for Systems Design and Optimization, Report No. 39, Kansas State University, 1972.

167a. Hwang, C. L., F. A. Tillman, W. K. Wei, and C. H. Lie, "Optimal Scheduled Maintenance Policy based on Multiple Criteria Decision Making", to be published.

175a. Jacquet-Lagreze, E., "Explicative Models in Multicriteria Preference Analysis", in M. Roubens (ed.), Advances in Operations Research, pp. 213-218, North-Holland, Amsterdam, 1977.

189a. Keeney, R. L. and A. Sickerman, "Assessing and Analyzing Preferences Concerning Multiple Objectives: An Interactive Computer Program", Behavioral Science, Vol. 21, No. 3, pp. 173-182, 1976.

197a. Kornbluth, J. S. H., "A Survey of Goal Programming", OMEGA, Vol. 1, No. 2, pp. 193-205, 1973.

204a. Ladd, E. R., "A Dynamic Programming Approach to Goal Programming", Ph.D. Thesis, Colorado State University, 1973.

211a. Lee, H. B., "Integer Programming and Nonlinear Integer Goal Programming Applied to Systems Reliability Problems", M.S. Thesis, Kansas State University, 1978.

219a. Lhoas, J., "Multi-criteria Decision Aid Application to the Selection of the Route for a Pipe-Line", in M. Roubens (ed.), Advances in Operations Research, pp. 265-273, North-Holland, Amsterdam, 1977.

225a. Loucks, D. P., "Planning for Multiple Goals", in C. R. Blitzer, P. B. Clark and L. Taylor (eds.), Economy-Wide Models and Development Planning, pp. 213-233, Oxford University Press, London, 1975.

238a. Masud, A.S.M. "A Study of Multiple Objective Decision Making-Methods and Applications", Ph.D. Thesis, Kansas State University, 1978.

239a. McMillan, C. Jr., Mathematical Programming, (Chapter 14, Mathematical Programming with Multiple Objectives) Wiley, New York, 1975.

255a. Oppenheimer, K. R., "A Proxy Approach to Multi-Attribute Decision Making", Management Science, Vol. 24, No. 6, pp. 675-689, 1978.

257a. Parthasarathy, T. and T. E. S. Raghavan, Some Topics in Two-Persons Games, American Elserier, New York, 1971.

273a. Raju, K. S., "Iterative Nonlinear Goal Programming and Application to Production Planning Problems", M.S. Thesis, Kansas State University, 1978.

279a. Rodder, W., "A Duality Theory for Linear Vector Optimum Problems", in M Roubens (ed.), Advances in Operations Research, pp. 405-407. North-Holland, Amsterdam, 1977.

301a. Schwartz, S. L. and I. Vertinsky, "Multi-attribute Investment Decisions: A Study of R & D Project Selection," Management Science Vol. 24, No. 3, pp. 285-301, 1977.

322a. Steuer, R. E., "ADEX: An Adjacent Efficient Extreme Point Algorithm for Solving Vector-Maximum and Internal Weighted-Sums Linear Programming Problems," SHARE Program Library Agency, Distribution Code 360D-15, 2.014, 1974.

322b. Steuer, R. E., "ADBASE: An Adjacent Efficient Basis Algorithm for Solving Vector-Maximum and Internal Weighted Sums Linear Programming Problems," (in FORTRAN), College of Business and Economics, University of Kentucky, 1974.

325a. Streeter, H. W. and E. B. Phelps, "A Study of the Pollution and Natural Purification of the Ohio River, Illinois Factors Concerned in the Phenomenon of Oxidation and Reaeration", Public Health Service Bulletin, Vol. 146 (1925).

327a. Tantasuth, V., "Goal Programming and Long Range Planning in Underdeveloped Countries", Ph.D. Thesis, Texas Tech University, 1975.

330a. Tell, B., "The Effect of Uncertainty on the Selection of a Multiple-Criteria Utility Model", in M. Roubens (ed.), Advances in Operations Research, pp. 497-504, North-Holland, Amsterdam, 1977.

333a. Theil, H., Optimal Decision Rules for Government and Industry, Rand McNally and Company, Chicago, 1964. (Chap. ).

337a. Trzeciak, J. M., "Computational Aspects of Linear Multiple Objective Optimization", Ph.D. Thesis, Iowa State University, 1976.

353a. Wehrung, D. A., D. S. P. Hopkins and W. F. Massy, "Interactive Preference Optimization for University Administrators", Management Science, Vol. 24, No. 6, pp. 599-611, 1978.

353b. Wei, W. K., "Optimal Scheduled Maintenance Policy based on Multiple Criteria Decision Making", M.S. Thesis, Kansas State University, 1978.

354a. Wendell, R. E., A. P. Hunter, Jr., and T. J. Lowe, "Efficient Points in Location Problems", AIIE Transactions, Vol. 9, No. 3, pp. 238-246, 1977.

357a. Wilhelm, J., "Generalized Solution Principles and Out-ranking Relations in Multi-Criteria Decision-making", European Journal of Operational Research, Vol. 1, No. 6, pp. 376-385, 1977.

307a. Simon, H. A., "A Behavioral Model of Rational Choice," Quarterly Journal of Economics, Vol. 69, No. 1, pp. 99-118, 1955.

157a. Himmelblau, D. M., Applied Nonlinear Programming, McGraw-Hill, New York, 1972. (Chapter 9, Evaluation of Constrained Nonlinear Programming Techniques).

Vol. 59: J. A. Hanson, Growth in Open Economies. V, 128 pages. 1971.

Vol. 60: H. Hauptmann, Schätz- und Kontrolltheorie in stetigen dynamischen Wirtschaftsmodellen. V, 104 Seiten. 1971.

Vol. 61: K. H. F. Meyer, Wartesysteme mit variabler Bearbeitungsrate. VII, 314 Seiten. 1971.

Vol. 62: W. Krelle u. G. Gabisch unter Mitarbeit von J. Burgermeister, Wachstumstheorie. VII, 223 Seiten. 1972.

Vol. 63: J. Kohlas, Monte Carlo Simulation im Operations Research. VI, 162 Seiten. 1972.

Vol. 64: P. Gessner u. K. Spremann, Optimierung in Funktionenräumen. IV, 120 Seiten. 1972.

Vol. 65: W. Everling, Exercises in Computer Systems Analysis. VIII, 184 pages. 1972.

Vol. 66: F. Bauer, P. Garabedian and D. Korn, Supercritical Wing Sections. V, 211 pages. 1972.

Vol. 67: I. V. Girsanov, Lectures on Mathematical Theory of Extremum Problems. V, 136 pages. 1972.

Vol. 68: J. Loeckx, Computability and Decidability. An Introduction for Students of Computer Science. VI, 76 pages. 1972.

Vol. 69: S. Ashour, Sequencing Theory. V, 133 pages. 1972.

Vol. 70: J. P. Brown, The Economic Effects of Floods. Investigations of a Stochastic Model of Rational Investment. Behavior in the Face of Floods. V, 87 pages. 1972.

Vol. 71: R. Henn und O. Opitz, Konsum- und Produktionstheorie II. V, 134 Seiten. 1972.

Vol. 72: T. P. Bagchi and J. G. C. Templeton, Numerical Methods in Markov Chains and Bulk Queues. XI, 89 pages. 1972.

Vol. 73: H. Kiendl, Suboptimale Regler mit abschnittweise linearer Struktur. VI, 146 Seiten. 1972.

Vol. 74: F. Pokropp, Aggregation von Produktionsfunktionen. VI, 107 Seiten. 1972.

Vol. 75: GI-Gesellschaft für Informatik e.V. Bericht Nr. 3. 1. Fachtagung über Programmiersprachen · München, 9.–11. März 1971. Herausgegeben im Auftrag der Gesellschaft für Informatik von H. Langmaack und M. Paul. VII, 280 Seiten. 1972.

Vol. 76: G. Fandel, Optimale Entscheidung bei mehrfacher Zielsetzung. II, 121 Seiten. 1972.

Vol. 77: A. Auslender, Problèmes de Minimax via l'Analyse Convexe et les Inégalités Variationelles: Théorie et Algorithmes. VII, 132 pages. 1972.

Vol. 78: GI-Gesellschaft für Informatik e.V. 2. Jahrestagung, Karlsruhe, 2.–4. Oktober 1972. Herausgegeben im Auftrag der Gesellschaft für Informatik von P. Deussen. XI, 576 Seiten. 1973.

Vol. 79: A. Berman, Cones, Matrices and Mathematical Programming. V, 96 pages. 1973.

Vol. 80: International Seminar on Trends in Mathematical Modelling, Venice, 13–18 December 1971. Edited by N. Hawkes. VI, 288 pages. 1973.

Vol. 81: Advanced Course on Software Engineering. Edited by F. L. Bauer. XII, 545 pages. 1973.

Vol. 82: R. Saeks, Resolution Space, Operators and Systems. X, 267 pages. 1973.

Vol. 83: NTG/GI-Gesellschaft für Informatik, Nachrichtentechnische Gesellschaft. Fachtagung „Cognitive Verfahren und Systeme", Hamburg, 11.–13. April 1973. Herausgegeben im Auftrag der NTG/GI von Th. Einsele, W. Giloi und H.-H. Nagel. VIII, 373 Seiten. 1973.

Vol. 84: A. V. Balakrishnan, Stochastic Differential Systems I. Filtering and Control. A Function Space Approach. V, 252 pages. 1973.

Vol. 85: T. Page, Economics of Involuntary Transfers: A Unified Approach to Pollution and Congestion Externalities. XI, 159 pages. 1973.

Vol. 86: Symposium on the Theory of Scheduling and its Applications. Edited by S. E. Elmaghraby. VIII, 437 pages. 1973.

Vol. 87: G. F. Newell, Approximate Stochastic Behavior of n-Server Service Systems with Large n. VII, 118 pages. 1973.

Vol. 88: H. Steckhan, Güterströme in Netzen. VII, 134 Seiten. 1973.

Vol. 89: J. P. Wallace and A. Sherret, Estimation of Product. Attributes and Their Importances. V, 94 pages. 1973.

Vol. 90: J.-F. Richard, Posterior and Predictive Densities for Simultaneous Equation Models. VI, 226 pages. 1973.

Vol. 91: Th. Marschak and R. Selten, General Equilibrium with Price-Making Firms. XI, 246 pages. 1974.

Vol. 92: E. Dierker, Topological Methods in Walrasian Economics. IV, 130 pages. 1974.

Vol. 93: 4th IFAC/IFIP International Conference on Digital Computer Applications to Process Control, Part I. Zürich/Switzerland, March 19–22, 1974. Edited by M. Mansour and W. Schaufelberger. XVIII, 544 pages. 1974.

Vol. 94: 4th IFAC/IFIP International Conference on Digital Computer Applications to Process Control, Part II. Zürich/Switzerland, March 19–22, 1974. Edited by M. Mansour and W. Schaufelberger. XVIII, 546 pages. 1974.

Vol. 95: M. Zeleny, Linear Multiobjective Programming. X, 220 pages. 1974.

Vol. 96: O. Moeschlin, Zur Theorie von Neumannscher Wachstumsmodelle. XI, 115 Seiten. 1974.

Vol. 97: G. Schmidt, Über die Stabilität des einfachen Bedienungskanals. VII, 147 Seiten. 1974.

Vol. 98: Mathematical Methods in Queueing Theory. Proceedings 1973. Edited by A. B. Clarke. VII, 374 pages. 1974.

Vol. 99: Production Theory. Edited by W. Eichhorn, R. Henn, O. Opitz, and R. W. Shephard. VIII, 386 pages. 1974.

Vol. 100: B. S. Duran and P. L. Odell, Cluster Analysis. A Survey. VI, 137 pages. 1974.

Vol. 101: W. M. Wonham, Linear Multivariable Control. A Geometric Approach. X, 344 pages. 1974.

Vol. 102: Analyse Convexe et Ses Applications. Comptes Rendus, Janvier 1974. Edited by J.-P. Aubin. IV, 244 pages. 1974.

Vol. 103: D. E. Boyce, A. Farhi, R. Weischedel, Optimal Subset Selection. Multiple Regression, Interdependence and Optimal Network Algorithms. XIII, 187 pages. 1974.

Vol. 104: S. Fujino, A Neo-Keynesian Theory of Inflation and Economic Growth. V, 96 pages. 1974.

Vol. 105: Optimal Control Theory and its Applications. Part I. Proceedings 1973. Edited by B. J. Kirby. VI, 425 pages. 1974.

Vol. 106: Optimal Control Theory and its Applications. Part II. Proceedings 1973. Edited by B. J. Kirby. VI, 403 pages. 1974.

Vol. 107: Control Theory, Numerical Methods and Computer Systems Modeling. International Symposium, Rocquencourt, June 17–21, 1974. Edited by A. Bensoussan and J. L. Lions. VIII, 757 pages. 1975.

Vol. 108: F. Bauer et al., Supercritical Wing Sections II. A Handbook. V, 296 pages. 1975.

Vol. 109: R. von Randow, Introduction to the Theory of Matroids. IX, 102 pages. 1975.

Vol. 110: C. Striebel, Optimal Control of Discrete Time Stochastic Systems. III. 208 pages. 1975.

Vol. 111: Variable Structure Systems with Application to Economics and Biology. Proceedings 1974. Edited by A. Ruberti and R. R. Mohler. VI, 321 pages. 1975.

Vol. 112: J. Wilhelm, Objectives and Multi-Objective Decision Making Under Uncertainty. IV, 111 pages. 1975.

Vol. 113: G. A. Aschinger, Stabilitätsaussagen über Klassen von Matrizen mit verschwindenden Zeilensummen. V, 102 Seiten. 1975.

Vol. 114: G. Uebe, Produktionstheorie. XVII, 301 Seiten. 1976.

Vol. 115: Anderson et al., Foundations of System Theory: Finitary and Infinitary Conditions. VII, 93 pages. 1976

Vol. 116: K. Miyazawa, Input-Output Analysis and the Structure of Income Distribution. IX, 135 pages. 1976.

Vol. 117: Optimization and Operations Research. Proceedings 1975. Edited by W. Oettli and K. Ritter. IV, 316 pages. 1976.

Vol. 118: Traffic Equilibrium Methods, Proceedings 1974. Edited by M. A. Florian. XXIII, 432 pages. 1976.

Vol. 119: Inflation in Small Countries. Proceedings 1974. Edited by H. Frisch. VI, 356 pages. 1976.

Vol. 120: G. Hasenkamp, Specification and Estimation of Multiple-Output Production Functions. VII, 151 pages. 1976.

Vol. 121: J. W. Cohen, On Regenerative Processes in Queueing Theory. IX, 93 pages. 1976.

Vol. 122: M. S. Bazaraa, and C. M. Shetty, Foundations of Optimization VI. 193 pages. 1976

Vol. 123: Multiple Criteria Decision Making. Kyoto 1975. Edited by M. Zeleny. XXVII, 345 pages. 1976.

Vol. 124: M. J. Todd. The Computation of Fixed Points and Applications. VII, 129 pages. 1976.

Vol. 125: Karl C. Mosler. Optimale Transportnetze. Zur Bestimmung ihres kostengünstigsten Standorts bei gegebener Nachfrage. VI, 142 Seiten. 1976.

Vol. 126: Energy, Regional Science and Public Policy. Energy and Environment I. Proceedings 1975. Edited by M. Chatterji and P. Van Rompuy. VIII, 316 pages. 1976.

Vol. 127: Environment, Regional Science and Interregional Modeling. Energy and Environment II. Proceedings 1975. Edited by M. Chatterji and P. Van Rompuy. IX, 211 pages. 1976.

Vol. 128: Integer Programming and Related Areas. A Classified Bibliography. Edited by C. Kastning. XII, 495 pages. 1976.

Vol. 129: H.-J. Lüthi, Komplementaritäts- und Fixpunktalgorithmen in der mathematischen Programmierung. Spieltheorie und Ökonomie. VII, 145 Seiten. 1976.

Vol. 130: Multiple Criteria Decision Making, Jouy-en-Josas, France. Proceedings 1975. Edited by H. Thiriez and S. Zionts. VI, 409 pages. 1976.

Vol. 131: Mathematical Systems Theory. Proceedings 1975. Edited by G. Marchesini and S. K. Mitter. X, 408 pages. 1976.

Vol. 132: U. H. Funke, Mathematical Models in Marketing. A Collection of Abstracts. XX, 514 pages. 1976.

Vol. 133: Warsaw Fall Seminars in Mathematical Economics 1975. Edited by M. W. Loś, J. Loś, and A. Wieczorek. V. 159 pages. 1976.

Vol. 134: Computing Methods in Applied Sciences and Engineering. Proceedings 1975. VIII, 390 pages. 1976.

Vol. 135: H. Haga, A Disequilibrium – Equilibrium Model with Money and Bonds. A Keynesian – Walrasian Synthesis. VI, 119 pages. 1976.

Vol. 136: E. Kofler und G. Menges, Entscheidungen bei unvollständiger Information. XII, 357 Seiten. 1976.

Vol. 137: R. Wets, Grundlagen Konvexer Optimierung. VI, 146 Seiten. 1976.

Vol. 138: K. Okuguchi, Expectations and Stability in Oligopoly Models. VI, 103 pages. 1976.

Vol. 139: Production Theory and Its Applications. Proceedings. Edited by H. Albach and G. Bergendahl. VIII, 193 pages. 1977.

Vol. 140: W. Eichhorn and J. Voeller, Theory of the Price Index. Fisher's Test Approach and Generalizations. VII, 95 pages. 1976.

Vol. 141: Mathematical Economics and Game Theory. Essays in Honor of Oskar Morgenstern. Edited by R. Henn and O. Moeschlin. XIV, 703 pages. 1977.

Vol. 142: J. S. Lane, On Optimal Population Paths. V, 123 pages. 1977.

Vol. 143: B. Näslund, An Analysis of Economic Size Distributions. XV, 100 pages. 1977.

Vol. 144: Convex Analysis and Its Applications. Proceedings 1976. Edited by A. Auslender. VI, 219 pages. 1977.

Vol. 145: J. Rosenmüller, Extreme Games and Their Solutions. IV, 126 pages. 1977.

Vol. 146: In Search of Economic Indicators. Edited by W. H. Strigel. XVI, 198 pages. 1977.

Vol. 147: Resource Allocation and Division of Space. Proceedings. Edited by T. Fujii and R. Sato. VIII, 184 pages. 1977.

Vol. 148: C. E. Mandl, Simulationstechnik und Simulationsmodelle in den Sozial- und Wirtschaftswissenschaften. IX, 173 Seiten. 1977.

Vol. 149: Stationäre und schrumpfende Bevölkerungen: Demographisches Null- und Negativwachstum in Österreich. Herausgegeben von G. Feichtinger. VI, 262 Seiten. 1977.

Vol. 150: Bauer et al., Supercritical Wing Sections III. VI, 179 pages. 1977.

Vol. 151: C. A. Schneeweiß, Inventory-Production Theory. VI, 116 pages. 1977.

Vol. 152: Kirsch et al., Notwendige Optimalitätsbedingungen und ihre Anwendung. VI, 157 Seiten. 1978.

Vol. 153: Kombinatorische Entscheidungsprobleme: Methoden und Anwendungen. Herausgegeben von T. M. Liebling und M. Rössler. VIII, 206 Seiten. 1978.

Vol. 154: Problems and Instruments of Business Cycle Analysis. Proceedings 1977. Edited by W. H. Strigel. VI, 442 pages. 1978.

Vol. 155: Multiple Criteria Problem Solving. Proceedings 1977. Edited by S. Zionts. VIII, 567 pages. 1978.

Vol. 156: B. Näslund and B. Sellstedt, Neo-Ricardian Theory. With Applications to Some Current Economic Problems. VI, 165 pages. 1978.

Vol. 157: Optimization and Operations Research. Proceedings 1977. Edited by R. Henn, B. Korte, and W. Oettli. VI, 270 pages. 1978.

Vol. 158: L. J. Cherene, Set Valued Dynamical Systems and Economic Flow. VIII, 83 pages. 1978.

Vol. 159: Some Aspects of the Foundations of General Equilibrium Theory: The Posthumous Papers of Peter J. Kalman. Edited by J. Green. VI, 167 pages. 1978.

Vol. 160: Integer Programming and Related Areas. A Classified Bibliography. Edited by D. Hausmann. XIV, 314 pages. 1978.

Vol. 161: M. J. Beckmann, Rank in Organizations. VIII, 164 pages. 1978.

Vol. 162: Recent Developments in Variable Structure Systems, Economics and Biology. Proceedings 1977. Edited by R. R. Mohler and A. Ruberti. VI, 326 pages. 1978.

Vol. 163: G. Fandel, Optimale Entscheidungen in Organisationen. VI, 143 Seiten. 1979.

Vol. 164: C. L. Hwang and A. S. M. Masud, Multiple Objective Decision Making – Methods and Applications. A State-of-the-Art Survey. XII, 351 pages. 1979.